MICROFINANCE
An Introductory Text

MICROFINANCE
An Introductory Text

Dr. H. Ramananda Singh
N. Dhaneshwar Singh

AKANSHA PUBLISHING HOUSE
NEW DELHI • GUWAHATI • VISAKHAPATNAM

AKANSHA PUBLISHING HOUSE
4649-B/21, Ansari Road
Darya Ganj, New Delhi - 110 002
Ph.: 23263193 / 9811582579 / 09435116718
Fax: 011-23263193
Email: ektabooks@yahoo.com
www.akanshapublishinghouse.com

Microfinance: An Introductory Text

First Published 2011
ISBN 978-81-8370-265-2

PRINTED IN INDIA

Published by Akansha Publishing House, New Delhi and Printed at Harmain Offset Press, Delhi.

Contents

Preface

Microfinance is recognized and accepted as one of the new development paradigms for alleviating poverty through social and economic empowerment of the poor, with special emphasis on empowering women. It provides opportunity to the poor for getting sufficient amount of credit easily to start any income generating activity. Microfinance not only deals with the credit part but also deals with savings and insurance part. It ensures the right to save and it is one of the most powerful weapons, which works for bringing the poor rural people into the financial mainstream. Thus, microfinance is often considered as one of the most effective and flexible strategies in the fight against the global poverty. It has proven to be a powerful tool to address issues of the poor. It is sustainable and can be implemented on massive scale necessary to respond to the urgent needs of those living on less than $1 a day, the world's poorest.

Now microfinance is one of fastest growing and evolving industries spreading across the globe with active participation of many stake holders such as Donors, MFIs, Govts., Formal financial systems, Community organizations, etc. With the rapid growth of microfinance industry, its operation expanded with diverse products/services, innovative delivery, use of information and technology and it has become more complex and competitive. Considering new developments, initiatives and innovative in microfinance sector in India and abroad, this book is designed to make understand the basic fundamentals, principles, and theories including recent innovations of microfinance. This book primarily focuses on students, researchers, practitioners of microfinance and rural financial services. This book is written in simple language and organized in precise form for better understanding of the readers.

This book comprises of twenty chapters. First chapter briefly highlights the history of microfinance. In the second chapter, definition of microfinance and its underlying philosophy are discussed. Third chapter deals with concept and assessment of Self Help Group and its progress in India. Various credit delivery models of microfinance such as SHG model, Grameen model, individual banking model, co-operative models are illustrated in Chapter Four. Chapter Five provides the global experiences and trends in various countries such as Bangladesh, Kenya, Ghanna, Uganda, Indonesia, China, Nepal etc. The emerging trends and issues of microfinance in India with special reference to SHG-Bank linkage programme are discussed in Chapter Six. The Seventh Chapter deals with demand, supply and growth of microfinance institutions (MFIs) in India along with example of some leading MFIs.

India has a large number of MFIs varying significantly in size, outreach and credit delivery methodologies. Presently, there is no regulatory mechanism in place for MFIs except for those that are registered as NBFCs. various legal and regulatory issues in Indian context are analyzed in Chapter Eight. Chapter Nine provides an in-depth understanding of various innovative products and credit delivery models being practiced in India.

Information Technology gives opportunities to MFIs for reducing costs of delivery and process management, besides bringing about transparent in operations. Chapter Ten highlights some experience on use of latest ICT in India and abroad for cost effective operation of microfinance. Chapter eleven focuses on management information system for MFI as it is one of the important tools for effective and efficient operation of MFI. Chapter Twelve discusses the issues, challenges and opportunities of microfinance.

There is Increasing participation of many formal financial intuitions (Banks/FIs) in microfinance through intermediaries (NGOs/MFIs). The rating of these intermediaries has become important while financing to these organisations. Various tools of rating for the performance of MFIs are illustrated in Chapter Thirteen with the caption "Credit Rating Models for MFI".

Most of the microfinance institutions (MFIs) strive to meet interrelated financial and social goals: managing a double bottom line where strong financial performance facilitates the fulfillment of a social mission. Monitoring and assessing social performance is emerging as a vital activity in the industry. Various social performance indicators and standards are discussed in Chapter Fourteen.

Chapter Fifteen focuses on Microinsurance in India and also discusses its problems, issues, challenges. Chapter Sixteen explains some key financial ratios/indicators for measuring the performance of MFIs.

All the MFIs are exposed to a great number of risks, both internal and external, that threaten effective services to clients, financial stability, and future sustainability. Chapter Seventeen deals with Risk Management for MFI.

Impact Assessment tools of Microfinance and Sustainability of microfinance are discussed in Chapter Eighteen and Chapter Nineteen respectively.

The last Chapter emphasizes on Women Empowerment through microfinance.

This book also provides some real-life cases /examples for better understanding to the reader.

We extend our gratefulness and wholehearted appreciation to those who are directly or indirectly associated with us in bringing out this book for their inspiration and support.

We also would like to extent our thanks to those authors of research papers and articles that we have referred in bringing out this book.

Finally, we hope the students, practitioners and researchers of the microfinance will find this book valuable. We welcome criticisms and suggestions from the readers for further improvement of this book.

Dr. H.Ramananda Singh
N. Dhaneshwar Singh

Abbreviations

ACCION	Americans for Community Co-operation in Other Nations
ACSI	Amhara Credit and Saving Institutions
ADB	Asian Development Bank
ADBN	Agricultural Development Bank of Nepal
AKRSP	Aga Khan Rural Support Program
APMAS	Andhra Pradesh Mahila Abhivruddhi Society
ARDC	Agricultural Refinance and Development Corporation
ARWP	Accelerated Rural Water Supply Programme
ASA	Activities for Social Alternatives
ASA	Association for Social Advancement
ASCRA	Accumulating Savings and Credit Associations
ATM	Automatic Teller Machine
BASIX	Bhartiya Samruddhi Finance Limited (BSFL)
BIMAS	Business Initiatives and Management Assistance
BKD	Badan Kredit Desa
BKK	Badan Kredit Kecamatan
BPR	Bank Perkreditan Rakyat
BRAC	Bangladesh Rural Advancement Committee
BRI	Bank Rakyat Indonesia
BSNL	Bharatiya Sanchar Nigam Limited
SBP	State Bank of Pakistan
CAMEL	Capital Adequacy, Asset Quality, Management, Earnings, and Liquidity Management
CAPART	Council for Advancement of People's Action and Rural Technologies
CFMS	Centralised Funds Management System
CFPA	Chinese Foundation for Poverty Alleviation
CGAP	Consultative Group to Assist the Poorest
CIDA	Canadian Internal Development Agency
CMF	Centre for Microfinance
CPSRB	China Postal Savings and Remittance Bureau

CRISIL	Credit Rating Information Services of India Limited
DECSI	Debit Credit and Saving Institution
DHAN	Development for Humane Action
DWACRA	Development of Women and Children in Rural Areas
EBS	Equity Building Society
EFT	Electronic Fund Transfer
FINCA	Foundation for International Community Assistance
FINGOs	Financial Intermediaries NGOs
FLDG	First Loss Default Guarantee
FSS	Financial Self Sufficiency
FWWB	Friends of Women World Bank
GIC	General Insurance Corporation
GOI	Govt. of India
GTZ	German Agency for Technical Corporation (Gesellschaft fur Technische Zusammenarbeit)
HHEP	Household Economic Portfolio
IA	Impact Assessment
IASC	International Accounting Standards Committee
IAY	The Indira Awas Yojana
ICT	Information and Communication Technology
IFAD	International Fund for Agricultural Development
IFAD	International Fund for Agricultural Programme
INFINET	Indian Financial Network
IRDA	Insurance Regulatory and Development Authority
IRDP	Integrated Rural Development Programme
IRDP	Integrated Rural Development Programme
JGSY	Jawahar Gram Samriddhi Yojana
KCC	Kisan Credit Cards
KEPP	Kenya Entrepreneurship Promotion Programme
KERUSSU	Kenya Rural Savings and Credit Cooperative Society Union
KFW	Kreditanstalt for Wiederafbu
K-Rep	The Kenyan Rural Enterprise Program
KSP	Koperasi Simpan Pinjam
KUD	Koperasi Unit Desa
KUSCO	Kenya Union of Savings and Credit Co-operatives
KVIC	Khadi and Village Industries Commission
KWFT	Kenya Women Finance Trust

KYC	Know Your Customer
LAB	Local Area Banks
LAN	Local Area Network or
LIC	Life Insurance Corporation of India
LPD	The Lembaga Perkreditan Desa
MAC	Mutually Aided Co-operative Society Act
m-Banking	Mobile Phone Banking
MCC	Microcredit Companies
MCP	Microcredit Program
M-CRIL	Micro-Credit Rating International Limited
MF	Microfinance
MDG	The Millennium Development Goals
MFDEF	Micro Finance Development and Equity Fund
MFDF	Microfinance Development Fund
MFIs	Microfinance institutions
MIFAN	Microfinance Association of Nepal
MIS	Management Information System
NABARD	National Bank for Agricultural and Rural Development
NBFC	Non Banking Financial Companies
NBFI	Non-banking Financial Institutions
NDS	Negotiated Dealing System
NGO	Non Government Organisation
NREG	National Rural Employment Guarantee
NRP	Nepal Rastra Bank
NSAP	The National Social Assistance Programme
OER	Operational Efficiency Ratio
OSS	Operational Self Sufficiency
PAR	Portfolio at Risk
PBOC	People's Bank of China
PDAS	Portable Devices Assistance
PLA	Participatory Learning and Action
PMRY	Prime Minister's Rozgar Yojana
POS	Point of sale devices
PP	Perum Pegadaian
PRA	Participatory Rural Assessment
PRI	Panchayati Raj Institutions
PRIDE	Promotion of Rural Initiatives and Development Enterprises

PROSHIKA	Proshikshan (Training), Shiksha (education) and Kaj (action).
PWR	Participatory Wealth Ranking
RBI	Reserve Bank of India
RCC	Rural Credit Cooperatives
REGP	Rural Employment Generation Programme
RFI	Rural Financial Institutions
RGVN	Rashtriya Gramin Vikash Nidhi
RMCC	Rural Mutual Credit Cooperative
RMDC	Rural Microfinance Development Center
RMK	Rashtriya Mahila Kosh
ROA	Return on Assets
ROSCA	Rotating Savings and Credit Association
RRA	Rapid Rural Appraisal
RRB	Regional Rural Bank
RRDB	Regional Rural Development Banks
RRSP	The Restructured Centrally Sponsored Rural Sanitation Programme
RTGS	Real Time Gross Settlement System
SACCOS	Savings and Credit Cooperatives
SCA	Service Centre Agencies
SCCS	Savings and Credit Cooperative Societies
SEBI	Securities an Exchange Board of India
SEF	Small Enterprise Foundation
SEWA	Self Employed Women's Association
SFC	State Financial Corporations
SFCL	Small Farmer Cooperatives Ltd
SFCLs	Small Farmers Cooperatives Ltd.
SFMS	Structured Financial Messaging Solution
SGSY	Swarnajayanti Gram Swarozgar Yojna
SHARE	Share Microfin Limited (SML)
SHG	Self Help Groups
SHPI	Self Help Promoting Institutions
SIDA	Swedish International Development Agency
SIDBI	Small Industries Development Bank of India
SKS	Swayam Krishi Sangham
SME	Small and Medium Enterprise
SPM	Social Performance Management
SRO	Self-Regulatory Organisations

SSI	Small Scale Industries
SWAN	State Wide Area Network
SWOT	Strength Weakness Opportunity Threat
TCP	Tshomisano Credit Program
TCR	Total Cost Ratio
TRYSEM	Training of Rural youth for Self–Employment
UID	Unique Identification
UN	United Nations
UNDP	United Nation Development Programme
USAID	United States Agency for International Development
UWFT	Uganda Women's Finance Trust
VB	Village Bank
WAN	Wide Area Network
WDB	Women's Development Businesses Group
WEEC	Women's Economic Empowerment Consort
WLL	Wireless in Local Loop
YDBP	Yayasan Dharma Bhakti Parasahabat

1

Microfinance: Historical Background

1.1. Informal Credit and Saving Institutions: Pre-19th Century

The word "microfinance" and its gradual ascent as a popular poverty alleviation tool may be relatively new to most of us, but the concept is not new. Informal credit and saving institutions for the poor have been around for decades, providing customers who were traditionally neglected by commercial banks, a way to obtain credit through co-operatives and development finance institutions. Some examples of these informal saving and credit groups that have operated for centuries are the " SUSUS" of Ghana, " TONTINES" of West Africa, "CHIT FUNDS" in India, "TANDAS" in Mexico, "ARISAN" in Indonesia, " CHEETU" in Sri Lanka and "PASANAKU" in Bolivia, as well as numerous savings clubs and burial societies found all over the world.[1] These informal groups are also known as Rotating Savings and Credit Association (ROSCAs). ROSCAs consist of a group of men and /or women who contribute to a collective fund and decide either by auction or collective decision, to contribute collected money to one of the group members. The other type of informal group is known as saving and credit cooperatives, (SACCOs).

One of the earlier and longer-lived micro credit organizations providing small loans to rural poor with no collateral was the Irish Loan Fund system. This began in the early 1700s by the notable author and nationalist Jonathan Swift. Swift's idea began slowly but by the early 1840s had become a widespread institution of about 300 funds all over Ireland. Their principal purpose was making small loans with interest for short periods up to 20 weeks. Despite small size of the loans, from as small as 4 pounds to a maximum of 10 pounds per person, the funds constituted one the larger financial organizations in Ireland. The idea of repayment was based on "Social Capital" so that if the borrower could find two other people to verify his or her trust, then they could secure the loan.

In the 1800s, various types of larger and more formal savings and credit institutions began to emerge in Europe, organized primarily among the rural and urban poors. These institutions were known as People's Banks, Credit Unions, and Savings and Credit Co-operatives. The concept of the credit union was developed by Friedrich Wilhelm Raiffeisen and his supporters. Their altruistic action was motivated by concern to assist the rural population to break out of their dependence on moneylenders and to improve their welfare. From 1870, the unions expanded rapidly over a large sector of the Rhine Province and other regions of the German states. The cooperative movement quickly spread to other countries in Europe and North America, and eventually, supported by the cooperative movement in developed countries and donors, also to developing countries.

Viewed purely from a historical perspective the origin of micro-finance could be traced back to the beginning of the co-operative movement in Germany, where the movement was started in 1944 in the field of co-operative-based credit system by the "Raiffeisen Societies" as well as "Rochdale Pioneers" in England. Similarly, the enactment of the Cooperative Credit Societies Act, 1904 could be considered as the beginning of micro-finance in India.[2]

In the late-19th Century, various types of larger and more formal savings and credit organizations began to emerge in Europe and were organized primarily among the rural and urban poor. These institutions were known as People's Banks, Credit Unions, and saving and Credit Cooperatives. In Indonesia, the Indonesian People's Credit Banks (BPR) or the Bank Perkreditan Rakyat opened in 1895. The BPR became the largest microfinance system in Indonesia with close to 9,000 units. Most of these institutions were owned by either Govt agencies or private banks and were mostly dependent on subsidies and grants of various rural development schemes. Over the years, these institutions became inefficient and widely discredited as a development intervention.

Beginning in the 1950s, development projects began to introduce subsidized credit programmes targeted at specific communities. Rural development banks suffered massive erosion of their capital base due to subsidized lending rates and poor repayment discipline and the funds did not always reach the poor, often ending up concentrated in the hands of the better-off farmers.

1.2. Origin of Modern Microfinance: Post-1970s

In the early 1970s, experimental programmes in Bangladesh, Brazil and a few other countries extended tiny loans to groups of poor women to invest in micro-businesses. This type of micro enterprise credit was based on solidarity group lending in which every member of a group guaranteed the repayment of all members.

The late 1970s and early 1980s saw the emergence of 'micro-enterprise lending" programmes, meaning and almost exclusive focus on credit for income generating activities (in some cases accompanied by forced savings schemes) and targeting very poor mostly women borrowers. The early focus of most micro enterprise lending programmes concentrated on proving that the poor were creditworthy.

However, the origin of institutionalized (modern) microfinance can be traced back to 1976 in Bangladesh when Professor Muhammad Yunus[3], head of Rural Economics Program at the University of Chittagong, launched an action research project at Jobra (a village adjacent to Chittagong University) to examine the possibility of designing a credit delivery system to provide banking services targeted at the rural poor. He proved that poor are not only bankable but also profitable business. Later on, he founded Grameen Bank which was largely focused on credit to poor especially to women, with saving mobilization as means to promote discipline. The Grameen Bank of Bangladesh is often referred to as the "flagship" of the new micro-enterprise lending movement. In 1980s, the Bank's founder, Dr. Mohammad Yunus of Bangladesh, referred to credit as a human right. Savings were conceived of as a method to ensure repayment, rather than as a service or end in itself.

Through the 1980s, the policy of targeted, subsidized rural credit came under a slow but increasing attack as evidence mounted of the disappointing performance of directed credit programmes, especially poor loan recovery, high administrative costs, agricultural development bank insolvency, and accrual of a disproportionate share of the benefits of subsidized credit to larger farmers. The basic tenets underlying the traditional directed credit approach were debunked and supplanted by a new school of thought called the "financial systems approach", which viewed credit not as a productive input necessary for agricultural development but as just one type of financial service that should be freely priced to guarantee its permanent supply and eliminate rationing.

Meanwhile, microcredit programmes throughout the world improved upon original methodologies and defied conventional wisdom about financing the poor. First, they showed that poor people, especially women, had excellent repayment rates among the better programmes, rates that were better than the formal financial sectors of most developing countries. Second, poor were willing and able to pay interest rates that allowed microfinance institutions (MFIs) to cover their costs.

By the late 1980s, the provision of credit to the poor had re-emerged as probably the most popular and widely acclaimed of all development initiatives. It was not until the mid-1990s that the term micro-enterprise lending began to be replaced by a new term that includes not only credit, but also saving and other financial services. Micro-enterprise finance or "Microfinance" emerged as the term of choice to refer to a range of financial services to the poor, that included not only credit, but also savings and other services such as insurance and occasionally pawning, or leasing. Thus modern microfinance became most popular terminology for providing financial services to poor. It has also become recognized as one of the effective tools for poverty alleviation.

1.3. History of Microfinance in India

Social banking has been prevailing in India since long. Institutional credit was perceived as a strategy for rural development and poverty alleviation by enhancing rural production and productivity in Independent India. Increasing access to credit for the poor and marginalized was more emphasized in Indian Plans. The role prescribed for the financial sector in India to achieve developmental goals dates to the pre-Independence days. There was a great need to replace costly informal credit with institutional credit. The All India Rural Credit Survey report of 1954 found that informal sources accounted for 70%, while the cooperative accounted for 6.4% and commercial banks just 0.9% of rural credit usage.

In 1960, India had made one the largest interventions in rural credit market and it was referred to as Social Banking Phase. Social Banking Phase was characterized by broadening the access to credit for poor and marginalized people and to section of people with no access to formal banking in India.

Phases of microfinance in India[4]

Phases	*Year*	*Features*
1	*2*	*3*
First phase: Social Banking	1960-1990	▪ Nationalization of commercial banks. Fourteen commercial banks were nationalized in 1969 and 8 commercial banks were nationalized in 1980. ▪ Lead Bank Scheme was initiated with district credit plans

(Contd...)

1	*2*	*3*
		▪ Expansion of the network of rural banking. RRBs were set up in 1976. NABARD was formed in 1982. Co-operative banking was structured and developed. SIDBI was established. ▪ Extensive disbursement of subsidized credits.
Second phase: Financial systems approach	1990-2000	▪ NGO-based MFIs were developed to provide microfinance products and services on not-for-profit basis. ▪ SHG-Bank linkage programme was initiated and rapidly replicated ▪ Innovative credit lending mechanisms based on "peer pressure" and "moral collateral" were developed.
Third Phase: Financial inclusion	2000 onwards	▪ Microfinance is seen as a business proposition and has commercialized. ▪ Development of for-profit MFIs like Non-Banking Financial Companies (NBFCs) and Non-banking Financial Institutions (NBFIs). ▪ NGO-MFIs are being legitimized. ▪ Customer's-centric/client-centric microfinance products and services are given importance. ▪ Policy regulations are increased.

In about 50 years, the policy directions of the Government of India have demonstrated the rapid expansion of rural banking network, priority sector lending and large subsidy-oriented credit programmes to serve the marginalized section of the society.

The All India Rural Credit Survey Committee recommended expansion of the co-operative credit system in 1954 to cater to the credit needs of the rural poor. The committee on co-operative Credit had proposed strong and stable institutional framework for strengthening of co-operatives in 1960 followed by the "Lead Bank Scheme" in 1969. The All India Credit Survey Committee in 1969 recommended the adoption of "Multi-agency Approach". It was the first time the Government of India has accepted the fact that the rural credit demand could not only be met from co-operatives along and the commercial banks have to play a vital role in meeting rural credit demand. The "Lead Bank Scheme" had started district credit plans which brought about a strong reform in the rural financial sector. Another important development in the India financial sector came out by nationalization of 14 commercial banks in the year 1969.

In 1975, the Regional RuralBanks (RRBs) were incorporated and "Agricultural Refinance and Development Corporation (ARDC) was set up. By mid 1970s, the banking sector was operating as a three-tier system where the first tier had consisted of commercial banks, the second tier consisted of the RRBs and cooperative banks had formed the third tier. By the same period 49% of all scheduled commercial banks had operated from rural areas.

In the 1980s, the concept of microfinance generated as a result of credit subsidization policy toward poverty-stricken farming community. During the same period, the concept of microenterprise credit arose which began with a motive to provide loans to poor people, especially women to invest in very small-scale business activities which had helped in accumulative assets and increase their household income. Realising the importance and need for rural financial services, the National Bank for Agriculture and Rural Development (NABARD) was set up in 1982. Loans available through micro credit scheme were more accessible to the poor people as compared to bank loans. Again in 1982, "Development of Women and Children in Rural Areas (DWCRA)" was started as a sub-scheme of Integrated Rural Development Programme (IRDP). Under DWCRA, Government of India introduced the provision of revolving fund to women groups for income-generating activities. In 1988, "Service Area Approach" was adopted and in 1989, market-oriented approaches for cooperatives were taken as per the recommendation of the Khusro Committee.

The scaling up of microfinance programmes in India was due to the effort led by the Self-Help Group Movement, where poor households from rural India are organised into homogenous groups of around 10-20 each, and pooled their money which was lent to the needy in the group in form of credit. In the year 1992, the major microfinance programme was initiated by NABARD by initiating the SHG-Bank linkage programme. By the mid 1990s, several mainstream banks began providing credit and savings facilities to SHGs and that had built credible financial discipline.

During early 1990s, the Non-government Organizations (NGOs) became instrumental in providing financial services to the poor and during late 1990s; many of the NGOs transformed themselves into formal financial institutions (MFI) in order to provide microfinance products like saving, credit, insurance, remittances etc.

In the year1993, "National Credit Fund for Women (Rashtriya Mahila Kosh)" was formed to provide credit (through NGO intermediaries) to self-employed women. An important microfinance movement developed in Andhra Pradesh in 1995 when State Government granted autonomy to cooperatives by passing "Mutually-aided Cooperative Societies Act". The "Local Area Banks (LABs)" were introduced in 1996 by Reserve Bank of India (RBI). The "Small Industries Development Bank of India (SIDBI)" took an important step in 1998 by setting up "SIDBI Foundation for Microcredit" with an initial capital of Rs. 100crores. In 2005, Government of India renamed it "Micro Finance Development and Equity Fund" with corpus fund of Rs. 200 crores to help in infusion of new capital to MFIs. Microfinance institutions (MFIs) became an integral part of microfinance from the year 2000 with RBI declared that the bank lending to MFIs is a part of priority sector lending.

Box-1: Lead Bank Scheme

The basic objective of the Lead Bank Scheme is that one of the commercial banks of Government of India will act as a lead bank in one district. The scheme had focussed on "Area Approach" for appropriate credit arrangement on the basis of local conditions. Under this scheme, one of the banks will carry out its operations as a lead bank in the under-banked district. It played as a leader in the expansion of banking facility and co-ordinating the activities of commercial banking, cooperative banking and other financial institutions. Through district surveys, it finds out the unbanked areas and extends banking branches in phased manner. Also in local areas, it develops integrated credit plans for input supply, processing, storage and marketing facilities.

Box-2: Service Area Approach

Under the "Service Area Approach" each branch of commercial banks operating in rural area and semi-urban area was assigned a specific area composed of cluster of villages within which the assigned branch would continue its operations, which would lead to a planned approach for economic growth of that area. It included five phases—i) identify the service area for each branch in semi-urban and rural areas, ii) assessment of potential activities and beneficiaries for credit lending, iii) development of annual credit plans, (iv) implementation of credit plans, and (v) monitoring the implementation of the programmes. The "Service Area Approach" led to higher concentration on the service areas for planned developments, organized and planned lending, and effective credit assessment and monitoring of loan uses.

NOTES

1. C.P.Mohan,"Microfinance & India's RRBs: The Best Fit", *Cab Calling*, Jan-Mar-2005, p. 26.
2. Dr. A.N. Sarkar, "Innovations in Microfinance", *Kurukshetra*, Vol 50, No. 2 , December 2001, p. 2.
3. Professor Muhummad Yunus was awarded Nobel Peace Prize in 2005 for his big contribution for poverty alleviation through his new innovative microfinance.
4. Debadutta K. Panda, *Understanding Microfinance*, Wiley-India.

2

Microfinance: Definition and Its Philosophy

2.1. Definition of Microfinance

Microfinance could be defined as a broad range of financial services such as deposits, loans, money transfers and insurance to the poor, low income households and micro-enterprises.

In order not to equate micro-finance merely as credit for micro-enterprises but include savings, consumption loans, housing loans and insurance services. It was in 1999 that the task force on micro finance set up by National Bank for Agriculture and Rural Development (NABARD) came up with a definition which has become the definitive one.

> " Microfinance is provision of thrift , credit , and other financial services and products of very small amounts to the poor in rural, semi-urban or urban areas for enabling them to raise their income levels and improve living standards". [1]

The term "micro credit" broadly refers to (very) small loans provided to low-income people and enterprises owned by them. This term has however been gradually replaced by microfinance which is broader and refers better to the variety of services that low-income people may now access in a growing number of countries.

Thus, Microfinance comprises micro credit as well as savings products, pensions, payment services, housing loans, insurance, emergency and other private loans, etc. to poor and low-income people and or the enterprises they own.

The scope of Microfinance now covers entire range of financial and non-financial services, including skill upgradation and entrepreneurship development, rendered to the poor for enabling them to overcome poverty.

Microfinance operations usually involve the following activities:[2]

a) Making small and flexible loans according to clients requirements, repayment capacities and cash-flows.
b) Providing secure deposit facilities to the poor, thereby allowing them to save as and when they have surplus.
c) Including collateral substitutes such as group guarantees and compulsory savings.
d) Encouraging repeat and larger loans based on repayment performance.
e) Continuous monitoring and following up to ensure timely repayment of loans.

2.2. Microfinance Institution (MFIs)

The term Microfinance Institution (MFI) is mostly used to refer to all types of formal and semi-formal institutions that offer microfinance services. These include the following institutions but are not limited:

Banks	Companies that fall under national banking laws with considerable microfinance activities.
Regulated MFIs (Non-Banking Financial Companies NBFCs).	Financial intermediaries that are subject to government or Central bank rules and regulation but are not banks.
Micro-credit Companies	Non-regulated companies involved in microfinance.
Credit (and savings) co-operatives and credit unions	Formally registered co-operatives and unions that provide microfinance services to their members.
Development NGOs and other non-profit organisations	Registered as society or non-profit organisation or trust that acts as intermediary or facilitator in microfinance activities.

Thus, MFI is a financial institution which can be a non-profit organisation, regulated financial institution or commercial bank that provides microfinance products and services to low-income clients.

Initially, microfinance was mostly provided by Non Governmental Organisations (NGOs) and other development oriented organizations that wanted to do more than just non-formal education, technical assistance etc. In recent years, there has been a tendency for these informal credit providers to transform into a formal and professionals micro finance institution. Some countries governments have established separate institutions for micro-finance to be regulated by the Central Bank. Regulation means in many cases that these MFIs are now allowed to capture savings and deposits from their clients and perform other financial services. More recently, the Commercial banks have taken microfinance into their portfolios more aggressively than before.

2.3. Microfinance: Banking with the Poor

Like everyone else, most poor people need and use financial services all the time. They save and borrow to take advantage of business opportunities, invest in home repairs and improvements, and meet seasonal expenses like school fees and holiday celebrations. The financial services available to the poor, however, often have serious limitations in terms of cost, risk and convenience. Moneylenders, for example, often charge exorbitant interest rates on loans. Buying goods on credit is far more expensive than paying in cash. Local rotating saving and credit circles take deposits and give loans only at rigid time intervals and in strict amounts, and often result in the loss of member's money.

In 1980s and 1990s, micro credit programmes throughout the world improved upon the original methodologist and bucked conventional wisdom about financing the poor.

a) First, it showed that poor people, especially women, had excellent repayment rates among the better programmes, rates that were better than the formal financial sectors of most developing countries.

b) Second, the poor were willing and able to pay interest rates that allowed microfinance institutions (MFIs) to cover their costs.

These two features—high repayment s and cost recovery interest rates—permitted some MFIs to achieve long-term sustainability and reach large numbers of clients. In fact, the promise of microfinance as a strategy that combines massive outreach, far reaching impact, and financial sustainability makes it unique among development interventions.

2.4. Microfinance and Poverty Alleviation

In the context of designing programmes for poor, microfinance is recognized and accepted as one of the new development paradigms for alleviating poverty through social and economic empowerment of the poor, with special emphasis on empowering women.[3] The operational framework of micro-finance therefore, essentially rests on the following premises:

a) Formation of self employment enterprise is a viable alternate means of alleviating poverty

b) Lack of access to capital assets/credit acts as a constraint on the existing and potential micro-enterprise and

c) The poor are capable of saving despite their poor income level.

Today, the microfinance industry and the greater development community share the view that permanent poverty reduction required addressing the multiple dimensions of poverty. Microfinance is visualized as a tool which can help in ensuring both livelihood security and promotion for the poor. Thus the concept of microfinance as a credit plus initiative to tackle the burden of poverty has become globally accepted.

Microfinance provides opportunity to the poor for getting sufficient amount of credit easily to start any income generating activity. Microfinance not only deals with the credit part but also deals with savings and insurance part. It ensures the right to save and it is one of the most powerful weapons, which works for bringing the poor rural people into the financial mainstream.[4]

2.5. Millennium Development Goals (MDG) and Microfinance

The Millennium Development Goals (MDGs) were set by world leaders at the Millennium Summit held in New York in 2000. The Millennium Development Goals (MDGs) are the World's time-bound and quantified targets for addressing extreme poverty in its many dimensions-income poverty, hunger, disease, lack of adequate shelter, and exclusion-while promoting gender equality, education and environmental sustainability. They are also basic human rights, the rights of each person on the planet to health, education, shelter and security. The goals are given bellow:

a) To reduce the proportion of people living in extreme poverty by half between 1990 and 2015 (defined as people living on less than $1 /day).

b) To enrol all children in primary school by 2015.

c) To make progress towards gender equality and empowering women by eliminating gender disparities in primary and secondary education by 2005.

d) To reduce infant and child mortality rates by two thirds between 1990 and 2015.

e) To reduce maternal mortality ratios by three-quarters between 1990 and 2015.

f) To provide access for all those who need reproductive health services by 2015.

g) To implement national strategies for sustainable development by 2005 so as to reverse the loss of environmental resources by 2015.

The world has made significant progress in achieving many of the Goals. Between 1990 and 2002, average overall incomes increased by approximately 21 percent. The number of people in extreme poverty decline by an estimated 130 million. Child mortality rates fell from 103 deaths per 1000 live births a year to 88. Life expectancy rose from 63 years to nearly 65 years. An additional 8 percent of the developing world's people received access to water. And an additional 15 percent acquired access to improved sanitation services.[5]

But progress has been far from uniform across the world- or across the Goals. There are huge disparities across and within countries. Within countries, poverty is the greatest for rural areas, though urban poverty is also extensive, growing and underreported by traditional indicators.

There have been global campaigned under the banner of the "Micro-credit Summit" led by some of the largest donor organizations in the world for promoting microfinance as strategy for poverty alleviation. Microfinance is often considered one of the most effective and flexible strategies in the fight against the global poverty. It has proven to be a powerful tool to address issues of the poor. It is sustainable and can be implemented on massive scale necessary to respond to the urgent needs of those living on less than $1 a day, the world's poorest.

For the international community, microfinance means reaching specific Millennium Development Goals (MDGs) in education, women's empowerment and health, among others. This means viewing microfinance as an essential element in any country's financial system. In this context a quote by Kofi Annan, Secretary General, UN, is also relevant:

> *"Micro-credit is a critical anti-poverty tool- a wise investment in human capital. When the poorest especially women, receive credit, they become economic actor with power. Power to improve not only their own lives but, in a widening circle of impact, the lives of their families, their communities and their nations".*

2.2.6 Two Schools of Thought in Microfinance

Micro finance brings the development sector and the business sector together around the goal of providing credit to the millions of poor people who do not have access to formal credit institutions. These two sectors are represented in the two main schools of thought in microfinance; one that favours serving the poorest of the poor and one that favours sustainability.[6] These goals are not mutually exclusive, but complementary to one another.

Pro-Poor School of Thought

The primary goal of the pro-poor school is to serve the poorest of the poor. These organizations look to microfinance as means to break the cycle of poverty and work with people to build stronger livelihoods. It can be riskier and more expensive to serve this group. The poverty camp is housed within the development sector. Non-profits and NGOs servicing this segment of the population often rely on grants and donor funding to sustain their programmes. Those in the pro-poor camp feel that unless they focus on the poorest of the poor, this group will not realize the benefit of microfinance.

Sustainability School of Thought

The primary goal of the sustainability school is to grow in scale and be financially self-sustaining, providing loans without grants or donor funding. The sustainability camp views the private sector, with socially conscious for profit organization as the future home of microfinance. These organizations look to sustainability and efficiency as a means to accessing the funding levels necessary to provide loans on a larger scale. However, self-sustainability is difficult, and many organizations seeking this as their primary goal will have to make difficult decisions. More stringent collateral requirements and practical favouritism to larger loans may lead sustainability-bound organizations away from serving the poorer clients that they originally served.

Both Development and Sustainability are two sides of the same coin and are most important two pillars of microfinance.

NOTES

1. NABARD (2000), "Summary and Recommendations of Task Force on Supportive Policy and Regulatory Framework for Microfinance." Mumbai. (Http://nabard.org/whats/ mftf.htm).
2. Sa-Dhan (2004), *Indian Experience of Microfinance: a sustainable banking solution for the poor*, Occasional Paper series.
3. Dr. A.N. Sarkar, "Innovations in Microfinance", *Kurukshetra*, December 2001, p. 2.
4. Rimjhim Mousumi Das, "Microfinance through SHGs: A boon for the rural poor", *Kurukshetra*, Feb-04, p. 43.
5. Jonathan J. Murdoch, "Empowerment of Women through Government", *Focus*, p. 7.
6. C.P. Mohan,"Microfinance & India's RRBs: The Best Fit", *Cab Calling*, Jan-Mar-2005, p. 27.

3

Microfinance and Self Help Groups (SHGs)

3.1. Concept of Self Help Groups

The Self Help Groups (SHGs) are usually informal groups where members have a common perception of need and importance towards collective action for a common cause. The common need here is meeting their emergent economic needs without being dependent on outside help. These groups promote savings among members and use the pooled resources to meet the emergent needs of their members, including the consumption needs. The number of members in SHGs is normally ranged from 10-20. The main objective of SHG is to inculcate the habit of thrift, saving, banking culture, that is availing the loan and repaying the same over a given period of time and in the process, gain economic prosperity through credit. In short, *a SHG is a group of about 10 to 20 people, usually women, from a similar class and region, who come together to form savings and credit organization.* They pooled financial resources to make small interest bearing loans to their members. This process creates an ethic that focuses on savings first. The setting of terms and conditions and accounting of the loan are done in the group by designated members.

A Self Help Group (SHG) is a small, economically homogeneous affinity group (10-20 members) of the rural poor voluntarily coming together:

a) To save small amounts regularly;

b) To mutually agree to contribute to a common fund;

c) To meet their emergency needs;

d) To have collective decision making;

e) To solve conflicts through collective leadership and mutual discussion; and

f) To provide collateral free loans on terms decided by the group.

A SHG is a registered or unregistered group of micro entrepreneurs with a homogeneous social and economic background, voluntarily coming together to save small amounts regularly and mutually agreeing to contribute to common fund to meet their emergency needs on mutual help basis[1]. The group members use collective wisdom and peer pressure to ensure proper end-use of credit and timely repayment thereof. In fact, peer pressure has been recognized as an effective substitute for collaterals. Moreover, financing through SHGs also reduces transaction costs for both lenders and borrowers.

Self Help Group (SHG) is an unregistered group of less than twenty people (any structure more than twenty has to be registered) from a homogeneous class who come together for addressing their common economic problems.[2] They are encouraged to make voluntary saving on regular basis. They use these savings to make interest-bearing loans to their members. This process i.e. saving, lending and recovering it back imbibes the essential of financial intermediation conditions and keeping financial accounts. This helps in building financial discipline and more importantly credit history for themselves. The group's members also learn to handle larger sums of money which are much beyond their individual savings. This process also makes them to understand the basic principle of banking that money has a time value and is a scarce resource.

The group which learn this basic process of savings, lending and recovering it back, are ready to be linked to the bank. Linking means access to the larger resources as well as the security of their saving when they have surplus. The banks loan amount adds to the small savings which the group had accumulated and thereby the availability of resources increases. The Banks are able to lend at the normal commercial rate of interest: there are no subsidies but the money comes back. The peer pressure among the group members ensures timely repayment as the group's own accumulated savings are part and parcel of the aggregate loans made by the group to their members and there are other members waiting as to when their demand for loan would be prioritized by the SHG. The conventional collateral is substituted by social security (more effective collateral i.e. peer pressure).

Self Help Groups have a number of advantages over co-operatives as there is no domination of rich, no interference of government, no politics and the like.

3.2. Characteristics and Principles of SHGs

SHGs exhibit certain distinct characteristic. They are participative and democratic in character. They follow the cooperative principles of collective endeavour for individual and community development by overcoming the deeply entrenched social bottlenecks and economic hurdles. There should be true democratic culture in which all the members must participate actively in the decision making process. Collective responsibility, leadership with fixed tenure, mutual trust and co-operative philosophy should be the drive force for SHG.

Some of the basic characteristics of SHG are:

a) SHG should be informal and small group of 10-20 members;

b) SHG members should be economically homogeneous and cohesive group of rural poor;

c) SHG should be formed voluntarily with common objective;

d) All members should agree to save small amount regularly and to contribute to a common fund;

e) SHG should meet their emergency need on mutual help basis;

f) Leaders should be selected in democratic way and on rotation for fixed tenure;

g) SHG should encourage participation in making collective decisions;

h) All conflicts should be solved through collective leadership; and

i) Provide collateral free loans on terms and conditions as decided by the group.

The basic principles on which the SHGs function are:

a) The members of the groups should be residents of the same area and must have an affinity. Homogeneity of relationship could be in terms of caste/occupation/gender or economic status (which is critical);

b) Saving first, credit thereafter;

c) SHGs should hold regular meetings;

d) SHGs should maintain record of financial and other transactions;

e) They should have norms regarding memberships, meetings etc.;

f) Group leaders should be elected by members and rotated periodically;

g) Transparency in operations of the group and participatory decision making;

h) Rates of interest on loans should be decided by the group; and

i) Group liability and peer pressure to act as substitute for traditional collateral.

3.3. Objectives of SHGs

The principles underlying the SHGs model include financing the poorest of the poor, ensuring excellent recovery level, and empowering women not just by meeting their needs for consumption and productive loans but also through more holistic educative programmes on issues such as sanitation and family planning. The SHGs or the Thrift and Credit Groups are mostly informal groups on rotational or need basis. SHGs are organized in the selected villages for economic and social development of the rural poor and women in particular.

The purpose of the Self Help Group is to organize poor specially women efficiently into a decision-making groups that manages saving, loan disbursements and repayment; carries out training in credit and micro-enterprise development and promotes mutual support and problem solving.[3]

Some of the major objectives of Self Help Groups are as given below:

a) To mobilize human, financial and other resources for development;

b) To provide group pressure and guarantee as an effective substitute for collateral security;

c) To reduce transaction costs significantly on small loans through voluntary and other contributions of the group;

d) To ensure payment of market rates of interest;

e) To achieve high loan repayment rates; and

f) To demonstrate financial commercial viability.

3.4. Modus Operandi and Dynamics of Self Help Group

Self Help Group is the building block of microfinance. It is one of the most essential elements of microfinance on which entire activities of microfinance are based. All philosophies and theories of microfinance are centred on Self Help Group. Success of microfinance largely depends upon the quality of SHG and how it functions. Thus SHG can be treated as core element of microfinance programme. Some of the basic working principles and functions that a SHG should follow are:

a) Group members usually create a common fund by contributing their small savings on a regular basis;

b) Group evolves a flexible system of working (sometimes with the help of NGOs) and manages pooled resources in a democratic way;

c) Loan requests are considered by group in periodic meetings and competing claims on limited resources are settled by consensus;

d) Loans are given mainly on trust with minimum paper with and without any security;

e) The loan amounts are small, frequent for shot duration and are mainly for conventional purposes;

f) The rates of interest vary from group to group and the purpose of loan. It is higher than that of banks but lower than that of moneylenders;

g) At periodic meetings, besides collecting money, social and economic issues are also discussed; and

h) Defaults are rare due to group pressure and intimate knowledge of the end use of credit.

3.5. Self Help Groups and Its Role

Self Help Groups are necessary to overcome exploitation, create confidence for the economic self reliance of rural poor, particularly among women. These groups enable them to come together for a common objective and gain strength from each other to deal with exploitation which they are facing in several forms. A group becomes the basis for action and change. It also helps building of relationship for mutual trust between the promoting organization and the rural poor to constant contact and genuine efforts. SHG could go all out for all round economic development. They can play pivotal role in:

a) Creating economic self-reliance of rural poor by meeting consumption and production credit needs as and when they arise. This will prevent exploitation of the poorer sections from non-institutional credit sources;

b) Development of group dynamics, building leadership quality to realize their potentiality and self-belief;

c) Assisting the members in getting access to the formal credit institution;

d) Setting viable norms for interest rates, repayment schedules, gestation period, extension, writing off bad debts;

e) Helping banks in recovery of credit by motivating members for prompt repayment of loans;

f) Procurement of high cost inputs that could not be bought individually;

g) Training of members in the use of extension services and Government support;

h) Building common infrastructure for the benefit of its members;

3.6. Features of SHG-Bank Linkage programme in India

The main aim of the SHG-Bank Linkage programme being implemented in India since 1992 is to tap the potential of the SHG concept to bring banking services to the doorsteps of poor.[4]

The important features of the product developed under the SHG-Bank linkage programme in India are as under:[5]

a) The members of the groups should be residents of the same area and must have an affinity. Homogeneity of relationship could be in terms of caste/occupation/gender or economic status (which is critical).

b) Saving first, credit later. Small fixed savings at a regular interval. It helps in building up financial discipline.

c) SHG should hold regular meetings

d) SHGs should maintain record of financial and other transactions

e) They should have norms regarding membership, meeting etc.

f) Group leaders should be elected by members and rotated periodically.

g) Transparency in operations of the group and participatory decision making

h) Rates of interest on loans should be decided by the group

i) Group liability and peer pressure to act as substitute for traditional collateral.

j) Shorter repayment period and progressive lending

k) The SHG deciding the quantum as also the terms and conditions for loans to members

l) No subsidies and no subsidization of interest

The meetings of the SHGs also serve as time and place for collection of regular savings and loan installments as also for consideration and sanction of loans. The attendance of the meeting is compulsory and absence attract fine. The fine so collected indicates that the "Group" is also able to ensure that it 'Will" prevail over the members. The groups were also encouraged to rotate the office bearers to avoid dominance of one /two persons.

This approach also helped in reducing the transaction cost of the both banks and the ultimate users of credit. It has provided the most essential minimum financial services at door steps in the true sense.

3.7. Assessing of Self Help Group

For any financing institution, appraisal is very important for ensuring the utility of the loan and repayment of the loan. Bankers generally appraise the project and the borrower. In case of SHG financing, most of the project appraisal norms like assessing the cost benefit and profits will not be workable due to the peculiarities of SHG financing. For considering a loan application for financing the Financer has to evaluate the capacity and character of the prospective borrower. SHG's also being customers have to be appraised before extending credit facilities. But then assessment of creditworthiness of a SHG is very different from that of an individual. SHGs are not to be assessed in terms of their ability to provide collateral or guarantees of net worth. The SHGs have to be assessed in terms of Group dynamics like cohesion, vibrancy, goal-oriented action, participation of members, democratic decision and collective leadership. The appraiser has to see whether the group is functioning, actually as a group, why the members have come together, whether it is for obtaining loan from bank or the group sees other purposes, what is the group discipline and whether it is sustainable.

For assessing a Self Help Group the important aspects that a financer should look into include[6];

(a) Norms for functioning : The SHG should have developed some kind of norms for its functioning the norms should be covering major areas of its functioning as well as the decision making processes, leadership etc., Norms generally relate to

i. Membership

ii. Meetings - time, periodicity

iii. Savings - amount, periodicity, rate of interest (return)

iv. Credit - procedure for sanction, ceiling amount, purposes, rate of interest to be charged, repayment period etc.

v. Fines - in case of default in attending meetings, savings and credit repayment. Group may also levy fine for any deviant behavior etc.

vi. Leadership - election or nomination of leaders, rotation of leaders etc.

vii. Personal/social improvement - minimum literacy level to be achieved, social work to be done etc.

The above norms may be written or oral. They may be decided in the initial meetings or they may evolve over a period of time depending upon the need of the group. The important aspects to be looked into are:

i. How norms evolved, whether by the consensus of the whole group.

ii. Whether the members are aware of the norms (even if they are oral) and understand them,

iii. Whether the norms are implemented.

(b) Meetings: The group decides the periodicity of the meetings i.e., weekly, fortnightly or monthly. They also decide on the time of the meeting. Decision on time and periodicity helps in regular conduct of meetings. The regularity in the holding of the meeting and the attendance during meeting gives an indication about groups functioning. Therefore, a Financer should see whether.

i. The meetings have been held regularly

ii. The attendance in the meetings

iii. The members are punctual and stay till the end of the meeting

iv. Are there any sanctions for the delinquent members?

The Financier can use his observations during the meetings and the meeting registers to get data on this appraisal aspect.

(c) Maintenance of Books: Whether group is maintaining the basic books that will give details of its functioning and accounts of the group is an important criterion to be judged. The books should give the details of number of meetings held, decisions taken in the meetings, amount of savings of the members and credit availed, the total savings of the group and repayments. Who maintains these books is another important criterion for judging the group. Do members maintain it; if not are they making efforts to achieve basic numeracy or literacy so that they can start doing it themselves. Therefore, the financer has to verify the following:

i. Whether details of meetings, proceedings, and attendance are maintained.

ii. Whether member-wise record of saving and credit are maintained.

iii. Whether the records are up-to-date.

iv. Whether all members are kept informed of their savings and credit balances from time to time.

v. In case of illiterate groups whether what is the system followed, does the group verify the books maintained by NGO/outsider.

vi. Whether systems have been developed to ensure safe custody of cash.

(d) Leadership: Two or three group members are elected as leaders or Initially the opinion leaders may be the leaders and over a period of time they are expected to be taking turns. The group leaders are expected to do the following activities:

i. regularly convene and conduct the meetings,

ii. help the group members in taking decisions,

iii. resolve conflicts,

iv. maintain books of account and

v. Approach bank branch for operation of accounts.

The aspects that are to be seen are:

i. Whether the leaders have been elected and rotated

ii. Whether they help in democratic functioning of the group

iii. Whether there is a conscious attempt to groom other members to take up leadership

iv. Are they marginalising the benefits (especially loans)

(e) Participation and Awareness of Group Members: Are the Members aware of the purpose of group formation, the operations and activities of the group i.e. the savings and the credit of the group as well as the individual member's savings and credit details.

i. Do they participate in group discussions and decision making

ii. Do they help solve the problem that are raised in the meetings

iii. Do they work cohesively and have transparent dealings

The democratic character of the group may be judged by attending one or two meetings and talking to individual members. The awareness level of members helps in healthy functioning of the group and resolution of conflicts within the group.

(f) Savings: The group decides on the amount of savings as also its periodicity. It has to be seen whether the saving, as decided upon, is regularly made, how the defaults are dealt with and whether the system is modified as per the requirements of the members.

(g) Credit: The following aspects to be looked into while assessing the credit function of the group:

i. The decision making process of selecting loanees.

ii. The system followed in assessing credit requirement of individual members and the amount to be sanctioned.

iii. The system of monitoring the credit.

iv. The repayment performance of members and incidence of defaults besides the effectiveness to deal with such defaults; whether the concept of 'peer pressure' is working.

(h) Self Reliance of the Group: Can the group function on its own without the support of the NGO is an important criterion for assessment? The level of dependency on the NGO/ promoter of the group and impact of withdrawal of NGO/promoter on the group is to be assessed.

3.8. Parameters for measuring SHG's Performance.

Rating of Indian SHGs is important for NGOs, financial intermediaries and banking institutions, particularly for disbursement of credit. So, it is necessary to assess the social and financial performance of the SHGs. The information requirement for analysis of the performance of SHGs is given as under:

a) General Information	▪ Name of the SHG ▪ Name of the Village ▪ Name of the block ▪ Name of the district ▪ Name and type of the implementing agency ▪ Name of the president/secretary ▪ Age of the group ▪ Purpose of formation of group ▪ Extent of bank linkage ▪ Monthly saving per member ▪ Total number of members
b) Homogeneity of members in the group	▪ Age group of members ▪ Sex of members (male, female or joint) ▪ Maritus status ▪ Education level ▪ Social category ▪ Economic category ▪ Area of residence
c) Management and dependence	▪ Dependence on NGO or intermediary ▪ Management type and structure
d) SB account credit –saving	▪ Total saving ▪ Total credit ▪ Total interest ▪ Cash in Bank ▪ Who handles the SB account ▪ Frequency of transactions by the SB account in a month
e) Group account	▪ Total saving ▪ Total loan disbursement to members ▪ Total interest ▪ Total fine ▪ Cash in hand
f) Meeting	▪ Frequency ▪ Regularity ▪ Attendance ▪ Degree of participation
g) Record keeping	▪ Maintained by whom ▪ Quality of maintenance ▪ Regularity
h) Leadership	▪ Type (democratic or autocratic) ▪ Tenure of leader ▪ Decision making
i) Credit/loan	▪ Internal credit (%)

		▪ Rate of interest (%) ▪ Purpose of loan ▪ Repayment period ▪ Method of sanctioning loans and selection of members eligible for a loan ▪ Total number of loans disbursed ▪ Fine to the defaulter ▪ Criteria for putting a fine ▪ Interest type i.e. simple or compound, fixed or variable etc
j)	Saving	▪ Saving account ▪ Periodicity ▪ Regularity ▪ Saving Type
k)	Productive activities	▪ Types of business, time period of business, initiation of business ▪ Donor agency/bank/group loan, how linkage is established, interest rate, time period of loan, amount of loan/grant etc. ▪ Detail activity of the business ▪ Detail of the profits
l)	Livelihood	▪ Past livelihood options ▪ Present livelihood options ▪ Change in economic position (income, asset position, BPL level etc) ▪ Change in social position (Participation, migration, decision making, employment etc)

3.9. Tools for Rating of Self Help Group

Based on the NABARD 's broad guideline for assessing the Self help Group, NABARD has developed a model tool for rating of SHG commonly known as NABARD Critical Rating Index (CRI) as given below:

(a) NABARD's RATING OF SELF HELP GROUPS

Sl. No.	Category	Criteria	Mark	Key
1	COMPOSITION	Membership is homogeneous	10	The rating is based on the judgment of assessing official
		No homogeneity in membership	5	
2	AGE OF THE GROUP	One year and above	10	There is no need to evaluate an SHG if it is less than six

(Contd...)

Sl. No.	Category	Criteria	Mark	Key
		Six months and above but less than a year	5	month old (ignore marginal shortfalls upto 1 month)
3	WEEKLY GROUP MEETINGS	Four meetings per month	10	The total number of meetings conducted during the last 3 months may be divided by 3 to arrive at average no. of group meetings.
		2-3 meetings per month	8	
		1 meeting per month	5	
4	ATTENDANCE	More than 90%	10	
		Between 70% and 90%	5	
		Less than 70%	3	
5	MINUTES BOOK	Written in detail	10	Peruse of minutes book pertaining to meetings held during the last 3 months.
		Maintained, but not in detail	5	
6	PARTICIPATION IN GROUP DISCUSSION	Participation by only a few members	5	Peruse minutes book (if rating is 10 for item 5)
		Participation by majority of members	10	Observe during a couple of group meeting Interact with members
7	SAVINGS (FREQUENCY)	4 times a month (by majority members)	10	**Step 1:** Take the average no. of members making saving during last 3 months.
		4 times a month (but not by majority)	8	**Step 2:** Compare this with the total no. of members
		2-3 times a month (by majority members)	8	**Step 3 :** Majority mean > 60%
		2-3 times a month (but not by majority)	5	**Step 4:** For average no. of meeting, follow rating given for item 3 above.
		1 time a month day (by majority members)	3	
		1 time a month (but not by majority)	1	
8	SAVINGS & LOAN RECOVERY(MODE	Collected in group meetings	10	Ascertain form group leaders and members in this

(Contd...)

Sl. No.	Category	Criteria	Mark	Key
	OF COLLECTION)	House - to house collection	5	regard also, peruse minute's book.
9	STYLE OF FUNCTIONING AND GROUP DECISIONS	Democratic and Transparent	10	Peruse minute's book, Interact with members, Observe in few group meetings, Ascertain whether periodical elections are conducted for the leadership and whether all decisions are in group meetings and on democratic lines.
		Decisions taken by few dominant member / members / group leaders	0	
10	SANCTION AND DISBURSEMENT OF LOANS	Selection of borrowers in group meetings	2	Ascertain the position from group leaders/ members
		Sanction and disbursement of loans in group meetings	2	Peruse minutes book (Each item will get marks shown against it, if the conditions are satisfied)
		Loan terms and conditions discussed in group meetings and recorded in minutes	2	
		Utilisation of loans reviewed regularly in group meetings	2	
		Recovery of loans reviewed regularly in-group meetings.	2	
11	INTEREST ON SHG LOANS	Uniform rate irrespective of source of funds	5	Peruse loan register.
		Different rates depending on source of funds	3	Ascertain from group leaders / members
		Interest rates vary according to the purpose of loan	5	
		Uniform interest rate for all purposes	3	
12	UTILISATION OF SAVING FOR LOANING	Above 80%	10	Compare savings outstanding on a given date with loans outstanding on
		Above 50% and upto 80%	5	

(Contd...)

Sl. No.	Category	Criteria	Mark	Key
				the same date to obtain the percentage. Nil mark for utilisation of savings below 50%
13	RECOVERY OF LOANS	Dues not recovered in respect of 10% or less of total no.of loan accounts	10	Even one installment unpaid without authorisation by the group is treated as dues not recovered. Count such accounts and compare them with total no. of loan a/c. Also, peruse minutes book for authorisation for non-payment
		Dues not recovered between 10% and 30% of total no.of loan accounts.	5	
14	BOOKS OF ACCOUNTS	Attendance cum minutes book	3	Each record / register, if maintained properly and upto date, will get marks shown against each.
		Savings Register	3	
		Loan Ledger	3	
		Bank Passbook	1	
15	BYLAWS / GROUP RULES	Known to all members	10	Ascertain from the member through interaction
		Known to most of the members	5	
		Not known to many members	0	
		TOTAL MARKS	**150**	

Selection Criteria of SHG for Credit Linkage

1. SHG scoring more than 120 marks out of maximum of 150 marks could be chosen for credit linkage.
2. SHG scoring less than 120 marks will have to be further developed before linkage. The areas for taken up after 3 months.

The norms for SHGs in a particular place may have to be developed keeping in view the local conditions. The above pattern is only a model and indicative one and could be used as the basis for developing suitable norms for financing SHGs is it banks or any other financing institution.

APMAS (Mahila Abhivruddhi Society, Andhra Pradesh) has also developed SHG rating tool based on NAPABARD's Credit Rating Index which is based on the following three broad parameters.[7]

(a) System and Self Management

i. Homogeneity of the group (same economic class, social class, neighborhood)
ii. Regularity of Meeting
iii. Meeting Attendance
iv. Quality of record system (Adequacy & timeliness)
v. Members participation in decision making
vi. Ability to enforce norms
vii. Financial transactions within the group
viii. Members awareness

(b) Social

i. Member awareness/ participation in social development activities
ii. Decision making ability of the group members
iii. Impact on status

(c) Financial

i. Regularity of savings
ii. Velocity of Internal Lending
iii. Repayment Terms
iv. Monthly Repayment pattern
v. Asset Quality
vi. Borrower Quality (nos. of defaulters in the group)
vii. External Loan Repayment
viii. Percentage of Production loan funds
ix. Portfolio distribution among members
x. Pattern of internal lending
xi. Average Idle Fund.

NOTES

1. Dr. Manoj Shankar Gupta, "Poverty Eradication through Micro-Finance/SHG", *Poverty and Sustainable Development*, p. 379.
2. Y.C.Nanda," Micro Finance- A route to Reach Rual Poor", *The Journal of Indian Institute of Banking and Finance*, October-December 2004, p.26.
3. Helzi Noponen, "The Internal Learning System for participatory Impact assessment of Microfinance", *National Bank News Reviews*, April-June 2002, p53.
4. H.S.Shylendra, "The SHG-Bank Linkage programme: An assessment and future strategies", Journal of Rural Development, Vol 23(4), pp 411-433 (2004), NIRD Hyderabad.
5. NABARD 2002, " mF in India-An Overview," Mumbai (http://nabard.org/roles/mcid/section1.htm
6. NABARD website. http://www.nabard.org/microfinance/assessmentmethods.asp
7. APMAS website http://www.apmas.org/RatingTools.aspx

4

Credit Delivery Models of Microfinance

4.1. SHG- Bank Linkage Model

Under this model, groups are formed by different agencies known as Self Help Promoting Institutions (SHPIs). These could be NGOs, Voluntary Associations, Government Agencies, Panchayati Raj Institutions, Vikas Volunteer Vahini (VVV), Clubs, Banks, and Co-operative Societies etc.

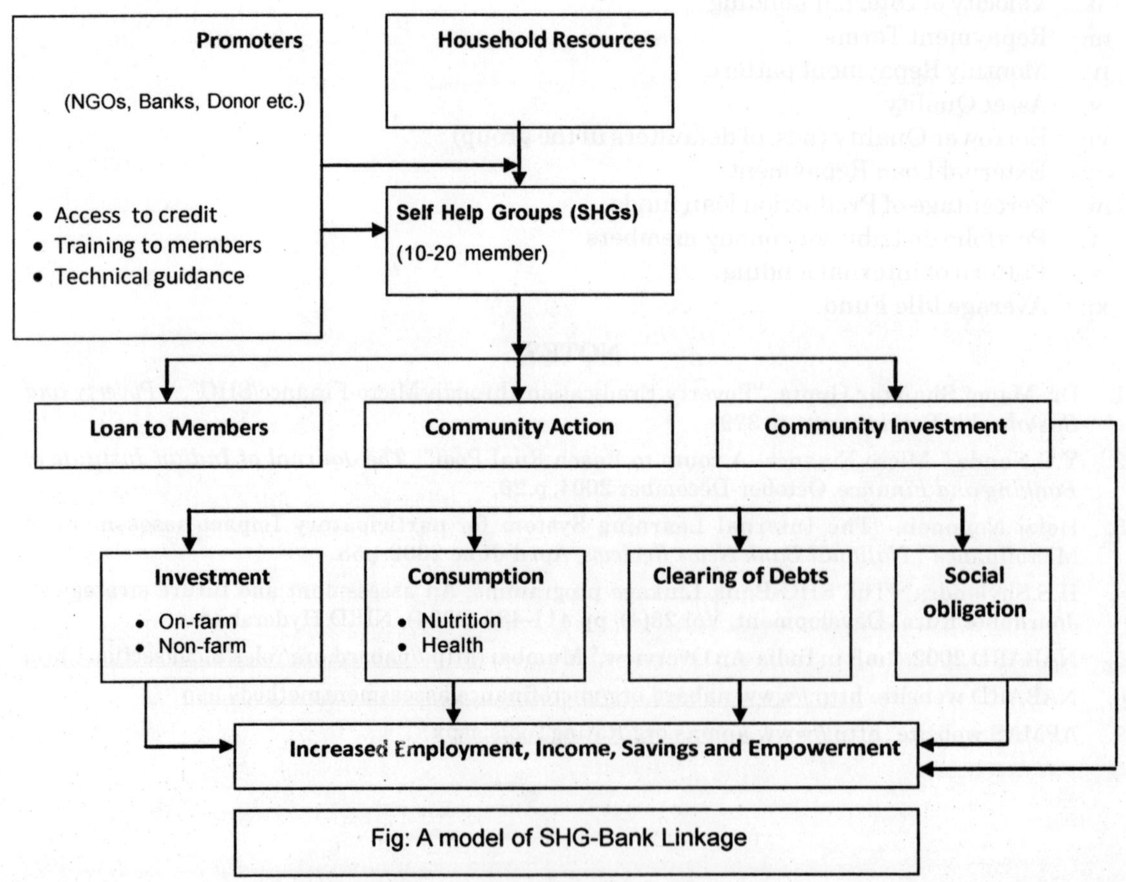

Fig: A model of SHG-Bank Linkage

The SHG model is indigenously developed in India. Unlike other models of micro-credit, the SHG model starts off with savings as a base. The model is like the Grameen model, but not as regimented. Mainstream banking has accepted this model for a nationwide bank linkage programme and it is quite popular with bankers who see potential in microfinance. The essential design elements of the SHG model are as follows:

a) Homogeneous affinity group of 15-20 members;

b) Regular meetings;

c) Regular savings;

d) Lending decisions are of the group;

e) Group selects their leaders; and

f) Group accesses external funds.

Group federates at Cluster/Block level. Most of the groups in India have been promoted by NGOs. The group tend to be dependent on the intervening agency for a long time to help them not only maintain accounts and conducts meetings, but also to manage the external interface with the bankers and others. The rate of growth SHG is not as fast as the Grameen groups, because of the heterogeneity of group formation. Since the design allows for flexibility and focuses on internal capability development, it may take a long time for penetration. Moreover not all promoters of SHGs have the same focus towards the poorest of the poor.

Since there is no single external agency channelling credit, there is every danger that the groups might wither away after a while. However, some of the agencies of the state have these as effective channels for delivering the programme funds of various line departments. Since there is no single apex body, and most of the groups are independent, there is every danger that they would get misused as the co-operative got misused in the past.

SHG tend to work better in areas where the credit culture is not severely damaged-particularly in the southern part of India. The Grameen model which is more disciplined-seems to work in areas where the credit culture is severely impaired- particularly in north and eastern parts.

The SHG model builds on the fact that India already has a large number of bank branches and this channel builds the "last mile" linkage with the lower-income customers[1].

Model-I: Banks promote SHGs and finance them directly

In this model, banks themselves take up the work of forming and nurturing the groups, opening their saving accounts and providing them bank loans. Here, the bank assumes to play the role of NGOs and ensure linkage to SHGs. Banks give loans directly to individual/SHG members on recommendations of the SHG and the NGO. The NGO assists the bank in monitoring, supervising and recovery of loans.

Model-II: NGOs facilitate the promotion of SHGs and Banks Finance SHGs.

In this model NGO acts as facilitators. NGO would organize the poor into SHGs, undertaking training for awareness building, entrepreneurship and skill training, help in arranging inputs, extension and marketing, introduce saving and internal lending, help in maintenance of accounts and link them with the banks for credit requirements. Banks directly provide loans to SHG with recommendation of the NGO.

Model-III: NGOs borrow funds from Banks/ FIs and provide services to SHGs/Clients

NGO forms SHGs and perform financial intermediation role as on –lender to SHGs after sourcing loan from Bank. In this case, besides acting as facilitator, the NGO also works as financial intermediary. Here the loan is given to NGOs by the bank for on-lending the SHGs/ Individuals. In this linkage model, NGO would be legally responsible for repayment and it would bear the risk of non-payment. Involvement of NGOs in micro-credit system would have positive influence as they are grass-root agencies with good information about borrowers, thus adverse selection and production of recovery could be avoided. At the same time, NGOs would be in a position to help rural poor, particularly women to being them above poverty line and create rural employment.

This SHG-NGO-Bank integration is very much essential to credit delivery, for self-employment and other business activities which could be an effective vaccine against poverty. The ultimate goal of this linkage programme is not just promotion of SHGs but the focus is poverty eradication. It is an established fact that micro-credit is an important means of poverty alleviation. The SHG route is one of the cost effective method of credit flow to the poor who need most.[2]

4.2. Grameen Model

In this model, financial assistance is provided to the individual in a group by the formal institution on the strength of group's assurance. In other words, individual loans are provided on the strength of joint liability/co-obligation. Joint liability is a method of providing guarantees for loans based on peer pressure in which members of a loan group agree to jointly guarantee the loans of all group members. If one member of the group defaults, the remaining group members are held responsible either for enforcing loan repayment by the defaulting member or for paying off the outstanding loan balance.

This microfinance model was initiated by Bangladesh Grameen Bank and is being used by some of Micro Finance Institutions (MFIs) in our country. SHARE microfinance Ltd, Activities for Social Alternatives (ASA) and CASHPHOR Financial and Technical Services Ltd. The Indian Banks have, so far not adopted this model perhaps because of its high delivery cost.

The Grameen Model which was pioneered by Prof Muhammad Yunus of Grameen Bank is perhaps the most well known, admired and practiced model in the world. The model involves the following elements.

a) Homogeneous affinity group of five

b) Eight groups form a Centre

c) Centre meets every week

d) Regular savings by all members
e) Loan proposals approved at centre meeting
f) Loan disbursed directly to individuals
g) All loans repaid in 50 instalments.

The Grameen model follows a fairly regimented routine. It is very cost intensive as it involves building capacity of groups and customers passing a test before the lending could start. The group members tend to be selected or at least strongly vetted by the bank. One of reasons for the high cost is that staff members can conduct only two meetings a day and thus are occupied for only a few hours, usually early morning or late in the evening. They were used additionally for accounting work, but that can now be done more cost effectively using computers. The model is also rather meeting intensive which is fine as long as the members have no alternative use for their time but can be a problem as members go up the income ladder.

The greatness of the Grameen model is in simplicity of design of products and delivery. The process delivery is scalable and the model could be replicated widely. The focus on the poorest, which is a value attribute of Grameen, has also made the model a favourite among the donor community.

However, the Grameen model works only under certain assumptions. As all the loans are only for enterprise promotion, it assumes that all the poor want to be self-employed. The repayment of loans starts the week after the loan is disbursed- the inherent assumption being that the borrowers can service their loan from the ex-ante income. Both these assumption could be questioned.

One way to look at the Grameen vs. SHGs question is the way time is spent in the group meetings. In case of Grameen, perhaps 70-80% of the time is spent in carrying out transactions whereas in SHG 70-80% of the time is spent on member interactions. In both cases, a lot of time is spent on counting and recounting currency notes and making accounting entries in passbooks. Some attempts have been made to automate the latter, including smart cards and hand-held terminals, but the time-savings are not good enough to enable the staff to hold more meetings per day than at present. SHG meetings tend to be less frequent, monthly not weekly. A bank worker need not attend every time, or even ever, as the group develops.

4.3. Co-operative Model

In common parlance, a co-operative is an autonomous association of people who are considered as the members of the co-operative. These members are united voluntarily to meet their common socio-economic and cultural needs. A co-operative is a democratically member-controlled institution. This has been initiated by Co-operative Development Forum (CDF), Hyderabad which has relied upon a "Credit Union" model involving saving first strategy. It has built up a network of Women Thrifts Groups (WTGs) and Men Thrift Group (MTGs). They are registered under Mutually Aided Co-operative Society Act (MACs) and mobilize saving resources from the members and access outside/supplementary resources from the institutional systems.

In the case of cooperatives, all borrowers are members of the organization either directly or indirectly by being members of primary cooperatives or associations which are members of the apex society. Creditworthiness and loan security are a function of co-operative membership within which member savings and peer pressure are assumed to be a key factor. There is now a large number of 'new generation' cooperative credit societies in India devoted specifically to providing financial services to the poor. Most of these are in Andhra Pradesh which was the first enacted a law permitting mutually aided-as opposed to traditional government-asisted-cooperative societies. Elsewhere, a number of well known programmes such as the SEWA Bank, Ahmedabad, the Indian Cooperative Network for Women, Tamil Nadu and the Annapurna Mahila Cooperative Credit Society in Mumbai have still survived under the traditional cooperative laws.

4.4. Individual Banking Model

Under the individual banking model, there are two sub models: one where joint liability groups are formed-thereby providing social collateral to the lending institution, the other being direct lending to individual clients. Both the models are appropriate for larger clients who either carry out enterprises that hire the other poor who want to be self employed. The reason why this works with larger clients is because the transaction size is large enough to justify the transaction costs. Village unit system of Bank Racist Indonesia is arguably the world's biggest and most profitable microfinance institution. They do not reach all the poor, may be only a few of the very poorest, and they do not use and never have used any form of group at all. In India, BASIX offers both individual lending products in addition to group lending.

The SHG and the Grameen models offer economics of transaction costs to the MFI, but at the cost of the members' time, because the unit of dealing is the 'group' rather than the individual. In contrast, MFIs offering individual loans incur high transaction costs for servicing their borrowers, particularly where they are engaged in farming, since it is difficult to locate a farmer, as compared to a weaver or a shop-keeper in a village.

4.5. Hybrid or Mixed Model

Some MFIs started with Grameen model but converted to the SHG model at a later stage. However, they did not completely do away with Grameen type lending and smaller groups. They are an equal mix of SHG and Grameen model. For example, BASIX uses a number of delivery channels and methodologies (including lending to SHGs) to provide financial services.

The Indian sub-continent is diverse and we need to understand why some things work in some areas and not in others. This has to be seen in the context of the overall fabric of the state, the alternate institutions and their growth. We also need to very closely examine why alternative models of reaching out the poor are not working in certain parts of country. Is it the absence of a sufficient number of appropriate social intermediaries? Is the cost of promoting appropriate delivery mechanism too high? The typology of the microfinance delivery mechanism is only a route taken to address the basis issue of poverty. Therefore, it does not matter what the typology or the ideology behind the typology is as long as the channel is appropriate for the social milieu and can deliver the services to the deserving people. If the objective is outreach, then growth should naturally happen. There are fast growing Grameen models and equally fast growing individual banking models.

Several governmental schemes are being routed through microfinance, including a very large project funded by the World Bank and being implemented in the state of Andhra Pradesh. Similarly organization like Hidustand Lever have looked at the potential of these groups as a channel for retailing and have launched a programme called ' Project Shakti' to tap the smaller villages through micro credit channel.[3]

4.6. Rotating Saving and Credit Association (ROSCA)

Rotating Saving and Credit Association (ROSCA) is a type of democratic association where a group of individuals (from 5 to 50 individuals), primarily women, join hand together for making a regular cyclical or periodical contribution to a common fund. The fund is then relented to one member in each cycle in the form of a loan. For example, if a group of 30 members contribute Rs.20 per month, continuously for 10 months, and then the collected amount of Rs.6000 is provided to one or more members in the form of loan. Selection of the member who is supposed to receive the loan is done by consensus, by lottery, by bidding or other agreed methods. Generally, outside financial intermediaries like NGOs are not involved in ROSCAs, and all the organisational operations are carried out by the members. Unlike credit unions, ROSCAs do not charge any interest on loans rather the interest is implicit. There are also limitations associated with ROSCA and some of the limitations are given below:

a) Inflexibility in structure and operations;

b) Selection of a member for provision of a loan;

c) Unavailability of a loan in urgency;

d) Unavailability of a loan of desired size;

e) High cost incurred in operations in meetings like refreshments, forgoing other works for attending meetings etc.; and

f) High risk due to high member dropouts, defaults and fraud.

4.7. Village Banking Model

According to ACCION, "Village Banking is a lending methodology in which clients-typically women-form groups of approximately 10-30 individuals that are automatically responsible for leadership, bye-laws, bookkeeping, fund management and loan super-vision. The group pools funds to use for business loans, savings, and mutual support, and members cross-guarantee individual loans."

The "Village Banking" Model was developed by FINCA International, based in USA. These "Village Banks" are community-based thrifts and credit associations with primary objective of improving the socio-economic status and living standards of the members through promotion of self-employment activities. Village banks are highly democratic, self-managed, grassroots organizations. They elect their own leaders, select their own members, create their own bylaws, do their own bookkeeping, manage all funds, disburse and deposit all funds, resolve loan delinquency problems, and levy their own fines on members who come late, miss meetings, or fall behind in their payments.

To eliminate the need for collateral (the poor man's obstacle to receiving bank loans), village banks rely on a variation of the *solidarity lending* methodology. It relies on a system of cross-guarantees, where each member of a village bank ensures the loan of every other member. This system gives rise to an atmosphere of social pressure within the village bank, where the cost of social embarrassment motivates bank members to repay their loans in full. The admixture of cross-guarantees and social pressure makes it possible for even the poorest people to receive loans. This method has proven very effective for FINCA, yielding a repayment rate of over 97% in its worldwide network.

The functioning of the "Village Banks" rests upon the member whereas the external agencies like NGOs, Banks etc. wok only as funders. The "Village Banking" Model is not in use in India.

Out of all models, three models, i.e. SHG model, Grameen Model and Cooperative Models are very popular and widely used in India.

NOTES

1. R. Srinivasan and MS Sriram, "Microfinance in India: Discussion", *IIMB Management Review*, June 2003.
2. Sabyasachi Das, "Self Help Groups & Micro Credit: Synergic Integration", *Kurukshetra*, August 2003.
3. R. Srinivasan and M.S. Sriram, "Microfinance: An introduction", *IIMB Management Review*, June 2003.

5
Global Experience of Microfinance

"Microfinance is not a charity. It is a way to extend the same rights and services to low-income households that are available to everyone else. It is recognition that poor people are the solution, not the problem"

– Kofi Annan, Secretary General, United Nations in 2004

5.1. Global Microfinance Scenario

Microfinance has gradually developed to be a worldwide movement, no longer being a subject matter of microfinance practitioners alone. Governments, donors, development agencies, banks, foundations, corporations, business communities, civil societies, researchers, universities, consultants, philanthropists and others are taking an increasing interest in it. It has been evidenced worldwide that microfinance helps the poor to overcome poverty, and not through charity. It is a financial system that serves the poor with financial services in a most effective and productive way.

The microfinance sector has grown over time with more and different types of actors becoming involved, with increasing numbers of geographic regions around the world being serviced, with new types of products and services being developed, and with ideas and technologies to support it.

The global picture regarding microfinance outreach is quite impressive. From a mere 7.6 million poorest families in 1997, the Micro Credit Summit Campaign reported an outreach of more than 92 million clients by December 31, 2004. This number includes 66.6million families who were among the poorest when they started with a program. Of these 66.6 million poorest clients, 55.7 million or 83.6 percent were served by the 52 largest individual institutions, all with 1, 00,000 or more clients. Among these largest MFIs, 79% are in Asia, 17% are in Africa and only 4% are in Latin America.[1]

Of the 3,164 institutions that had reported to the Micro Credit Summit Campaign by 31 December, 2004, 1628 were in Asia, 994 in Africa, 388 in Latin America and Caribbean, 48 in North America, 34 in the Middle East, 72 in Europe and the Newly Independent states. The increase in the number of institutions reporting from 618 in 1997 to 3164 in 2004 is definitely an indication of an impressive growth in the field of microfinance.

According to the United Nations, 2.7 billion people in the world today – almost half of the world's population – struggle to live on less than $2 a day. It is difficult for people in the developing world to get access to credit by conventional means because banks generally require the security of collateral loans. Through microfinance services, micro loans enable micro entrepreneurs to acquire working capital, equipment, tools, materials, inventory, or other means to start or expand income-producing businesses.

Prof. Yunus recently estimated that There are 1.2 billion poor in the World. Recently experts warn that due to indiscriminate flow of resources to the micro-finance programmes and rapid growth of micro-finance institutions (MFIs), the campaign to help 100 millions poorest people throughout the world may get derailed from the course of action set by the Micro credit Submit. Even Prof. Yunus also warned saying that. "The point is not to pour in such much money that it kills the existing initiatives, but to help build more and more grass-root organizations and create institutions and policies". Another expert, Mr. Ismail Seregeldin of the World Bank, also said, " We warn of the danger of measuring progress by how much money is available for micro finance, because if you do so you risk killing it. Mobilising money is not the problem the real problem is how to structure the system".[2]

UN resolution: "International Year of Micro-finance"

Micro-finance has proven to be powerful tool to address the issues of the poor. With more than 1.2 billion people around the world living on less than $1 per day, the United Nations has declared the year 2005 as the "International Year of Micro credit" the goal is to reach 100 million of poorest families by the year 2005.

United Nations declared year 2005 as the international Year of micro-credit focusing on following areas:[3]

a) Assessment and promotion of the contribution of micro-credit and micro-finance towards achieving the goals as contained in Millennium Development Goals (MDGs), particularly targets related to having the proportion of the people living in extreme poverty by 2015 and promoting gender equality and empowerment of woman.

b) Promotion of awareness and understanding of micro-credit and micro-finance, their role in poverty eradication including achieving the MDG and how they empower people and contribute to communities

c) Identification of critical measures for Government to optimally stimulate sustainable, pro-poor financial sectors and build collective vision and strategies that position micro-credit and micro-finance as integral part of country's financial system.

d) Increase of the capacity of the micro-credit and micro-finance service providers to be more effective and efficient at addressing the needs of poor and very poor people, and strengthening the capacity of donors and Governments to support those institutions by following good practice of micro credit and micro-finance principles.

Major Funding Agencies

Major Funding Agencies for microfinance are Kreditanstalt for Wiederafbu (Kfw), Swedish International Development Agency (SIDA), Canadian Internal Development Agency (CIDA), World Bank, Asian Development Bank, International Fund for Agricultural Development (IFAD), Consultative Group to Assist the Poorest (CGAP), USAID, GTZ etc.

5.2. Microfinance in Bangladesh

BRAC, Grameen Bank, ASA and PROSHIKA are the four principal MFIs operating in Bangladesh. While the Grameen Bank has a special status in the banking set-up of the country, the other three are Non-Government Organizations (NGOs). By the end of December 2001, these MFIs had an overall membership of over 105 lakh people, of which over 88 percent were women[4]. They had disbursed a total amount of Tk.4356 core.[5]

BRAC: (Bangladesh Rural Advancement Committee) is the largest NGO of the Bangladesh with total membership of 41.38 lakh[6]. Initially, it was set-up in 1972 as a relief organization and empowerment of the poor, especially women, in the rural areas of the country. Besides providing microfinance to its clients it also works in the fields of literacy, legal education and human rights.

Grameen[7] Bank: which is the largest provider of micro credit in the country, had its origins in an action research project in 1976 and was formally recognized as a bank in 1983 through an ordinance issued by the Government. Although termed a bank, it does not have a scheduled status from the central bank of the country, the Bangladesh Bank. The Grameen Bank provides loans to the landless poor, particularly women, to promote self-employment and make them income earners. As at the end of December 2001, it had a membership of 23.78 lakh and cumulative, micro credit disbursement of Tk. 14,653 crore.[8]

With an ambitious aim of alleviating poverty and empowering women in rural Bangladesh, Grameen Bank starts its operation in full fledge since 1983 under the dynamic leadership of Dr. Muhammad Yunus, a professor of Economics at Chittagong University of Southern Bangladesh. Yunus says, *"I became aware that there was much that could not be solved by following the teachings of development economics. I decided to go out among the common folk in countryside to see for myself"*.[9]

While informing about the start of Grameen Bank, Yunus (1997) informs that Grameen Bank started its life in the tiny village of Jobra by lending 50 taka ($1.50) to Sophia Khatoon who worked seven days a week making bamboo stools which she sold to moneylender who provided credit to buy her raw materials. She paid the moneylender interest to the tune of 10 percent a day-more than 3,000 per cent a year. With her loan from the Grameen Bank it took

Sophia Khatoon only a few months to establish her own self-employment and increase her income five fold. In this time she repaid her loan with interest at the bank rate. Then, Yunus was trying to make a link between bank and the poor people in that village but the banks are tied to their procedures and will advance loans only to those people have collateral or guarantor. Finding it impossible to get credit without collateral, Yunus himself began as guarantor of the poor and took loan of $ 300. In 1976, he disbursed the loan to the poor people that was the starting of Jobra Grameen Bank Prakalpa (Jobra Grameen Bank Project) then the project was under the Rural Economics programme of Chittagong University. He , then, put forward a proposal to the Central Bank of Bangladesh and got the permission to operate the programme but with one condition that he had to prove within two years that poor are worthy for the loan and can repay the money. Dr. Yanus started in Tangail District and found the system working well. Dr. Yunus one day finally asked himself, "why am I running after banks? Why don't I set up a bank that will work only for the poor?" In 1983, after a lot of running around, he received permission from the government to set up a bank. Thus the Grameen (rural) Bank was born as an independent financial institution.[10]

Grameen Bank started revolution in the sector of poverty alleviation, women empowerment and micro-enterprise. Success of Grameen Banks is mainly due to:

a) Intensive discipline, supervision and servicing considerable delegated authority from the staff.

b) The rigorous selection of borrowers and their projects with the assistance of staff members

c) The powerful peer pressure exerted on these individuals by the groups

d) The repayment scheme based on 50 weekly instalments contributes to its viability.

Grameen Bank credit delivery system has the following features:

a) Extend banking facilities to poor men and women;

b) Eliminate the exploitation of the poor by money lenders;

c) Create opportunities of self-employment for the vast multitude of unemployed people in rural Bangladesh;

d) Bring the disadvantaged, mostly the women from the poorest households, within the fold of an organizational format which they can understand and manage by themselves;

e) Reverse the age-old vicious circle of low income, low saving and low investment, into virtuous circle of low income , injection of credit , investment, more income, more saving, more investment more income;

f) There is an exclusive focus on the poorest of the poor;

g) Borrowers are organized into small homogeneous groups;

h) Special loan conditionality which are particularly suitable for the poor;

i) Simultaneous undertaking of a social development agenda addressing basic needs of the clientel;

j) Raise the social and political consciousness of the newly organized groups;

k) Focus increasingly on women from the poorest households, whose urge for survival has a far greater bearing on the development of the family;

l) Encourage their monitoring of social and physical infrastructure projects-housing, sanitation, drinking water, education, family planning etc.;

m) Design and development of organization and management systems capable of delivering program resources to targeted clientele; and

n) Expansion of loan portfolio to meet diverse development needs of the poor, e.g. credit for building sanitary latrines, credit for installation of tube wells that supply drinking water and irrigation for kitchen gardens credit for seasonal cultivation to buy agricultural inputs loan fro leasing equipment/machinery, et cell phones purchased by Grameen Bank members, finance projects undertaken by the entire family of a seasoned borrower etc.

The underlying premise of Grameen is that, in order to emerge from poverty and remove themselves from the clutches of users and middlemen, landless peasants need access to credit, without which they cannot be expected to launch their own enterprises, however small these may be.

In defiance of the traditional rural banking postulate whereby " no collateral (in this case, land) means no credit", Grameen Bank experiment set out to prove – successfully that lending to the poor is not an impossible proposition: on the contrary, it gives landless peasants the opportunity to purchase their own tools , equipment, or to the necessary means of production and embark on income-generating ventures which will allow them escape from the vicious cycle of low income , low saving, low investment , low income". In other word, the banker's confidence rest upon the will and capacity of the borrowers to succeed in their undertaking activities.

The mode of operation of Grameen Bank is as follows. A bank branch is set up with a branch manager and a number of centre managers and covers an area of about 15 to 22 villages. The manager and the workers start by visiting villages to familiarize themselves with the local milieu in which they will be operating and identify the prospective clientele, as well as explain the purpose, the functions and the mode of operation of the bank to the local population. Groups of five prospective borrowers are formed: in the first stage, only two of them are eligible for, and receive, a loan.

The group is observed for a month to see if the members are conforming to the rules of the bank. Only if the first two borrowers begin to repay the principal plus interest over a period of six weeks, do the other members of the group become eligible themselves for a loan. Because of these restrictions, there is substantial group pressure to keep individual records clear. In this sense, the collective responsibility of the group serves as the collateral on the loan.

Loans are small, but sufficient to finance the micro-enterprises undertaken borrowers: rice husking, machine repairing, purchase of rickshaws, buying of milk cows, goats, cloth, pottery etc. The rate on loan recovery is currently 95 per cent-due to group pressure and self-interest , as well as the motivation of borrowers.

Although mobilization of savings is also been pursued alongside the lending activities of the Grameen Bank, most of the latter's loan able funds are increasingly obtained on commercial terms from the central bank, other financial institutions, the money market, and from bilateral and multilateral aid organizations.

The most important feature is the recovery rate of loans, which is as high as 98%. A still more interesting feature is that of advancing credit without any collateral security. To obtain loan, potential borrowers must form a group of five, gather once a week for loan repayment meeting etc. The formation of groups, the key unit in the credit programme is the first necessary step to receive credit. Loans are initially made to two individuals in the group, who are then under pressure from the rest of the members to repay in good time. If the borrowers default, the other members of the group may forfeit their chance of a loan. There have been occasions when the group has decided to fire or expel a member who has failed to attend weekly meetings or wilful defaulted on repayment of loan. The Grameen Bank has provided an inbuilt incentive for prompt and timely repayment by the borrower, i.e. gradual increase in the borrowing eligibility of subsequent loans.[11]

As on April 2005, the Grameen bank had 1456 branches, covering over 1,687 villages with staff strength of 13,492. The Total number of borrowers was 4.48 million out of which 96 per cent were women. Total amount of loan disbursed by Grameen Bank since inception is TK 228.27 billion (US$ 4.79 billion). Out of this Tk 206.29 billion (US$ 4.29 billion) has been repaid. Current amount of the outstanding loans stands at Tk 21.98 billion (US$ 346.33 million). Projected disbursement for 2005 is Tk 33.00 billion (US$ 455.8 million). End of the year outstanding loan is projected to be at Tk 27.0 billion (US$ 448 million). The recovery rate has been at 98.91 percent.

ASA (Association for Social Advancement): It was established in 1978. Initially, it was involved in the area of legal and human rights. It later changed its focus to economic empowerment of the poor through micro credit delivery system. Its micro credit programme started in 1991 and had membership of 15.79 lakh in December 2001.[12] It is now reputed to be the most cost-effective MFI in the world.

PROSHIKA: it was established in 1976. It derives its name from three Bengali words namely, Proshikshan (Training), Shiksha (education) and Kaj (action). Since inception, the organization has been working for the empowerment of the poor through credit and other inputs like development training, education, health and social forestry. It had 24.48 lakh members.[13]

While ASA and Grameen Bank are pure MFIs, the other two institutions have adopted the "Credit Plus" approach in their activities. Besides microfinance, BARC and PROSHIKA have significant strides in the fields of education, health, nutrition, environment and organization building.

The MFIs of Bangladesh place a great deal of importance to group solidarity and cohesiveness. Grameen Bank has formulated sixteen decisions, which are a sort of rules, which the members have to abide by. Besides the start of every meeting, the members dutifully recite all the decisions in once voice. Similarly, BRAC has its own eighteen principles, which are in rhythmic form and the members also recite the same at the start of every meeting, in PROSHIKA, even the loan is given in the name of the group. The system and procedures of the MFIs are quite simple and in tune with the requirement and capabilities of their clients. The interest rate calculations are extremely simple and are known to even the illiterate borrowers. Repayment is on weekly basis and the borrower clearly knows the amount required to be repaid. Documentation is minimal.

5.3. Microfinance in Indonesia

Indonesia has been one of the first countries to develop commercial microfinance in Asia, with regulated financial institutions providing the bulk of microfinance services. Bank Rakyat Indonesia (BRI) units have been in existence for twenty years, and some forms of 'People's credit banks' or BPRs, have appeared more than a century ago. Microcredit is defined by Bank Indonesia, the central bank, as a loan below Rp.50 million (US$5,373), a financial product provided by formal and semi-formal financial providers in Indonesia. In addition to the success of commercial microfinance providers, Indonesia has also been a favourable ground for the development of numerous subsidised government programmes, local and community-based financial institutions, cooperatives and NGOs.

As of 2003, 31.2 million poor people were living in Indonesia, and represented 17.4% of the population. Approximately 20% of Indonesia's 214 million people depend on micro- and small-scale businesses to earn a living, but only 10 million out of 42 million microenterprises have access to credit from formal financial institutions.

During the financial crisis 1997-98, commercial microfinance providers such as BRI units and BPRs have shown resilience and growth in savings mobilization when the whole banking sector was collapsing. Micro savings have proven to be a valuable safety net for low-income population and micro entrepreneurs.

Several studies have demonstrated that there is still an unmet demand for microfinance services, as a majority of rural households still do not have access to a source of funds from a semi-formal or formal institution. The regulated microfinance providers, BRI Units and BPRs, tends to cover mostly the upper levels of the microenterprise market, in district and sub-district towns, with loans of more than Rp. 3 million (US$320), while NGOs, cooperatives, and village-based institutions (BKDs) reach a lower end of the market but still have a limited outreach in rural areas.

Indonesia has had a long history of commercial microfinance, starting a century ago with the Badan Kredit Desa (BKD or Village Credit Organisation), village-owned banks offering microcredit on commercial terms. Approximately 5,000 BKDs operate in Indonesia now a day. Sustainable microfinance in the banking sector began in 1970 with the opening of Bank Dagan Bali (BDB); a private bank in Bali specialized in commercial microfinance, which built it success on the knowledge of microfinance clients and on state-of-the art savings products. BDB was closed by Bank Indonesia in 2004 due to governance and liquidity problems.

Another significant player in the formal microfinance market is the state-owned pawning company, Perum Pegadaian, serving million of low-income people. With these three main players (BRI, BPRs, and Pegadaian), the formal financial sector is the dominant force in microfinance, and outperforms the semiformal and informal sectors by a large margin.

Bank Rakyat Indonesia (BRI): BRI which acts as Micro-finance institution and is now the largest financially sustainable intermediary in the developing world. BRI's approach to micro-finance making its services widely available and the financial intermediary profitable helped the country reduce the incidence of poverty from about 40 percent of the population in mid 1970s to about 11 percent in 1996.

In 1984, in the wake of new financial reforms undertaken by the government, Bank Rakyat Indonesia transformed its sub-branches ('Unit Desa') network operating at sub district level. The outlets were transformed from loss-making channeling agent for the government subsidized credit program for rice cultivation (BIMAS) into commercial microfinance intermediaries. The unit network is now the largest and one of the most profitable rural micro banking networks in the developing world.

When the East Asian economic crisis began and poverty in the country started to rise in 1997, BRI concentrated on financing poor people, who had lost their jobs, for pursuing informal sector enterprises. It also gave secured and tailor-made deposit services to poor people in times of crisis. During the financial crisis, most of BRI microfinance clients kept their trust in the financial services offered by BRI units; clients maintained and even increased their savings levels. BRI continued its wide outreach, high repayment rate and profitability even during the 1997-98 East –Asian Economic Crisis. The BRI Unit Desas unaffected success during the crisis were in sharp contrast with BRI heavy losses on its corporate portfolio, which meant that BRI became technically bankrupt, and had to be rescued by a public restructuring and refinancing program, as for the rest of the banking industry.

As a direct consequence of the financial crisis, 82 commercial banks were closed, 13 were nationalised and others recapitalised or merged into a larger financial institution, the newly established Bank Mandiri. The BRI unit's network saved BRI from being merged into this larger bank. With bank closures, many small depositors lost their savings, sustaining a severe crisis of confidence towards financial institutions.

World Bank says about this Bank and its operation that "Programme succeeded because the bank loaned at market rate, used income to finance their operations, kept operating cost low and devised appropriate savings instruments to attract depositors. BRI adopted demand-led commercial financial system approach in sharp contrast to supply led system approach for financing poor households under its microfinance programme. While implementing supply-led subsidized lending approach during 1970s and early 1980s, BRI had significant loan loses and over dues".[14]

The Bank Rakyat Indonesia units (BRI Units), or sub-branches, were first established in the 1970s under a government scheme (BIMAS) to provide agricultural inputs for rice cultivation. Unprofitable until 1983-84, the BIMAS was discontinued and the system was restructured with support from the World Bank and USAID. It transformed into the most successful rural network for microfinance provision managed by a commercial bank. The BRI units built their success on demand-based financial products and the development of individual profit centres (originally called Unit Desa). The KUDEDES product, an individual loan, requires collateral and can be used for working capital and investment purposes. The SIMPEDES savings product allows unlimited withdrawals, attracts competitive interest rates and is guaranteed by the government. Each BRI unit is treated as a profit centre, financially self-reliant and subsidy independent. At the end of September 2004, BRI was operating 4,049 units, and 325 branches. BRI partial privatisation was a success, with an IPO and share listing on the 10th November 2003, and shares oversubscribed 15.4 times. The government sold approximately 30% of BRI capital.

At the end of September 2004, BRI had 87% of its loan portfolio in micro, small and medium enterprises, while the corporate lending represented the remaining 13%. 31% of the Rp.58, 119 billions (US$ 6.2 billions) in loan outstanding was related to the microenterprise sector, or Rp. 18,146 billions (US$ 1.9 billion).

BPRs or People's Credit Banks

The generic term for small financial institutions in Indonesia is Bank Perkreditan Rakyat (People's Credit Bank, or BPR), which were introduced by Bank Indonesia in 1978. After the 1988 financial reforms of PAKTO 88, new secondary banks were established, also called BPRs. Specific requirements for the licensing of pre-existing BPRs (capital, size of deposits) were set but never fully respected. Today, BPRs includes licensed financial institutions, mostly privately-owned, that meet the criteria specified in the 1992 Banking law, and number 2,148 in 2004 (accounting for 15% of the microfinance market), and almost 9,000 public rural financial institutions that are not licensed, and can be categorized as generic BPRs, which include village-owned BKDs of Java and Madura, and the Lembaga Dana dan Kredit Pedesaan (LDKPs) or Rural Fund and Credit Institution, owned mostly by provincial governments (or in some cases by villages).

BPRs offer loan, savings and term deposits, but no checking accounts. They serve the middle segment of the microfinance market, generally chosen by clients who cannot provide enough collateral to access BRI loans. They have mixed results and generally low financial performance, weak management and lack internal auditing and supervision.

BPRs do not directly target micro entrepreneurs and have been pushed by Bank Indonesia's regulations to do more conservative, collaterised lending.

With the licensing of BPRs, these small financial institutions operating at local level can have a public or private ownership, which entails several differences:

a) Public BPRs usually don't compete with one another as they cover different locations. In fact they operate in contexts of quasi monopolies. In contrast, private BPRs compete with one another.

b) Public BPR are more efficient in mobilising savings, and provide smaller loans than private BPRs.

c) Public BPRs have linkages with commercial banks, in contrast with private ones, which are more recently established, mostly present in urban or semi-urban areas.

d) Public BPRs are more profitable than private BPRs, with high returns among BKDs. The public LDKP seems to be the most successful.

As of March 2004, they were 2,148 regulated BPRs reaching 2.4 million borrowers and 5 million depositors, with a 77% loan to deposit ratio, while keeping a low 8% non-performing loan (NPL) ratio. 61% were registered as limited liability companies, 36% as government enterprises, and the rest as cooperatives. As of March 2004, licensed BPRs had Rp.13, 430 billion (US$1.4 billion) in assets, from which Rp. 9,431 billion (US$1 billion) was in loans outstanding. They had also mobilised Rp.2, 665 billion (US$284 million) in savings, and Rp.3, 360 billion (US$360 million) in time deposits. In 2003, they collectively made Rp.429 billion (US$46 million) in profit, posting a 25% return on equity, and 3.4% return on assets.

Perum Pegadaian

Perum Pegadaian (PP) is a large state-owned pawning company providing microfinance services to more than 15 million customers in 2004 through 812 branches. During that year, PP provided Rp.10, 450 billion (US$1, 1 billion) in loans, and generated a profit of Rp.230 billion (US$24.7 million). Pegadaian offers fast and efficient financial services, allowing clients to turn their valuables temporally into cash without having to sell them. PP provides generally small loans, 88% of PP loans in 2001 were less than Rp.500, 000 (US$66).

Semi-formal Financial Sector

The semi-formal financial sector is composed by thousands of non-bank financial institutions, such as Badan Kredit Desa (BKDs, or village credit organisations), and LKDP, finance and insurance companies, cooperatives and credit unions, and NGOs. These institutions are not directly regulated by Bank Indonesia but registered and licensed by other state authorities and/or regional governments. The semi-formal sector reaches approximately 1 to 2 million clients.

Established more than a century ago, **BKDs** were among the first microcredit institutions in Indonesia. They are village-owned organisations located on Java and in Madura. BKDs are generally small organisations operating at village level, with disparities of performance among them. They generally suffer from poor performance, weak management capacity and are restrained by village bureaucracy.

BKDs are supervised and administered through BRI's branches, on behalf of Bank Indonesia, who reimburse BRI for the expenses related to the supervision. Managed by village leaders,

BKDs offer savings and credit products to their clients. Compulsory savings are required in order to borrow. Loans are typically of a small size, without collateral, and are processed quickly. They are not allowed to mobilise voluntary savings. They usually open one day a week, the amount deposited by clients is transferred to the BKD account at BRI. BKDs finance their lending requirements through mobilised earning on deposits, compulsory savings and borrowings from BRI.

LKDP are 'rural credit fund institutions', which takes different forms such as Badan Kredit Kecamatan (BKK), strong in Java, and LPDs in Bali. They are supervised by local provincial governments.

BKK Central Java is one example of a successful 'generic BPR', an LDKP system, owned by the provincial government. It was born as a credit institution to target the poor; and was allowed to accept savings only after 1984. It uses typical microfinance techniques, i.e. loans unsecured and character-based, small initially, then increased gradually according to repayment performance, loans paid in equal installments, no collateral but mandatory savings. It received technical assistance from USAID.

The Lembaga Perkreditan Desa (LPD) of Bali is considered the best LDKP system in Indonesia, despite the strong local competition. It was established in 1988 as village-owned financial institutions, with an economic and a social role in the community. It received technical assistance from USAID and GTZ. LPDs are seen as profitable entities, which rely on savings and deposit as the main source of funding. LPD differ from the provincial government controlled institutions (LKDPs) by being owned by local community organisations. The glue of customary obligations and relationships is a significant factor in holding these small financial institutions together. In mid-1999, 910 LPD served some 545,000 clients, which meant that more than 80% of the Balinese population was reached by LPDs, a level unrivalled anywhere. The Balinese LPD and the BKKs account for a substantial part of the LDKPs that have not converted to BPR status.

Cooperatives are seen as highly politicised and used as government funding vehicles. Government-sponsored village unit cooperatives (Koperasi Unit Desa or KUD) were established during the colonial period and seen by the constitution and Pancasila as one of the pillars of the Indonesian state. However, under the Suharto regime, they were mainly used for political purposes, and never seen as real people's institutions but as instruments of government control on rural people, and on pressure to achieve agricultural production targets. Two types of cooperatives involved in microfinance exist, the credit and savings cooperatives, Koperasi Simpan Pinjam (KSP), and savings and credit units (Unit Simpan Pinjam, USP) of multipurpose cooperatives. Most cooperative are highly subsidised and used as government' funds channels. However a few grassroots cooperatives have demonstrated stronger results.

An independent credit union movement, supported by the Credit Union Coordination Board of Indonesia (Badan Kordinasi Koperasi Kredit or BK3I), appear more successful. In addition, INKOPDIT (Induk Koperasi Kredit) or the Credit Union Central of Indonesia has started a microfinance program in 2004, which build up the capacity of self-help groups, progressively transformed into cooperatives.

NGOs

A vast majority of NGOs remains unsustainable and dependent on donors' funds to operate. A few NGOs have ventured in commercial microfinance by setting up their own BPRs, as did Bina Swadaya, one of the largest NGOs, or by starting their own commercial bank (Yayasan Purba Danarta in Central Java). Some NGOs use a modified Grameen Bank methodology, such as Yayasan Mitra Usaha (YMU) reaching 12,000 clients, and Yayasan Dharma Bhakti Parasahabat (YDBP) reaching 100,000 members. YDBP uses BPRs to expand its microfinance activities, having acquired four BPRs; it plans to open new BPRs or branches to sustain its expansion. YDBP is the fastest growing and largest NGO-MFI in Indonesia, while serving exclusively women and keeping a relatively high repayment rate (95%).

Bina Swadaya (Self-Reliance Development Foundation) has helped self-help groups to link with banks, especially in many of the most disadvantaged areas of Indonesia. It worked in the poorest villages targeted by the IDT government program developed in the 1990s. Bina Swadaya has also set up its own BPRs and since 2002 has adapted the ASA methodology from Bangladesh in 7 of its 21 branches.

PPSW works exclusively with women on a wide range of issues, such as economic and social development, migrant workers, reproductive health and education. In microfinance, PPSW aims to raise women's income through the development of community-based organisations and cooperatives. PPSW has set up in 2001 and since then financed a secondary cooperative, KOPPERTI, to serve a network of primary cooperatives, which are based on the aggregation of self-help groups.

5.4. Microfinance in Kenya

The Kenyan Microfinance industry is one of the oldest and most established in Africa. Two of the current six to ten big players in the MFI market in Kenya started operating as early as the 1980s. The Kenyan microfinance market was traditionally characterised by a similarity in lending methodology, with the majority of MFIs doing group based lending, often with a second tier guarantee group known as 'chikola' groups. This landscape is now changing with more diverse methodologies emerging every day as new MFIs enter the market.

Savings and Credit Cooperatives (SACCOS)

The SACCOS system is a mutual membership organization. It involves pooling of voluntary savings from members in the form of shares. The savings/shares form the basis for extending credit to members. Credit is usually based on three times the level of savings/shares. SACCOs are regulated by the Co-operatives Societies Act. SACCO societies respond to peoples need for food and food production, housing, education, small enterprise, transport, medical care, clothing and expenses in marriage, birth and death. Additionally, they instil thrift, self-reliance, democratic principles, social concern, leadership and management. SACCOs have grown rapidly over the years. There were over 4,000 SACCOs with 2.9 million members; share capital of Kshs 29 billion and credit out-reach of Kshs 22 billion in 1999. A number of the SACCOs are increasingly getting interested in offering a limited range of banking services. Few SACCOs are already offering such services; however, the legitimacy of their bank operations is a critical issue. SACCOs are mainly organized as workplace or cash crop based savings and credit associations whereby people with a common bond, e.g. by working together in the same company or institution, save regularly, thus building enough deposits for lending within the group. There are two main umbrella SACCOs namely, Kenya Union of Savings and Credit Co-operatives (KUSCO) and Kenya Rural Savings and Credit Cooperative Society Union (KERUSSU).

MicroStart partnered with five MFIs: Equity Building Society (EBS), Women's Economic Empowerment Consort (WEEC), Business Initiatives and Management Assistance (BIMAS), Kenya Entrepreneurship Promotion Programme (KEPP), and World Concern Kenya.[15]

Rotating Savings and Credit Associations (ROSCAs) and Accumulating Savings and Credit Associations (ASCRAs) are also locally known in Kenya as 'merry-go-rounds', *itega* or *giteti*. Some of them are registered at the Ministry of Social Affairs, others are not. As self-regulation or group-based rules provide the most decisive regulatory framework for ROSCAs and ASCRAs (in mobilizing, rotating, accumulating and disbursing money), they are all labelled as informal here whether registered or not.

Commercial Banks

The number of banking institutions actively involved in the provision of microfinance is increasing. These include the Post Bank, K-Rep Bank, the Kenya Commercial Bank (KCB), the Co-operative Bank of Kenya, Equity Building Society (EBS) and Family Finance Building Society. These institutions have, in the past, channelled funds from organisations such as USAID, the OPEC Fund, the IFC and DANIDA to the microfinance and small enterprise sector.

NGO-MFIs

At the end of the 1990s, the sector was dominated by NGO-MFIs, which still play a large role in terms of the number of institutions. There are about 130 NGOs who practices some form of micro financing in Kenya. About 20 of them practice pure micro financing and can be labelled as NGO-micro-finance institutions (NGO-MFIs) while the rest practice micro financing alongside social welfare activities. Some of the major players in the NGO sector are K-Rep Development Agency (KDA), Faulu Kenya, Kenya Women Finance Trust (KWFT), Pride Kenya, PRIDE Africa (Sunlink services), WEDCO (formerly a program of CARE International), Small and Medium Enterprise Programmes Limited (formerly of the National Council of Churches of Kenya), Machakos Catholic Diocese, Kenya Small Traders and Entrepreneurs Society (KSTES), Business Initiatives and Management Assistance (BIMAs), Ecumenical Loans Fund (ECLOF) and Vintage Management Services. Faulu and WEDCO, two of the major institutions have meanwhile changed institutional charter from international NGO into a microfinance company, registered in Kenya with limited liability under the Companies Act.

The Kenyan Rural Enterprise Program (K-Rep)

K-Rep initially focused on lending funds provided by USAID and other donors to smaller organisations such as the National Council of Churches in Kenya (NCCK), KWFT, and Tototo among others. K-Rep transformed into a bank serving nearly 40,000 active clients and, by the end of 2002, had a portfolio of US$15 million. K-Rep Bank was the first NGO to become a bank in Africa. K-REP was designed as an intermediary NGO in 1984 to provide credit and technical assistance to other NGOs in Kenya. In the early 1990s, K-REP recognized a potential danger in combining the provision of financial services (loans and deposits) with non-financial services (training and technical assistance). This problem arose from the difficulty in assessing the cost of non-financial services, leading to such costs undermining the financial sustainability of the institution. This resulted in the organization adopting a minimalist approach (loans without training or technical assistance). The targeting philosophy of this approach was to offer financial services to existing entrepreneurs, not people that could be trained to become an entrepreneur. The minimalist approach was one of the main results of the adoption of a business-oriented approach as opposed to the integrated approach, in which financial service provision was only a minor and often ill-defined part of a wide range of programmes and services. Driven by the motivation of self-sustainability, K-REP reduced the number of NGOs it supported from twelve to four. The number was subsequently increased to five with the addition of KWFT. These five all promoted the minimalist approach. For donors, including Dutch CFAs, this meant that there was little scope for them to finance non-financial services of micro-finance agencies. The only remaining subsidy object was product development or financial institutional innovation.

Kenya Women's Finance Trust (KWFT)

(KWFT) was incorporated as a non-profit trust in 1982 and has grown into a leading MFI serving over 50,0000 active clients with a portfolio of over US$6 million at the end of 2002.By the early 1990's, interest in and knowledge of the microfinance industry had grown substantially and the "minimalist" group-based Grameen lending approach was adopted by many MFIs. Kenya Women Finance Trust (KWFT) was founded in 1981 as an affiliate of Women's World Banking (WWB) by professional women in Kenya to provide financial services to women in the country. KWFTs stated mission is to advance and promote the direct participation of economically active women in viable business to improve their economic and social status, by providing financial and non-financial services. The KWFT credit schemes aim to provide women with credit and technical assistance as a means of facilitating their integration into development. KWFT lending is directed to women under two group-based schemes and a pilot scheme for lending to individuals:

a) Type I: Biashara Lending Scheme (BLS)

The *Biashara* Lending Scheme gives loans to individual members through their groups. Loan amounts range from Ksh.10, 000 to 50,000. Once a group is formed and registered, members go through training in loan application and repayment procedures. In order to qualify for a loan, each woman in the group saves Kshs. 200 per week for eight weeks. After this, three women out of five become eligible for a loan. Four weeks later, during which time the borrowers would have started repaying weekly, the remaining two women in each group of five also, receive a loan. Loans are repaid weekly for a total of 52 weeks. The average annual interest rate of 18.57% is a flat rate, equivalent to approximately 33% on a reducing balance.

The BLS targets women groups that have business ventures. Women entrepreneurs organize themselves into six groups of five. Loans are given to individual women through these groups.

b) Type II: Uaminifu Lending Scheme (ULS)

The *Uaminifu* Lending Scheme (ULS) gives credit to existing groups (merry-go-rounds, *itega, giteti*, who in turn lend to individual group members. Security for the credit is provided by group savings and the co-guaranteeing system of members. Eligibility for a *Uaminifu* Loan depends on the following aspects:

i) Having members who are currently running small and micro-enterprises;
ii) Being registered with the Ministry of Culture and Social Services as a self help group;
iii) Having at least 10% of the total amount they intend to borrow as a group;
iv) Having or agreeing to open a bank account for depositing members savings; and
v) Having the intention and capacity to continue facilitating access to credit for members.

Preference is given to group members who operate manufacturing businesses and innovative ventures, especially those with a potential for creating substantial employment.

In a mid-term review of KWFT by order of DFID, it was concluded that, In essence, KWFT effectively has one group-based credit methodology with two versions which may be referred to as products. It was also observed that, the two products are becoming increasingly similar.

In particular, there are no significant process differences from the loan application stage. The evaluators also refer to the incidence of phantom members in *Uaminifu* groups that compelled KWFT to even screen individual group members of merry-go-rounds.

c) Type III: Barclays Bank of Kenya Credit Line Scheme (CLS)

The Credit Line Scheme (CLS) is the newest scheme of KWFT and is implemented in collaboration with Barclays Bank of Kenya. The Trust provides management skills, training and other technical services to clients while the bank meets their credit needs. Interest and bank charges are levied at commercial rates. To be eligible for CLS, the following criteria have to be fulfilled:

i) the applicant must be a member of KWFT;
ii) the applicant must be 100% owner of the business;
iii) the applicant must be running the business on a full-time basis;
iv) the applicant should operate the business in permanent buildings (rented premises must;
v) the applicant have a lease to cover the loan repayment period);
vi) the applicant must have been in operation for at least one year; and
vii) the applicant should be easily accessible to both KWFT staff and bank officials.

SunLink, PRIDE Africa

Mission and Objectives

PRIDE means Promotion of Rural Initiatives and Development Enterprises. PRIDE Africa is a micro finance and information group registered in the United States with operations in different countries in East Africa, including Tanzania, Uganda, Zambia and Kenya. PRIDE Africa microfinance operations in Kenya are through its SunLink Services project, which was originally conceived as a research and development project in 1995. Its major role was to involve the commercial banks in Kenya in providing financial services to the poor. With time, the project has evolved from a research project to a microfinance service provider, commencing its operations in 1999 in Nairobi.

Post Bank

Post Bank has five regional offices in Nyeri, Mombasa, Kisumu, and Nakuru, with its head office based in Nairobi. The bank has 58 directly controlled branches and sub-branches countrywide and also operates through 356 Post Offices and 99 Postal Agents on an agency basis. Post Bank is currently collaborating with MicroPED and MicroSave-Africa, two of the major microfinance support organizations in the country, in training a broad range of its staff in microfinance, conducting research on new products, and developing a strategy for marketing these services. The bank is a founder member of the Kenyan Association of Micro Finance Institutions (AMFI), a voluntary network of leading MFIs deeply involved in developing a legal framework for licensing, regulation, and supervision of the evolving microfinance industry.

5.5. Microfinance in Uganda[16]

In Uganda, some of the leading MFIs are, namely, the Foundation for International Community Assistance (FINCA), the Foundation for Credit and Community Assistance (FOCCAS), and the Promotion of Rural Initiatives and Development Enterprises (PRIDE),[17,18] Uganda Women's Finance Trust (UWFT), Volunteer Efforts for Development Concerns (VEDO), The Poverty Alleviation Credit Trust and UGAFODE. The brief profile of these MFIs along with theirs lending methodologies and experiences are given as under:

FINCA

FINCA is one of oldest best practice MFIs in Uganda. Its microfinance programme is mainly targeted to poor female entrepreneurs through its group lending program. FINCA's methodology is called Village Banking. The average first loan to individuals is $82. First loans are 50,000 to 100,000 USH and the loan cycle is 16 weeks. FINCA lends to the group (the external account) and the group makes its decisions to lend to the members (the internal account). Payments are weekly. In addition to loans, voluntary savings and mandatory savings, it offers a five week mandatory training program and low-cost group disability and life insurance. FINCA has established the widest outreach among the non-governmental organizations. Members make many of their own decisions about loan appraisal, fines, and penalties for lateness and poor repayment behaviour within their internal account.

FOCCAS

FOCCAS is a rural-based institution targeting poor rural women. It follows group lending methodology. In addition to credit and voluntary and mandatory savings, FOCCAS places a strong emphasis on non-formal education. Through the group lending process, it incorporates information on health, nutrition, family planning, HIV/AIDS prevention, and business management.

PRIDE Africa

Based on experienced learned in Kenya and Guinea, PRIDE could successfully established its operation Uganda within a short period of time. It follows Grameen model with some modifications. Under its model, an interested person has to form a 5 persons "enterprise group". After this process of self selection, PRIDE would then put together 10 groups to form a 50 persons Market Enterprise Committee. Within the 5 persons group, members will select officers and likewise the 50 persons group would have a leadership comprised of the chairmen of each smaller group. After each 50 persons group is registered and the 5000 USH per person membership fee is paid, the group is assigned a specific day and hour to come to the branch once a week to attend a meeting. For 8 weeks the group undergoes training, engages in cross visits to other groups, and each member opens an individual bank account in the bank with a minimum of 10,000 USH. In addition, at each weekly meeting the members must each put 2500 USH into the Loan Insurance Fund. Thus, there are 3 levels of loan security: the LIF, the members' savings, and the 5 persons solidarity group mechanism. In the 8th week 2 peoples from each 5 persons group who are not officers (not the chairman or secretary) receive the first loans, presently capped at 150,000 USH. These two begin paying back in the 9th week and will repay principal and interest weekly for 25 weeks. The effective interest rate is considerably higher than 30%. In addition, the member must continue putting 2500 USH per week into the LIF. In the 10th week, 2 more members put in their applications which are appraised in the 11th week, and they receive their loans in the 12th week. The process continues until the last person in the 5 persons group (the chairman) receives his or her loan in the 16th week. Pride calls this the 8-4-4system. No lending takes place in the interim weeks reserved for appraisals and approvals. There is no discount for early repayment.

UWFCT

Uganda Women's Finance Trust established in 1984 was the first institution to offer micro-finance services in Uganda. It offered credit and savings to groups and to individual women entrepreneurs through nine branches. It also allows men to participate as long as they don't compose more than 20 percent of a group nor assume any leadership positions.

VEDCO

Volunteer Efforts for Development established in 1992 provide integrated financial services i.e. in addition to credit, they also provide training, savings and credit promotion, agricultural and marketing services. Groups were formed of 5 to 8 people. Loan size range from 120,000 to 700,000 (maximum) Loans below 300,000 must be secured by 30% of the loan amount in savings (roughly a 3:1 ratio) and loans above that require 40% in savings.

The Poverty Alleviation Credit Trust in Masindi

The Poverty Alleviation Credit Trust in Masindi established in 1996 mainly through Grameen Trust funding and strictly follows Grameen methodology. Loans are given to group consisting of 5 members for a term of 50 week.

UGAFODE - Kampala (an Opportunity International affiliate)

UGAFODE initially started with individual lending but later on switched to group lending in 1996. The present method involves finding preexisting groups, building them to 50 or so within which self-selected solidarity groups of 5 to 9 persons are formed. They operate up to 50 Kms from Kampala but largely in northern Kampala and among roadside traders, and also Entebbe road. Ugafode's first loan maximum is 300,000 USH, and overall max is 2,000,000 USH; the loan period is 4 to 6 months, with 30 day grace period, repayment weekly, biweekly or monthly; interest is 4% per month flat rate. There is a not' refundable application fee of 1000 USH plus 2% commission of amount of loan up front. Compulsory savings are required up to total of 10% of the loan amount. Local council leaders must endorse the loans.

An important lesson learned from Ugafode's experience is that using church groups as a base from which to build local groups is dangerous in terms of repayment culture. Churches are associated with charity and Ugafode's early attempt to build on these showed higher tendencies to default.

5.6. Microfinance in Ghana

Currently, there are three broad types of microfinance institutions operating in Ghana. These include:[19]

a) Formal suppliers of microfinance — rural and community banks, savings and loans companies and commercial banks.

b) Semi-formal suppliers of microfinance-credit unions, financial nongovernmental organizations (FNGOs), and cooperatives.

c) Informal suppliers of microfinance - Susu collectors and clubs, rotating and accumulating savings and credit associations (ROSCAs and ASCAs), traders, moneylenders and other individuals.

In terms of the regulatory framework, rural and community banks are currently regulated under the Banking Act 2004 (Act 673), while the Savings and Loans Companies are currently regulated under the Non-Bank Financial Institutions(NBFI) Law 1993 (PNDCL 328). On the other hand, the regulatory framework for credit unions is still being developed to reflect their dual nature as cooperatives and financial institutions. The rest of the players such as FNGOs, ROSCAS, and ASCAs do not have explicit legal and regulatory frameworks, and are largely unregulated.

Major challenges of microfinance inappropriate institutional arrangements, poor regulatory frame work, inadequate capacities, lack of coordination and collaboration, poor institutional linkages, lack of linkages between formal and informal financial institutions, inadequate skills and professionalism, and inadequate capital etc.

One of the unique schemes of microfinance in Ghana is the programme for Susu by the Barclays Bank of Ghana (BBG)Ltd. BBG launched a micro banking scheme in December 2005 which establishes a formal link between modern finance and susu (one of Africa's most ancient forms of banking) collection in an unconventional mobile initiative across the country. The scheme aims to extend microfinance to some of the least affluent in Ghana, like the small trader at the market or the micro-entrepreneur selling from road-side stalls. Though their individual income is apparently too small for 'high street' banking, collectively it estimated at about a $150 million economy thriving below the traditional banking radar. Ghana's 4,000-strong Susu Collectors offer basic banking to the needy. For a small fee they personally gather the income of their clients and return it at the end of each month, providing greater security for their client's money. In addition, with finance from Barclays the Susu Collectors are able to provide their clients with loans, helping them to establish or develop their business.

Some of the institutions which are actively engaged in microfinance in Ghana are Microfinance and Small Loans Center (MASLOC), The Ghana Microfinance Institutions Network (GHAMFIN), Association of Rural Banks (ARB); Association of Financial NGOs (ASSFIN), Ghana Cooperative Credit Unions Association (CUA) and Ghana Cooperative Susu Collectors Association (GCSCA)

5.7. Microfinance in Ethiopia

Most of the MFIs operate both in the rural and urban areas mainly centering their head office in Addis Ababa. Debit Credit and Saving Institution (DECSI) and Amhara Credit and Saving Institutions (ACSI) take more than 65% share in serving clients served in the market.[20]

One of the largest MFIs in Ethiopia Amhara Credit and Saving Institution (ACSI) shows that ACSI has served more than half a million clients. Over 6 million loans have been disbursed worth Birr 1.5 billion. By 2005, the institution was operationally and financially self sufficient at 119.9% and 115.3% respectively. ACSI is among a few MFIs that are able to achieve the highest efficiency at the lowest cost per borrower. The operating cost was as low as five cents in 2005.ACSI also has a high portfolio quality, as delinquency rates are around 1.9%. Ethiopian microfinance has made remarkable progress over the past decade, reaching almost two million clients in a country of 77 million people.[21]

There are about 27 MFIs according to the National Bank of Ethopia. Some of them are Amhara Credit and Saving Institutions (ACSI), Debit Credit and Saving Institution (DECSI), Oromia Credit and Saving Share Company (OCSSO) and OMO.

5.7. Microfinance in South America

Bolivia is the poorest country in South America. The gross domestic product per capita is about US$800 (World Bank, 1997). The two largest urban FOs, BancoSol and Caja Los Andes, accounted for more than one-third of the clients and for more than half the portfolio outstanding. Bolivia has the most advanced microfinance sector in Latin America and has been a model worldwide. Apex organizations—second-tier wholesaling mechanisms that lend and offer non financial assistance to retailing microfinance organizations—have not been responsible for this success.

The story of Latin American microfinance institutions basically begins in the 1980s with the advent of socially-driven NGOs making loans to poor micro entrepreneurs.[22] The growth of these early microfinance institutions (MFIs) was funded largely by grants and soft loans from donors and governments in the region.

By the early 1990s, a few leading MFIs had reached full financial sustainability. In 1992, one of the leaders among all of these pioneering institutions—the Bolivian NGO, PRODEM—

converted into the first regulated MFI in Latin America: BancoSol, a regulated commercial bank. The door was now thrown open and the regulation of many other MFIs followed in quick succession.

The *Cajas Municipales*, a group of municipally owned MFIs in Peru became regulated in 1993. The Accion International affiliate, Corposol of Colombia, became regulated in 1994, changing its name to Finansol and failing in 1995-96 in what is still the most spectacular bankruptcy in the field of Latin American microfinance. Happily, a succession of many other NGOs went on to become regulated MFIs that grew rapidly and prospered. For example, in 1995, the IPC affiliates in Bolivia and El Salvador were licensed to accept deposits, becoming the well-known and highly-respected Caja Los Andes and Financiera Calpiá.

1995, another Accion International affiliate,the NGO, ADEMI, became the commercial bank Banco ADEMI. Many more successful cases of upgrading or conversion into a regulated financial institution have followed. There have also been numerous successful cases of downscaling, in which regulated commercial banks or *financieras* (small banks) enter into the microfinance field. For example, under the auspices of an IDB Global Loan to Paraguay, the German technical assistance firm, IPC, taught 53 Paraguayan *financieras* how to adapt their consumer lending methodology in order to successfully make loans to microenterprises. Three commercial banks in Chile have also downscaled successfully into micro credit and now dominate the microfinance market in that country. More recently, the large commercial banks, Banco Solidario of Ecuador and Banco de Trabajo of Peru as well as the giant commercial bank, Banco de Crédito of Peru have all successfully entered into micro lending on a large scale. And two Guatemalan banks, Bancafé and Banrural, have shown that even commercial banks can reach very poor micro entrepreneurs with that most unbanker-like product: village banking in which groups of 15-40 poor women are organized into small cooperatives and provided with credit, savings, and other services.

Microfinance has been far slower to develop in the largest 4 economies in Latin America: Brazil, Mexico, Argentina, and Venezuela. These 4 countries and Uruguay are at the bottom of the list as the only 5 countries with penetration rates of under 1%. This is a huge failing since more than half of Latin America's micro entrepreneurs live in these 4 largest countries. Unfortunately, there has simply been a lack of strong NGOs growing up in these large country markets. For various reasons, these NGOs have not been successful at achieving the kinds of scale seen in the leading microfinance markets of Central America and the Andean region. Nor have they excited the interest of many commercial banks to enter into microfinance, particularly in view of the strong presence of state development banks in the large country markets. Nonetheless, at least 2 rising stars have emerged in the large countries. Compartamos, a Mexican NGO which became regulated in 2001, now serves over 200,000 clients, mainly using a village banking methodology. And Banco do Nordeste, a state development bank with a successful micro credit program that serves the destitute areas of Northeast Brazil, has now topped the 100,000 client mark. While these are still drops in the bucket compared to the 10 million micro entrepreneurs in Mexico and the 19 million in Brazil, the rapid growth of these 2 programmes gives hope that these two giant markets may finally be yielding to the microfinance revolution. Latin American microfinance has blossomed into a $1.5 billion industry with an expected annual growth rate of 20%.[23]

5.9. Microfinance in Brazil[24]

Brazil represents a significant market for microfinance, considering the sheer size of the country in physical, population, and economic terms, even before investigating other characteristics. Brazil has the world's fourth-largest land area, which spans 8.5 million square kilometers. It is the fifth most populous country in the world, with over 174 million inhabitants. And with a total GDP of R$ 1.18 trillion (US$ 503.9 billion) in 2001, Brazil has the largest economy in Latin America, as well as the eighth-largest economy in the world. The context for microfinance in Brazil is distinguishing, as the overall financial sector is highly developed when compared to many other countries with microfinance industries. An advanced banking sector currently offers microfinance substitutes and may provide micro credit in the near future. Other types of credit are more widely accessible to micro entrepreneurs, and include consumer credit, credit cards, store credit, supplier credit, moneylender credit, and loans from personal relations. Microfinance currently plays a small but growing role in Brazil's overall financial sector. There are 121 microfinance institutions (MFIs) operating in Brazil, serving 158,654 active clients with an overall active portfolio of R$ 138.8 million as on 2001. Although the overall industry has grown substantially in recent years, many MFIs are experiencing slow growth or are even contracting. Nine MFIs have over 2,000 current clients. Most MFIs are considerably smaller. Four waves of institution types emerge when considering the historical evolution and leadership of MFIs in Brazil. Brazilian MFIs demonstrate average levels for key performance indicators when compared to their peers in other countries. Potential demand for microfinance in Brazil is expansive. There are 8.2 million microenterprises in Brazil eligible for microfinance. Overall microfinance penetration in Brazil is 2.0% of potential demand. There is a strong need for financial services in Brazil, but the country has a unique demand profile.

Brazilian micro entrepreneurs are highly experienced with financial products when compared to counterparts in other countries with emerging microfinance markets. Several industry-level challenges face the microfinance industry. The regulatory environment continues to affect the microfinance sector, despite considerable advances in recent years. The lack of a demonstration effect hinders the industry, as Brazilian MFIs have not had examples of unqualified success from which they can be inspired. The macroeconomic environment stunted the development of microfinance during hyperinflation, and continues to hurt the industry through high interest rates.

Portosol was formed with Porto Alegre municipal and Rio Grande do Sul state government support in 1996. Portosol, considered to be one of the most successful Brazilian microfinance NGOs, drew national attention to microfinance and inspired many other municipal and state governments to create local MFIs. After an initial stage of rapid growth, Portosol experienced a decline in active clients from a peak of 2,400 in December 1999 to a recently stabilized level of approximately 2,100 active clients. Portosol continues to grow its active portfolio size despite a stable number of active clients through its popular *troca de* cheque service, which offers immediate cashing of post-dated checks to existing clients.

Banco do Povo de São Paulo is a partnership between the state and municipal governments of Sao Paulo formed in 1998. This entity offers loans to local micro entrepreneurs at a highly subsidized rate of 1% per month. The program is growing rapidly in less than four years of operation. It already serves 9,521 current clients. The average loan size of Banco do Povo de São Paulo is R$ 1,696.

Banco do Nordeste

Banco do Nordeste is a government development bank based in Ceara that provides over 70% of bank financing in the Northeast region. Through its fast-growing *Credi Amigo* program launched in 1998, the bank serves 54% of the current microfinance clients in Brazil. The *Credi Amigo* program targets low income clients (with a current average loan size of R$ 584) in urban areas using a solidarity group methodology. The bank has an aggressive growth strategy and makes commercially based decisions within the framework of a state development institution.

More than 2000 the average loan size for the six top MFIs in the Northeast is R$ 642, much lower than the average loan sizes of Portosol in the South (R$ 1,866), Banco do Povo de São Paulo in the Southeast (R$ 1,696) and Banco do Povo de Goias in the Center-West (R$ 1,113).

5.10. Microfinance in South Africa

The Small Enterprise Foundation, Marang Financial Services, Women's Development Businesses, Paradigm Shift are among the largest MFIs in South Africa. Brief profiles of these MFIs are given as under.

Small Enterprise Foundation

Small Enterprise Foundation (SEF) is South Africa's oldest and best-known pro-poor MFI. SEF has been active since 1992 and targets residents of rural villages in the Limpopo and Mpumalanga, where poverty levels are amongst the highest in South Africa. As of June 2009, SEF had 57,425 clients and an outstanding loan portfolio of R89 million (average loan size of R2023 per client). SEF provides small loans through two programmes: the Micro credit Program (MCP) and the Tshomisano Credit Program (TCP). Both use the Grameen methodology of solidarity groups of five members, but TCP specifically targets the poorest women whereas MCP does not. SEF originally started with MCP, but in 1996 discovered the poorest members of target communities were not participating and instead better-off people dominated in hopes of obtaining larger loans at a later stage. In response, SEF developed the Participatory Wealth Ranking (PWR) to identify the poorest members of a community. This approach, regarded as a major contribution to poverty targeting worldwide, identifies households earning less than half of the poverty line and only the women of these households are eligible to join TCP.

It is compulsory for every SEF client to save at every biweekly meeting (savings are held at Post Savings Bank branches) but clients may withdraw whenever they wish. The minimum amount saved is R10 per person per biweekly meeting. After the first loan, 10% of subsequent loans is required as up-front savings. Social performance monitoring is performed by SEF through the participatory method of interviewing clients before each loan cycle about their food consumption and housing. Also measured are each client's savings in burial societies and a loan officer's estimate of the value of the client's business. This approach encourages the loan officer and client to have in-depth conversations about the client's financial progress. The results of these conversations are summarized in quarterly reports.

Marang Financial Services

Marang Financial Services is a non-profit MFI dedicated to making financial services accessible to poor households in South Africa. The organization grew out of the collapse of the Get Ahead Foundation and Rural Finance Facility in 2000 and built upon the experience, infrastructure and personnel of the two organizations. Marang serves approximately 24,000 clients, mainly women, via 23 branches and 19 satellite offices in five provinces (Eastern Cape, Gauteng, KwaZulu Natal, Limpopo and Mpumalanga). Marang currently offers group enterprise loans using the solidarity lending methodology. These loans are offered to groups of between five and eight women between the ages of 18 to 70 who are unable to secure loans from the formal financial sector due to a lack of acceptable collateral. An individual enterprise loan is being developed. Both women and men will be eligible for this loan product provided they are South African citizens ages 21 years or older and have operated their business for at least 24 months. Marang is also considering offering a micro-insurance product that will insure clients and their families against death, disability and other possible mishaps. Ten percent of the loan amount must be deposited into the loan group's bank account as an initial compulsory savings. Subsequently, clients are expected to regularly deposit a minimum of R20 into this account. The money belongs to the clients but should not be withdrawn during the duration of the loan unless the group experiences repayment problems beyond its control.

Women's Development Businesses Group[25]

Women's Development Businesses Group (WDB) is composed of three organizations: WDB Micro Finance, the WDB Trust and WDB Investment Holdings. All three groups work together to help South African women build a sustainable way out of poverty. The primary development tool is micro-credit for the poorest. WDB was established in 1991 and has 27 branches operating in Eastern Cape, KwaZulu Natal, Limpopo and Mpumalanga. The core business of WDB Group is WDB Micro Finance, which provides micro credit to women in rural South Africa in order to improve their livelihoods through economic empowerment. As of year end 2009, WDB Micro Finance currently served over 45,000 clients through two micro loan programmes. The Poverty Alleviation program engages the poorest of the poor in income generating activities to enable them to lift themselves out of poverty. This program offers basic financial skills and credit management training and loans of between R 300 to R 4000. The Enterprise Development program is designed for women who are ready to graduate from basic income generation to operating a business or enterprise. The women in this program are assigned a business mentor and receive more substantive business skills training. The program provides loans of between R 5000 to R 10 000.

The WDB Trust is responsible for capacity building and fund raising for the WDB Group and creating development projects to improve the lives of poor rural women. The WDB Trust developed an ICT program that links women to technology through computer based literacy training as well as a Business Development program that provides women entrepreneurs with skills to help them run their businesses more efficiently. WDB Investment Holdings manages a portfolio of investments and distributes the profits to the WDB Trust for disbursement to the Group's social development programmes. Since 1997 the group has distributed over R45 million to the Trust. WDB Investment Holdings also ensures the economic empowerment of women within its underlying investments through placements, skills transfer and supply chain opportunities for SMEs.

Paradigm Shift

Paradigm Shift is a non-profit, Christian organization based in the United States. Paradigm Shift is committed to empowering churches and ministries to provide meaningful Christian discipleship and economic development in South Africa. Paradigm Shift's mission is to train churches in developing countries to provide business training, micro loans, mentoring and discipleship to the urban poor. Paradigm Shift functions much like a consulting firm by providing curriculum, training, reporting and ongoing support to the partner church. The micro credit portion of the Paradigm Shift program offers micro loans to entrepreneurs to be invested in income generating activities. In order to receive a loan, an entrepreneur must own and operate a small business for at least three months, complete an introductory business training course, socially collateralize the micro loan with four to seven other entrepreneurs and commit to attending 18 weekly meetings.

Paradigm Shift's goal is to see the Gospel message communicated by partner churches as they focus on meeting both physical and spiritual needs in their communities. The purpose of the program is two-fold: to create opportunities for entrepreneurs to develop and expand their small businesses so they can better provide for their families and to offer intentional avenues of discipleship which communicate God's hope, love and redemption for participating entrepreneurs. This integrated approach is designed to have a long-lasting impact on the life of each church volunteer, entrepreneur and his/her family.

5.11. Microfinance in China

Microfinance is not a new phenomenon in China. It was introduced in October 1993 as part of a government scheme in poverty alleviation. The first experiment with Microfinance in China was based on the successful Grameen Bank model of loan delivery, targeting poor rural women in Xiling Township, Hebei Province. Then, many similar programmes supported by the Chinese government and international NGOs have sprouted in the rural areas with the reports of varying degrees of success. Parallel to these microfinance programmes, the government has been providing loans for rural development through the Agricultural Bank of China, but non-performing loans and bad debts have plagued this institution since it was officially restored in 1979. Lack of manpower and network support from sub-branches at the grassroots level prevented the banks from allocating poverty relief loans to individual households. NGO type microfinance programmes in China possess the advantage of good relationship with the borrowers at grassroots level over the larger banks and therefore are able to fill the gap where the larger banks failed. Like microfinance programmes in other countries, those in China, which are run by government supported financial institutions, started by providing subsidized credit to the poor.

Three categories of microfinance programmes define the present microfinance landscape in China:[27]

a) Project-based microfinance funded by international NGOs such as UNDP, World Bank, USAID, etc and local governments. Chinese Foundation for Poverty Alleviation (CFPA) operates their microfinance programmes with both international and local funding. Qinghai Community Development Project is also NGO based organisation having mircrofinance programmes.

b) Programmes run by government dominated funds via the Agricultural Banks.

c) Programmes run by the Rural Credit Cooperatives using their own deposits and the People's Bank of China refinancing facility.

In China, microfinance only consists of microcredit operations and does not include savings, insurance or transfer payments. In rural areas, microfinance institutions (MFIs) tend to target clients from farming households and rurally-based microenterprises whilst in urban areas the institutions focus on laid-off and unemployed workers and urban-based microenterprises.[28]

The Chinese microfinance industry can be divided into the following categories:

Public-interest Microfinance

Public-interest MFIs are operated by non-government organizations (NGO) or the government and their principal objective is to reduce poverty and promote social development. The main difference between NGO and governmental MFIs is that NGO MFIs pursue self-sustainability whereas sustainability is not a goal of governmental MFIs. .

Mutual Microfinance

In recent years, an emerging mutual fund model in rural communities has received significant attention from governments and donor agencies. Chinese civil society has a long history of mutual funds, known as Hehui, or ROSCA in the west. Mutual funds were created by farmers themselves, or with support from the government or international development organizations. An example of such a fund is the rural community revolving fund which was created with the support of the State Council's poverty alleviation office. External supporters also provide technical assistance and additional funds, and act as policy coordinators. Loan capital for mutual fund operations is usually mainly provided by the fund members themselves. Mutual funds are managed by, and in the interests of, the fund members. In 2007, the Chinese Banking Regulatory Commission (CBRC) permitted the registering of a new type of mutual fund, known as a rural mutual credit cooperative (RMCC). RMCC is the only form of mutual financial institution recognized by financial regulators.

Commercial Microfinance

The term 'Commercial Microfinance' refers to the microfinance services provided by formal financial institutions. The objective of commercial microfinance is to achieve commercial sustainability as opposed to poverty alleviation. As a result microfinance products from these providers tend to be targeted towards the mid/low income market segment. Commercial microfinance providers include rural credit cooperatives (RCC), rural commercial banks, rural cooperative banks, village banks (VB), lending companies (LC), urban commercial banks, postal savings banks and microcredit companies (MCC). However RCCs, VBs, and MCCs are the main players in this sector. MCCs are a new type of microfinance provider and were first created in 2005 as a pilot program initiated by the People's Bank of China (PBOC). With the exception of MCCs, all commercial microfinance providers are registered financial institutions.

The existing financial infrastructures which seek to meet the Chinese government's aim to reduce poverty in rural areas and its recent proclamation on developing 'a new socialist countryside' may have a crowding-out effect on existing and potential services provided by the NGO type of microfinance programmes. These programmes are usually under international rhetorical pressure to move away from subsidies and donor funds to achieve self sustainability.

China Postal Savings and Remittance Bureau (CPSRB) already have 36,000 offices around China, with 70% of the offices based in rural areas. With deposits reaching 1.22 trillion yuan (US$150.4 billion), the China Postal Savings Bank is looking into ways to mobilize their enormous deposits and expand its business to lending activities in the future. This will result in direct competition with the Rural Credit Cooperative where rural clients will certainly benefit by getting better services, but this may pose an untimely threat to the survival of NGO microfinance programmes in China, which are currently solely dependent on lending activities.

In terms of regulation, NGO microfinance programmes are, in theory, illegal. However they have compromised informally with local governments on their activities. Local governments have permitted them to continue their operations and sometimes even to charge higher loan interest rates. The ambiguity and lack of a clear and legal financial role for the NGO microfinance programmes, and the inefficiency of microfinance programmes run by commercial banks, can undermine the sustainability of the microfinance movement in China. Given the differences in the legal and regulatory framework, and existing poverty alleviation policies in China, the path that the NGO microfinance programmes are taking in China could lead to a different course than that of the Grameen Bank.

Formal regulations for the operation of NGO microfinance programmes need to be developed for them to be recognized within the organization status quo, otherwise these programmes will continue to remain 'illegal' in their operations. NGO microfinance programmes in China are therefore neither organizational nor institutional in status. Some microfinance programmes have taken the lack of regulations as an opportunity to innovate and improve their programmes.

The Chinese Foundation for Poverty Alleviation (CFPA) has recently launched a new loan product at the Xiapu site and the Funding the Poor Cooperative (FPC), run by the Rural Development Institute of the Chinese Academy of Social Sciences, is working on a trial commercial microfinance concept where loaned funds are owned by a community, consisting of not more than five members. The CFPA has also used this lax but compromising regulatory environment to obtain institutional recognition and is currently preparing a proposal for the establishment of an independent commercial institution from its current project situation. With the regulatory framework lagging behind in China, it is already difficult to accord any organizational status to these NGO programmes, and scarcely an institutional status. However, in order to push the authorities to pay more attention to the development of a sound microfinance regulatory framework in China, strong initiatives at the bottom level, as seen in the CFPA, are being taken to influence higher level policy making. NGO type microfinance programmes have a long and difficult path to tread to achieve commercial status in China, given that the focus on large-scale commercial microfinance is on re-hauling the RRCs. NGO microfinancers must therefore find their own way to achieve some form of non-commercial sustainability in their programmes as they possess many unique characteristics and concepts, such as grassroots relationships with their clients, community building, and the ultimate goal of poverty alleviation, that the management of RCCs is still struggling to include in its corporate management.

5.12. Microfinance in Nepal

The microfinance sector in Nepal has expanded and became more diversified in recent years and apart from serving the poor, particularly women, may also fill the gap left by the progressive withdrawal of commercial banks from rural areas, due to the insurgency and cost savings measures. Diversification has come from the commercialisation of leading NGOs and their transformation into rural microfinance banks. They compete with pre-established public Regional Rural Development Banks, using the same Grameen Bank methodology as many of the smaller Nepali microfinance institutions.

The Rural Microfinance Development Center (RMDC), an apex institution modelled over the PKSF in Bangladesh, provides wholesale fund to these regulated organisations, as well as to the best performing microfinance institutions in Nepal, among them are large NGOs and cooperatives. In parallel, the restructuring of the Agricultural Development Bank of Nepal as resulted in the establishment of Sana Kisan Bikas Bank, another apex organisation that provides wholesale loan to the Small Farmers Cooperatives Ltd., which has graduated from credit groups promoted under the Small Farmers Development Project. In addition, thousands of smaller NGOs and community-based organisations are also involved in microfinance but lack the institutional capacity and scale to reach sustainability. The Rural Self Reliance Fund, operated by the Central Bank of Nepal provides wholesale lending to them, while the Centre for Microfinance (CMF) acts as the central focal point for microfinance in Nepal, providing information sharing, capacity building and consultancy services.

In the early 1960s, the cooperative movement became the first vehicle of microfinance in Nepal, as 13 cooperatives provided flood victims access to financial services adapted to their specific needs. In parallel, rural finance institutions were established such as the Agricultural Development Bank of Nepal, which aimed at providing credit and marketing support to agriculture.

In 1974, the two state-owned commercial banks, Nepal Bank Ltd. and Rastriya Banijya Bank were directed by the central bank, Nepal Rastra Bank, to invest at least a portion (first 5% to increase as high as 12%) of their deposit liabilities in the 'small sector'. This marked the beginning of the directed credit system in Nepal. In 1976, the scope of the small sector was broadened to include agriculture, cottage industry and services, and has since then been called the 'priority sector'. The credit didn't reach the poor, as only influential and well-connected people, with collateral, were able to access the program. This led to the development of targeted initiatives, such as the Intensive Banking Program in 1981, initiated by the government and the central bank, through partnerships with commercial banks. Under this approach, group guarantee for loan repayment were used instead of physical collateral.

Starting in 1975, the Small Farmers Development Program, implemented by the Agricultural Development Bank of Nepal, mobilised farmers groups using a credit plus approach, and was the first experience of group-based lending in Nepal. Unfortunately, it failed due to political pressure for a fast expansion, overemphasis on credit, high delinquency levels and the overall not satisfactory performance of the system.

In 1982, the Cottage and Small Industries Project and the Production Credit for Rural Women all provided new directions to priority sector lending, focusing on project viability rather than collateral, and therefore provided a financing window to the poor through commercial banks collaborating with local development organisations. The commercial banks perceived this program as more of an obligation towards the central bank than a business interest.

In 1990, the government of Nepal established the Rural Self-Reliance Fund (RSRF), with the objective of providing wholesale loans to NGOs, cooperatives and other financial intermediaries for lending to the poor. The Microfinance Department of NRB acts as the secretariat of the RSRF and management committee headed by the NRB deputy governor oversees the fund.

In 1992, the government of Nepal, following a recommendation from the NRB, established Regional Rural Development Banks (RRDB) in each of the five development regions of Nepal, modelled on the Grameen Bank methodology. The majority of the ownership is in the hands of government, Nepal Rastra Bank (the central bank) and public commercial banks, while other private commercial banks have small equity stakes. During the same period, private initiatives led by NGOs, such as Nirdhan and the Center for Self-help Development, also used the Grameen Bank methodology, resulting in a generally more efficient and successful replication. In the 1990s, with technical assistance from GTZ, local branches of ADBN under the Small Farmer Development Program, started to be reorganised into federations of small farmers groups, the 'Small Farmer Cooperatives Ltd (SFCL); each operating as an autonomous cooperative.

With the promulgation of the Development Bank Act in 1995, Nirdhan was the first NGO (1998) to transfer its microfinance portfolio into an autonomous microfinance rural bank (Nirdhan Utthan Development Bank). Since 2000, three other microfinance rural banks were created through the same process first initiated by Nirdhan, with DEPROSC Development Bank in 2000, Swabalamban Bikas Bank Ltd and Chhimek Bikas Bank in 2001. Acknowledging the poor performance of the RRDBs under public ownership, the central bank started a restructuring program, which will lead ultimately to the privatization of the five RRDBs. With a view to provide a source of wholesale fund to regulated microfinance institutions, the Rural Microfinance Development Center (RMDC) was established in 1998, and later on opened its lending to other microfinance providers. In 2001, the Small Farmer Development Bank was established under the Development Bank Act to provide wholesale funds to Small Farmers Cooperatives Ltd. (SFCLs).

In Nepal, Microfinance Development Banks, which were previously regulated under the Development Bank Act 1995, are now regulated by the recently introduced 'Bank and Financial Ordinance 2004'. The two apex organizations, RMDC and Sana Kisan Bikas Bank (Small Farmer Development Bank), as well as the five RRDBs, the four private rural microfinance banks have come under the umbrella of the new ordinance promulgated in 2004. Some other microfinance institutions come under the 'Financial Intermediary Act 1998', amended in 2002, which provides a limited banking license to NGOs.

Microfinance practices reflect the diversity of landscape and population density in Nepal. In the Terai region (plain); more densely populated, with better transport infrastructure and easier access to clients; the Grameen Bank model has been adapted by a large number of organisations. It is also a region where traditional financial organisations, such as commercial and development banks, operate. In the hills and mountains, community-based organisations, such as Self Help Groups, Credit and Savings Associations and Cooperatives, seem the most adapted to the remoteness and isolation of local communities.

The Center for Microfinance in Nepal has registered 2,345 savings and credit cooperatives in Nepal, but only 20 are licensed and report to the NRB. These 20 mobilized a total of US$ 22.7 million in around 110,560 savings accounts, while lending out US$ 18.8 million reaching around 61,700 borrowers. Thousands of NGOs facilitate or provide financial services to their members in Nepal, but only 47 of these are licensed by NRB as Financial Intermediary NGOs (FINGOs). Their outstanding loan portfolio in January 2005 was US$ 3.2 million with some 35,550 borrowers. Mobilized deposits were not published by NRB in January, even if, an amendment to the Financial Intermediary Societies Act (1999) in 2002 allow FINGOs to collect micro-savings.

Grameen Bank Methodology

First introduced to Nepal in the early 1990s, the Grameen Bank methodology has been adapted by a large number of organizations, mostly operating in the Terai region (plain), where the population is dense and road, market and other infrastructures are comparatively more developed than in the hills and mountains. The methodology is based on peer groups of five members incorporated into centres of up to ten groups. Weekly meetings are used to collect compulsory payments from members to contribute to the group's fund - incorporating both savings and loans. The group fund, managed by the group, may be used to make additional loans to members. Loans are made initially to two members, then to two others and finally to the last member, with a four to eight week interval between each disbursement. The group members guarantee each others loan repayments. Microfinance providers using the Grameen methodology will typically offer general loans, seasonal loans, specific loans (sanitation, housing) and the loans issued from the group fund. Savings products are generally the compulsory group fund savings, and any additional personal, voluntary savings. In recent years, several leading microfinance providers have started to move away from the traditional Grameen model, to focus on new practices for Nepal, such as a streamlining of operations, the introduction of customer friendly products, and a strong emphasis on institution and staff capacity building. New products have also been offered to clients by several organisations, such as micro insurance covering risks related to health, life and livestock.

Community-Based Model

Community-based models, such as the methodology implemented by Savings and Credit Cooperative Societies (SCCS), provide a wide range of savings and loan products to their members. They tend to serve a well-off population but also the poor, with a stronger emphasis on the disadvantaged in the case of organisations established by development programmes. They commonly require compulsory savings, but also offer individual or group saving products, deposits, and festival and educational savings services. Loans provided by SCCS have a minimum term of 3 months and can be extended for more than 18 months, covering specific purposes, such as agriculture, microenterprise, housing, or, in some cases, emergency or social reasons. In addition, as successfully demonstrated in India, self-help Groups can be linked to commercial banks, an approach taken by the Banking with the Poor Program implemented by the Rastriya Banijya Bank (RBB). Despite the institutional challenges and necessary methodological adjustments to be made, RBB has lent directly to self-help groups under this program.

Small Farmers Co-operatives

Small Farmers cooperatives were also initiated under the Small Farmers Development Program of the Agricultural Development Bank of Nepal (ADBN), which was the first Nepali program to use a group-based methodology. The program has faced major difficulties in terms of portfolio quality (38% NPL) and the dependency of groups towards ADBN loan capital. GTZ has supported methodological changes to the ADBN, which is also under restructuring phase, led by the ADB. Under a joint Nepali-German program, RUFIN, GTZ has provided technical assistance to the ADBN in transforming the groups into sustainable Small Farmers Development Cooperatives (SFCLs), now largely financed by an apex bank. Despite the recent successes in revitalizing the program, problems still persist such as decapitalization and sustainability issues.

Village Bank Model

The Village Bank model was also used in Nepal, with the Women Empowerment Program of Pact Nepal, between 1998 and 2001. Adapted from the model used in Latin America, village banks are community-managed credit and savings associations designed to provide financial services to members living in rural areas. This methodology focuses on empowering relatively large groups of people (20-40 in Nepal) in building their own financial institution, with a savings first approach. First, the village bank promoters, in this case local NGO partners of Pact Nepal, provided training to the village banks, focusing on building the capacity of membership and management committees. The promoters also lend fund capital to build up the 'external account' of the village bank, which is then on lent to members. Repayments from members are collected by the village bank, which repay its main obligation to the promoters. In parallel, the village bank members build up their 'internal account' through savings and on lend internally this fund. This model was successful in Nepal, as it combined training in literacy and business development with financial services and was able to obtain a large outreach at low cost. However, of the few weaknesses, was the dependency created by the financial links between village banks and promoters.

Other group and individual lending methodologies

The two public-owned commercial banks, Nepal Bank Ltd. and Rastriya Banijya Bank, representing 95% of the rural branches of commercial banks in Nepal, are reducing their presence in rural areas. Their branches were considerably weakened by the consequences of the local conflict and the growing pressure from the restructuring program supported by the World Bank. Under the deprived sector requirement, commercial banks can choose to provide equity or wholesale funds to microfinance institutions, or lend directly to the poor. In the later case, they typically provide loans not exceeding Rs.30,000/- to individuals or groups, most often in the context of a government-sponsored program (Intensive Banking Program for example). Government programmes such as the Micro-Credit Project for Women (MCPW) provide opportunities for NGOs to borrow wholesale funds for loans to groups of poor people. With the introduction of this program, the Financial Intermediary Societies Act 1998 enabled NGOs to provide micro credit to their group members. With the first amendment of the Act, NGOs were also able to acquire a limited banking licence from the central bank and act as Financial Intermediaries NGOs (FINGOs), and therefore acquired the possibility to mobilize savings of their members.

Funding and Supporting Organisations

The Rural Self-Reliance Fund (RSRF) was established in 1990 by the government of Nepal to support organisations providing financial services at a grassroots level in rural areas. These included: Savings and Credit Cooperatives, NGOs, and Grameen replications. RSRF is currently managed by Nepal Rastra Bank, with a portfolio of Rs.19.2 million outstanding as of mid January 2004. The Rural Microfinance Development Centre Ltd. (RMDC) provides wholesale funding to regulated microfinance organisations that comply with a strict set of criteria related to their institutional capacity, focusing on the poor and financial performance. As of June 2004, RMDC had Rs.133 million in loans outstanding, in majority with private Grameen Bank replications.

Another apex organisation, Sana Kisan Bikas Bank (Small Farmer Development Bank) was established in 2001 by the Agricultural Development Bank of Nepal (ADBN) to outsource the wholesale funding to Small Farmers Cooperatives Ltd (SFCL), which was formed after the transformation of Small Farmers Development Projects, promoted under the Small Farmers Development Project, into cooperatives. SKBB is owned by: ADBN, the Ministry of Finance, two commercial banks, and a group of SFCLs. It is envisaged that SFCLs majority ownership will grow over time. In Nepal USAID focuses on education, gender and microfinance programmes. It has provided substantial funding to Pact Nepal for the Women Empowerment Program until 2001. USAID will continue to promote microfinance and education through recent grants to World Education to support the WEEL project (Women Economic Empowerment and Literacy) and to Save the Children under the IGP grant program.

The Center for Microfinance is one of the key organisations supporting microfinance in Nepal. It aims at strengthening the microfinance sector through capacity building, research and consultancy services. It is also involved in policy development, an innovation catalyst (partner in a micro insurance pilot scheme), and impact assessment. CMF currently partner with ImpAct, an international project focusing on the social impact of microfinance, funded by the Ford Foundation and implemented by three UK universities. The Institute for Integrated Development Studies (IIDS), established in 1990, is an independent research institute, under NGO status, focusing on development issues in Nepal.

Over the years, local microfinance networks have been established in Nepal, such as the Microfinance Association of Nepal (MIFAN), the Grameen Replications Network and several cooperative networks and federations. However, they are now mostly inactive, due to a lack of funding and the diversity and geographical isolation of their members. Plan International, an international NGO, encourages the creation of a national microfinance forum, which would involve policy makers, Academics and microfinance providers: this forum would focus on issues such as product development, pro-poor methodologies, regulations and standards.

5.13. Microfinance in Pakistan

In the 1960s and 1970s, subsidized microcredit was provided in rural areas, but failed to reach the poor due to an unsustainable system, which was prone to abuse and diversion of funds to higher income groups. In the 1980s, the Aga Khan Rural Support Program (AKRSP) was established in the northern region to build community-based organizations and infrastructure, and assist in resource mobilization through credit and savings. The success of the AKRSP led to the creation of Pakistan's other Rural Support Programmes (RSPs), which formed the primary approach to microfinance during the 1980s and part of the 1990s. Those RSPs made a major contribution to the microfinance sector by accessing lines of credit from commercial banks to provide microcredit to low-income people living in rural areas. Similarly, the Orangi Pilot Project (OPP) developed an individual lending methodology adapted to urban slums, by targeting entrepreneurs in Karachi region. In the 1990s, learning from international best practices, NGOs specialized in microfinance started their operations, such as Kashf Foundation, Taraqee and Damen. The outreach of microfinance institutions and other rural organizations providing financial services has been limited due to a narrow institutional base, slow progress on sustainability and efficiency benchmarks.

Since 2000, the microfinance landscape in Pakistan has changed considerably. This change can be credited primarily to the government's growing interest in the microfinance sector. It was this interest that resulted in:

a) The creation of the apex funding body, the Pakistan Poverty Alleviation Fund (PPAF)
b) The formulation of the MFIs ordinance 2001, regulating the creation of commercial microfinance banks, such as The First MicroFinanceBank (created by the AKRSP) and the Khushhali Bank, a retail microfinance bank issued from a public-private partnership.

In the last two years, Pakistan microfinance providers have posted faster growth in terms of outreach, with 'transformed' or 'created' dedicated microfinance organizations starting to realize their full potential through a conducive regulatory environment. Other organizations are also benefiting from the dissemination of best practices and the availability of funds to finance their expansion.

The MFIs Ordinance 2001 was promulgated by the Government of Pakistan to support the development of the microfinance sector by introducing the concept of microfinance banks. Under this ordinance, microfinance banks created with the necessary amount of capital, can offer microfinance services, including savings deposits, to the general public. In addition, the State Bank of Pakistan (BSP) introduced additional prudential regulations related to microfinance operations. This ordinance and the relevant prudential regulations of the BSP, regulate The First Micro Finance Bank and the Khushhali Bank.

The majority of microfinance organizations operating in Pakistan, particularly RSPs, use community-based organizations as conduits for their financial services. This methodology produces the highest outreach. The largest microfinance provider is the NRSP, with national coverage. However, RSPs find it difficult to view microfinance activities as anything other than a supporting component of their larger, integrated program, resulting in difficulties to separate costs specific to microfinance. Other organizations use the solidarity group model, adapted from the Grameen Bank to the Pakistan context, the best example being Kashf Foundation. Organizations such as this are the fastest growing providers of microfinance in Pakistan and post the best 'portfolio quality' ratios. Finally, some organizations use a mix of individual lending and partnerships with community-based organizations. It seems that the organizations using this methodology are the most viable programmes, if self-sufficiency ratios are compared. Some NGOs, like Kashf Foundation and the Orangi Pilot Project, now specialize in microfinance and have reached a substantial and growing number of clients.

In the **formal sector**, two commercial banks, the Bank of Khyber and the First Women Bank, provide microfinance services to low-income clients, directly through their branches, or as wholesale funds to partner MFIs. The microfinance specific ordinances promulgated in 2000 and 2001 by BSP allowed for the establishment of two specialized microfinance institutions, the Khushhali Bank, a retail microfinance bank jointly owned by public and private banks, and the First MicroFinanceBank Limited, established from the transformation of the microfinance activities of the Aga Khan Rural Support Program. Orix Leasing and Network Leasing are two leasing companies involved in microfinance by providing leasing products to low-income clients. Some leasing companies strive to increase their share in the microfinance market by proposing other financial products, and potentially to set up their own microfinance banks. Network leasing has already been granted a license to set up a microfinance bank, which was due to start operations in July 2004. The new institution, called Network-MFB, will start at the district level, with plans to become a national institution.

Pakistan also has a rating agency, JCR-VIS, which has initiated ratings of NGOs and specialized microfinance organizations, such as The First MicroFinanceBank. NGOs are rated on a corporate governance scale while the full credit rating of MFIs applies only to institutions regulated by BSP. They are described as 'microfinance banks' and can mobilize commercial sources of funds.

NOTES

1. H.I.Latifee, "*The future of Microfinance: Visioning the Who, What, When, Where, Why, and How of Microfinance Expansion over the next 10 years*" Grameen Trust Bangladesh.

2. Pankaj Naithani, "Micro-financing the Self Employment Activities-A see-saw of Ideas", *Kurukshetra,* vol. 49, No-10, July 2001, p13.
3. Dr. Amrit Patel, "Micro-Credit and Role of Banks- Need for Initiatives and Commitment", *Kurukshetra,* February 2004, p6.
4. Bangladesh Bank(2002): Annual Report 2000-01 referred by Navin Bhatia & Anju Bhatia, "Microfinance Institutions of Bangladesh: Lessons for India", *Kurukshetra,* February 2004.
5. Taka is the unit of currency in Bangladesh. 1 US $ = 57 Taka..
6. BRAC(2002): *Annual Report 2001.*
7. Grameen in Bengali language means—village.
8. Grameen Bank: *Annual Report 2001.*
9. Yunus, Mohammad, (1997), "Grameen Bank Story: Rural Credit in Bangladesh", in Aired Krishna, Norman Upoff & Milton Jessant ed. *Reasons for Hope: Instructive Experience in Rural Development,* pp. 9-24, Connecticut: Kumara Press.
10. Md. Saiful Islam, "Who Benefits, How benefits: The political Economy of Grameen Bank's Microcredit Programme in Rural Bangladesh: A Theoretical Overview", *Indian Journal of Social Development,* vol-4 No 1, Jun-04, pp. 1-17.
11. G.K.Murthy, "Micro Finance in India", *Banking Finance,* October 2005, p.23.
12. ASA (2002): *Annual Report 2001.*
13. PROSHIKA (2001): *Activity Report July 2000-June 2001.*
14. Dr. Amrit Patel, "Micro-Credit and Role of Banks-Need for Initiative and Commitment", *Kurukshetra,* February, 2004, p7.
15. Enterprising Solutions Global Consulting,LCC, *UNCDF microfinance programme impact Assessment 2003,* New York.
16. Tom Dichter, Ephraim Kamuntu (1997), *UNDP Microfinance Assessment Report for Uganda.*
17. Jessical. L Jacobson (1999*), Uganda: The Provision of Microfinance in the Wake of Conflict"*, Johns Hopkins University - School of Advanced International Studies.
18. Dr. Johnson P. Asiama(2007), *Microfinance in Ghana and overview,* Bank of Ghana.
19. Befekadu B Kereda (2007), *Outreach and Financial Performance Analysis of Microfinance Institutions in Ethiopia,*UNCC,Addis Ababa.
20. Letena Ejigu (2009),*"Performance Analysis of Sample Microfinance Institution of Ethopia"*,University Business School, Punjab University. Addis Ababa, *"Trend Challenges and other issues in microfinance development in Ethopia"*, Alisei Publishing (2005),
21. Alvaro Ramirez, *"The microfinance experience in Latin America and the Caribbean"*.
22. Jansson, Tor, *"Financing Microfinance"*, September, 2003, available from the Inter-American Development Bank, Washington, D.C.
23. Simeon Nichter,Lara Goldmark,Anita Fiori (2002*), Understanding Microfinance in Brazelian Context*. BNDES microfinance
24. www.wdb.co.za
25. www.shiftingparadigms.org
26. Lilan Lau(2008*), Poverty and Sustainability Issues of Microfinance in China: A Case Study in Fuan Fujian Province,* Working paper, Centre for East and South-East Asian Studies, Lund University, Sweden.
27. Sun Tongguan, *The Policy and Legal Framework for Microfinance in China,* Rural Development Institute of CASS.

6
Microfinance in India

"Microfinance in India is approaching a historic 'tipping point' that could lead to a massive poverty reduction in the next five to ten years"

– Grameen Foundation US in 2005.

6.1. Rural Financial Infrastructure in India: An Overview

The financial sector in India incorporates a vast network of commercial banks, co-operative banks, and regional rural banks (RRBs), as well as other financial institutions such as development finance institutions, state-level finance cooperations, nonbank finance companies, insurance companies, provident funds and mutual funds.

Reserve Bank of India (RBI), the Central bank of the country and Ministries of Finance and Rural Development are guiding banking and the flow of credit for rural development and microfinance. The National Bank for Agriculture and Rural Development (NABARD) is an apex development bank engaged in supporting and promoting agriculture and rural development in an integrated manner.

As at the end of March 2001, there were 296 commercial banks operating in India. This included 27 public sector banks, 31 private, 42 foreign and 196 regional rural banks. Further there were 67 scheduled co-operative banks consisting of 51 scheduled urban co-operative banks and 16 scheduled state co-operative banks.[1]

There are more than 1,60,000 retail credit outlets in the banking and cooperative sectors, augmented by another 37,000 non bank finance companies. There are currently 1,10,000 co-operative societies or branches of cooperative banks, over 45,000 branches of the 27 public sector commercial banks and another 4,700 branches of 55 smaller private sector banks. The 196 rural regional banks have 14,400 branches in rural areas.[2]

Financial services to the poor are also available from the village or (town) neighbourhood-level agents of NBFCs. The Regional Rural Banks (RRBs) in particular, were established specifically in order to meet the credit requirements of the poor-small and marginal farmers, landless workers, artisans and small entrepreneurs and should, therefore, have emerged as a major source of microfinance. A total of 1,40,000 institutional outlets serving the rural sector and poor implies the availability of one outlet for every 5,600 persons –in theory, a very favourable ratio for catering to the financial need of the poor.[3]

Financial Sector Reforms

1991 marked a watershed in the history of Indian economy. Faced with a balance of payment crisis, the Indian Economy undertook an extensive reform programme ushering an era of deregulation, liberalization and gradual globalization coupled with a liberalized exchange rate management system and devaluation of the rupee exchange rate. The roadmap of the financial sector reforms was traced largely by two committees under the chairmanship of Shri M.Narashimham. The Committee on the Financial System and the Committee on Banking Sector Reforms are popularly known as the Narashimham Committees I and II. Narashimham Committee-I defined its approach to ensure that the financial services industry operates on the basis of operational flexibility and functional autonomy with a view to enhancing efficiency, productivity and profitability".

Narashimham Committee-II was entrusted with the task of evaluating the extent of implementing of reforms recommended by the Narashimham Committee-I in 1991 and mandated to chart the course of future reforms required to further strengthen the banking sector in India and to bring the efficiencies of the system up to international standards.

Table: Formal Financial Institutions in Rural India[4]

Type of institution	*Number*	*Rural/semi-urbanBranches*
Commercial Banks	106	32,854
Regional Rural Banks	196	14,142
State Co-operative Banks	28	789
District Co-operative Banks	367	12,128
Primary co-operative credit societies		92,000
State Land Development Banks	19	1,154
Primary land development banks	745	686
Total	1461	153753

Population (per retail outlet): 4,700 as of March 1999.

Rural credit system in India has been evolved from the year 1904, when the first primary Agriculture Credit Society was organized and thereafter expanding it through the nationalization of 27 commercial banks including State Bank and its seven subsidiaries and the establishment of 196 Regional Rural Banks to meet rural credit demand. Rural credit structure in India has completed almost 98 years and serves around 120 million rural households residing in about six lakh villages.[5]

India has a large and diverse network of rural credit institutions. It is widely recognized that Rural Financial Institutions (RFIs) play an important role in credit dispensation for development of the agricultural sector. They are recognized as vehicles through which poverty alleviation schemes are implemented by Government.

Earlier committees like the All India Rural Credit Survey (1954), the All India Rural Credit Review Committee (1969) and the Agriculture Credit Review Committee (1989) had emphasized the need to have a strong, vibrant and dynamic rural credit delivery system.[6] National Bank for Agricultural and Rural Development (NABARD) instituted an Expert

Committee on Rural Credit scenario and suggests a plan of action for "more effective rural credit". The significant issues of concerned addressed by the expert committee were:

a) Poorest of the poor are left our of the formal credit system- Institutions comprising of Commercial Banks, RRBs and the Co-operative have a large network with an outlet for a population of under 5000 on an average, a large number of rural poor, particularly weaker sections of society, marginal farmers and women continue to remain inaccessible.

b) High value, high-tech agriculture, off-farm activities and rural enterprises are not adequately financed by the RFIs.

c) The linkages with research, extension, input supplies, marketing and processing are weak.

d) The legal and regulatory mechanisms are inadequate, giving rise to non-financial viable institutions.

In the post nationalisation period the banking sector witnessed substantial amount of resources being earmarked towards meeting the credit needs of the poor. The banking network underwent an expansion phase without comparables in the world. The branch expansion was synergised with massive manpower recruitment drive for manning such branches. Credit came to be recognized as a remedy for many of the ills of the poverty. Credit packages and programmes were designed based on the perceived needs of the poor. Programmes also underwent qualitative changes based on the experiences gained. Besides the programmes initiated by the Central Government, a large number of credit-based programmes were introduced by the state governments with large resource allocations. While the underlying objectives were laudable and substantial progress was achieved, credit flow to the poor, and especially to poor women, remained low.[7] The problem of recovery of rural credit has become a constant source of anxiety for the financing institutions and a large chunk of bank's funds remains unloaded. The basic causes include weather conditions, drought and floods as well as the socio-political involvement in which the rural credit institutions functions.[8] Over the period of functioning, many banks face structural weaknesses mainly due to democratic character, non professional management, community ideological commitments and political interference. Co-operative being the 'local area bank' any fraudulent deal or bad loaning, people are very much sensitive and react instantly on the working of the society. The faith and confidence shaken, market has observed dramatic collapse and crash.

Poverty and Rural Credit System

Due to its sheer size of population of around 1000 million, India ranks among the top 15 economies of the world. However, around 260 million households are living below the poverty line. It is further estimated that of these households, only about 20% have access to credit from the formal sector.[9]

Indian accounts for an estimated 40 percent of the world's poor. India continues to have highest concentration of poverty of any country with more than 285 million people-about 26 percent of the population living below the official poverty line.

Poverty has been one of the persisting social evils haunting the rural masses in India. It has also remained the biggest challenge in India's development efforts to bring about a perceptible change in the quality of like of its millions people. A large chunk of the rural masses are living below poverty line and the task of uplifting them has become the constitutional responsibility of the Union, State and Local Governments.[10]

The following table represents data in respect of trends in poverty in India.

Trends in Poverty in India[11]

Region	*Percentage of population in India*					
	1973-74	*77-78*	*83-84*	*87-88*	*93-94*	*99-2000*
1. Rural	56.40	54.10	45.7	39.1	37.3	27.1
2. Urban	49.0	45.2	40.80	38.2	32.4	23.6
3. Combined	54.9	51.3	44.5	38.9	36.0	26.10

The table shows a perceptible decline in poverty ratio in the 1980s which was the combined result of acceleration in the growth rate' of GDP, spread of Green Revolution, increased allocations for poverty alleviation programmes and strengthening of public distribution system for good grains.[12] It is also distressing that in 10 states well over 40% rural population are poverty stricken , Arunachal Pradesh, Assam, Bihar (44.3%), Manipur, Meghalaya, Mizoram, Nagaland, Orissa (48.01%), Sikkim and Tamil Nadu.[13]

All India Debt and Investment Survey Report of the RBI, 1981-82, categorically revealed that 76.7 percent of poorest of the poor having assets up to Rs. 1,000 did borrow from non-institutional agencies.[14] The All India Debt and Investment Survey, 1991, reports that approximately 24 % of the Rural Households accessed debt either from formal or informal sources. Out of these, 36 % had to still depend on informal credit channels viz, moneylenders, shopkeepers, relatives etc. for meeting their credit needs.[15]

Rural credit system has been experienced with huge over dues due to repayment problems. Chronic over dues and poor recovery only hamper the development banking. The major internal and external factors which have been weakening the rural credit system are:

a) Inappropriate systems/inadequate procedure followed in regard to identification and selection of borrowers;

b) Ineffective supervision and monitoring over the end use of credit;

c) Inadequate rural orientation of staff and lack of positive relationship between bankers and the borrowers; and

d) Inefficient working of production units due to traditional production practices in uneconomic land holding.[16]

In India, the enactment of the Co-operative Societies Act in 1904 was the beginning of micro-finance. The objectives of the enactment were to provide credit to the farmers and combating the problems of usury and indebtedness to the village moneylenders.[17]

In India, numerous government schemes have tried to provide various subsidized services to the poor households. However, various studies have exposed the limitation of these programs, showing the lack of access of mainstream financial services for these poor households and their over-dependence on the local money lenders in meeting their consumption and micro-enterprise demands. According to an estimate, only 16% credit usage was met by the formal sources, while the remaining 84% was met by the informal services.

Increase involvement of banks in rural credit in post nationalization era was considered as integral part of the socio-economic development efforts in the rural area. However, despite having wide network or rural bank branches in the country and implementation of many credit linked poverty alleviation programmes, a large number of the very poor continue to remain outside the fold of the formal banking system. Various studies also suggested that the policies, systems and procedures and the saving and loan products often did not meet the needs of the very poor.

NABARD refinances the microfinance sector loans by banks, but doesn't undertake direct financing. Thus, its ability to promote innovations and establish any "missing link" units is very limited. NABARD also played a complementary role in popularizing the Kisan Credit Cards (KCC) as it was tasked to formalize and familiarize the KCC among farmers. As on March 2003, about 3.13 crore cards have been issued with NABARD pushing the Regional Rural Banks and Cooperative Banks. Moreover, as part of its promotional role, NABARD has also joined hands with the ICICI Bank and the National Stock Exchange to establish the Commodities and Derivatives Exchange of India. The institution also intends to take up a 30 percent stake in the Agriculture Insurance Company of India with General Insurance Corporation of India and four other insurance companies.[18]

Commercial banks were not in rural business until they were nationalized 35 years ago. Public sector banks today are the major players in rural banking and agricultural lending. However, after the implementation of Financial Sector reforms in 90s, they have gone slow in rural branch expansion. At the same time, private sector banks have very little exposure to rural finance. Though some of the older among them have branches (1,099) in rural areas, their association with rural areas is negligible. The manner, in which they have been spreading their branch network to cover bigger cities, is an indication of their strong preference for urban-oriented business.[19] The new generation banks with their IT-driven banking operations are yet to venture into rural areas with computerized services.

Small Industries Development Bank of India (SIDBI) mainly uses the network of State Financial Corporations (SFCs) and commercial Banks to extend microfinance sector loans in rural and small towns. It also faces the same constraints. State Financial Corporations (SFCs) largely concentrate on the upper end of SSIs and that too in urban areas. However, through their district branches, a small proportion of lending is done to the microfinance sector. Their lengthy and stringent procedures inhibit the poor.

Regional Rural Banks

Regional Rural Banks was established in 1975 by Govt of India on the recommendation of Working Group on Rural Banks (1975). The objective of RRBs is to grant loans and advances to the small and marginal farmers, agricultural labourers, artisans and other categories of poor people desirous of pursuing productive programme. As on 31st March 2002, there were 196 RRBs with a network of 14,350 branches spread over in different parts of the country.[20]

Regional Rural Banks (RRBs) are located in rural areas, have low CD ratio but are suffering immensely from lack of skill, incentives and infrastructure support. As can be seen from above, while there is no dearth of institutions and branch network in urban and rural areas, this physical outreach does not translate into access to credit by microfinance sector producers.

However, wherever, mainstream finance institutions are engaged in financing small borrowers their experience is characterized by a number of factors. Their institutional design and mandate, which determines their procedures, do not suit the poor. The poor find their procedures cumbersome, complicated and unsuitable for the local environment. They have also failed to provide a mix of credit for both consumption and productive loans. Therefore, poor feel alienated in dealing with them. They feel scared to go to them. Repeat loans, except for crop production are rare, even for the borrowers who have repaid fully. Further, even though the many of loans extended to the poor by the public sector financial institutions are subsidized, their ultimate cost to the borrowers is high which includes payment to the middle men, wage and business loss due to time spent in getting the loans approved.

6.2. Rural Credit Flow and Government Initiatives

Early Initiative-Development Finance in India

The role for the financial sector in India to achieve developmental goals dates to the pre-Independence days. There was a great need to replace costly informal sources accounted for 70%, while the co-operative accounted for 6.4% and commercial just 0.9% of rural usage.

The Lead Bank Scheme was introduced in 1969, thereby starting a process of district credit plans and coordination among the different financial intermediaries. The same year also saw the nationalization of 14 commercial banks. As a result of these initiatives, the share of formal financial sector in rural credit usage rose to 30% in 1971. The Regional Rural Banks (RRBs) were conceptualized in 1975 to augment the delivery of financial services in rural areas. This resulted in the creation of one of the largest networks of banks in the world. Not surprisingly, the All India Debt and Investment Survey of 1981 found that in total credit, the share of the formal financial sector has risen to over 60%.

Subsidised Credit for Development

The Government initiated the Integrated Rural Development Programme (IRDP) in 1980-81 with the objective of directing loans to poor self –employed people through the banking sector. NABARD was established in 1982. In the same year the government also introduced the Development of Women and Children in Rural Areas (DWACRA) scheme as a part of IRDP, IRDP is estimated to have reached over 5 million (5.5 crore) poor families till 1999. Later, it was transformed into Swarnajayanti Gram Swarozgar Yojna (SGSY). IRDP, despite its immense outreach, experienced very low repayment rates and accounted for 40 million defaulters, which ruled out long-term sustainability of the programme.

The formal financial sector was criticized for being supply driven during this phase with the major characteristics exhibited during this phase being:[21]

a) Development of a large banking network, including cooperative banks and innovations such as RRBs;

b) Focus approach on credit;

c) Lending targeted at the 'Priority sector" such as agriculture and weaker sections of the population;

d) Interest rates ceiling; and

e) Subsidies.

The financial services for the poor were viewed as a social obligation. Given the high rates of default, a formal loan waiver was announced by the government in the year 1989 which had a negative impact on credit discipline. The decision also reinforced the long-held view among the mainstream financial institutions that lending to the poor was not a profitable business.

Box-3: Economic Reforms and a New Generation of Financial Institutions

In the year 1991, India faced a balance of payment of crisis. The foreign currency reserve fell to very low levels, affecting the country's ability to met foreign debt obligations. The crisis, however, propelled the government to introduce structural changes in the economy, commonly referred to as the Economic Reforms of 1991, gradually resulting in greater autonomy to the financial sector. As a result, new generation private sector banks such as UTI Bank, ICICI Bank, IDBI Bank (all established in 1994) and HDFC Bank (early 1995) emerged. The Narsimhan Committee report of 1991 also recommended phasing out of interest rate concessions and around the same time, the Brahm Prakesh Committee recommended reducing the state involvement in cooperative banks.

Emergence of Microfinance

It was around this time that the first self-help groups (SHGs) started emerging in the country, mostly as a result of non-governmental organization (NGO) initiatives. MYRADA was one of the pioneers of the concept of SHGs in India. These SHGs were large enough for the banks to have transactions with, and were also very responsive and flexible to the needs of their members. While MYRADA did not directly intervene in the credit market for the poor, it facilitated banking with micro institutions established and controlled by the poor. These early initiatives were largely responsible for the emergence of the modern microfinance sector in India.

The early nineties also witnessed the rise of several microfinance institution (MFI) initiatives-some prominent MFIs such as SHARE were conceived during this period. In 1992, the SHG-Bank linkage programme was formally launched by NABARD which circulated guidelines to banks for financing SHGs under a pilot project aimed at financing 500 SHGs across the country through the banking system. By March 1993, the banks had financed about 600 SHGs. The good repayment rate gave the confidence to continue financing SHGs in the coming years. This encouraged the Reserve Bank of India (RBI) to include financing SHGs as a mainstream activity of banks under their priority sector lending in 1996. The Government of India bestowed national priority to the programme through it's recognition of microfinance, and mentioned it in the Union Budget of 1999. Since then, the bank-SHG linkage programme has become an innovative strategy for mainstreaming rural banking.

Concurrently, in 1993, the Rashtriya Mahila Kosh (RMK) was established to accelerate the flow of credit to self-employed women in the unorganized sector. It is worth mentioning here that the SEWA Cooperative Bank, operating in Gujarat with similar objectives since 1974, is arguably the first microfinance programme in India. The Bank has been viable right from its inception and is an ideal example of a community –owned sustainable financial service delivery vehicle. MF received greater recognition in 1998 when SIDBI set up the Foundation for Micro-credit with an initial capital of Rs. 100 crores. The same year also saw the formation of Sa-Dhan as an apex level association of community development finance institutions. The passing of the Mutually Aided Co-operative Societies Act and many new MF initiatives came up under the MACS Act. In addition to the success of the SHG-Bank linkage programme, alternative MF initiatives following Grameen and /or SHG methodology or at times individual lending models have also been successful, though on a smaller scale.

Box-4: Relevance of Microfinance in the Liberalized Scenario

Liberalisation in the banking sector and a policy thrust, in the form of priority sector lending requirement, has made it easy for individuals to take loans. However, even today, a significant proportion of India's population, especially in rural areas, has difficulty in accessing small loans from formal financial institutions and banks. This is due to a paucity of appropriate loan delivery and maintenance structures, which make it costly for these institutions to service such clients.

The Vyas Committee, in its interim report states that the present saving and credit products offered by the banking sector are perhaps not suitable, and that the poor need timely financial services at affordable costs rather than subsidized credit. This makes access to credit for the poor an important impact issue for the microfinance sector.

There has been growing consensus among microfinance practitioners that, in addition to credit, the poor need an entire range of financial services including saving, insurance and fund transfers. Savings and to an extent insurance, are mechanism which allow the poor, individually or in groups, to save and build a resource pool which can be drawn upon during times of need. Effective transfer services enable people to remit money across geographies. In India, where work-related migration is widespread, cheap money transfer services assume importance. Saving, insurance and money transfer services enable the poor to smoothen their cash flows across time and space.

Another critical impact issue in microfinance is livelihood promotion and maintenance. By providing convenient access to capital, microfinance provides the opportunity to the poor to take up income-generation activities. The success of these activities depends also on environmental and technical factors. However, access to capital is an important and sometimes determining constraint. The poor are also most vulnerable to risks. Prima Facie, it appears that microfinance enables the poor to diversity their risk management strategies and overcome phase of distress. Finally, microfinance also plays a role in improving the social status of the underprivileged, especially women.

The theory of underdevelopment views poverty as a product of the vicious circle of low per capita income, low savings, and consequently low capital formation and productivity and so on. In Rural areas, it arises mainly from unemployment, under employment and low earnings. Development of social infrastructure like education, skill and training, is crucial to enable rural people to be gainfully employed, besides paying special attention to encourage self-employment on large scale through provision of micro-credit.[22] Hence, poverty alleviation was one of the thrust areas in India's Ninth Five Year Plan (1997-2000).

Since independence numerous government schemes have attempted to provide subsidized services including credit based programs of varying nature to the poor households. Besides the Central Govt. programs, the State Govt's also introduced credit based programs with large resource allocations specifically for poverty alleviation.

Government initiatives for Rural credit and rural development

Government of India has also taken a number of steps to improve the flow of institutional credit to the small and marginal farmers in particular and other rural population in general. The expansion of the branch network of the nationalized banks, establishment of the Regional Rural Banks (RRBs), the priority sector and other targets (agricultural loan, loans to weaker sections etc) for commercial banks, the Differential rates of interest scheme, programmes like, TRYSEM, DWCRA, ICDP, SITRA, IRDP, SGSY etc were intended to improve the access of the rural people to credit and to improve their incomes. Some of the major schemes implemented by the Ministry of Rural Development are as follows:

Notwithstanding the impressive progress that has been made by the country on different fronts, poverty continues to be a matter of the serious concern. The effect of large percentage of the poor on the country's development is obvious. It is in this context that the self-employment programs acquire significance, Swarnjayanti Gram Swarojgar Yojana (SGSY) is the single self–employment program for the rural poor. Launched on April 1, 1999 the program replaces the earlier self-employment and allied programs –Integrated Rural Development Programme (IRDP), Training of Rural youth for Self –Employment (TRYSEM), Development of Women and Children in Rural Areas (DWCRA), Ganga Kalyan Yojana (GKY), Million Wells Scheme (MWS), SITRA, GKY and MWS which are no longer in operation. SGSY is an innovative and carefully thought-out Yojana. It takes into account all the strengths and weaknesses of the earlier self-employment programs. It offers the perfect balance of credit and subsidy.

a) Swarnjayanti Gram Swarozgar Yojana (SGSY): In the past multiplicity of development programmes in the rural areas failed to focus on the core issue of poverty alleviation through creation of sustainable income generating opportunities. On the recommendations of the Hashim Committee, the Govt. of India, therefore restructured all the poverty alleviation programmes under an one-umbrella scheme called "SGSY" from April 1999. The focus of the scheme is on group approach and organizing the poor into Self-Help Groups.[23]

It aims at bringing the assisted poor families above the poverty line by organizing them into Self-help Groups (SHGs) and by providing them income generating assets through a mix of bank credit and government subsidy. It is a holistic programme covering all aspects of self-employment like organization of rural poor into SHGs and their capacity building, training, planning of activity clusters, infrastructure development, financial assistance through bank credit, subsidy and marketing support etc. It also emphasizes the cluster approach in development of micro enterprises in identifying key activities.

The banks and other financial institutions are closely associated and involved in the implementation of the programme starting with preparation of project report for each key activity for the selection of swarozgaris and post project monitoring etc. The funds are shared between the Centre and State in the ratio of 75:25.

The SGSY is being implemented by the District Rural Development Agencies (DRDA), with the active involvement of Panchayati Raj Institutions (PRIs), the Banks, The line Department and Non-Government Organisation (NGOs). Since its inception and upto end – March 2005 a total allocation of Rs. 7,634 crore was made available by the Centre and States and the latest available data reveals that up to November 2004 over 46 lakh Swarozgaris have been benefited. The latest Union Budget has made provision of Rs. 862 crore for SGSY for the year 2005-06.[24]

It is envisaged that 50 percent of the Groups formed in each Block should be exclusively for women who will account for at least 40 percent of the Swarozgaris. Under this Scheme, Women are encouraged in the practice of thrift and credit which enables them to become self reliant. Through assistance in the form of Revolving Fund, bank credit and subsidy, the Yojana seeks to integrate women in the economy by providing opportunities of self employment.

b) Sampoorna Grameen Rozgar Yojana (SGRY): The SGRY was launched on September 25, 2001 by merging the ongoing schemes of Jawahar Gram Samriddhi Yojana (JGSY) and Employment Assurance Scheme (EAS). It aims at providing additional wage employment in all rural areas and thereby food security and improve nutritional levels along with the creation of durable community, social and economic infrastructure in rural areas. The scheme envisages generation of 100 crore man days of employment in a year. The scheme is exclusively implemented by the Panchayati Raj Institutions (PRIs). Right from its inception up to end-March 2005, SGRY has generated about 230 crore man-days. The total outlay in 2004-05 for SGRY was Rs. 4,590 crore of which cash, food grains, and special components were Rs. 4,050 crore, Rs. 260 crore and Rs. 280 crore respectively. Union Budget 2005-06 has made provision of Rs. 3,600 crore for the above scheme.

c) Integrated Rural Development Programme (IRDP): This programme is a major part of the Government's strategy to alleviate rural poverty by creating self-employment opportunities and productivity assets which would enable the beneficiaries to rise above the poverty line. The IRDP aims to identify rural poor families, find means to augment their income and provide work on sustained basis. Under this scheme, families living below the poverty line are provided income generative assets through subsidy and institutional credit. Accordingly, from 1980-81 to 1997-98, the programme assisted 24.39 lakh families by providing subsidy totalling Rs. 430.40 crores and bank credit to the extent of Rs. 1357.25 crores. There were many loopholes in implementation of the programme. Wrong identification of families and supply of substandard assets were quite common. The role of after care support or monitoring was not given any importance. As a result many of the poor beneficiaries sold off the asset soon after obtaining it.[25] The problem with IRDP was that it incorporated a substantial element of subsidy (35-50% of each family's project cost) and this resulted in extensive malpractice and miss utilisation of funds. This situation led bankers too to view the IRDP loan as a politically motivated handout and they largely failed to follow up with borrowers. This affected the credibility of micro-borrowers in the view of bankers and ultimately, hindered access of poor to banking services.

d) The Jawahar Gram Samridhi Yojana (JGSY): The programme has been launched with effect from April 1, 1999 with the twin objectives of creation of demand driven community village infrastructure and generation of supplementary employment (for the unemployed poor) in the rural areas. Wage employment under the JGSY is extended to Below Poverty Line families. It is stipulated that 30 percent of the employment opportunities should reserved for women.

e) Rural Employment Generation Programme (REGP): REGP was launched in 1995 with the objective of creating self-employment opportunities in the rural areas and small towns, is being implemented by the Khadi and Village Industries Commission (KVIC). Under REGP, entrepreneurs can establish village industries by availing of margin money assistance from the KVIC and bank loans, for projects with a maximum cost of Rs. 25 lakh. Since the inception of REGP, up to 31 March 2004, 1,86,252 projects have been financed and 22.75 lakh job opportunities created. A target of creating 25 lakh new jobs has been set for the REGP during the Tenth Plan. 8.32 lakh employment opportunities have already been created during 2003-04. For 2004-05, a target of creating 5.25 lakh job opportunities has been fixed.

f) Prime Minister's Rozgar Yojana (PMRY): PMRY started in 1993 with the objective of making available self-employment opportunities to the educated unemployed youth by assisting them in setting up any economically viable activity. So far, about 20 lakh units have been set up under PMRY, creating 30.4 lakh additional employment opportunities. The target for additional employment opportunities under the Tenth Plan was 16.50 lakh. PMRY is meant for educated un-employed youth with family income of up to Rs. 40,000 per annum, in both urban and rural areas, for engaging in any economically viable activity.[26]

g) The Indira Awas Yojana (IAY): aims at providing assistance for the construction of houses for people Below the Poverty Line in rural areas. Under the Scheme, priority is extended to widows and unmarried women. It is stipulated that IAY houses are to be allotted in the name of women members of the household or alternatively, in the joint names of husband and wife.

h) The National Social Assistance Programme (NSAP): The NSAP which came into effect five years ago represents a significant step towards introducing a National Policy for Social Assistance benefits to households Below the Poverty Line, with a major focus on women. It has three components, namely, the National Old Age Pension Scheme, The National Family Benefit Scheme and the National Maternity Benefit Scheme. The National Maternity Benefit Scheme is exclusively aimed at assisting expectant mothers by providing them Rs. 500 each for the first two live births. (This Scheme has since been transferred to Ministry of Health and Family Welfare). Under the National Old Age Pension Scheme, Central Assistance of Rs. 75 per month is provided to women and men who are 65 years of age and above and have little or no regular means of subsistence from their won sources of income or through financial support from the Self-Help Groups. Under the National Family Benefit Scheme, Central Assistance of Rs. 10,000 is extended to the bereaved family in the case of death of the primary breadwinner due to natural or accidental causes. Women are also beneficiaries under this Scheme.

i) RRSP: The Restructured Centrally Sponsored Rural Sanitation Programme which was launched with effect from 1st April 1999 provides for the construction of sanitary latrines for rural households. Where individual household latrines are not feasible, provision exists for construction of village sanitary complexes exclusively for women, to ensure privacy and dignity. Up to 10 percent of the allocated fund can be utilized for construction and maintenance of public latrines for women.

j) ARWP: Under the Accelerated Rural Water Supply Programme, training is being imparted to women to enable them to play an active role using and maintaining hand pumps for supply of drinking water. Women are also represented in village level committees and are actively involved in the selection of sites for hand pumps and other sources.

Many programmes which were started by the government enthusiastically but they were not able to achieve their objectives. The reason behind this is poor follow up, lack of management and participation from the Government as well as people. No programme can ever get its ultimate result unless and until there is co-ordination and co-operation between government and the beneficiaries.[27]

India's main poverty program, the Integrated Rural Development Programme, incorporating a substantial element of subsidy had negative consequences for the financial sector, due to the misuse of funds and poor repayment rates (35%). It undermined the credibility of microfinance and hindered the recycling of loanable funds by commercial banks. It has been revamped as the SGSY. Likewise, the network of primary co-operatives and RRBs proved to be a failure.

In the union budget 2005-06, Govt of India has come up a very ambitious plant called "Bharat Nirmal". It is a plant for building the infrastructure mainly in rural India. The plan is to be implemented during next four years. It comprises the provision of irrigation, roads, water supply, housing, rural electrification and rural telecom connectivity. The targets set under this plan are:[28]

i) To bring and additional one crore hectares under assured irrigation;

ii) To connect all village having population of 1000 (or 500 in hilly/tribal areas) with a road;

iii) To construct 60 lakh additional house for the poor;

iv) To provide drinking water to the remaining 74,000 habitations that are uncovered;

v) To reach electricity to the remaining 1,25,000 villages and offer electricity connection to 2.3 crore households; and

vi) To give telephone connectivity to the remaining 66,822 villages, Panchayat Raj Institutions would be fully involved in planning and implementation of these projects.

(k) National Rural Employment Guarantee Bill 2004 (NERG): has been introduced in Parliament in December 2004 to provide at least 100 days of guaranteed wage employment every year to each household. The other major employment generation programmes currently in vogue are Swaranjayanti Gram Swarozgar Yojana (SGSY), Sampoorna Gramin Rozgar Yojana (SGRY), Rural Employment General Programme (REGP), and Prime Minister's Rozgar Yojana (PMRY). These programmes cater to the needs of the diverse groups of poor section of the society, especially in rural areas.

The lack of proper supervision and design deficiencies of the above poverty related programmes led to the following problems:

i) High defaults and leakages in poverty-related programmes;

ii) The poorer of the poor still remain outside the banking fold; and

iii) The perception that the very poor are not bankable remains.

However, these programmes were more in the nature of poverty alleviation schemes and not so much for improving the access of the bypassed rural population to the financial services.

6.3. Issues of Rural Finance

The Banking sector, after nationalization, witnessed substantial amounts being earmarked for credit programs specifically directed to the poor. There was a massive branch expansion especially in the rural areas. Credit was often recognized as the remedy for many ills of poverty. Despite the large resource allocations were made both in the form of grants/subsidies as well as credit from banks, the poorest as well as women remained out of the banking system because of the following reasons:

a) System and procedure of the banking system are too rigid;

b) Absence of consumption credit;

c) Savings as a financial product are not yet recognized;

d) Too many resources are put in the Poor's hands under government –sponsored programmes with decisions resting with others; and

e) The perception that the very poor are not bankable remains.

A study made by Price Waterhouse Coopers, a reputed investment consultant, shows the following pattern of credit usage by the rural poor:[29]

a) 63 percent of total credit availed by the rural poor is used for consumption purposes with only 37 per cent used for productive use;

b) the overall share of organized sector in credit flow to the rural poor is around 16 percent;

c) non-availability of credit for consumption needs from the organized sector with very high cost to the borrowers;

d) Delay in sanction of loans by the organized sector; and

e) Very high rate of default under the government sponsored programmes has led to reluctance on the part of the banks to extend credit to rural poor.

Some of issues of rural finance are given as under:[30]

a) Like other developing countries in India too, for long the general belief was that poor required cheap and may subsidized credit and they did not save and would be unable to provide any margin for loans.

b) The credit requirement of the marginal farmers, agricultural labour, artisans, petty traders, etc are often small, urgent and frequent. The cost structure, procedures and systems obtaining in the banking system make the transaction costs for small financial operations quite high.

c) Poor credit discipline in rural credit is another issue. The rural credit is generally considered "developmental lending" which has a negative connotation in the mind of the banker from returns and recovery point of view. The problem was further compounded as the rural borrowers could not clearly distinguish between the "Grants" provided by the Government and credit provided by the Banks.

d) Inadequate manpower in the rural branches. Most of bank staffs don't like to post in rural branches because of low incentives and parks, poor infrastructure in rural areas.

e) Poor also find it difficult to approach banks. The documentation and formalities were very complex for them.

f) Though the interest rates on bank loans are low, the real transaction cost of the borrower is quite high if taken into the account of travelling expenses, loss of wages, payment to self appointed 'middlemen' etc.

g) Rural credit is more rigid and lacks flexibility and user's friendliness. On the other hand, informal lending is more flexible in terms of quantum of loan, collateral requirement, period of loan and the purpose of loan.

h) Further, there had also not been much innovations or attempts to develop appropriate products or efforts to adapt the delivery system to meet the requirement of the rural poor as a client group.

The bypassed rural poor wanted a product which could offer broadly the following facilities:

a) Opportunities to keep safe their occasional surplus in the form of thrift.

b) Access to consumption loans to meet emergent requirements.

c) Hassle-free access to financial services.

The inability of the credit institutions to deal with the credit requirements of the poor effectively has led to the emergence of micro-finance or micro-credit system as an alternative credit system for the poor. [31]Usually, credit institutions provide finance for productive purposes but sometimes poor people need money for consumption or for emergency purposes, which many time cannot be catered by the formal credit system or government sponsor and poverty alleviation schemes. In rural India, it can be seen that the poorer sections of the society and destitute cannot avail of the credit from banks and other formal institutions due to their inability to deposit collateral security and mortgage property. At this point of view, micro-financing or group lending is being looked upon as the instrument that can be considered as the golden stick for poverty alleviation vis-à-vis rural development.

6.4. Evolution of Microfinance in India

The post-nationalization period in the banking sector witnessed substantial amount of resources being earmarked towards meeting the credit needs of the poor. The banking network underwent an expansion phase without comparables in the world. The branch expansion[32] was synergized with massive manpower recruitment drive for manning such branches. Credit came to be recognized as a remedy for many of the ills of the poverty. Credit packages and programmes were designed based on the perceived needs of the poor. Programmes also underwent qualitative changes bases on the experiences gained besides the programmes were introduced by the states governments with large resource allocations.

While the underlying objectives were laudable and substantial progress was achieved, credit flow to the poor and especially to poor women, remained low. This led to initiatives that were institution led, that attempted to converge of the existing strengths of rural banking infrastructure and leverage this to better serve the unbanked poor. The pioneering efforts at this were made by National Bank for Agricultural and Rural Development (NABARD), which was vested with the enviable task of framing appropriate policy for rural credit intuitions and their development initiatives.

During the eighties, NABARD conducted a series of research studies in association with MYRDA[33] (an NGO from South India) and also independently which showed that despite having a wide network of rural bank branched that implemented specific poverty alleviation programs and self-employment opportunities through bank credit for almost two decades, a very large number of the poorest of the poor continued to remain outside the fold of the formal banking system.

These studies also showed that the existing banking policies, system and procedures, and deposit and loan products were perhaps not well suited to meet the most immediate needs of the poor. It also appeared that what the poor really needed was a better access to these services and products, rather than cheap subsidies credit.

Against this background, a need was felt for alternative policies, systems and procedures savings and loan products, other complementary services, and new delivery mechanism which would fulfil the requirements of the poorest, especially of the women members of such households, The emphasis therefore was on improving the access of the poor to micro Finance (MF) rather than just micro-credit.[34]

NABARD's launching of its pilot phase of the SHG-Bank linkage program in 1992 can be considered as the landmark development in the Microfinance scenario of India. The strategy involved forming small, cohesive and participative groups of the poor, encouraging them to pool their thrift regularly and using the pooled thrift to make small interest bearing loans to members and in the process learning the nuances of financial discipline. Subsequently, bank credit also becomes available to the Group, to argument its resources for lending to its members. The promotion and bank linking of SHGs has not been viewed as a credit program but as part of an overall arrangement for providing financial services to the poor in a sustainable manner and also an empowerment process for the members of these SHGs.

The NABARD led Pilot Project which commenced with the support of the Reserve Bank of India, from 1992 onwards aimed at promoting and financing 500 SHGs across the entire country, the SHG-Bank linkage strategy has come a long way. The strategy includes financing of SHGs promoted by external facilitators like NGOs, bankers, socially spirited individuals and government agencies and also promotion of SHGs by banks themselves and financing SHGs directly by banks or indirectly where NGOs and similar organizations act as financial intermediaries as well.

The pilot phase was followed by the setting up of a Working Group of NGOs and SHGs by the Reserve Bank of India in 1994, which came out with wide ranging recommendations on internalization of the SHG concept as a potential intervention tool in the area of banking with the poor. The Reserve Bank of India accepted most of the major recommendations and advised the banks to consider lending to the SHGs as part of their mainstream rural credit operations. Based on very successful feedback of the pilot run of the Program, NABARD in 1998 crystallized its Vision for providing access to 100 million of rural poor through linking of 1 million SHGs by 2008 (which was achieved in March 2004).

In recent years, microfinance institutions (MFIs) have emerged as promising institutions to meet the consumption and micro enterprise demands of the poor. However, the varied demands of the low income households and diverse regional provocations have led to the emergence of multiple models in community based baking in India. These ranges from homespun self help groups (SHGs) and co-operatives to adapted models like that of Grameen Bank of Bangladesh or for –profit corporate models.

The Task Force on Supportive Policy and Regulatory Framework of Microfinance" inter alia recommended the formulation of a "National Policy on Micro Finance". The National Policy on Microfinance should emphasize on encouraging initiatives and participation of different types of institutions in micro-finance, bringing the micro-finance activities, irrespective of the type of institutions involved, within the regulation and supervision by competent authorities, creating policy environment for closer linkages of the microfinance sector with the formal banking channels, and making available equity, start-up capital and capacity-building funds for the existing and prospective institutions engaged in microfinance.[35]

NABARD is one of the key players in the SHG-Bank linkage Programme. It is, in fact, the chief promoter of the programme. The success achieved so far could be attributed to a considerable extent to the continued efforts made by NABARD to mainstream the programme.

At the same time, the onus for the future success and sustainability of the programme to a great extent lies with NABARD. The main aim of the programme is to tap the potential of the SHG concept to bring banking services to the doorsteps of poor, especially the women who have been neglected by the formal financial agencies in the past.[36] Through the linkage Programme, NABARD would like to realize the vision of empowering the rural poor by improving their access to the formal credit system in a cost-effective and sustainable manner.

In India, microfinance has enabled the poor to have a greater access to financial services, particularly credit. It has achieved several social development objectives like gender sensitization, empowerment and poverty alleviation by diversifying their livelihoods and especially contributed largely towards raising their incomes. It has also allowed the poor to accumulate assets and has contributed towards their security. Further, microfinance has also had a very significant social impact. In areas with sound microfinance programmes, the quality of life of the poor has improved significantly.

Shift to the New Paradigm

Now, the microfinance "approach" has engendered a new relationship between the banks and poor. A relationship which is based on sound business principles enables the poor to approach banks as "customers" and not as "beneficiaries". SHG-Bank linkage programme marks a watershed in the history of rural banking in India. The Banks have reported 95% on-time repayment by the SHGs across the country; and they have reported very low NPAs (Non Perfoming Assets). The mantra of this miracle is nothing but banking through groups.[37]

Actors	*Roles*
The poor	✓ Perceived thrift as their strength as also as the bonding factor among themselves;
	✓ Realised that timely and adequate credit was preferable and productive than subsidies and doles;
	✓ They needed hassle-free delivery mechanisms.
NGOs	✓ Acted as catalysts of change
	✓ Combined social and economic agenda with synergistic effect
	✓ Recognised sustainability as the core factor in development
Banking System	✓ Accepted SHG-Bank linkage as a cost effective means of reaching the poor
	✓ Accepted peer pressure as collateral substitute for excellent recovery of loans
Government	✓ Formulated supportive policy framework
	✓ Encouraged routing of social programs through SHGs
Reserve Bank of India	✓ RBI policy pronouncements on micro-Finance led to increased involvement of banks

(Contd...)

Actors	*Roles*
	✓ Liberalized interest rates and deregulated interest rate structure for micro credit, leading to flexibility in lending rates
NABARD	✓ Provided inputs in capacity building for banks and partner agencies
	✓ Promoted the idea of organizing thrift and credit groups among the NGOs as an add-on activity and encouraged linking them with banks
	✓ Provided loan-able funds to banks and financial support to eligible MFIs to ease the fund flow position to the sector.

6.5. Government of India: Initiatives for Development of Microfinance Industry

In order to provide an enabling environment for realizing the latent potential of microfinance in India, a close scrutiny of policy issues such as capital constraints, legal and structural constraints and socio-cultural constraints is required. It is necessary that the microfinance sector displays strong and consistent growth so that a majority of the poor have access to institutional financial services.

Since 1999, the sector has been advocating on various critical issues to policy makers at the central and state levels, the Reserve,Bank of India (RBI), national commissions and committee etc. In 1999, NABARD formed a task force to bring out the conceptual policy framework encompassing issues in policy, regulation, financing and capacity building for the sustainable growth of microfinance in the country.

Later on in 2002, the Association of Microfinance Institutions in India, Sa-Dhan, represented the sector in the RBI informal group on funding issues and in the same year, Sa-Dhan was a part of the empowered Committee housed aspects of microfinance in India. In 2004, the Vyas Committee on "flow of credit to agriculture" formed by RBI also assessed the role of microfinance and MFIs in credit delivery to the poor. This report finds that the number of new SHGs formed has been growing by nearly 20 percent annually. This raises the hope that it should be possible to achieve a compounded annual growth rate of 20 percent over the next five years in improving the outreach of microfinance initiatives, which could allow the microfinance programme to reach almost 75 percent of the total poor households (80 million or eight crore) in the next five years.

In pursuance of the proposal contained in the union budget 2000-2001, a Microfinance Development Fund (MFDF) of Rs. 100 crores was established by NABARD with an initial corpus of Rs. 80 crore, contributed equally by the Reserve Bank of India and the National Bank. The funds are to be utilised for scaling up the SHG-linkage programmes and supporting other innovative credit delivery model, keeping following broad objective:

a) Support financial services to the rural poor, particularly women, who have not been able to secure the needed services from the formal financial system.

b) Provide laudable and capacity building funds in respect of SHGs and various types of other grass roots level micro-finance institutions.

c) Support all initiatives for up-scaling of the SHG-Bank linking programmes.

d) Built up expertise in micro-finance activities.

e) Evolution of regulatory and supervisory mechanisms for microfinance institutions as and when required.

Box-5: Microfinance Development and Equity Fund (MFDEF)

Recognising the need for upscaling the micro-finance interventions in the country, the Hon'ble Union Finance Minister, while presenting the budget for the year 2000-01, announced the creation of a Micro Finance Development Fund (MFDF) with initial contribution of Rs.100 crore, to be funded by Reserve Bank of India and NABARD (Rs.40 crore each) and the balance Rs.20 crore to be contributed by commercial banks. In the Union Budget for 2005-06, the Government of India had decided to re-designate the existing MFDF as Micro Finance Development and Equity Fund (MFDEF) and raised its corpus from Rs.100 crore to Rs.200 crore with the similar ratio of contributions. The MFDEF is managed and administered by NABARD. The objective of MFDEF is to facilitate and support the orderly growth of the microfinance sector through diverse modalities for enlarging the flow of financial services to the poor, particularly for women and vulnerable sections of society consistent with sustainability. The Fund is utilised to support interventions to eligible institutions and stakeholders. The major components of the assistance include promotional grant assistance to Self-Help Promoting Agencies, training and capacity building for microfinance clients and stakeholders of SHG-Bank Linkage Programme, funding support to MFIs, Management Information System (MIS) for microfinance, research, studies and publications.

In the UN International Year of Microcredit-2005, the Government of India has acknowledged the role of MFIs in financial intermediation and in the Union Budget 2005, it has accorded "Banking Correspondent" status to MFIs and strengthen the National Microfinance Fund under NABARD with an incremental corpus of Rs. 100 crore and re-designated it as Microfinance Development Equity Fund (MEDF). This fund will support the activities like:

a) Training and exposure to SHG members, partners, NGOs, banks and government agencies.

b) Provide start-up funds to MFIs and meet their operational deficits.

c) Meet the cost of formation and nurturing of SHGs.

d) Design new delivery mechanisms.

e) Promote research, management information systems and dissemination of best practices in microfinance.

In May 2005, the Annual Credit policy Statement RBI 2005 -06 also mentioned the financial intermediation role played by MFIs. These are all clear indications of the changes that are happening in the policy regime towards microfinance and microfinance institutions.

Union Budget (2005-06)

Announcement on Microfinance[38]

a) The programme of linking Self-Help Groups (SHGs) with the banking system has emerged as the major micro-finance programme in the country. 560 banks including 48 commercial banks, 196 RRBs and 316 co-operative banks are now actively involved in the programme. The target for credit-linking has been increased from 2 lakh SHGs in 2004-05 to 2.5 lakh SHGs in 2005-06.

b) Since Micro Finance Institutions (MFIs) prove small scale credit and other financial services to low income households and small informal business, Government has decided to promote MFIs in a big way. This would be done by identifying MFIs and classifying, rating and empowering them to intermediate between lending banks and beneficiaries.

c) Commercial banks may appoint MFIs as "Banking Correspondents" to provide transaction services on their behalf.

d) For infusion of new capital into MFIs, the existing Micro Finance Fund would be re-designated as "Micro Finance Development and Equity Fund". The Corpus of this fund would be increased from the existing Rs. 100 crore to Rs. 200 crore. The fund would be managed by a Board consisting of representatives of NABARD, commercial banks and professionals with domain knowledge. The Board will be asked to suggest suitable legislation, and accordingly, a draft bill would be introduced in the Parliament in 2005-06.

e) RBI would be requested to open a window to enable qualified NGOs engaged in micro-finance activities to use the External Commercial Borrowing (ECB). Detailed guidelines containing necessary safeguards will be issued by RBI.

6.6. Progress of SHG-Bank Linkage Program

Self Help Groups (SHGs) have become the common vehicle of development process as SHGs converges all development programmes. SHG-Bank Linkage Programme launched by NABARD way back in 1992 envisaging synthesis of formal financial system and informal sector has become a movement throughout the country. It is considered as the largest microfinance programme in terms of outreach in the world and many other countries are keen to replicate this model. At present, a large number of Self-Help Group Promoting Institutions (SHPIs), all the banking agencies and MFIs are pursuing this programme for the upliftment of the poor. This is also recognized as a part of priority sector lending and normal banking business by Reserve Bank of India. Thus, it is synonymous with microfinance programme of the country. This programme is also the main contributor towards the Financial Inclusion process in the country. As on 31 March 2009, there are more than 61 lakh saving-linked SHGs and more than 42 lakh credit-linked SHGs and thus, about 8.6 crore poor households are covered under the programme.

NABARD has been playing a leading role in the microfinance programme for two decades now. It has been catalysis the banking system in the country to join hands progressively with informal delivery channels to give SHG-Bank linkage the necessary momentum. NABARD has been instrumental in facilitating various activities under microfinance sector, involving all possible partners in the arena. It has been encouraging the voluntary agencies, bankers, and socially spirited individuals, other formal and informal entities and also government functionaries to promote and nurture SHGs. The focus in this direction has been on training and capacity building of partners, promotional grant assistance to Self Help Promoting Institutions (SHPIs), Revolving Fund Assistance (RFA) to MFIs, equity/ capital support to MFIs to supplement their financial resources and provision of 100% refinance against bank loans provided by various banks for microfinance activities.

SHG-Bank-Cumulative Progress (1992-2009)
(Physical and financial terms)

Up to end March	*SHGs financed*	*Bank Loan (Rs. million)*
1992-99	32,995	571
1999-00	1,14,775	1,930
2000-01	2,63,825	48,09
2001-02	4,61,478	10,263
2002-03	7,17,360	20,487
2003-04	10,79,091	39,042
2004-05	16,18,456	68,985
2005-06	22,38,565	1,13,975
2006-07	29,24,973	1,23,665
2007-08	36,25,941	1,69,999
2008-2009	42,24,338	2,26,798

Source: NABARD, *Status of Microfinance in India.*

As may be seen from table, as on 31st March 2009, the bank loans aggregating Rs.2,26,798 million were disbursed to 43,24,338 SHGs. Around 77.80 percent of the SHGs linked were exclusively women SHGs. Various studies revealed that the on –time repayment of SHG loans to banks was over 90 per cent.

As on 31 March 2009, total number of 42,24,338 SHGs were having outstanding bank loans of Rs. 22,679.85 crore as against 36,25,941 SHGs with bank loans of Rs. 16999.90 crore as on 31 March 2008 with a growth rate of 16.5 % (No. of SHGs) and 33.4% (Bank Loan outstanding with SHGs). The share of SHGs under SGSY was 9,76,887 SHGs (23.1%) with outstanding bank loans of Rs. 5,861.72 crore (25.8%) as against 6,16,978 groups (25.2%) with outstanding bank loans of Rs. 4,816.87 crore (28.05%) as on 31 March 2008.

As on 31 March 2009, total 61,21,147 SHGs were having saving bank accounts with the banking sector with outstanding savings of Rs. 5,545.62 crore as against 50,09,794 SHGs having savings of Rs. 3785.39 crore as on 31 March 2008, thereby having growth rate of 22.2% and 46.5% respectively. Thus, more than 8.6 crore poor households were associated with banking agencies under SHG-Bank Linkage Programme. As on 31 March 2009, the

Commercial Banks had the maximum share of SHGs' savings of 35,49,509 SHGs (58%) with savings amount of Rs. 2772.99 crore (50%) followed by Regional Rural Banks having savings bank accounts of 16,28,588 SHGs (26.6%) with savings amount of Rs. 1989.75 crore (35.9%) and Cooperative Banks having savings bank accounts of 9,43,050 SHGs (15.4%) with savings amount of Rs. 782.88 crore (14.1%).The share under SGSY in the total savings was 15,05,581 SHGs with savings of Rs.1,563.39 crore forming 24.6 % of the total SHGs having savings accounts with the banks and 28.1% of total savings amount.[39]

SHG movement has clearly brought out the need for multi-level support to effectively empower the rural poor. The mere purveying of the credit which largely follows a product approach has been found to be woefully inadequate to cause economic progress. The key factor for success of the SHG movement are group synergy, enhanced social capital, strategic interventions by facilitators resulting in inculcating thrift habits, gradual improvement in financial management abilities and acceptance of democratic process of decision making. These key factors reveal the approach that is needed to develop quality clients among the poor. The poor has responded to this approach by proving that they are excellent "Repayment Masters".

6.7. Regional Spread SHG-Bank Linkage

The spread of the SHG-bank linkage has shown significant progress in recent years. States such as Andhra Pradesh, Tamil Nadu, Karnataka, Uttar Pradesh, Maharashtra and Kerala maintained their high growth trends. The details are given in the following Table. [40]

Positive Trends in Cumulative Growth in SHGs in Linked to Banks

Region	*March 2001*	*March 2002*	*March 2003*	*March 2004*	*March 2005*	*March 2006*	*March 2007*	*March 2008*	*March 2009*
Northern region	9,012	19,321	34,923	52,396	86,018	1,33,097	1,82,018	1,34,783	1,66,511
North Eastern	477	1,490	4,069	12,278	34,238	62,517	91,754	1,03,424	1,17,812
Eastern Region	22,252	45,892	90,893	1,58,237	2,65,628	3,94,351	5,25,881	7,53,048	9,33,489
Central Region	28,851	48,181	81,583	1,27,009	1,97,365	2,67,915	3,32,729	3,26,763	3,32,116
Western Region	15,543	29,318	42,180	54,815	96,266	1,66,254	2,70,447	4,46,550	3,93,499
Southern Region	1,87,690	3,17,276	4,63,712	6,74,356	9,38,941	12,14,431	15,22,144	18,61,373	22,80,911
All India	2,63,825	4,61,478	7,17,360	10,79,091	16,18,456	22,38,565	29,24,973	36,25,941	42,24,338

It is seen from the above that highest concentration is southern region with 18,61,737 SHGs (54%) followed by eastern region with 9,33,489 SHGs (22%).

During the period April 2005 to March 2006, 620109 new SHGs were financed by banks to the tune of Rs. 44.99 million by way of loans. Cumulatively, banks have lent Rs. 113.97 billion to 2, 238,565 SHGs.

6.8. Partner Agencies in SHG-Bank Linkage Program

During the year 2005-06, 44,362 of 547 banks participated in the SHG-bank linkage program Agency-wise number of SHGs financed are given in Table below.

Agency-wise Distribution of Number of SHGs[41]

(Amount Rupees million)

Agency	*Comulative up to 31 March 2009*			
	SHGs		*Bank loan*	
	No	*%*	*Amount (Rs. In lacs)*	*%*
CBs	2831374	67.02	1614942.80	71.20
RRBs	977834	23.15	522441.61	23.03
Co-operatives	415130	9.83	130599.84	5.77
Total	4224338	100	2267984.25	100

44,362 branches of 545 banks (commercial banks-47, Regional Rural Banks-158 & Co-operative Banks -340) situated in 583 districts in the 30 states of the country are participating in the programme.[42]

About 32.98 million poor household have gained access to formal banking system through SHG bank linkage programme. Nearly 90% of the group are women groups.

Commercial Banks (CBs)

The SHG-Bank linkage program became a part of business for all the 27 public sector banks and 20 private sector banks. SBI credit linked the highest number of the SHGs (142,034) during 2005-06, followed by Indian Bank (30,632) and Canara Bank (18,445). During the year, many more banks registered impressive growth in SHG-Bank Linkage. These were Indian Overseas Bank, Punjab National Bank, Andhra Bank, Bank of India and Bank of Baroda. The private sector banks which significantly supported SHG financing were ICICI Bank Ltd (6,746), Dhanalaxmi Bank (1,201) followed by the Lord Krishna Bank (1,181).

The share of Commercial Banks in total SHGS financed by different agencies were 53 percent of total SHGs (22,38,566 SHGs) and 61 percent of total bank loan (Rs.11,397 million).

Regional Rural Banks (RRBs)

All the 196 RRBs in the country participated in the SHG-Bank linkage program.

During the year 2005-06, maximum number of SHGs have been linked by Pragjyotish Goanlia bank in Assam (9,190 SHGs) followed by Bolagnir Anchlik Gramya Bank (7,278 SHGs) in Orissa and Karnataka Vikas Gramin Bank (5,819 SHGs) in Karnataka. The other RRBs showing significant achievement were Pansian Gramin Bank in Tamil Nadu, Nagarjun

Gramin Bank, Sri Rayalseema Gramin Bank and Shri Vishakha Gramin Bank in Andhra Pradesh, Kalahandi Anchalik Gramya Bank in Orissa and Pragati Gramin Bank in Karnaka.

The share of Commercial Banks in total SHGS financed by different agencies were 33 percent of total SHGs (22,38,566 SHGs) and 29 percent of total bank loan (Rs.11,397 million).

Co-operative Banks

NABARD has been supporting capacity building, exposure and awareness creation initiatives among the co-operatives to mainstream SHG-Bank linkage in the Co-operative banking sector. Cooperative Banks, though comparatively late starters, have begun making forays into MF sector on a large sector. The amendments made by many of the States in their respective Co-operative Societies Acts enabled Co-operative banks to take up the activity of promotion and nurturing of SHGs. Influenced by the pioneering performance of District Central Cooperative Banks (DCCBs) like Hoogly (West Bengal), Chandrapur (Maharashtra) and South Canara (Karnataka) in the SHG-Bank Linkage programme, many other DCCBs also evinced keen interest in SHG-Bank Linkage Programme.

The number of partners for the SHG-Bank linkage in the Co-operative banking sector increased to 340 up to March 2006.

The overall portfolio at risk (NPA) of the programme was 1.36% which was very commendable for a programme that was 13 years old and growing at a fast pace. The NPAs under SHG Portfolio of the Commercial Banks was at a level as low as 0.93 % as against an overall NPA ratio of 2.65% for their normal lending activities. The NPAs under the SHG Portfolio of the RRBs was 2.32% as against an overall NPA ratio of 8.70 % for their normal lending activities. The NPAs under the SHG Portfolio of the Co-operative Banks was 2.14 % as against an overall NPA ratio of 18.84 % for their normal lending activities. 41,630 (.e 76%) rural branches lend to SHGs.

6.9. SHG-Bank Linkage Problems and Issues

Programmes in terms of reaching physical targets have been successful and there is a positive impact being experienced by the poor in terms of getting easy access to formal saving and credit facilities leading to improvements in their socio-economic conditions.[43]

However, programme is faced with problems like uneven spread across and within different states, inadequate response from the banks, rapid promotion of SHGs leading to large number becoming defunct and prevalence of high rate of interest charged to ultimate borrowers raising questions about the ability of the intervention for poverty alleviation.

Some problems which hinders the progress of SHGs are lack of awareness, lack of commitment, lack of efforts on the part of implementing agencies, lack of good and viable NGOs, lack of motivation for women in forming SHG, lack of nursing and management , lack of proper training to banks, NGOs and government officials, lack of coordination between bank and block officials, non-delegation of adequate powers to branch mangers, weak credit structure of banks and no effective follow up after sanction of loan.[44]

The focus on group solidarity in SHGs in India is missing. It still has not been institutionalized. In the present form, group cohesion and solidarity is largely dependent upon the NGO that has been involved in shaping group. The financing agencies, the banks have no role in strengthening the groups or in ensuring that it remains cohesive. As such, the danger of the groups disintegrating is very real. Since 1999, with launching of Swarnajayanti Gram Swarojgar Yojana (SGSY), where financing has primarily to take place in groups, the Government agencies have also jumped in the arena for forming groups. This has further complicated the issue of group solidarity as the SGSY groups for the poor are being formed for the purposed of getting credit under which there is an element of subsidy from the Government. Subsidy goes against the philosophy of the microfinance[45] and has the danger of having a negative demonstrative effect on the other groups formed by NGOs.

While NGOs have primarily been instrumental in forming and nurturing the SHGs, it is the banks which primarily have the responsibility of financing them. The involvement of two separate agencies necessitates that some form of collaboration between the two should exist so that their energies are directed towards a common goal. Such collaborative mechanism is yet to take shape.

The MFIs of Bangladesh are noted for reaching out to people but in India, the SHG office bearers have to visit the banks for carrying out various transactions. It will not be unusual for a new SHG to find that getting an account opened with the bank is a Herculean Task involving several visits to the bank and considerable man-hours. The documentation and formalities required for getting loans is also not standardized, varying from bank to bank and state to state.[46]

Banks role

For the linkage programme to success, the banks and co-operatives must become much more proactive. The RBI's guideline for commercial banks to treat SHG financing as priority sector lending as well as to include microfinance under their corporate planning is a welcome measure. The initiatives have given new impetus for the involvement of financial institutions.

While in those areas where NGOs are present the banks can take the help of NGOs in promoting SHGs, in other areas banks must come forward on their own to form and nurture SHGs. The banks have to provide physical and financial resources for the purpose. The banks have to provide physical and financial resources for the purpose. For this to happen on a massive scale, the banks need to create SHG cells in their zonal or district level officers for providing continued thrust and monitoring. Like specialized officers, they should recruit and post professional trained in microfinance and SHG concept in rural branches so that they are able to promote and mange SHGs in significant numbers. The Banks must come out with new saving and credit products to suit the changing needs of the SHGs including extending cash credit facilities, SHGs must not be seen by the banks only as agencies for promoting loan business. Launching easy and convenient saving products can also go a long way in ensuring livelihood security for the poor.

NGO role

The credit both for introducing SHGs as financial intermediaries for the poor as well as for the results achieved so far under the linkage programme in major way goes to the NGOs in the country. NGOs have emerged as the major Self Help Promoting Institutions (SHPIs).

Some have taken up SHPI role as an add-on activity under NABARD initiative. NGOS have been able to attain this because of their strengths in social intermediation process, concern for the poor and ability to innovate for realizing their goals. To a great extent, the future success of the programme also depends on the evolution of the role of NGOs in the field of microfinance.

A large number of NGOs are either trying to promote or even transform themselves into full fledged microfinance institutions (MFIs). However, NGOs should increase their outreach uniformly by widening and deepening the SHGs Base within and across the villages. In order to avoid any unnecessary duplication and competition in SHG formation, NGOs operating in a particular area or district must coordinate among themselves before during the scaling up. Such a coordination would not only help in orderly growth of SHGs but also in increasing outreach of SHGs in villages untouched so far by any NGOs.[47] Through such coordination NGOs will also be in a position to exchange ideas about best practices.

NGOs should try linking their SHGs with nearby financial institutions as more and more banks are also trying for such linkages. Linking SHGs with the banks would enable them to automatically get integrated with the financial system. A large number of NGOs these days are trying to federate their SHGs at block or district level. The SHGs must be nurtured to mature as financial intermediaries capable of meeting various savings and credit needs of the poor.

6.10. SHGs-Bank Linkage: Future Strategies

SHG promotion and nurturing is a time consuming process. Any kind of target fixing in SHG promotion goes against the basic principles of SHG formation. Apparently, the SHG-Bank linkage Programme is tending towards becoming target oriented. NABARD has claimed that they have been able to cross the target of one million SHGs set for 2008 by 2004 itself.[48] While one can set bigger goals for the programme but target-based approach is not consistent with the basic nature of SHG formation which may have deleterious impact on the sustainability of the Programme. There are fears being expressed that the programme, if implemented in a target based way, may end up like the earlier Integrated Rural Development Programme (IRDP) under which a large number of programme participants were unable to pursue any viable projects leading to high repayment problem.[49]

While exceeding of the physical target could be considered as an indicator of success, but for the reason mentioned above the recent growth also needs careful analysis for identifying the quality of the SHGs being formed. At the same time, NABARD has to ensure that SHGs formed for the purpose of saving and credits are not hijacked by other agencies and programmes. There are now efforts to adopt group-based approach in many of the government based programmes like SGSY and Swa-Shakti. NABARD should take adequate care so that even if some integration has to be attained between SHGs and such programmes, it is done without harming the basic principles and structure of SHGs.

The key to future success lies in retaining the basic character and strength of SHGs along with integrating them appropriately with outside system to meet the needs of the members in enduring way. This calls for highly co-ordinated efforts among all the stakeholders at different levels.[50]

For the linkage programme to succeed, the banks and co-operatives must become much more pro-active. The RBI's guideline for commercial banks to treat SHG financing as priority sector lending as well as to include microfinance under their co-operate planning is a welcome measure.

The quality of book-keeping could be another issue. Once the size of operations starts growing, the need for better house-keeping could not be over-emphasised. The Self-Help Group Promoting Institution (SHPI) would be required to keep an eye on the house-keeping and constantly upgrade the skills and improve the internal checks and balances. There is need for installing an early warning system so that the corrective action could be taken. The numbers should not become the main consideration. The important thing is to have sustainable Self-Help Groups.

6.11. Socio-Economic Impact of SHG Programme on Women[51]

Some of the benefits of women's SHG are:[52]

a) inculcation of spirit of self-effort and self-reliance among women;

b) enabling a forum for women to exchange ideas and experiences;

c) providing opportunities to women in productive work;

d) fostering spirit of cooperation among women;

e) promoting awareness;

f) providing opportunities to acquire skills; and

g) instilling confidence.

Economic Empowerment

a) Increase in Assets (livestock and consumer durables);

b) Increase in Income; and

c) Impact on poverty alleviation.

Social Empowerment

a) Improvement in confidence;

b) Treatment within family;

c) Communication skill; and

d) Other behavioural changes.

Studies conducted by NABARD have revealed that nearly 31% of the household members of the SHGs were landless agriculture labourers and 54% were small and marginal farmers. Further, nearly 70% of the loans were used for income-generating purposes. Average net income of the households in the post-SHG situation is increased by nearly 33%. About 64% of the incremental income of the SHG-member household was generated from non-farm and off farm activities. The involvement in the SHG has helped in improving the self confidence to be relatively more assertive even in confronting social evils and problems situations.[53]

In fact SHG-Bank linkage programme has changed rural credit from a position of dominance of supply side consideration to a more healthy demand oriented service system.

NOTES

1. Vepa Kamesam, "Indian Economy-Financial sector Reforms and Role of RBI", May 15, 2002. (http://www.rbi.org.in)
2. Women's World Banking, *Macro environment and Legal and Regulation Framework in India*, March 2002.
3. Sanjay Sinha, "Financial Services for Low income Families: An appraisal", *IIMB Management Review*, June 2003.
4. Alfred Hanning," How to regulate and Supervise Microfinance: Key Issues in an Internal Perspective", the case of India (by Prakash Bakshi), *High Level Policy Workshop*, World Bank, Kampala, November 1999.
5. S. Kanthimathinathan, "Rural Credit at cross-roads", *Kurukshetra*, Feb-04, p. 33.
6. Dr. Medha Dubhashi, "Expert Committee on Rural Credit", *Kurukshetra*, 2004, p. 29.
7. http://www.un.org.in/iawg/icecd/section1.htm
8. Dr. K.Sivaloganathan, "Problems in the recovery of rural credit", *Kurukshetra*, Feb-04, p. 36.
9. G.K.Murthy, 'Micro Finance in India', *Banking Finance*, October 2005 p. 23.
10. Dr. H.D.Dwarakanath, "Savings and credit movement in Andhra Pradesh—Participation of Rural Women", *Kurukshetra*, August 2003, p. 31.
11. Planning Commission, *Economic Survey*, Govt. of India, Ninth Five Year Plan, 1997-2000, vol.15.
12. Dr. Bimla Kumari, "Amartya Sen's Strategy of Poverty Reduction and its relevance to India", *Poverty and Sustainable Development*, p. 39.
13. Dr. Amal Mandal, "Poverty Eradication in Rural India: Relfection on Methodology", *Kurukshetra*, August, 2003, p. 5.
14. Dr. A.R. Patel, "Micro-Finance and Micro-finance institutions –need for bank's initiative and commitment", *National Bank News Reviews*, April-June 2002, p. 35.
15. J.C.Mishra & R.K.Ṭhanvi, "Indian Banking System and Microfinance", *Kurukshetra*, February 2004, p. 13.
16. Sabyasachi Das, "Self Help Groups & Micro credit: Synergic Integration", *Kurukshetra*, August-2003, p. 26.
17. Y.C.Nanda, " Micro Finance- A route to Reach Rural Poor", *The Journal of Indian Institute of Banking & Finance*, October-December 2004, p. 23
18. G.Srinivasan, "Rural Credit Delivery: Reaching the Unreached", *Kurukshetra*, Vol 51, No 10, August 2003.p.11.
19. Dr. N.K.Thingalaya "Rural Financing: Compatibility of Regional Rural Banks", October-December 2004, p. 31.
20. Dr. T, Srinivas Prasad, "Regional rural Banks: Performance Evaluation", *Kurukshetra*, August 2003, p. 20.
21. Fisher T, Sriram MS: 2002, "Beyond Micro-credit" Vistaar Publication.

22. V.Nirmala. K.Sham Bhat and P.Buvaneswari, "SHGs for Poverty Alleviation in Pondicherry", *Journal of Rural Development*, Vol 23(2), p. 204 (2004), NIRD, Hyderabad.

23. Dr. A.N.Sarkar, "Innovations in Microfinance: Linked Development Programmes", *Kurukshetra*, December 2001, p. 3.

24. Dr. Ahurosh Raravikar, "Union Budget 2005-06: A leap towards Bharat Nirman", *CAB CALLING*, Jan-Mar-05, pp. 50.

25. Deb Kalipada, "Development and Disparities, Rawat Publications, Jaipur, 2001 referred by Dr. Sabanna S.Talwar", SHG, Women and Poverty Alleviation in Karnataka State", *Poverty and Sustainable Development*, p. 636.

26. *Economic Survey: 2003-04 & 2004-05*, Government of India and Union Budget 205-06, Government of India.

27. Rimjhim Mousumi Das, "Microfinance through SHGs: A boon for the rural poor", *Kurukshetra*, Feb-04, p. 45.

28. Dr. Ashutosh Raravikar, "Union Budget 2005-06: A lead towards Bharat Nirman", *Cab Calling*, January-March 2005.pp. 44-45.

29. G.Srinivasaan, "Rural Credit Delivery-Reaching the Unreached", *Kurukshetra*, August 2003, p. 12.

30. Y.C.Nanda , " Micro Finance- A Route to Reach Rural Poor", *The Journal of Indian Institute of Banking and Finance*, October-December 2004, pp. 23-25.

31. Sabyasachi Das, "Self Help Groups & Micro credit: Synergic Integration", *Kurukshetra*, August 2003, p. 25.

32. The rural and semi-urban banking network in India includes about 33,000 branches of scheduled commercial banks, 14,500 branches of Regional Rural Banks and 92,000 Primary Agricultural Co-operative Societies.

33. MYRADA- Mysore Resettlement and Development Agency.

34. NABARD 2002, " MF in India-An Overview," Mumbai (http://nabard.org/roles/mcid/section1.htm.)

35. NABARD (1996), *Linking of Self Help Groups with Banks*, Mumbai.

36. NABARD 2002,"Micro Credit Innovations Department (MCID) update." Mumbai (http:// nabard.org/roles/mcid/introduction.htm) by the formal financial agencies in the past.g services to the doorsteps of poor.

37. J.C.Mishra and R.K.Thanvi, "Indian Banking System and Microfinance", *Kurukshetra*, February, 2004, p. 13.

38. *Union Budget 2005-06*, Government of India.

39. NABARD, "Progress of SHG Bank Linkage in India 205-06", website of NABARD.

40. NABARD 2006,"Regional Spread of SHGs Linked as on 31st March 2006." Mumbai (http [:/nabard.org/roles/mcid/statewise.htm).

41. NABARD, *Progress of SHG-Bank Linkage in India, 2005-06*, p. 11

42. NABARD," Highlights 203-04" (Http://www.nabard.org/oper/oper_highlights.htm).

43. Puhazhendhi, V. and K.J.S.Satyasai (2001)," Economic and Social Empowerment of Rural Poor through Self Help Groups." *Indian Journal of Agricultural Economics*, 50(3), July-September, pp. 450-51.

44. Dr. Manoj Shankar Gupta, "Poverty Eradication through Micro-Finance/SHG", *Poverty and Sustainable Development*, p. 379.

45. Jayaraman, B (2001): *Occational Paper 20—Micro Finance Retrospect and Prospects*, NABARD, Mumbai.

46. Navin Bhatia & Anju Bhatia, "Microfinance Institutions of Bangladesh: Lessons for India", *Kurukshetra*, February 2004, p. 21.

47. Osborne Matthew Luke (2003), Why do Self Help Group Sometimes Fail? A Short Study of Non -Functioning Self Help Groups in Three Project Areas, Bangalore, MYRADA.

48. NABARD 2004," NABARD and Microfinance." Mumbai (htpp://nabard.org/roles/mcid/introduction.htm).

49. Mahajan, Vijay and Bharti Gupta Romola (2003) "Microfinance in India: Banyan Tree and Bonsai." A review Paper for World Bank, New Delhi, World Bank (Unpublished), quoted in "The SHG-Bank Linkage Programme: An assessment and Future strategies by H.S. Shylendra in *Journal of Rural Development* Vol 23(4), p. 418.

50. H.S.Shylendra, "The SHG-Bank Linkage programme: An assessment and future strategies", *Journal of Rural Development*, Vol 23(4), pp 411-433 (2004), NIRD Hyderabad

51. V. Puhazhendhi & K.J.S. Satyasai, "Empowerment of Rural Women through Self Help Groups-An Indian Experience", *National Bank News Review*, April-June 2002, p. 39-47.

52. Jha A.K. (2000), Lending to the poor: Designs for credit, Economic and Political Weekly, 35 (8 and 9):606-209, referred by V.M.Rao, "Women Self Help Groups, Profiles from Andhra Pradesh & Karnataka, *National Bank News Review*, April-June-2002, p. 63.

53. Y.C.Nanda, "Micro Finance- A Route to Reach Rural Poor", *The Journal of Indian Institute of Banking & Finance*, October-December 2004.

7
Growth of Microfinance Institutions (MFIs) in India

7.1. Demand for Microfinance Industry in India

In the absence of any sophisticated methodology to estimate the size of the market, players in the MF sector have resorted to rough estimations and lack of the envelope calculations. Given that there are 75 million poor households in India, of which 60 million are in rural areas and 15 million in urban, estimates of the size of the market vary from setting average financing requirement of Rs. 2000 per poor household to Rs. 6,000 in rural and Rs. 9000 per urban household. This works out to a MF demand of around Rs. 50,000 crores. And this does not include housing, which can be estimated at another Rs. 1,000 crores annually. Apart from micro-credit, they require savings and insurance also. Meanwhile, bank advances to weaker section aggregated Rs. 9700 crore during 1997-98. MFIs and SHGs are estimated to have provided about Rs. 137 crore (cumulative up to September 1998).[1] The above scenario, suggest a vast unmet gap in microfinance industry.

M-CRIL, a leading micro-credit rating agency provides a conservative estimate for the annual demand at $ 9.8 bn (Rs. 480 bn) based on 60-70 million poor families with an average household credit demand of Rs. 8,000.

Another estimate from the prominent microfinance practitioner, Vijay Mahajan [2]at $ 30 Bn weights India with 10% of the estimated global aggregate demand of $ 300.[3]

Considering the number of households per segment, the weighted average annual credit demand per household is $ 420 (Rs. 21K) for non-agriculture population and $ 1,300 (Rs. 65K) for agriculture population. The overall annual credit demand for households with income below $2 per day (Rs. 100) therefore amounts of $57Bn to $101 Bn (Rs. 2,833Bn-Rs.5,064 Bn). Similarly assuming $2 K (Rs. 100K) as the average housing loan required and taking average repayment period of five years, we can infer an annual housing credit demand of $12Bn-$15 Bn (Rs.592Bn-Rs.740Bn). Therefore, the overall annual cumulated credit demand (micro-credit and housing) would be in the range of $71Bn -$119 Bn (Rs. 3,562Bn – Rs.5,962 Bn).

7.2. Supply for Microfinance in India

Currently, roughly 66% of the formal supply is disbursed through the Self Help Group-

Bank linkage route, largely financed by the National Bank for Agriculture and Rural Development (NABARD) while the rest comes from microfinance institutions (MFIs) increasingly backed by commercial banks. The increase in credit flow to SHGs over the previous year is 61%, showing a growth in the average credit disbursed to SHGs.

Sa-Dhan, an association of 139 community development finance institutions states that the total portfolio outstanding its members has risen 2.5 times from $90Mn (Rs. 4.3 Bn) in 2004 to $210 Mn (Rs. 10.6 Bn) by March 31st 2005. The Client outreach during the same period rose by 96% from .3 million to 6.48 million. Despite these efforts, the World Bank estimates that the Indian microfinance activity currently reaches only 4% of the poor.[4]

Up to March 31st 2005, a grant total of 1.62 million SHGs, representing 24.3 million poor families or approximately 121.5 million people[5], have received cumulative loans of over $ 1.4 bn (Rs. 68Bn) from commercial banks.

In a sample study of 40,000 households cited by Sa-Dhan, the "moneylender' is still supreme, holding average outstanding loans at $418 (Rs.20, 908). Similarly, a 2003 national government survey found that 22% of all cultivator households access credit from informal sources and only 27% from formal sources.[6]

It clearly appears that, in spite of the rapid growth in the past two years, the supply of credit is well below demand. There was a total credit supply of $1.5 Bn (Rs. 75 Bn) in non-agriculture, of $ 25.1 Bn (Rs.1253Bn) in agriculture and none in rural housing.[7]

Therefore, the annual supply-demand gap of credit is in the range of $45 to 93Bn (Rs. 2,234 – 4,629 Bn).[8]

7.3. Microfinance Institutions in India

Microfinance has evolved as a development approach to benefit the economically underprivileged facing difficulty in accessing institutional finance. Government initiatives to make credit accessible to the poor, growth of SHG-Bank linkages and the success of Grameen Bank in Bangladesh and its replicas the world over, have all contributed to the rise of microfinance sector in India.[9]

A range of institutions in public sector as well as private sector offers the micro finance services in India. They can be broadly categorized in to two categories namely,

i) Formal institutions;

ii) Informal institutions.

The formal category comprises of Apex Development Financial Institutions, Commercial Banks, Regional Rural Banks, and Co-operative Banks that provide microfinance services in addition to their general banking activities and are referred to as micro finance service providers.

On the other hand, the informal institutions that undertake microfinance services as their main activity are generally referred to as Micro Finance Institutions (MFIs). While both private and public ownership are found in the case of formal financial institutions offering microfinance services, the MFIs are mainly in the private sector.

The microfinance service providers include apex institutions like NABARD, SIDBI and Rashtriya Mahila Kosh (RMK), Friends of Women World Bank (FWWB), Council for Advancement of People's Action and Rural Technologies (CAPART), Rashtriya Gramin Vikash Nidhi (RGVN). At retail level, commercial Banks, Regional Rural Banks and Co-operative banks also provide micro finance services.

International donors

Some of the important International donors are given below:

a) IFAD-International Fund for Agricultural Programme;

b) UNDP-United Nations Development Programme;

c) DFID-World Bank and Department for International Development; and

d) UK (DFID).

The Vyas Committee's interim report finds that the number of new SHGs formed has been growing by nearly 20% annually (section 6.8, table 6.1 of the Vyas Committee's interim report). This raises the hope that it should be possible to achieve a compounded annual growth rate of 20% over the next five years in improving the outreach of microfinance initiatives, which could allow the microfinance programme to reach almost 75% of the total poor households (80 million or eight crore) in the next five years.

The realization among commercial entities that the bottom of the pyramid is a profitable market extends to the financial sector. Many banks including foreign ones have shown an increasing willingness to provide retail micro finanace services. ICICI Bank has taken a lead with its microfinance initiatives. Other private sector banks such as UTI Bank, ABN Amro and HDFC Bank have started exploring the microfinance sector. However, some of them perceive a reputation while dealing with MFIs.

7.4. NGOs: Changing Role from Social Intermediary to Financial Intermediary

Most NGO-led microfinance is with poor women, for whom access to small loans to meet dire emergencies is a valued outcome. Thus quick and high customer satisfaction is the Unit selling Proposition (USP) that has attracted NGOs to this trade.

To many NGOs, microfinance is a way to financial sustainability. Especially for medium-to large NGOs that are able to access bulk fund form SIDBI, the interest rate spread could be an attractive source of revenue, superior to uncertain, highly competitive and increasingly difficult-to-rise donor funding. Only a few NGOs might ever become full fledged MFIs that combine savings and credit (if not insurance), but in the interim, credit retailing itself can yield attractive dividends without much regulatory burden.

A large number NGOs decided to become financial intermediaries, borrowing from wholesale institutions such as the RMK and SIDBI and lending in retail to their constitutions. Thus what was earlier a facilitator, enabler or welfare/service provider role, changed to a lender role. Most NGOs did not see that this role, if it had to be played seriously, needed changes in their attitudes, competencies and systems. They did not bring about these changes and in the early years at least, suffered delinquency and default.[10] There is not much scope for NGOs in financial intermediation roles to be able to make surplus large enough to run their other activities. Nor is the possibility of 'time-sharing' of staff involved in microfinance so easy, since the work flow is intense and time-bound and any loading of staff with other work show up in the form of delinquency or default. Thus many NGOs have figured that they should not be financial intermediaries and so have taken to the role of forming SGHs and linking those with banks. NABARD's encouragement of this model has also has a lot to do with the change in the role of NGOs to social intermediation—that is forming groups and hand-holding them on an ongoing basis. However, NABRD has not been paying NGOs for this work, at all initially and inadequately lately. More recently, other source of funds have come up including Swaran Jyanati Swarojgar Yojana (SJSY), SIDBI Foundation for Micro Credit (SFMC) and the ICICI Bank, all of whom are now paying NGOs for the valuable role of social intermediation.

The growth of microfinance is visible in many aspects. There are more than 2000 NGOs involved in the NABARD SHG-Bank linkage program. Out of these, approximately 800 NGOs are involved in some form of financial intermediation. Further, there are 350 new generation co-operative providing thrift and credit services.[11] The growth of community institutions has taken place with the role to take social and financial intermediation. A numbers of community banks have come into existence at village and block levels call "Federation of Self Help Groups'. The inadequacies of the formal financial system to cater to the needs of the poor and the realization of the fact that the key to success lies in the evolution and participation of community based organizations at the grassroots level led to the emergence of new generation of MFIs.

One kind of MFI is an NGO engaged in promoting Self-Help Groups (SHGs) and their federations at a cluster level and linking SHG with Banks under the Scheme. Examples are Myrada in Karnataka, which has promoted Sangmitra, a company of its village saving and credit sughas, PRADAN with has established a large number of SHGs and federated them under Damodar in Bihar, Sakhi Samiti in Rajasthan.

Box-6: SEWA Bank

The microfinance initiative in private sector can be traced to the initiative undertaken by Ms. Ela Bhat for providing banking services to the poor women employed in the unorganized sector in Ahmedabad city of Gujarat State. Shri Mahila SEWA (Self Employed Women's Association) Sahakari bank was set up in 1974 by registering it as an Urban Co-operative Bank. Since then, the bank is providing banking services to the poor self-employed women working as hawkers, vendors, domestic servant etc. As on March 2003, the MFI had a membership of 30,000 seventy per cent of whom are from urban area. The deposit and loan portfolio stood at Rs. 623.9 million and Rs, 133.6 million respectively. Though the MFI is making profit, yet the SEWA bank model of MFI has not been replicated elsewhere in the country.

Another kind is NGO-MFI directly lending to the poor borrowers, who are either organized into SHGs or into Grameen Bank type of groups after borrowing bulk funds from Small Industries Development Bank of India (SIDBI), RMK, and Friends of Women's World Bank (FWWB). Examples in this category are Rashtriya Gramin Vikas Nidhi (RGVN) which runs credit and savings programme in Assam and Orissa on the lines of Grameen Bank, Bangladesh. Also we have SHARE in AP, ASA in Tamil Nadu under this category.

There are MFIs which are specifically organized as co-operatives, such as over 500 Mutually Aided Cooperative Thrift and Credit Societies (MACTS) in AP, promoted among others by Co-operative Development Foundation (CDF) and the SEWA Bank in Gujarat which also runs federations of SHGs in nine districts.

Then we have MFIs, which are organized as Non-Banking Financial Companies (NBFC) such as BASIX, CFTS Mirzapur, SHARE Microfin. Ltd and Sarvodaya Nanofinance Ltd.

7.5. Microfinance Interventions through Different Organizations

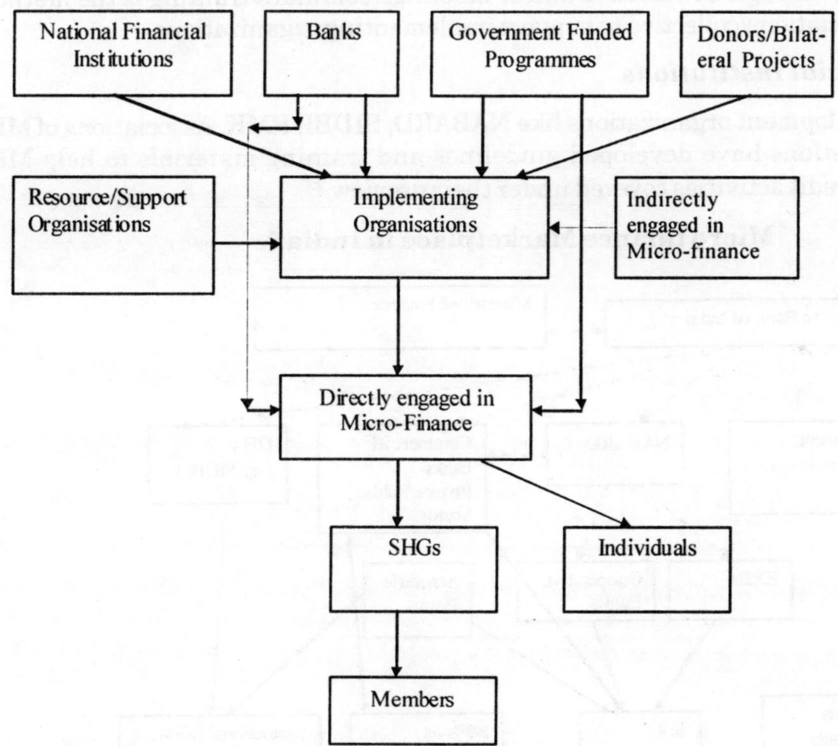

(a) Organisations Implementing Microfinance Activities

Organisation implementing microfinance activities can be categorised into three basic groups.

i) Organisation which directly lend to specific target groups and are carrying out all related activities like recovery, monitoring, follow-up etc. Some of these organizations are graduating to become exclusive MFIs, but such cases are few.

ii) Organisations that only promote and provide linkages to SHGs and are not directly involved in micro lending operations.

iii) Organisations which are dealing with SHGs and plan to start microfinance related activities.

(b) Resource Organisation or Support Agencies

These are the organizations that provide support to implementing organizations. The support may be in terms of resources or training for capacity building, counselling, networking, etc. They operate at state/regional or national level. They may or may not directly involve in micro-finance activities.

A few associations to bring such MFIs on one platform have also been initiated in India. Experience sharing through newsletters and or meetings/seminars/training is the methods adopted by the associations/collective to support implementing organizations.

(c) Formal Financial Institutions

Banks and development organizations like NABARD, SIDBI, RMK, Associations of MFIs etc. These organizations have developed guidelines and training materials to help MFIs implement micro-credit activities covered under their preview.[12]

Micro finance Marketplace in India[13]

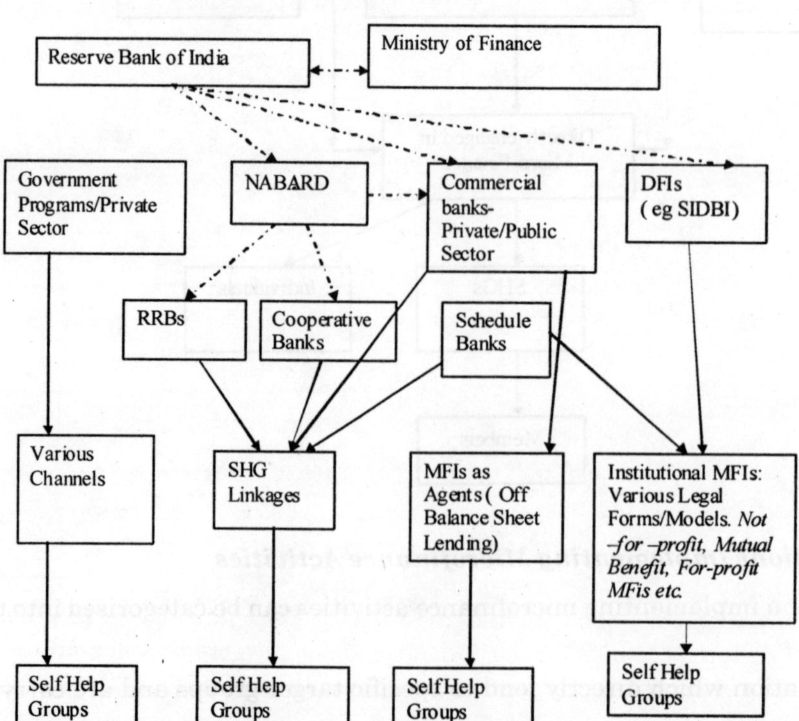

7.6. Profile of Some Large NGO –MFIs in India

Microfinance Institutions (MFIs) are the financial institutions that offer small-scale financial services in both the forms – credit and savings, especially to the poor in rural, semi-urban and urban areas. These financial services are meant to help them in undertaking economic activities, mitigating vulnerabilities to income shocks, smoothening consumption, increasing savings and supporting self-empowerment. There are a number of microfinance institutions in India, which play some pivotal roles to the development of India. India's microfinance sector is fragmented with more than 3000 microfinance institutions (MFIs). The top 10 MFIs in India are estimated to account for almost 74 per cent of the total loans outstanding. It can be added here that the total loan outstanding of Indian microfinance sector lies between Rs. 160-175 billion. As on March 31, 2009, almost 17 Indian microfinance companies have more Rs. 1 million outstanding loans. The brief profile and performance of top 10 MFIs in India is given as under:

1. SKS Microfinance Ltd (SKSMPL): It was started as NGO in 1998 with its headquarter at Hyderabad and later on transformed into an NBFC in 2005. Since transformation, SKS has been successful in creating a for-profit model of microfinance using commercial funds that is scalable. Delivering services at the doorsteps of its members and following clear-cut processes, SKS has been able to ensure a repayment rate of over 99% on its loan. In July 2009, Bajaj Allianz made a strategic investment of $10million (INR 50 crore) in SKS Microfinance which was the first-ever investment by an insurance company in an Indian microfinance institution. In November 2008,SKS raised equity worth $75 million (Rs.366 crore), the largest equity raised by an MFI in the world. SKS was ranked as Number 1 MFI in India and number 2 in the world by MIX market, world's leading business information provider for MFI industry.

Name	SKS Microfinance Ltd
Headquarter	Secunderabad, Andhra Pradesh
Legal Status	Pvt. Ltd. Company (NBFC)
Lending Model	JLG
Number of Branches	1,413
Loan Outstanding (Rs. Mn)(As on September 30, 2008)	18,227
Borrowers(As on September 30, 2008)	2,590,950
Net Worth (Rs. Mn)(As on September 30, 2008)	2,395
Portfolio Yield (%)(Apr 1-Sep 30, 2008)	23.40
OSS (%)(Apr 1-Sep 30, 2008)	126.49
Current Portfolio (%)(As on September 30, 2008)	99.14
Debt to Net Worth (Times)(As on September 30, 2008)	7.37

2. Spandana Sphoorty Financial Ltd (SSFL): is one of the largest microfinance institutions (MFI) in the world. Spandana provides micro-credit and credit plus services to low-income households and individuals to improve their quality of life. It was promoted by Padmaja Reddy in 1998.

Name	Spandana Sphoorty Financial Ltd
Headquarter	Hyderabad, Andhra Pradesh
Legal Status	Public Ltd. Company (NBFC)
Lending Model	JLG, Individual
Number of Branches	696
Loan Outstanding (Rs. Mn)(As on September 30, 2008)	11,987
Borrowers(As on September 30, 2008)	1,668,807
Net Worth (Rs. Mn)(As on September 30, 2008)	1,225
Portfolio Yield (%)(Apr 1-Sep 30, 2008)	27.43
OSS (%)(Apr 1-Sep 30, 2008)	132.02
Current Portfolio (%)(As on September 30, 2008)	98.88
Debt to Net Worth (Times)(As on September 30, 2008)	7.04

3. Share Microfin Limited (SML): It started its operation for poor in 1989 as not-for-profit society. It was the first microfinance institution (MFI) in India to obtain a Non-Banking Financial company (Non-deposit) licence. SHARE has adopted a for-profit approach to create social returns by channelling funds form development institutions and commercial banks as collateral-free loans to Joint Liability Groups (JLGs). JLGs are central to the Grameen lending methodology that SHARE has replicated.

Name	Share Microfin Limited
Headquarter	Hyderabad, Andhra Pradesh
Legal Status	Public Ltd. Company (NBFC)
Lending Model	JLG, Individual
Number of Branches	666
Loan Outstanding (Rs. Mn) (As on September 30, 2008)	8,568
Borrowers(As on September 30, 2008)	1,231,556
Net Worth (Rs. Mn)(As on September 30, 2008)	1,448
Portfolio Yield (%)(Apr 1-Sep 30, 2008)	27.49
OSS (%)(Apr 1-Sep 30, 2008)	152.45
Current Portfolio (%)(As on September 30, 2008)	99.32
Debt to Net Worth (Times) (As on September 30, 2008)	5.03

4. Asmitha Microfin Ltd (AML): Established in the year 2002 and was registered as a public limited company with the Registrar of Companies. It was also registered with the Reserve Bank of India under section 45/1A as an NBFC (Non Deposit accepting). Asmitha follows the credit methodology of self help group lending wherein the loans are disbursed to the members of a group after the joint undertaking of liability by all the members within the group.

Name	Asmitha Microfin Ltd
Headquarter	Hyderabad, Andhra Pradesh
Legal Status	Public Ltd. Company (NBFC)
Lending Model	JLG
Number of Branches	363
Loan Outstanding (Rs. Mn)(As on September 30, 2008)	4,944
Borrowers(As on September 30, 2008)	694,350
Net Worth (Rs. Mn)(As on September 30, 2008)	475
Portfolio Yield (%)(Apr 1-Sep 30, 2008)	17.43
OSS (%)(Apr 1-Sep 30, 2008)	121.04
Current Portfolio (%)(As on September 30, 2008)	99.80
Debt to Net Worth (Times)(As on September 30, 2008)	9.92

5. *Shri Kshetra Dharmasthala Rural Development Project (SKDRDP):* It is founded in the year 1982 on the occasion of the installation of 39 feet monolithic statue of Lord Bahubali in Dharmasthala. SKDRDP is active at present in the state of Karnataka and more intensely in west coast where it is engaged in intensive fight against poverty, ignorance, illiteracy, alcoholic abuse, gender discrimination, division of villages on the lines of caste, creed and money power. It started microfinance operation since 1992. The funds provided under the programme are called as 'pragathinidhi'. The members availing Pradthi Nidhi pay back in weekly instalments.

Name	Shri Kshetra Dharmasthala Rural Development Project
Headquarter	Dharmasthala, Karnataka
Legal Status	Trust
Lending Model	SHG
Number of Branches	22
Loan Outstanding (Rs. Mn)(As on September 30, 2008)	4,060
Borrowers(As on September 30, 2008)	612,482
Net Worth (Rs. Mn)(As on September 30, 2008)	157
Portfolio Yield (%)(Apr 1-Sep 30, 2008)	12.02
OSS (%)(Apr 1-Sep 30, 2008)	100.46
Current Portfolio (%)(As on September 30, 2008)	99.68
Debt to Net Worth (Times)(As on September 30, 2008)	29.81

6. Bhartiya Samruddhi Finance Limited (BSFL) : Started in 1997, it is a regulated non-banking finance company (NBFC) registered with the Reserve Bank of India, through which credit and technical assistance is delivered to almost 4,50,000 clients. It is the flagship of the BASIX Group, an Indian-based microfinance institution and one of the industry leaders in institutional development and mainstream financial sector linkages. Through its "Livelihood Triade" strategy, BSFL provides microfinance, institutional development and agricultural and business development services. In its microfinance operations, BSFL works in rural areas, offering individual and group-based micro credit and insurance products. It also makes general purpose loans to self-help groups, which deliver credit and other services to poor women. Samruddhi's presence extends to over 5,000 villages in 28 districts spread over seven states: Andhra Pradesh, Karnataka, Orissa, Maharashtra, Madhya Pradesh, Jharkhand and Rajasthan.

Name	**Bhartiya Samruddhi Finance Limited**
Headquarter	**Hyderabad, Andhra Pradesh**
Legal Status	**Public Ltd. Company, (NBFC)**
Lending Model	**Diversified**
Number of Branches	**87**
Loan Outstanding (Rs. Mn)(As on September 30, 2008)	**3,882**
Borrowers(As on September 30, 2008)	**457,668**
Net Worth (Rs. Mn)(As on September 30, 2008)	**317**
Portfolio Yield (%)(Apr 1-Sep 30, 2008)	**17.89**
OSS (%)(Apr 1-Sep 30, 2008)	**108.97**
Current Portfolio (%)(As on September 30, 2008)	**99.00**
Debt to Net Worth (Times)(As on September 30, 2008)	**11.59**

7. Bandhan: Bandhan was set up to address the dual objective of poverty alleviation and women empowerment. The microfinance activities are carried on by Bandhan Financial Services Pvt. Ltd (BFSPL), incorporated under the Companies Act, 1956 and also registered as a Non Banking Financial Company (NBFC) with the Reserve Bank of India (RBI).

Name	**Bandhan**
Headquarter	**Kolkata, West Bengal**
Legal Status	**Society**
Lending Model	**JLG**
Number of Branches	**385**
Loan Outstanding (Rs. Mn)(As on September 30, 2008)	**3,389**
Borrowers(As on September 30, 2008)	**851,713**
Net Worth (Rs. Mn)(As on September 30, 2008)	**435**
Portfolio Yield (%)(Apr 1-Sep 30, 2008)	**26.32**
OSS (%)(Apr 1-Sep 30, 2008)	**175.40**
Current Portfolio (%)(As on September 30, 2008)	**99.92**
Debt to Net Worth (Times) (As on September 30, 2008)	**7.07**

8. Cashpor Micro Credit (CMC): It was started in December 2002 as subsidiary section 25 company of Cashpor Financial and Technical Services (CFTS). Cashpor has been working with an objective to reduce poverty in eastern U.P. and Western Bihar through the provision of micro finance services to the rural poor women.

Name	Cashpor Micro Credit
Headquarter	Varanasi, Uttar Pradesh
Legal Status	Section 25 Company
Lending Model	JLG
Number of Branches	247
Loan Outstanding (Rs. Mn)(As on September 30, 2008)	1,431
Borrowers(As on September 30, 2008)	303,935
Net Worth (Rs. Mn)(As on September 30, 2008)	93
Portfolio Yield (%)(Apr 1-Sep 30, 2008)	28.78
OSS (%)(Apr 1-Sep 30, 2008)	109.71
Current Portfolio (%)(As on September 30, 2008)	98.00
Debt to Net Worth (Times)(As on September 30, 2008)	14.72

9. Grama Vidiyal Micro Finance Pvt Ltd (GVMFL): Grama Vidiyal is a microfinance institution, operating in the Tamil Nadu area of South India. Since 1993, Grama Vidiyal, in partnership with Activist for Social Alternatives (ASA), has provided small loans to women without access to formal typically have daily incomes of less than INR 80 per day. In 2007, Grama Vidiyal transformed from a charitable trust to a regulated Non-Bank Financial Company (NBFC). Its status as an NBFC brings Grama Vidiyal under the purview of government regulation and but will permit the firm to take a larger amount of equity capital.

Name	Grama Vidiyal Micro Finance Pvt Ltd
Headquarter	Tiruchirappalli, Tamil Nadu
Legal Status	Pvt. Ltd. Company (NBFC)
Lending Model	JLG
Number of Branches	126
Loan Outstanding (Rs. Mn)(As on September 30, 2008)	1,316
Borrowers(As on September 30, 2008)	288,311
Net Worth (Rs. Mn)(As on September 30, 2008)	231
Portfolio Yield (%)(Apr 1-Sep 30, 2008)	32.46
OSS (%)(Apr 1-Sep 30, 2008)	141.53
Current Portfolio (%)(As on September 30, 2008)	99.54
Debt to Net Worth (Times)(As on September 30, 2008)	4.95

10.Grameen Financial Services Pvt Ltd (GFSPL): Grame Koota was visualized in 1997 based on the book "Give us credit" by Alex Counts, which gives an account of the impact of micro credit on the lives of the poor in Bangladesh and the United States. It is a microfinance institution (MFI) based in Bangalore, India that was founded in 1999. It is a division of Grameen Financial Services (P) Ltd and began its operation with funding from Grameen Trust. Grameen Koota provides credit to low-income households through 62 branches in Karnataka and Maharastra. It is one of the first MFIs in the world to use MIFOS, an open source management information system that aids in monitoring of borrowers and portfolios.

Name	Grameen Financial Services Pvt Ltd
Headquarter	Bangalore, Karnataka
Legal Status	Pvt. Ltd. Company (NBFC)
Lending Model	JLG
Number of Branches	62
Loan Outstanding (Rs. Mn)(As on September 30, 2008)	1,287
Borrowers(As on September 30, 2008)	153,453
Net Worth (Rs. Mn)(As on September 30, 2008)	127
Portfolio Yield (%)(Apr 1-Sep 30, 2008)	18.77
OSS (%)(Apr 1-Sep 30, 2008)	106.41
Current Portfolio (%)(As on September 30, 2008)	99.98
Debt to Net Worth (Times)(As on September 30, 2008)	10.51

7.7. Microfinance Outreach in India

MF outreach in the country is insufficient, geographically limited and not informally organized- factors which limit its impact.

One of the important objectives of the nationalization of banks in 1969 was to ensure credit delivery to the rural and informal sector. Even though almost 560 banks including 48 commercial banks, 196 regional rural banks (RRBs) and 316 co-operative banks are now actively involved in microfinance[1], the sector needs more credit support and related assistance. During last three years, many Indian and foreign banks have intervened in the microfinance sector with innovative downscaling strategies. In the absence of enough rated microfinance companies who could act as mass retailers of micro credit, commercial banks depend on NGO and MFIs as their sales agents through partnership models and securitization. Currently ICICI Bank, ABN Amro, UTI Bank and HDFC Bank use such innovations for credit delivery to the sector. ICICI Bank is the first commercial bank to enter the micro-credit market and the share of the bank in total disbursement by the end of fiscal 2004-05 is estimated to be close to 40% cent.

The picture of microfinance sector in India is diverse as the country itself, it is characterized by distinct delivery models and legal structures.

Indian MFIs are predominantly NGOs i.e. nearly 80 percent of MFIs operate under the society/trust form which is for the not-for-profit sector with a clear development agenda. Apart from this, other important legal forms are being used by Indian MFIs. Ten percent of organizations operate under the Company structures; five percent are Section 25 companies; two per cent as local Area Banks. The focus of NGO-MFI on the not for profit legal structure is one of the critical impediments in the sector. The diversity and lack of regulation and standardization are significant limitations to the growth of the sector. Moreover, none of these legal structures are allowed to take savings which is also as important as credit. The poor households also have high demand for saving services, social security services like insurance and other financial services. Since a large part of their saving demand is unmet, the poor turn to informal and often unreliable sources to save. Currently, these issues have been taken to various policy makers for policy changes and amendments.

In case of operating models, the SHG model constitutes the major operating for with nearly 65 per cent MFIs, followed by the Grameen model with a 20% share, joint liability groups with 8per cent and individual with 7 per cent.

Microfinance outreach in the country is insufficient, geographically limited and not formally organized. On the other hand, geographically speaking, 70 percent of the Indian microfinance sector is skewed towards the southern states of Andhra Pradesh, Karnataka, Tamil Nadu and Kerela.

7.8. Microfinance: Roles and Future Strategies of NABARD

The prominent among the various initiatives and innovations that have taken place in fostering the growth of microfinance sector with the active involvement of NABARD include:[2]

a) Bank Credit to Self-Help Groups;

b) Creation of Credit and Financial Service Fund;

c) Grant Support to NGOs;

d) Support to RRBs;

e) Support to Farmers Clubs;

f) Revolving Fund Assistance to NGO;

g) Development initiative for North Eastern Region and KBK region of Orissa;

h) Capacity Building for partner institutions;

i) Creation of Micro Finance Development Fund; and

j) Establishing collaboration with external donor agencies (viz KFW/GTZ, IFAD) in the area of SHG-Bank Linkage programme.

Other promotional supports to be provided are:

a) Need based training and exposure of the bank personnel;

b) Generating best practices and disseminating them;

c) Building case studies highlighting the commercial aspects of banking with the poor through SHGs; and

d) Encouraging the cooperative banking system to expand its participation.

Creating enabling environment

As NGOs have become one the major players in the whole programme and are likely to play a significant role in future, it is necessary that legally their role is clearly recognized and clarified. NABARD is also experimenting with direct refinancing of NGOs. In order for the programme to attain both credibility and accountability, NABARD on a priority basis should make effort to get necessary legal provision enacted with reference to NGOs as recommended by the Task Force on Microfinance. Among other things, the recommended provisions include inserting amendments to the RBI Act and Societies Acts for providing due recognition to microfinance activities of NGOs. This may help the NGOs in revolving their difficulties in pursuing an activity like microfinance by being charitable institutions.

Capacity buildings

In terms of capacity building of various players, NABARD has played a major role till now through various sensitization and training programmes. The training programmes should now become more focused and aim towards professionalizing the microfinance sector in general and NGOs in particular. Attempts have already been made in identifying the thrust areas of such training programmes aimed at improving the relevant knowledge, attitude and skills of the various stakeholders.

Microfinance Development and Equity Fund[3]

There is now an urgent need of micro credit providers to shift from a minimalist approach- that is offering only financial intermediation- to an integrated approach to poverty alleviation taking a more holistic view of the client including provision of enterprise development services like marketing infrastructure, introduction of technology and design development. In this context, setting up of the Micro Finance Development Funds marks an important step: Pursuant to the announcement of the Union Finance Minister in his budget for the year 2000-01. This fund of Rs. 100 crores has been created in NABARD to support broadly the following activities:

a) Giving training and exposure to SHG members, partner NGOs, banks and government agencies;

b) Providing start-up funds to micro finance institutions and meeting their initial operational deficits;

c) Meeting the cost of formation and nurturing of SHGs;

d) Designing new delivery mechanisms; and

e) Promoting research, action research, management information systems and dissemination of best practices in microfinance.

This fund is thus expected to address institutional and delivery issues like institutional growth and transformation, governance, accessing new sources of funding, building institutional capacity and increasing volumes.

7.9. Performance of MFIs as per M-CRIL Rating

Micro-Credit Rating International Limited (M-CRIL)'s analysis of the performance of microfinance in India covers 69 MFIS until June 2002.

Microfinance in India is broadly characterized by a small number of large MFIs that are relatively strong and large number of relatively small and weak organizations. By model, the Grameen MFIs are substantially larger than the other types in terms of credit with more than three times the average number of borrowers and nearly 2.7 times the average portfolio of all sample MFIs. A few of the prominent Grameen programmes in the country are growing fairly fast compared to others. IBPs (Individual Banking programmes) have much larger loans outstanding per borrower as well as far higher individual savings. This is both because some of the more prominent and also because they have a very high saving orientations.

Financial Performance of MFIs

Indian MFIs are going through a massive growth phase, sparked by increased international attention in 2005 (UN Year of Micro-credit) but more pertinently, a new and better access to relatively low cost capital from banks led by ICICI Bank.

Below are some highlights about Indian microfinance market:

1) ***Market leaders:*** A mix Market Survey[4] found that large MFIs (seven institutions from their sample of 28) dominate the market. Large MFIs hold 81% of the overall loan portfolio and serve 67% of borrowers. The three largest institutions, which along covered 54% of borrowers, are NBFC based in south India.

2) ***Efficiency, productivity and outreach:*** In 2004, the average Indian MFI spent less than two thirds of the amount that it cost the average South Asian Institution to serve each borrower. Moreover, whereas the average South Asian MFI served 219 borrowers per staff member, Indian institutions reached 439 borrowers per staff member[5]. While microfinance in India does not reach the per capita volume it does in Bangladesh. Indian medium and large scale e MFIs demonstrated some of the highest sustained growth rates over the years 2003 and 2004, many averaging 100%. Over this period, outreach in the sector more than doubled, the number of borrowers served grew by 108% while the loan portfolio increased by 139%.

3) ***Asset Quality:*** Institutions sometimes undertake aggressive write-offs to sanitize their portfolio and only write-off ratio will reveal genuineness of PAR. With 4% of their portfolio at risk over 30 days and 0.5 % of write off ratio, Indian MFIs maintain good portfolio quality. Sa-Dhan states PAR over 60 days as 2.2% suggesting that a significant amount of repayments are received form significant borrowers after 30 days. Soundness of asset quality can be inferred from Sa-Dhan's study which states a Current Repayment Rate of 97.7% for Indian MFIs, much high to its benchmark of 90%.

4) ***Leverage:*** Indian MFIs also enjoy unprecedented access to financing by banks and other financial institutions, making them among the most highly leveraged institutions in the world. According to M-CRIL,[6] the average Capital Adequacy Ratio (CAR) of Indian MFIs is 18 % while the median of 17.3% indicates that 50% of the MFIs have a CAR below this

level. As many as 49 MFIs (45% of the total) have CAR below 12%- the minimum level specified for non-banking finance companies (NBFCs) by the Reserve Bank of India. It is therefore questionable for future growth, how Indian MFIs can attract further investment with such a thin layer of capital to allow loss absorption in case of default. Such a high leverage raises questions about the ability of MFIs to access good rating for their existing portfolio in order to use mainstream financial instruments such as securitization. While largest MFIs (with portfolio above Rs. 10 crores) are the most susceptible to envisage securitization, 7 out of 8 largest MFIs display a CAR < 20% in India.

5) ***Debt-Equity:*** Similarly as per debt-equity estimates of leverage estimation, the average debt-equity ratio for Indian MFIs rated by M-CRIL[7] during 2003-05 was as high as 11.8 (excluding MFIs with negative net worth). This is much greater than the relatively prudent ratio of 7:1. While low debt-equity of most MFIs restricts their growth (due to their limited ability to borrow for operations); the bloated debt-equity ratio increases the sector risk of the MFI model of microfinance. However changes in this ratio are more significant in absolute value like increasing trends may denote an MFI exhausting its fund raising capacity while decreasing trends suggest that it does not sufficiently leverage the funds that it may not have sufficiently leveraging the fund sources.

6) ***Profitability:*** While most MFIs are close to attaining full operational self-sufficiency, large institutions have exceeded the mark. The data also suggests medium and large MFIs enjoy high returns on equity. The Micro Credit Ratings International Ltd. (M-CRL), Micro Finance Review 2003 (revised February 2004) analyses the performance of MFIs in the Asian region as seen through 110 ratings conducted by M-CRIL from September 1998 to June 2003. According to this study, 23 of the 110 MFIs rated out of which 104 were Indian) have generated sufficient profits to contribute to their capital from internal accruals.

Sa-Dhan in its study on sample of 74 MFIs states Operational Self Sufficiency 110% (FY 2005) against its benchmark of 10%. While most MFIs are close to attaining full operational self-sufficiency, large institutions have exceeded the mark.

7) ***Return on Equity:*** The ROE ratio is an important tool for shareholders to determine how much income their investment is generating, relative to the risk involved, and how it compares with alternative investment. MIX survey, on 28 Indian MFIs has indicated an ROE of 10.2 %. The optimal Range as per ACCION is more than 15% indicating that the Indian MFIs do not present an attractive opportunity.

8) ***Return on Asset:*** The ROA measures the net income earned on the assets of a credit and saving institutions. It differs from ROE ratio since it measures the return on all funds used to finance the institution (equity and liabilities), not only on the fund owned. As per the MIX date, Indian MFIs have ROA of 1.5 %. The optimal range as per ACCION is more than 3% indicating that the Indian MFIs are still lagging behind on the profitability front.

Though the outreach of the microfinance sector is still very limited (at most 5%) in relation to demand, the sector is growing at 20-30% per year and there are a number of organizations striving for sustainability.

There have been NGOs which gradually metamorphosed into lending institutions, developmental professionals who have set up microfinance companies and banks that have experimented with working exclusively with groups and therefore have microfinance branches.

7.10. Growth Strategies

The SHG movement enjoys immense political and non-government support in India. Union Finance Minister P.Chidambaram had words of praise and promise in his budget speech 2005-06. He proposed to extend the SHG-Bank group linkage to cover another 85,000 SHGs in 2006-07.

At the moment, in terms of credit outlay, the sector is divided between bank-linked SHG members and MFIs clients at a ratio of 3:1. Both channels are growing rapidly but as the sector penetrates the national consciousness, more investors, entrepreneurs and professionals are attracted to the MFI model. Current trends suggest that the market division between the largely state bank financed SHG and private bank financed MFI route will reverse in the next few years.

There are three main expansion strategies for microfinance institutions:

i) ***Horizontal Growth:*** the MFI chooses plain vanilla products (usually just loans) and replicate across all branches to expand their client base and geographic coverage.

ii) ***Vertical Growth:*** The MFI chooses to maintain a particular client profile and geographic coverage but diversity its products and services instead. Thus catering to changing needs of the customer, the MFI converts itself from a standardized retailer into a full service local financial institution. The MFI is now a ' Credit Plus" provider offering insurance, savings, money transfer, remittance, larger loan size, individual consumer loans, personal loan products and ancillary business services such as connecting clients to previously non-existent or inaccessible markets and livelihood opportunities.

iii) ***Franchisee:*** the MFI appoints a local entrepreneur as its franchisee and allows her to conduct business under an established name and methodology.

ANNEXURE-1

Microfinance Stakeholders in India

1. Apex & Regulatory Intuitions

1. National Bank of Agriculture & Rural Development (NABARD)
2. Small Industrial Development Bank of India (SIDBI)
3. Reserve Bank of India (RBI)
4. Ministry of Home Affairs, Government of India
5. Registrar of Societies and Trusts
6. Registrar of Cooperative State/Capital
7. Registrar of Companies
8. Central Board Direct Taxes
9. Insurance Regulatory Development Authority
10. Ministry of Finance, Government of India
11. CAPART
12. RGM
13. RMK
14. FWWB

2. Microfinance related Legislations in India

1. Society Registration (Various Acts) and same for Trusts
2. Foreign Contribution Regulation Act (FCRA 1976) and amendments
3. Banking Regulation Act, 1949
4. Banking Companies Acquisition Act, 1970 and 1980
5. Non-Banking Finance Company Regulations till date
6. The Reserve Bank of India (RBI) Act 1934 and amendments till date
7. Income Tax Act, 1961
8. Companies Act, 1956
9. IRDA Act 1999
10. State Cooperative Acts (several)
    - i) Multi State Cooperative Act
    - ii) Parallel Cooperative Act (like Mutually Aided Cooperative Societies Act (MACs) Act etc)

3. Capacity-building, Consultancy Services & Technical support

1. Centre for Micro Finance (CMF), Institute for Financial Management and Research , Chennai
2. EDA Rural System
3. Intellecap (Intellectual Capital Advisory Services Pvt. Ltd.)
4. M-CRIL
5. MicroSave India
6. Sa-Dhan
7. District Rural Development Agency (DRDA)
8. Bankers Institute of Rural Development (BIRD)
9. COMAT
10. Indian Gramen Services (IGS)
11. Media Lab Asia
12. n-logue
13. Rural Innovations Network (RIN)
14. Development Alternatives
15. Appropriate Rural Technology Institute (ARTI)
16. Banking with the Poor
17. ARAVALI (Association for Rural Advancement through Voluntary Action and Local Involvement)
18. All India Association for Micro Enterprise Development (AIAMED)
19. Credit and Development Forum (CDF) India
20. Creditwatch India

4. Donor/Funding Agencies

1. ACCION International
2. Action Aid
3. Acumen Fund
4. Asian Development Bank (ADB)
5. Alter Fin
6. Bill & Melinda Gates Foundation

7. CARE India
8. Consultative Group to Assist the Poor (CGAP)
9. Department for International Development (DFID)
10. FINCA International
11. Ford Foundation
12. Freedom from Hunger
13. Friends of Women World Banking
14. GTZ
15. IFAD (International Fund for Agricultural Development)
16. World Bank Microfinance Rating and Assess Fund
17. Okiocredit
18. Planet Finance
19. Shell Foundation
20. Shorebank Advisory Services
21. Social Initiative Group
22. USAID
23. Unitus

5.Venture Capital Funds

1. Aavishkar
2. Bellwether
3. Blue Orchard Finance
4. Lok Capital
5. Grameen Capital India (GCI)

6. Research Institutions & Colleges offering courses focused on Development / microfinance

1. Centre for Development Studies
2. Centre for Micro Finance, Institute for Financial Management and Research, Chennai
3. FDI India (Entrepreneurship Development Institute of India)
4. Indian Institute of Management Bangalore- Microfinance Incubator
5. Indian Institute of Management –Ahmedabad

6. Indian School of Microfinance for Women
7. Institute for Development Policy and Management
8. International Food Policy and Research Institute (IFPRI)
9. Institute of Rural Management , Anand
10. Xavier Institute of Management , Bhubaneswar
11. Indian Institute of Forest Management, Bhopal
12. Overseas Development Institute (ODI).

NOTES

1. Summaries and Recommendation of the Task force or Supportive Policy and Regulatory Framework for Microfinance, 1999.
2. Vijay Mahajan is Chairman and Founder Board Member of BASIX, a permier livelihood promotion institution.
3. Mehan, Jennifer, *Tapping Financial Markets for Microfinance*, Grameen Foundation USA Publication Series, 2005.
4. Basu, Priya, Lead Economist, Finance & Private Sector, World, Debate: Cap the interest rate on microfinance? *The Economic Times* 21 March 2006.
5. Average size of a family is taken as five members.
6. Chidambaram P., Governement of India *Union Budget 2004-05*.
7. Centre for Micro Finance at Institute of Financial Management and Research, October 2006, "Microfinance in India: Current Trends and Challenges".
8. *Ibid.*
9. Occasional Paper series, "Indian Experience of Microfinance a sustainable banking solution for the poor", Sa-Dhan, December 2004 (http://www`.sa-dhan.org)
10. Vijay Mahajan, "Microfinance in India: Discussion", *IIMB Management Review*, June 2003.
11. Website of Sha-Dhan , "Emergence of MFIs and the growth of Microfinance Sector in India", www.shadhan.com. Sa-Dhan- The Association of Community Development Finance Institutions (biggest Apex Body of Microfinance Institutions in India).
12. United Nation," Micro Finance Interventions: MF in India-An Overview", (http://www.un.org.in/iawg/icecd/section1.htm).
13. Y.S.P.Thorat and Ramesh S. Arunachalam, "Regulation and Areas of Potential Market Failure in Microfinance", referred in, *Microfinance in India Current Trends and Challenges*, CMF & IFMR, October 2006.
14. *Economic Survey 2004-05.*
15. NABARD, "Annual Report 2000-2001" referred by Dr. A.N. Sarkar, "Innovation in Microfinance" *Kurukshetra*, 2Dec-2001.p. 7.
16. Jagdish Capoor, "Development Issues in Micro Credit" *RBI*, Mar 16, 2001 (http://rbi.org.in)
17. Performance and Transparency: A Survey of Micro Finance in South Asia. CGAP, World Bank & Mix-Market.
18. Mix Market 2004 data as of October 18, 2005.
19. Technical Note 2: Equity and Leverage in Indian MFIs, M-CRIL, Gurgaon, India. September 2005.
20. Technical Note 4: Financing microfinance in India, M-cril, Gurgaon, India, April 206.

8
Legal and Regulatory Framework for MFIs

8.1. Evolution of the Different Types MFIs

Poor people, especially women, have demonstrated that they are excellent borrowers, when provided with efficient, responsive loan services at commercial rates. When lending, savings and other financial services are offered in an efficient and financially sustainable way, these services have a real impact on helping poor people build income and assets, manage risk and work their way out of poverty.

The spectrum of Institutions operating in the microfinance industry has become increasingly more diverse. This is in part due to the recent entrance of several private mainstream commercial banks, finance companies and insurance firms into microfinance, either as retailers or wholesalers. Additionally, some NGOs have transformed into regulated, for-profit structures, owned and governed by shareholders, in part due to pressure from the microfinance community, donors in particular.

The increased range of institutional types within the industry indicates the need for an expansive set of policies and regulations to encourage its continued growth.[1]

8.2. Building Financial System that Works for the Poor

Strong institutions mean financially sustainable institutions that can provide the poor with continued access to financial products and services. Financial sustainability will be achieved increasingly through wholesale financing arrangements, commercial borrowings, and or broad-based saving mobilization rather than concessional funds. Saving mobilization is the key as it is a highly valued service to poor people. Savings can become the dominant source of funds for the micro-loan portfolio, if the necessary legal structures and capabilities are in place.

Financial systems need to encourage a range of institutional types to enter and expand sound, efficient and financially sustainable microfinance operations. The government's role in encouraging this burgeoning industry should not be as a retailer of microfinance services but rather as the creator and supervisor of regulations and norms that encourage sound and responsive microfinance operations across the range of regulated legal structures.

Funds have flowed to MFIs through advances from banks (either on their own accord or through directed credit programs), linkage programs between self-help group and banks and wholesaling by apex agencies, notably SIDBI and Friends of Women's World. Because of the role of the RBI, NABARD and the directed credit programs, the banking system overall has great role in microfinance. Donors funded the NGOs initially, but public sector second tier organizations have since entered the market with the provision of bulk loans. NABARD has begun to refinance commercial bank loans to self help groups.

8.3. Legal Framework and Regulatory Environment

Regulation is the provision of rules while supervision is the monitoring and enforcing of the rules. Regulation and supervision can be done by different entities as done in India where RBI makes the rules and NABARD enforces them on financial intermediaries in the rural sector. Supervision is the key element of as regulation without supervision is pointless and will violate fundamental principles such a providing a level playing field for the market participants.

A serious problem currently facing the RBI is the number of institutions applying for Non-Banking Finance Company (NBFC) status.

India has a large number of MFIs varying significantly in size, outreach and credit delivery methodologies. Presently, there is no regulatory mechanism in place for MFIs except for those that are registered as NBFCs. As a result, MFIs are not required to follow standard rule and it has allowed many MFIs to be innovative in its approach particularly in designing new products and processes. But the flip side is that the management and governance of MFIs generally remains weak, as there is no compulsion to adopt widely adopted systems, procedures and standards. Since the sector is unregulated, not much is known about their internal health.

All of the banking legislation affects the microfinance sector. The Reserve Bank of India Act established the RBI, and includes also a Section-I that lays out the regulatory framework for the nonbank finance companies. The Banking Regulation Act covers commercial banks, including local area banks. The Regional Rural Banks Act covers RRBs and Cooperative Act covers cooperatives.[2]

Existing legal framework and Banking law[3] for financial system in India are as under:

(i) ***Reserve Bank of India Act.*** The Reserve Bank of India establishes the central bank. It is of interest to the question of the regulation of microfinance in that under a 1997 Amendment it contains provisions for the establishment and operations of non-bank finance companies (Chapter III-B, Sections 45-I). The non-banking institution can be a company, a corporation or a cooperative society. A non-bank financial company (NBFC) is a non-banking institution that is a company and takes deposits. NBFC are registered under this Act (Second Schedule). Legislation is in preparation to subject NBFC to regulation and supervision using CAMEL (Capital Asset Management Liabilities) quarterly reporting (draft Financial Companies Bill).

(ii) ***Banking Regulation Act of 1949*** covers banking companies. It does not apply to primary agriculture credit societies, co-operative land mortgage banks and any other co-operative society (section 2). It is not directly relevant to microfinance, other than the fact that it covered local area banks and commercial banks which are involved in linkage operations and have in some cases small portfolios devoted to microfinance. The Banking regulation Act provides the basis for the licensing of local area banks and mutual benefit societies.

(iii) ***National Bank for Agriculture and Rural Development Act of 1981***

(iv) ***Company Act of 1956:*** provides the basis for the incorporation of local Area Banks, Non-Bank Finance Companies, non-for-profit Section 25 companies and Nidhis under Section 620.

(v) ***Mutually Aided Co-operative Society Act in 1995 (Andhra Pradesh).*** SEWA Bank is registered as co-operative society, but is regulated by the RBI from which it obtained a banking license.

(vi) ***Societies Registration Act of 1860 and Indian Trust Act-*** This acts cover semi-formal institutions engaged in microfinance but do not provide a basis for any form of regulation. There is a tax problem in that societies and trusts cannot engage in for profit activities, including financial services.[4]

(vii) ***Local Area Banks***

The Local Area Bank Scheme was introduced in August 1996 pursuant to the announcement of Finance Minister. Following this guidelines for setting up of LABs in the private sector were announced by the Reserve Bank of India (RBI) on 24th August 1996. The minimum start up capital of a LAB was fixed at Rs. 5 crore.[5]

The LABs could be included in the second Schedule of Reserved Bank of India Act, 1934 subject to the fulfilment of the eligibility criteria laid down in Section 42 (6) of the said Act. Only four LABs are functioning at present. These are:

a) *Coastal Local Area Bank Ltd:* established on 27 the December 1999 with an area of operation comprising three contiguous districts via, Krishna, Guntur and West Godavari with its head office at Vijayawada (Andhra Pradesh).

b) *Capital Local Area Bank Ltd.:* established on 14th January 2000 with its area of operation comprising three districts viz. Jalandhar, Kapurthala and Hoshiapur with its head office at Phagwara (Punjab).

c) *South Gujarat Local Area Bank Ltd.:* established on 3rd October 2000 with an area of operation comprising three contiguous districts viz Navasari, Surat and Bharuch with its head office at Navsari (Gujarat).

d) *Krishna Bhima Samruddhi Local Area Bank Ltd:* established on 28th February 2001 with an area of operation comprising three districts of Mahbubnagar in Andhara Pradesh and Raichur and Gulbarga in the state of Karnataka with its head office at Mahbubnagar (Andhra Pradesh).

The license of Vinayak Local Area Bank Ltd, Sikar (Rajasthan) established on 21st October 2000 was cancelled by Reserve Bank on 16th January 2002 as major irregularities were noted in its functioning.

It was presumably due to the setbacks encountered in the channelisation of credit through cooperatives, rural branches of commercial banks and RRBs that the new concept of a Local Area Bank emerged. The concept was attractive in that it sought to involve local leadership in mobilization of local resources for profitable lending in a compact area. It sought to combine the kind of local knowledge presumed to be the special feature of cooperative with the professional ethos of a commercial bank.

Central banks and bank superintendence are beginning to see the importance of understanding the nature of microfinance. This awareness has led to, in some cases, the modification of conventional regulatory requirement to fit the needs of microfinance operations. These special features of microfinance include the limited size of the microfinance market in relation to the financial sector as a whole, the replacement of traditional collateral by the demonstration of the portfolio quality, high transaction costs, different approaches to branching and delivery systems, lack of scale and sophistication to deal with typical reporting requirements.

The key dimensions in policy, banking regulation and supervision adapted to the needs of microfinance include the removal of interest rate ceilings, the evaluation of portfolio risk by looking at aggregate portfolio quality, with rigorous standards on loan loss provisioning and reserve and at the adequacy of systems, rigorous but simplified reporting requirements, and flexibility in branching operations.

Shared performance standards, transparency and accountability are keys for building solid and responsive financial services for poor households-for both regulated and unregulated microfinance institutions.

The finance minister's comment that he is not in favour of a separate regulator in micro-credit and the best way for lending institutions to promote micro-credit disbursals is to use intermediaries is in tune with the ground reality in India. In fact, one doubt if having a regulator to supervise a host of small institutions would be efficient or even cost-effective. The scale surely does not warrant the creation of an independent regulator.

In India, the most successful work, especially in rural areas is being carried out by non-regulated sources- NGOs and informal finance mechanisms of self help groups (SHGs). NGOs support SHG groups and also borrowers directly and are increasingly pursuing financial intermediation. This model has proved far more successful than the structured format with set targets of the kind most commonly seen in the formal banking sector. The latter has just not been able to deliver and has instead created the Indian paradox of excess funds with banks and lack of access to funds for micro-finance.

Given this, the intermediary role of MFIs becomes paramount. Intermediaries are more capable of identifying effectively with the specific needs of special borrowers than banks and financial institutions. The Finance Minister stated that if there has to be a regulator, it should be only for deposit-taking institutions. It is logical, as the relevant regulation is one that protects depositors in this sector. That, too, must not be overly stringent, or it may scare away potential proposals for setting up MFIs. The NGO-MFI network is capable of effective delivery on the fronts of outreach and sustainability. However to ease the constraints for growing the scale of activity, a conducive policy environment would be a prerequisite.

The cost of regulation to an institution can be such that it moves away from the poor and the rural areas. As for instance, in Bolivia where most of the growth in outreach has come over the past five years from unregulated financial institutions. At the micro level, geographical and localized imperatives play a significant role in shaping the outcomes. Consider the fact that for Bangladesh's successful Grameen Bank, key factors include its participatory process, coupled with willingness to innovate and a committed pragmatic leadership.

Essentially, microfinance poses the challenge of offering flexible credit instruments to match diverse requirements of low-income borrowers, without burdening lenders with excessive cost of monitoring end-use of funds. Stepping up regulation would be to the contrary.

8.4. MFIs and Its Legal Structure

Legal structures need to be build or adapted to enable a subset of strong microfinance NGOs to convert into regulated financial institutions that can mobilize public savings and rapidly expand commercial funding. This is necessary because many of larger microfinance institutions will increase their reliance on these sources of funds in the near future. These legal structures are extremely important to protect savers, investors and the banking industry. While becoming regulated institutions is helpful in terms of seeking commercial funds and investments, it is essential in terms of mobilizing public savings.[6]

Several features must be present for these legal structure to encourage the growth of the microfinance sector, including: relatively low minimum capital requirements, appropriate capital adequacy ratios (generally more conservative than for commercial banks), flexible ownership structures, high performance standards, and appropriate tax treatment. Finally, prudential regulation must be coupled with strong supervision. The systems of supervision for commercial banks are not easily transposed onto the microfinance industry.

With the current phase of expansion of the SHG-Bank linkage program and other MF initiatives in the country, the informal micro finance sector in India is now beginning to evolve. While there is no published data on private MFIs operating in the country, the number of MFIs is estimated to be around 800. The geographical distribution of MFIs is very much lopsided with concentration in the southern India where the rural branch network of formal banks is excellent. It is estimated that the share of MFIs in the total micro credit portfolio of formal & informal institutions is about 8 per cent.

a) NGO- MFIs

There are a large number of NGOs that have undertaken the task of financial intermediation. Majority of these NGOs are registered as Trust or Society. Many NGOs have also helped SHGs to organize themselves into federations and these federations are performing non-financial and financial functions like social and capacity building activities, facilitate training of SHGs, undertake internal audit, promote new groups and some of these federations are engaged in financial intermediation. The NGO MFIs vary significantly in their size, philosophy and approach. Therefore, these NGOs are structurally not the right type of institutions for undertaking financial intermediation activities as the byelaws of these institutions are generally restrictive in allowing any commercial operations. These organizations by their charter are non-profit organizations and as a result face several problems in borrowing funds from higher financial institutions. The NGO MFIs, which are large in number, are still outside the purview of any financial regulation. These are the institutions for which policy and regulatory framework would need to be established.

b) Non-Profit Companies as MFIs

Many NGOs felt that combining financial intermediation with their core competency activity of social intermediation is not the right path. It was felt that a financial institution including a company set up for this purpose better does banking function. Further, if MFIs are to demonstrate that banking with the poor is indeed profitable and sustainable, it has to function as a distinct institution so that cross subsidization can be avoided. On account of these factors, NGO-MFIs are of late setting up a separate Non-Profit company for their micro finance operations. The MFI is prohibited from paying any dividend to its members. In terms of Reserve Bank of India's Notification dated 13 January 2000, relevant provisions of RBI Act, 1934 as applicable to NBFCs will not apply for Non Profit Company.

a) License under Section 25 of Companies Act, 1956

b) Providing credit not exceeding Rs.50,000 for a business enterprise and

   Rs. 1, 25,000 for meeting the cost of a dwelling unit to any poor person

c) Not accepting public deposits.

c) Mutual Benefit MFIs

The state Co-operative Acts did not provide for an enabling framework for emergence of business enterprises owned, managed and controlled by the numbers of their own development. Several State Governments therefore enacted the Mutually Aided Co-operative Societies (MACS) Act for enabling promotion of self-reliant and vibrant co-operative Societies based on thrift and self-help. MACS enjoy the advantages of operational freedom and virtually no interference from government because of the provision in the Act that societies under the Act cannot accept share capital or loan from the State Government. Many of the SHG federations, promoted by NGOs and development agencies of the State Government, have been registered as MACs. Reserve Bank of India, even though they may be providing financial service to its members, does not regulate MACS.

d) For Profit MFIs

Non Banking Financial Companies (NBFC) are companies registered under Companies Act, 1956 and regulated by Reserve Bank of India. Earlier, NBFC were not regulated by RBI but in 1997 it was made obligatory for NBFC to apply to RBI for a certificate of registration and for this certificate NBFC were to have minimum Net owned funds of Rs. 25 lakhs and this amount has been gradually increased. RBI introduced a new regulatory framework for those NBFC who want to accept public deposits. All the NBFCs accepting public deposits are subjected to capital adequacy requirements and prudential norms. There are only a few MFIs in the country that are registered as NBFCs. Many MFIs view NBFC more preferred legal form and are aspiring to be NBFCs but they are finding it difficult to meet the requirements stipulated by RBI. The number of NBFCs having exclusive focus on MF is negligible.

Categories of providers	*Legal framework governing their activities*
Domestic commercial Banks: -Public sector Banks -Private sector Banks & -Local Area Banks	i) RBI Act 1934 ii) Bank Regulation Act 1949 iii) SBI Act iv) SBI Subsidiaries Act v) Acquisition & transfer of Undertaking Act 1970
Regional Rural Banks	i) RRB Act 1976 ii) RBI Act 1934 iii) BR act 1949
Co-operative Banks	i) Co-operative Societies Act ii) BR Act 1949 (AACS) iii) RBI Act 1934 (for Scheduled Banks)
Co-operative Societies	State Legislation like MACS.
Registered NBFCs	RBI Act 1934 Companies Act 1956
Unregistered NBFCs	Sec. 25 of Companies Act.
Other providers like societies, trusts etc.	Societies Registration Act'60 Indian Trust Act Chapter IIIC of RBI Act'34 State Moneylenders Act.

Legal Forms o MFIs in India[7]

Types of MFIs	*Estimated number*	*Legal Acts under which registered*
1) Not for Profit MFIs a) NGO-MFIs	400 to 500	Societies Registration Act, 1860 or similar Provincial Acts, Indian Trust Act, 1882.
2) Non-profit Companies	10	Section 25 of the Companies Act, 1956
3) Mutual Benefit MFIs a) Mutually aided Co-operative Societies (MACS) and similarly set up institutions	200 to 250	Mutually Aided Co-operative Societies Act enacted by State Government
4) For Profit MFIs a) Non-Banking Financial Companies (NBFCs)	6	Indian Companies Act, 1956, Reserve Bank of India Act 1934.

*The estimated number includes only those MFIs, which are actually undertaking lending activities.

Summary Legal Framwork for Institutions Engaging Directly or Indirectly in Microfinance

Category of Institution	*Type of Instituttions*	*Legal Framework: Licensing*	*Action Allowed*	*Minimum Capital Requirement*
1	*2*	*3*	*4*	*5*
Banks	Schedule Commercial Banks	Reserve Bank of India Act	Fully Banking, enumerated in Section 6. Must respect priority sector lending target (40% bank credit) of which 25% to weaker sections: local area banks may operate only in designated areas.	Rs. 100 crores.
Commercial MFIs	Regional Rural Banks (RRBs) Non-Bank Finance Companies (NBFCs)	Regional Rural Banks Act of 1970 Section 45-I(f) of RBI Act. NBFC Rules	Opening A/c , saving, lending only in rural areas. Only time deposits with one year maturity	Rs. 2 crores.
	Local Area Banks	Banking Regulation Act of 1949.	Deposit mobilization is allowed (current, recurring, savings and time deposits) No upper limit, although in practice max. is 10 to 12 times net owned funds.	Rs. 5 crores
Mutual Benefits MFIs	Urban Cooperative Banks	State or Multi-State Cooperative Act	Deposits allowed with an upper limit on deposits: Can take current, recurring, savings and time deposits.	Rs. 50 lakhs.
	Mutually Aided Cooperative Societies	Incorporated under AP MACS Act: RBI licenses under Banking	Funds from members in the form of share capital, deposits, debentures, loans and other contribution:	None

(Contd...)

1	*2*	*3*	*4*	*5*
		Regulation Act. And Cooperative Societies Rules of 1966.	Public savings as allowed in byelaws. (Raising share capital from government is not allowed)	
No-Profit MFIs	Section 25 Companies	Companies Act 1956.	Can take current, recurring , saving and time deposits	None
	NGOs	No licensing (Registration under the Societies Act or Indian Trusts Act)	Lending is not allowed under these acts, but is conducted on the basis of inclusion of lending in status submitted as part of the registration process under these Acts. (Deposit collection technically not allowed, limited by covenants under the RBI Act).	None

8.5. MFIs and Policy Framework

a) Capital requirements

NGO-MFIs, non-profit companies MFIs and mutual benefit MFIs are regulated by the specific act in which they are registered and not by the Reserve Bank of India. These are therefore not subjected to minimum capital requirements, prudential norms etc. NGO-MFIs to become NBFCs are required to have a minimum entry capital requirement of Rs. 20 million. As regards prudential norms, NBFCs are required to achieve capital adequacy of 12% and to maintain liquid assets of 15% on public deposits.

b) Foreign Investment

Foreign investment by way of equity is permitted in NBFC-MFIs subject to a minimum investment of $500,000. In view of the minimum level of investment, only two NBFCs are reported to have been able to raise the foreign investment. However, a large number of NGOs in the development- empowerment are receiving foreign fund by way of grants. At present, over Rs. 40,000 million every year flows into India to NGOs for whole range of activities including microfinance. In a way, foreign donors have facilitated the entry of NGOs into micro finance operations through their grant assistance.

c) Deposit Mobilisation

Not for profit MFIs are barred, by the Reserve Bank of India, from mobilizing any type of savings. Mutual benefit MFIs can accept saving from their members. Only rated NBFC-

MFIs rated by approved credit rating agencies are permitted to accept deposits. The quantum of deposits that could be raised is linked to their net owned funds.

d) Borrowings

Initially, bulk of the funds required by MFIs for on lending to their clients was met by apex institutions like National Bank for Agriculture and Rural Development (NABARD), Small Industries Development Bank of India (SIDBI) and Rashtriya Mahila Kosh (RMK). In order to widen the range of lending institutions to MFIs, the Reserve Bank of India has roped in Commercial Banks and regional Bank of India to extent the credit facilities to MFIs since February 2000. Both public and private banks have been given operational freedom to prescribe their own lending norms keeping in the view the ground realities. The intention is to augment flow of micro credit through the conduit of MFIs. In regard to external commercial borrowings (ECBS) by MFIs, not-for-profit MFIs are not permitted to raise ECB. The current policy effective from 31 January 2004, allows only corporate registered under the Companies Act to access ECB for permitted end use in order to enable them to become globally competitive players.

e) Interest Rates

Interest rates are deregulated not only for private MFIs but also for the formal banking sector. In the context of softening of interest rates in the formal banking sector, the comparatively higher interest rate (12 to 24 per cent per annum) charged by the MFIs has become a contentious issue. The high interest rate collected by the MFIs from their poor clients is perceived as exploitative. It is argued that raising interest rates too high could undermine the social and economic impact on poor clients. Since most MFIs have lower business volumes, their transaction costs are far higher than that of the formal banking channels. The high cost structure of MFIs would affect their sustainability in the long run.

f) Collateral Requirements

All the legal forms of MFIs have the freedom to waive physical collateral requirements from their clients. The credit policy guidelines of the RBI allow even the formal banks not to insist on any type of collateral and margin requirement for loans up to Rs. 50,000.

8.6. Regulation and Supervision of MFIs

Following Committees have examined the road map for regulation and supervision of MFIs[8]:

a) Task Force (appointed by NABARD) Report on Regulatory and Supervision Framework for MFIs.

b) MFIs, 1999.

c) Working Group (constituted by Government of India) on Legal & Regulation of MFIs, 2002

d) Informal Groups (appointed by RBI) on Micro Finance which studied issues relating to (i) Structure & Sustainability, ii) Funding (iii) Regulations and (iv) Capacity Building, 2003

e) Advisory Committee (appointed by RBI) on flow of credit to agriculture and related activities from the Banking System, 2004.

To address the issue of need for a differential regulatory framework, the latest committee sought answers to the following questions and concerns facing private MFIs in the Country:

a) Is non-existence of a separate differential regulatory framework a critical bottleneck hindering the growth of the sector?

b) Will MFIs be sustainable in medium term? If so, will they continue to focus on the poor?

c) Is access to public / member deposit the key issue for their sustainability?

d) Can MFIs finance loans for income generation at interest rates, which are sustainable by the rural poor?

e) Is it possible to evolve commonly agreed standards for MFI sector covering performance, accounting and governance issues, which can open up possibilities of self-regulation?

f) Has the sector reached a critical mass where regulation becomes important?

The Committee observed that while a few of the MFIs have reached significant scales of outreach, the MFI sector as a whole is still in evolving phase as is reflected in wide debates ranging around (i) desirability of NGOs taking up financial intermediation, (ii) unproven financial and organizational sustainability of the model, (iii) high transaction costs leading to higher rates of interest being charged to the poor clients, (iv) absence of commonly agreed performance, accounting and governance standards, (v) heavy expectations of low cost funds, including equity and the start up costs, etc.

The current debate on development of a regulatory system for the MFIs focuses on three stages. Stage one - to make the MFIs appreciate the need for certain common performance standards, stage two - making it mandatory for the MFIs to get registered with identified or designated institutions and stage three - to encourage development of network of MFIs which could function as quasi Self-Regulatory Organisations (SROs) at a later date or identifying a suitable organisation to handle the regulatory arrangements. The Committee recommended that while the MFIs may continue to work as wholesalers of micro-credit by entering into tie-ups with banks and apex development institutions, more experimentation have to be done to satisfy about the sustainability of the MFI model. Such experimentation needs to be encouraged in areas where banks are still not meeting adequate credit demand of the rural poor.

In regard to offering thrift products, the Committee felt that, while the NGO-MFIs can continue to extend micro credit services to their clients, they could play an important role in facilitating access of their clients to savings services from the regulated banks. As regards allowing NGO-MFIs to access deposits from public / clients, the Committee considers that in view of the need to protect the interests of depositors, they may not be permitted to accept public deposits unless they comply with the extant regulatory framework of the Reserve Bank of India. As no depositors' interest is involved where they do not accept public deposits, the Reserve Bank of India need not regulate MFIs.

As regards the high interest rates being charged by the MFIs, the Committee felt that the lenders to MFIs may ensure that these institutions adopt a 'cost-plus- reasonable-margin' approach in determining the rates of interest on loans to clients.

Major recommendations of High Level Committee headed by Deputy Governor Shri Vepa Kamesam on August 6, 2003: on issues related to (i) Structure & Sustainability (ii) Funding (iii) Regulations and (iv) Capacity Building are as follows:

(i) Structure & Sustainability Issues

a) Grant funding may be discouraged for purposes other than those defined as capacity building.

b) Interest rates on small loans (less than Rs. 2 lakh) from commercial banks to individual may be de-regulated.

c) Bank may be permitted to partner with MFIs/other agencies to offer (third party banking), which will increase outreach without additional investments and permit flexibility in terms of location and service.

(ii) Funding Issues

a) An autonomous and professionally managed National Micro Finance Equity Fund may be set up with an initial subscription of Rs. 200 crore (to be raised to Rs.500 crore over 2-3 years) with contribution by banks which may be treated as Weaker Section lending under Priority Sector.

b) RBI should evolve special credit rating tools for MFIs in India and build up MFI information Bureu for providing information.

c) Commercial banks/RRBs may provide 10% of their loans to MFIs as grants for capacity building and these grants should be reimbursed by NABARD from Micro Finance Development Fund.

d) While all NBFC-MFIs registered with RBI may be allowed to raise deposits subject to their obtaining minimum credit rating under the special credit rating tools developed for MFI sector, Non-Banking Finance Companies (NBFC-MFIS) or registered with RBI.

e) A separate category of NBFCs be created for attending to microfinance business with entry capital requirement of Rs. 25 lakhs for MFI needs to be urgently created.

f) The amount of deposits mobilized by any such MFI should not exceed Rs. 5000/- per depositor and all such deposits may be covered by the guarantee of Deposit Insurance & Credit Guarantee Corporation (DICGC).

(iii) Regulatory Issues

For SHGs

a) SHGs may not lend outside the Group.

b) SHGs may decide on some cap on borrowings per Member.

c) Group to decide on apportioning of income earned during a year.

d) Pass Books may be issued to each SHG Member.

e) A rating matrix by lender to assess SHGs while making credit decisions to be made mandatory. The rating exercise to be done by the lender (NGO/MFI/bank) on a yearly basis to ensure no slippage in the ratings.

For NGOs*

a) Those NGOs who opt to transform into section 25 companies to repay the deposits and come out of the deposit portfolio. Others who opt to continue to accept deposits to transform themselves into NBFCs or cooperatives and work within relevant rules.

b) Broad guidelines for a rating matrix for NGOs are devised. Each lender to evolve its own rating matrix based on these guidelines. Rating exercise to be repeated annually to avoid slippage in rating. Rating to be done by accredited agencies in case of NGOs with borrowings of above Rs. 2 crores.

For Micro Credit Institutions (MCIs)

a) Company Law Board to allow SHGs to be members of Section 25 companies.

b) There will be no ceiling in respect of loan amount extended by Section 25 companies to SHGs, however SHGs, to provide credit not exceeding Rs. 50000 per member of the SHG.

c) To encourage more flow of donations/contributions donors to be exempted from income tax under Section 11C of the IT Act.

d) All income and interest on loans to be recognized on an accrual basis.

e) MFIs may build up loan loss reserves (2% of total assets to begin with and up to 10% over a period of 10 years), suitable exemption to be provided under IT Act for creation of loan loss reserves.

f) Legal status of institution with details of borrowings is disclosed. Details of borrowings, details of loans and classification of loans and method of deferring and amortization to be disclosed.

g) Institute of Chartered Accountants of India be involved in developing an effective audit mechanism.

h) Loan granted by SHGs to individual members not to exceed Rs, 50,000. Transparency in rate/method of fixation of interest, it may cover costs of management /administration, cost of funds, rate of inflation and loan loss.

i) Savings of SHGs promoted by Section 25 companies be maintained with permitted organizations.

j) Complete income tax exemption for Section 25 companies purveying micro credit (to the donor and to the receiver). Government to consider complete exemption from IT for income earned, as the main purpose of the organization is to empower the poor.

For Micro Finance Institutions (NBFC)

a) Minimum entry-level capital requirement for micro finance NBFCs which are involved exclusively in financing SHGs be reduced to Rs. 25 lakhs from Rs. 200 lakhs at present. However, such NBFCs may not be allowed to accept deposits until their capital is raised to Rs. 200 lakhs.

b) Capital adequacy norms should be more stringent compared to formal financial Institutions as all the loans provide by MFIs are collateral free loans. A minimum capital adequacy ratio of 10% of the risk weighted assets is suggested.

c) All income and interest on loans should be recognized on accrual basis. All accounts where interest/installment is overdue for more than 45 days (to be moved to 30 days norm by 2007); to be treated as NPAs.

d) The organization should provide adequate provisioning to take care of loan losses; to begin with it should be 2% on the standard assets. Exemption to be provided under IT act for the loan loss reserves created. These guidelines to be more stringent when compared to formal institutions as all the loans provided by NBFCs are collateral free loans.

Based on the recommendations of the Advisory Committee on Flow of Credit to Agriculture and Related Activities from the Banking System (Vyas Committee), in the Annual Policy Statement for the year 2004-05, it has been announced that, in view of the need to protect the interest of depositors, microfinance institutions (MFIs) would not be permitted to accept public deposits unless they comply with the extant regulatory of the Reserve Bank.

(iv) Capacity Building Issues

a) Each bank could establish an exclusive micro financé cell to design strategies of the bank and creating an enabling environment to develop micro finance as core business of poverty lending.

b) RBI shall facilitate setting up of business incubation fund through SGSY programme for providing venture capital support.

c) SHGS may be networked into community-based organization at cluster/federation level.

d) Rural Infrastructure Development Fund (RIDF) funds may also be used for SHG promotion.

e) An innovation Fund for research & development may be initiated.

f) Common performance standards based on key financial and non-financial indicators may be evolved.

g) Microfinance resource centers with exclusive focus on capacity building may be set up in five different regions.

NOTES

1. Rajeev Ahuja and Johannes Jutting, "System Promoting Sustainable Financial Services to the Poor and Poorest", *Focus*, pp-2-4.
2. The term "Cooperative" covers a range of institutions, both formal (state-owned cooperative banks) and semi-formal (cooperative societies), therefore regulated and unregulated.
3. Draft Paper of Women's World Banking "Micro Environment and legal regulatory Framework India, March 2002, and a draft report on World Bank report on the microfinance industry in India.
4. www.indianlegaleagle.com and www.indialawinfo.com, www.mitrabharathi.com. www.worldbank.org.
5. A report of the Review Group on the Working of the Local Area Bank Scheme headed by Shri G.Ramachandran , Former Finance Secretary, Government of India, Reserve Bank of India, September 2002.
6. Rajeev Ahuja and Johannes Jutting, "Systems Promoting Sustainable Financial Services to the Poor and Poorest, *Focus*, p. 03.
7. Extracts from an article written and presented at APRACA Seminar at Manila on Regulation of MFIs in July 2004 by K.Muralidhara Rao, General Manager, NABARD, Mumbai.
8. http://www.nabard.org/microfinance/mf_institution.asp.

9

Innovative Products and Services of Microfinance

9.1. Innovative Credit Delivery Models

(a) ICICI Partnership Model[1]

Traditional models of MFIs financing have tended to exhibit low leveraging capability owing to the organization-based approach as against an asset-based. The partnership model pioneered by ICICI Bank attempted to address the following key gaps:

- Separating risk of the MFI from the risk inherent in the micro finance portfolio.
- Providing a mechanism for banks to continuously incentivise partner MFIs, especially in a scenario where the borrower entered into a contract directly with the bank and the role of the MFI was closer to that of an agent.
- Inability of MFIs to provide risk capital in large quantum which limited advances from banks despite a greater ability of the letter to provide implicit capital.

The loans are contracted directly between banks and underlying borrower, i.e. it does not reflect on the balance sheet of the MFI (this feature is similar to the SHG-Bank linkage model). The MFI continues to service the loans until maturity. In other words, the bank relies on the MFIs field operations for collection and supervision. The key difference then, between this and the financial intermediation model does not lie in the operating methodology, but in the manner in which the financial structure has been designed.

This structure primarily attempts to separate the risk of the MFI from the risk of the underlying portfolio. Why this is important? Because when the bank lends to the MFI, it has no recourse to the underlying borrowers. On the other hand, if the bank lends directly to the borrowers without the fund entering the MFI's balance sheet, it has recourse to the borrowers. So, at least in theory, if the particular MFI's goes bankrupt or close down for any other reason, the Bank can appoint another agency to recover the dues from borrowers. In addition, since the loans are not reflected on the balance sheet of MFI, it requirement for regulatory capital ceases to exist. Therefore, the lending paradigm shifts from being organization-based to being asset-based. This shift has crucial implications for rating, pricing and consequent marketability.

MFI provide guarantee (typically a first loss default guarantee) though it shares the risk of portfolio with the bank up to a certain defined limit. A first loss default guarantee (FLDG) makes the provider of the guarantee liable to bear losses up to a certain specified limit, say the first 10 percent or 20 percent of loss on the portfolio. An FLDG forces the guarantor to prevent any losses at all as it is affected adversely right form the start. The quantum and pricing of the FLDG will reflect the operating capability and maturity of the MFI.

In this model, the MFI collects a service charge from the borrowers to cover its transaction cost and margin. ICICI Bank also provide over draft (OD) facility to the MFI equivalent to the amount which the MFI is liable to provide as the FLDG. The OD represents funds committed, but not utilized. The OD is drawn only in event of default. On default, the MFI is liable to pay a penal rate of interest on the amount drawn down form the OD facility. The OD facility in effect, assumes the character of mezzanine equity permitting the MFI to leverage it for wholesale funding. In this manner, through the OD facility, the bank enables the MFI to provide explicit capital.

With the partnership structure, ICICI Bank is working with more than 30 MFIs in India accounting for loans outstanding of approximately US$ 150 million. Under the partnership model, loans are contracted directly between the bank and final borrower i.e. loans are not reflected on the balance sheet of the MFI. The MFI continues to originate, monitor and recover the loans until maturity in exchange for service fees.

Additionally, the MFI must share the risk inherent in the portfolio generated by it. This risk sharing can take different forms but here we emphasize only two mechanisms:

a) The MFI can open a locked saving (fixed deposit) account amounting to a certain percentage of the portfolio (generally 10-15%) and create a lien in favour of the bank. When security is provided in this form, this amount should be deducted from the capital base of the MFI.

b) The MFI can open an overdraft account offered with the bank, not to be used until default occur.

This mode of risk sharing has been termed First Loss Default Guarantee (FLDG). This means that if the FLDG is set 10% (predefined by the bank and MFI) then the first 10% of defaults is to be borne by the MFI.

(b) Local Agents

Although MFIs have been recognized as the key purveyors of micro finance in India, one cannot rule out the potential of new service delivery configuration that combine a local agent and various technological aids for ease of transaction. Some models that have made use of the local agent idea in the past include the Life Insurance Corporation of India's use of agents to sell insurance policies and commercial banks pygmy deposit scheme which used agents for the function of saving collection. The key challenge in developing scaled agent-based models is to be able to control agent fraud and create incentives for the agents that are aligned to the objectives of the provider. The emergence of connectivity and transaction devices increases the scope of agent-based model.

(c) Credit Franchisee

Another agent model that ICICI Bank is working on at block level (Kiosk is a transaction platform for an agent at village /cluster level) is the Credit Franchisee Model. The credit franchisee is envisaged to provide asset-backed loans (auto, gold, fixed deposit) and other financial services. The credit franchisee will be located in the places that are likely to be under-served from a financial services perspective, but would not be able to support a branch-based model of outreach in a viable manner. The credit franchisee is an entrepreneur who contributes equity, has a good understanding of the local market conditions, credit needs and credit history of individuals and who is willing to enter into risk-sharing arrangement with the bank.

(d) Loan Securitization

Efforts are on to develop a secondary market for securitized papers to expand the investor horizon and consequently lower the cost of funding these assets on a continual basis. In this regards, ICICI Bank is actively working with Credit Rating Information Services of India Limited (CRISIL), the premier credit rating agency in India, to develop a smooth and scaleable process for rating the underlying customer assets on an ongoing basis.

In India, in the absence of a secondary market for microfinance securities, people often use the term synonymously with portfolio sales. The first step of a securitization is the buy-out of a micro-finance loan portfolio against a purchase consideration calculated by computing the net present value of receivables at an agreed discount rate. The originator (MFI) or a third party (such as USAID or Grameen Foundation USA) provides partial credit protection i.e. credit enhancement to the investor (Bank) in the form of guarantee or over collaterisation etc. amounting to a certain percentage of the receivables under the portfolio by way of lien on fixed deposit.

The MFI continues to service the loan portfolio in exchange for service fees. Although ICICI has purchased several microfinance portfolios, there have been only two securitization deals. In 2004, the largest ever securitization deal in microfinance was signed between ICICI Bank and SHARE Microfin Ltd, a large MFI operating in rural areas of the state of Andhra Pradesh. Technical assistance and the collateral deposit of $ 325 K (93% of the guarantee required by ICICI) were supplied by Grameen Foundation USA. Under this agreement, ICICI purchased a part of SHARE's microfinance portfolio against an agreed discount rate. The interest paid by SHARE is almost 4% less than the rate paid in commercial loans. The other deal as conducted by ICICI Bank and BASIX in 2004 for a part of their portfolio amounting to $ 842 K (Rs. 42.1 Mn). After this deal, BASIX felt that reporting requirement imposed by ICICI was too demanding and decided to raise funds henceforth by other means.

Starting in the fiscal year of 2005, RBI allowed NGO-MFIs to borrow up to US$5 million during a year from external commercial sources through an authorized dealer under the automatic route. In March 2006, RBI came out with comprehensive guidelines on loan securitization, enabling a clean separation of assets between the originator and the owner and clearly defining roles of other parties involved in a securitization deal. Such policy milestones are shaping the fast paced thriving sector today.

(e) Equity Funding

Few MFIs receive much equity funding, and few large institutions invest in equity. The exception to this latter rule is the Bellwether Fund, which has invested millions of dollars into microfinance start-ups. Foreign private equity funds entering the sector include ACCION Equity Fund and LoK Capital.

(f) Charitable Grants

MFIs receive charitable grants from numerous domestic and international donors. Two types of grants are used: Operating grants which can only be used to meet operating costs and capital grants which go straight into an MFI's equity.

(g) Micro-Insurance: Contributing to a secure future

Microfinance also facilitates the provision of insurance for the poor. Though the scale of outreach is limited compared to credit and savings, there are examples where provision of insurance has helped the poor in coping with unforeseen events. The most notable example of an MFI providing insurance is that of SEWA Bank. Mainstream insurance providers such as Aviva Life Insurance, ICICI Lombard and Max New York Life have displayed an increasing willingness to develop product suited to MFIs.

Box-7: Life Insurance for Poor: The Basix Initiative

Aviva Life Insurance, a joint venture between Dabur and Aviva Plc, has tied up with BASIX to provide the rural poor and the MFI security against uncertainties such as death. Credit Plus is a yearly renewable term insurance scheme, which provides death cover on a group basis. Credit Plus provides assurance to BASIX borrowers (mainly the rural poor) that, in the event of their untimely death, their families would receive some financial payment and the outstanding loan would also be cleared.

Box-8: Facilitating Money Transfers: The Adhikar Experience

Adhikar, an NGO working in Orissa, has an innovative money remittance service for workers from the state working in distant Gujarat. With support from research and innovative fund of CARE India's Credit & Savings for Household Enterprises (CASHE) project, Adhikar set up Shramika Sahajoga in August 2002, exclusively to look after remittance services for migrant workers. The Shramika Sahajoga has a bank account in Tangi, Orissa and at Gandhidham in Corporation Bank and it is through these accounts that the money is transmitted from Gandhidham to Orissa. The bank provides instant credit in Orissa against a cheque deposited in Gandhidham for free. This considerably reduces the time taken to transfer money.

Shramika Sahajoga also facilitates the family members of migrant workers in forming SHGs for savings and credit activities. The many benefits of this programme are:

a) Smooth, safe and cost effective transfer of money of migrant workers to their
a) families at home.
b) Establishment of a viable MFI for the families of migrant workers of Orissa.
c) Economic development of migrant workers and their families as a result of savings
a) promotion among them.
d) Increase social networking arising out of group activities.

ICICI Lombard's weather insurance scheme is an example of the recent movement towards insuring farm produce against the vagaries of the Indian monsoon. BASIX, one of the India's largest microfinance institutions with nearly 60,000 borrowers in nine states, bought a bulk insurance policy from ICICI Lombard and provided cover to 250 groundnut and castor farmers in Andhra Pradesh through its KBS Local Area Bank.

(h) Weather insurance index

In India, the area-based crop insurance programme has been the traditional products for managing yield risk for farmers. However, the effectiveness of this programme has been debatable. It has experienced prohibitive costs due to the field inspections and loss adjustment to be made. As per the report of the Task Force on Agriculture set up by Government of India, all the crop insurance schemes were ineffective in estimating the probability of risks covered, leading to claim payouts in the range of four to five times of the premium collected. If crop insurance is to give protection at the level of the model yields, the premium might be as high as 30 percent as against the current 1-3.5 percent, accordingly to the study by the Task Force.[2] Index based insurance products, where payouts are based on a verifiable index; provide an opportunity to provide insurance to farmers and the rural poor without incurring the high overheads of loss adjustment and supervision typical of traditional crop insurance products. Since the index provides a transparent mechanism to compute payouts, claims settlement can be immediate. Moreover, it takes care of moral hazard challenge as rainfall, unlike yield is not affected by the action of the insured.

The claim s settled on the basis of transparent index. The index is crated by assigning weightage to critical time periods. The past weather data is mapped on this index to arrive at a normal threshold index. The actual weather data is then mapped to the index to arrive at the actual index level. In case there is a material deviation between the normal index and the actual index, compensation is paid out to the insured on the basis of pre-agreed formula.

ICICI Lombard General Insurance Company has customized the weather insurance product to cover the following:

i) Groundnut, castor and cotton crops in Andhra Pradesh.

ii) Oranges in Jhalawar, Rajasthan

iii) Apples in Himachal Pradesh

iv) Wheat in Madhya Pradesh

v) Mustard and coriander in Rajasthan.

(i) Savings and Investment products

It has been observed that although the demand for saving products is very high among the poor, few options of saving with the formal sector are available. The ratio of deposit accounts to total population in rural areas is about 18%. The corresponding ratio for urban areas is likely to be about 100%.[3] The regulator prohibits institutions other than banks and approved

Non-Bank Financial Companies (NBFCs), from collecting savings. This concern is justified in the context of schemes and agencies that have defaulted on their commitment to savers.

In order to provide poor households an avenue to save their surplus within the current regulatory environment, one option that ICICI Bank is exploring is to enable clients of MFIs to invest in mutual funds with the MFI/outreach channel facilitating access to the Asset Management Company. The objective is to provide a safe avenue for savings, an ability to earn returns with little or no volatility and to use MFI/outreach channel as the facilitator and not as "mobiliser of savings". Money Market Mutual Funds (MMMF) typically known as liquid funds would be the most suitable product that could be offered through MFI/outreach channel. The MMMF provides a legal saving option, as MFI/outreach channel can act as agents and sell units of the MMMF to its members.

(j) Training Institutes

Over the last decade, various resource units specializing in imparting training to MFIs have emerged. These include organizations like Indian School of Micro Finance for Women, Dhan Academy of Micro-Finance, M-TRIL, EDA Rural Systems and Bankers Institute of Rural Development (BIRD). In additions, resource centers have emerged at a regional level to impart training to local NGO/MFIs. Examples of this category would be People's Education and Development Organisation (PEDO) in Rajasthan, Centre for Youth in Social Development (CYSD) in Orissa and Mahila Abhivruddhi Society, (APMAS), Andhra Pradesh.

ICICI Bank plans to establish a national level Financial Services School in collaboration with MicroSave India. The School will impart training to MFI staff and senior management through a network of regional training resources across the country. The training process will be characterized by a combination of class room level teaching in the regional language, field visits and monitoring for a certain period of time.

(k) Mobile Phone Banking

Mobile phones have become mobile wallets by facilitating electronic payments in exchange for goods and services. Mobile Phone Banking (m-Banking) has assumed tremendous significance under the circumstances and this development in m-Banking has positively affected the microfinance industry also with usages like facilitating savings deposits, loan repayments and other funds transfers.

"*m-Money*" is money that can be accessed and used via mobile phone. Today, mobile subscribers in markets such as South Africa, in Kenya, Philippines, Japan, and elsewhere are beginning to use mobile money for transactions and services including domestic and international remittances, bill payment, payroll deposit, loan receipt and repayment, and purchases of goods and services ranging from prepaid airtime to groceries to bus tickets to micro insurance. Some examples of m-Money are: M-Peas in Kenya, G-Cash in Philippine, m-check in India etc.

(l) Micro Insurance and Natural Calamities

Every serious illness, every accident and every natural disaster threatens the very existence of poor people and usually leads to deeper poverty. Poor need more insurance coverage as they are generally prone to various kinds of risks. Microinsurance is the term used to refer the insurance to the low income people. Microinsurance is a low value product with less premium and benefits.

There is a clear need for evolving cost-effective and sustainable insurance products for the clients of the Micro-finance programmes. The National Bank should encourages and facilitate development and pilot testing of such products in association with stakeholders including insurance company.[4]

9.2. Innovative Projects of NABARD

(a) Grain Banks and SHGs

To explore the possibilities of monetizing the saving-in-kind in the form of grains, a pilot Project was implemented in 17 tribal villages of Kerpai & Nakrundi Gram Panchayats of Thuamul Rampur Block of Kalahandi district in Orissa. Members of SHGs can save both in cash and kind depending on the convenience. Loans also can be provided either in cash or in the form of grains. Three grain banks have been established in Islet, Sikergunda and Maltipadar tribal villages in two blocks of Kalahandi district, Orissa. 29 SHGs are participating. NABARD has sanction grant assistance of Rs. 0.38 million. Encouraged by the successful establishment and maintenance of the Grain Banks by SHGs formed by tribal communities, NABARD sanctioned another project in the pre-dominantly tribal areas of Chhattisgarh state involving a grant assistance of Rs. 0.24 million for construction and establishment of 5 grain banks each in Mylibeda and Meerkatola villages of Bastar and Kanker districts involving SHGs.

(b) Project on Processing Cards

With a view to reducing paper work, saving time and maintaining up to date records, a Pilot project was launched for providing processor cards to active clients like KCC holders and SHGs as also automation of bookkeeping of groups. It is expected to test the acceptability and adaptability of IT in rural areas, as also address MIS needs in rural banks. It is being implemented in 5 branches of Sri Visakha Grameen Bank in Andhra Pradesh and 5 branches of Krishna Grameen Bank, Karnataka. Grant of Rs. 3.5 million has been sanctioned of which Rs. 1.91 million has been released.

(c) Project on "e-Grama"

NABARD has part funded establishment of 13 Village Information Centres (e-grama centres) through an NGO in Davanagare district of Karnataka to help SHGs/villages to have access to Information Communication Technology. These e-grama centres make available information on areas like weather conditions, crop inputs, product prices, land records etc. Besides this, add –on services like bookkeeping of SHGs, DTP, scanning etc. are also being provided. The NGO has facilitated setting up 50 centres (including 13 with NABARD assistance). Commercial banks and RRB are extending necessary credit support to entrepreneurs. Grant assistance of Rs. 0.21 million has been released by NABARD during the year 2005-06.

(d) Setting-up of Computer Munshi

Proper bookkeeping of SHGs is one of the grey areas owing to the illiteracy among the group members. NABARD sanctioned financial assistance of Rs. 0.61 million to PRADAN—an NGO to develop system and local resources to address the issue. It involves training skilled local youth in computer operations and specially designed software to maintain SHG accounts. The project is being implemented in 4 districts (9 units) in Jharkhand and 1 district (1 unit) in Orissa. So far, 10 youth have been trained and their services are being availed of by 1220 SHGs in these states. Grant assistance of Rs. 0.49 million has so far been released under the project.

(e) Social Security System for SHG Members

Another innovative project which has been approved by NABARD entails creation of community based social security system for members of SHGs in rural areas for improving their livelihood and securing them from uncertainties of like. The project components include provision of a package of health insurance, life insurance etc. for SHG households by paying premium generated through discounts offered by service providers like grocery shop, cloth merchant etc. in the project area for SHG members in rural areas. It is being implemented through an NGO (Organisation for Awareness of Integrated Social Security, OASIS) in two villages covering 500 poor households from Betul district of Madhya Pradesh state , involving a grant assistance of Rs. 0.80 million.

(f) Next level of microfinance: Micro-Enterprise Promotion by SHGs

NABARD has initiated a pilot project for promotion of micro-enterprise by members of matured SHGs in 9 select districts across the country, viz. Ajmer (Rajasthan), Chandrapur (Maharashtra), Kangra (Himachal Pradesh), Madurai (Tamil Nadu), Mysore (Karnataka), 24 North Parganas (West Bengal), Panchmahal (Gujarat), Puri (Orissa), and Rae-Bareilly (Uttar Pradesh), in association with Marketing and Research Team (MART) as technical partner. The project will adopt 3M Model approach (Micro-finance, micro-market and a micro-planning methodology) developed by MART. In this project, NGOs act as Micro-Enterprise Promotion Agencies (MEPA) and assist members of matured SHGs to take up income generating activities on a sustainable basis. Survey of villages and SHGs by NGOs has been undertaken and micro Business Development Plans have been prepared for each district wherein potential activities have been mapped for the benefit of SHGs/members of SHGs, who would set-up their micro enterprises based on these activities. Promoting micro-enterprise is a complex issue which needs more holistic approach of appreciating skills levels, entrepreneurial spirit and dynamism, understanding markets, technology etc. This task has to be handled with care in order to ensure that genuine concerns do not lead to failure of micro Enterprises & increased debt burden and in turn to default. It brings into play the need for a hand holding strategy to enable the SHG members to cross over micro enterprise stage.

(g) Support to MFIs

Rating of MFIs

With a view to promoting flow of commercial loans from banks to MFIs, a scheme was launched by NABARD during 2005-06 to provide financial support to banks towards rating of MFIs by CRISIL. This scheme has since been revised to be operational up to 31 March 2008 and banks can now avail the services of other credit rating agencies viz. M-CRIL, ICRA, CARE & Planet Finance including CRISIL. Further the quantum of assistance has been increased to 80% of the cost upto a maximum of Rs. 80,000/-. This scheme would help MFIs in accessing commercial loans form banks. Those MFIs which have a minimum loan outstanding of more than Rs. 50.00 lakh (Rupees fifty lakh only) would be considered for rating and support under the scheme.

Capital / Equity Support to MFIs

In view of the announcement made by the Finance Minister in his Union Budget 2005-06, a scheme called "Capital/Equity Support to MFIs from Micro Finance Development and Equity Fund (MFDEF)" has been announced under which capital/equity support to various types of MFIs would be provided by NABARD to enable them to leverage capital/equity for accessing commercial and other funds form Banks. This would help MFIs in providing financial services at an affordable cost to the poor.

(h) Kisan Credit Cards (KCC)

The Kisan Credit Card (KCC) Scheme introduced in August 1998, to provide adequate and timely credit support in a flexible, hassle-free and cost effective manner, has so far covered about six crore farmer throughout the country. The scope of KCC was broad-based to cover term loans for agriculture and allied activities as also small quantum of consumption loan.

9.3. Other Innovative Approach

(a) BASIX Apana Bazar

It is an idea of enabling poor people to procure and distribute among themselves various items of daily consumption. A village of 100 poor families would be buying between half to one million rupees worth of food and provisions a year. Finally, if one is concerned about livelihoods, micro-credit needs to become macro and for that you need to something about increasing the absorption capacity.

(b) BASIX "Our Way": Basix has launched an initiative in retail mutual marketing called " Our Way" where it has encouraged, trained and financed SHG federations to act as wholesales for not one but any number of companies and capture the margins as well as bargain for higher discounts on the strength of their ownership of demand. This will enable low-income households will get things 5-10% cheaper.

SBI in the public sector and the ICICI Bank in the private sector, are looking out for emerging markets.

It does not take much analysis to figure out that the market for financial services for the 50-60 million poor households of India, coupled with about the same number who are technically above the poverty line but are severely under-served by the financial sector which is a very large one. Moreover, as in any emerging market, though perceived risks are higher, the returns are much greater. The traditional commercial markets of corporate, business, trade, and now even housing and consumer finance are being sought by all the banks, leading to price competition and wafer thin spreads.

(c) Post Office

The vast infrastructure of the Indian Postal Service must be exploited to scale up microfinance activity under the Business Correspondent or some other channel. A stable and conducive policy environment is necessary for other initiatives such as single credit bureau, biometric IDs or smart cards and weather stations. The sector at this stage needs a laissez faire environment; policy makers should be on continuous vigil and deliver concurrent improvement in policy and regulation. All organizations engaged in microfinance should be brought together under a single legal status and regulatory authority. Reacting to the high cash transaction and absorption necessitated by the popular partnership model, the regulator should pronounce certain capital adequacy ratio requirements and insist on standardized quality audit.

Further, bank-groups are motivated by a number of cross-selling opportunities in the market, for deposits, insurance, remittances and eventually mutual funds. Since the larger banks are offering all these services now through their group companies, it becomes imperative for them to expand their distribution channels as far and deep as possible, in the hope of capturing the entire financial services business of household. Banks and insurance companies have realized that NGOs offer a gateway to the large market of the lower-income households and that accounts for why a number of them, the ICICI Group leading are establishing business alliance with NGOs. It is a good thing that is happening as long as this enables the spread of financial services to the under-served at competitive rates.

FMCG (Fast moving consumer goods) companies like Hindustan Levers and Phillips have realized the potential of this big market and are actively using SHGs as entry points.

Microfinance is driven a demand pull rather than a supply push. Microfinance has been attractive to the lending agencies because of demonstrated sustainability and of low costs of operation.

NOTES

1. Bindu Ananth, Bastavee Barooah etc, " A Blueprint for the delivery of comprehensive Financial Services to the poor in India", CMR & IFMR, *Centre of Micro Finance Working Paper*, December 2004.
2. Vyas Committee Report (RBI).
3. Duggal and Singhal, "Extending Banking to the poor in India", *Working paper series*.
4. Dr. A.N.Sarkar, "Innovations in Microfinance: Linked Development Programmes", *Kurukshetra*, Dec-2001, p. 8.

10
Microfinance and Information Technology

10.1. Management Information System (MIS)

Technology gives opportunities MFIs for reducing costs of delivery and process management, besides bringing about transparent in operations. It assumes significance because of the manpower-intensive nature of business, underlying financial risks and regulatory sensitiveness. The aspects of the microfinance business where technology plays a key role include Management Information System (MIS), cash handling, data capture and subsequent management. In order for MFIs to grow rapidly, operations must be supported by robust and scaleable systems. Several providers have emerged to cater to the microfinance market.

Adoption of computer-assisted lending operations is an imperative need. A multinational company engaged in agri-business has made a very successful innovation in disseminating farm knowledge through computers placed in Kiosk called "e-Chou pals" in backward district Dhar in Madhya Pradesh. It has over 3363 such installations, reaching out to over 24 lakh farmers. This initiative also creates a direct marketing channel for the farmers' produce, eliminating wasteful intermediation and multiple handling, thus reducing transaction cost and making logistic efficient.[1] It is surprising to note that no MFIs seem to have entered into any collaborative action with this programme so far. MFIs can be an effective partner in such programmes. Kishan Credit cards can be made IT compatible, as debit card, on an experimental basis.

10.2. IT Infrastructure in Rural India

India now has a population of over 1 billion of which its rural population is approximately 70%. Much of the rural population does not have access to common infrastructure like connectivity, electricity, health and drinking water. Complex characteristics of rural India include inaccessible terrain and geographically dispersed hamlets/villages.

ICT is one of most important infrastructure for connecting people and places beyond the geographical boundaries. There have been debates on role of Information and Communication Technology (ICT) in developing a connectivity backbone in rural India to address urban-rural divide. ICT has been recognized as an infrastructure in developed countries and its use has shown the path of rapid socio-economic development.[2] However, in developing countries, especially in India, ICT interventions are still on concept stage. Many pilot projects are experimented in isolation and scaling up strategy is yet to be formulated.

Despite many initiatives taken up, India stands as per the report, 37th among 82 nations with network readiness index (NRI) as 3.89 (7 Point scale), 70th for ICT infrastructure. This indicates that a lot of improvement is needed in the national scenario.

In order to improve ICT infrastructure in rural areas, various policies and reforms such as "National Telecommunication Policy", "Indian IT Policy", "Indian Infrastructure Policy" and "Policy on Convergence" have been formulated by the Govt. of India in the recent past. National Telecom Policy (NTP99) was framed in 1999 with an objective to increase teledensity of 7 per 100 by 2007 and 15 by 2010. A very important decision came up in this policy was Universal Service Obligation (USO). Under this policy it is aimed at ensuring universal access to every citizen at affordable prices. Information, Communication and Entertainment Bill (ICE) was also another milestone in the history of Indian telecommunication having special focus on private service providers in the areas of ISP, Paging, VSAT and public mobile trunk operators.[3]

Telecom growth in India has been fuelled by wireless growth. The wireless subscriber base has grown from 1.6 million in 1999 to 90.14 million in March 2006 and is nearly double the subscriber base of 50.18 million of fixed service users. The mobile sector grew at 72.6 percent in comparison to 8.6 percent growth in the fixed sector over the year between March 2005-06.[4]

Another initiative of Government of India to improve ICT infrastructure in rural India and last mile connectivity is State Wide Area Network (SWAN) projects under e-governance which are being implemented in various states. Under this scheme, optical fibre line will be provided up to block level and last mile connectivity through radio link. This will enable provide connectivity backbone for e-governance at all the levels.

Mere provision of hardware and software components will not help the rural population draw benefits, but a systematic and convergent approach of policy makers, business drivers would be necessary for its use. Innovations are necessary for adoption of this technology since it can be viewed as a tool to improve the efficiency and effectiveness of the process that exist for the development of rural population and economy. Such processes could be providing basic information to the public for good governance, creating an atmosphere of transparency in pricing, marketing products, providing education and addressing disaster mitigation issues etc. Reaching the rural population where the other infrastructure relating to connectivity like rail, road is limited can be made possible through ICT infrastructure.

Bharatiya Sanchar Nigam Limited (BSNL) already has around 0.5 million village public telephones in rural India. Based on this, one estimate says that if wireless system with 10 km ranged is installed at the existing fibre connected rural exchanges; 80-85% of the villages could be connected. About 70% of the Indian land-mass is covered by optic fibre with cellular networks gradually coming up along national highways[5]. Companies such as Vortes and Neuraosynaptic have built a variety of devices designed to work within Internet Kiosk such as ECG monitors, digital stethoscopes and biometric/ low cost ATMs.

10.3. Leveraging ICT: Breakthrough for Rural Outreach

Some of innovative business model for rural outreach by leveraging the existing rural ICT infrastructure in India are given as under:

(a) e-choupal

ITC International Business Division has conceptualized the e-Chou pal as chain of internet Kiosk to facilitate procurement of specific commodities. These kiosks are connected through VSATs and are managed by the farmers, selected form within community and trained, known as "Sanchalaks". Each kiosk is a part of a hub and spoke model with the ITC Procurement Centre as the hub and the e-Choupal as the spokes. The investment in each kiosk is around Rs. 2.50 lakhs. At the kiosks, the "Sanchalaks" help the farmers readily access the different agricultural crop-specific websites that ITC has created in the relevant local language. E-choupals are set up with solar power backup and VSAT connectivity. They also provide access to local market (*mandi*) prices and global market price information on various agricultural products to allow farmers to compare prices. In fact, farmers view ITC as treating with greater respect and dignity than is the case in traditional *mandi* interactions.

The Farmers can learn online the best farm practices for their crop, the prevailing price and price trends for the crop in the Indian and world markets, and the local weather forecast. Moreover, if the farmer decides to sell his goods in the ITC procurement centre, the kiosk operator issue him a referral slip, which the farmer uses to sell his goods in the centre. As a direct marketing channel, virtually linked to the mandi system for price discovery, e-choupl\al aims to eliminate wasteful intermediation and multiple handling. It currently has 4700 installations covering 28,000 villages in 6 states.[6]

(b) n-Logue

It is promoted by TeNeT Group, IIT Chennai research group headed by Professor Ashok Jhunjhunwala. The core innovation at the heart of n-Logue's operations is a WLL technology, Cordect, which provides joint wireless Internet and voice connectivity. N-Logue is the second largest organization in this field, supporting over 500 rural IT-Kiosk. The focus of the company is to drive Internet and Telecom services in small towns and rural areas of India, thereby realizing its vision of 'significantly enhancing the quality of life of every rural Indian by driving the digital revolution profitably'.

(c) e-Grama

NABARD has part funded establishment of 13 Village Information Centres (e-grama centres) through an NGO in Davanagare district of Karnataka to help SHGs/villages to have access to Information Communication Technology. These e-grama centres make available information on areas like weather conditions, crop inputs, product prices, land records etc. Besides this, add on services like bookkeeping of SHGs, DTP, scanning etc. are also being provided.

(d) Computer Munshi

Proper bookkeeping of SHGs is one of the grey areas owing to the illiteracy among the group members. NABARD sanctioned financial assistance of Rs. 0.61 million to PRADAN—an NGO to develop system and local resources to address the issue. It involves training skilled local youth in computer operations and specially designed software to maintain SHG accounts. The project is being implemented in 4 districts (9 units) in Jharkhand and 1 district (1 unit) in Orissa. [7]

The pioneering breakthroughs in adopting ICT solutions have been made by MFIs which have attained financial and institutional stability and sustainability enabling them to have well defined MIS systems and a clear vision of what IT can do for their organizations. These organizations have been able to either raise funds from donors or fund them from their own funds-e.g. SEWA (Self Employed Women's Association) Bank, or else take assignment to develop IT software like BASIX (Bharatiya Samruddhi Financial Services) has done with International Finance Corporation(IFC). Some of MFIs who have successfully integrated ICT and MIS into the design and planning of the MFI and its operations are BASIX and Swayam Krishi Sangham (SKS), The Activists for Social Alternatives (ASA), Development for Humane Action (DHAN) Foundation etc.

Though ICT is mainly adopted by the New and Large MFIs, yet there is a small but increasing trend of small MFIs adopting ICT primarily with support from partner agencies (such as CARE's CASHE programme) and or from SIDBI.

(e) Internet Kiosks

An infrastructure of village-level kiosks is being promoted across the country by Internet service providers, public-private partnerships and agribusiness corporate. Several participants have been engaged in this task. ITC, n-logue, Drishtree and Development Alternatives (Tara Haat), have built more than 6,000 internet kiosks using technologies such as Wireless in Local Loop (WLL) and VSAT Terminals. By far the most successful of these initiatives has been the one launched by ITC, both commercially and in terms of number of kiosks on the ground.

In partnership with these kiosk network owners, ICICI Bank proposes to finance individual entrepreneurs (usually high-school graduates) who own and operate the kiosk. The entrepreneur invests around Rs. 5,000 and ICICI Bank finances the remaining Rs. 55,000 to purchase the operating license and equipment (including a PC, local language software, power backup, web camera and printer) from the Internet service provider. The online applications currently involve connectivity based service like e-governance, e-mail, Internet Chat, agricultural extension, and video conferencing with hospitals for preliminary diagnosis. Given the low investment required in the channel, the kiosks are expected to break even within the first year of operation of the kiosk. Kiosk needs catchments of about 5,000 people to be financially viable unit with the current applications, translating in to one kiosk in every cluster of four to five villages.

The strategy is to reach the poor at their doorsteps by delivering a suit of financial services through these kiosks. Currently, financial services have been rolled out in about 900 kiosks by ICICI Bank. Products such as Life & General Insurance (Weather insurance, personal accident insurance etc), Investment Services (Stocks, Bonds, Mutual Funds), gold purchase, credit products including micro-loans, agricultural loans, consumption loans and transaction and bill payment services and derivatives for small farmers (coffee options, soybean futures) can currently be delivered through these kiosks.

(f) Online Banking

As new areas of business open up and demand for remote banking services rise, technology, particularly information technology, emerges as an important variable in profitable banking operations. The backbone of any banking system is its payment and settlement systems. Important initiative in these areas includes Electronic Fund Transfer (EFT), Real Time Gross Settlement System (RTGS), to substantially mitigate settlement risks and collapse of markets, Centralised Funds Management System (CFMS), the Negotiated Dealing System (NDS), and the Structured Financial Messaging Solution (SFMS). SFMS is the backbone for all message-based communication over the Indian Financial Network (INFINET), which was started as a closed use group communication network for banks in India with PSBs as members. The INFINET has been operational for two years and its membership was thrown open to other banks and FIs in 2000-01. It may be pointed out that with effect from February 15, 2002 a screen based negotiated dealing (NDS) has been introduced to further facilitate trade in government securities.

According to an April 2006 McKinsey India Survey, rural India has the potential to become a US $ 599 billion market by the year 2020. It remains to be seen whether today's MFIs, bank, lenders and investors have the tenacity, dexterity and wit to retain first mover advantage.

Box 8: New Technology Introduction for Microfinance

Innovation	*Current status*
Mobile Phone Payments (cell phones become electronic wallets, using sms technology)	**Philippines:** Globe Communication and SMART have introduced cell phones to store and transfer electronic cash for payments. Being introduced to Rural Banker's Association of Philippines. **Kenya:** M-Pesa has partnered with Vodafone, Faulu-Kenya (Local MFI) and CBA (local bank). The M-Pesa system supports money transfer, cash withdrawal and deposit at retail outlets, and disbursement and payment of loans **South Africa:** the Wizzit banking facility allows low income account holders to use their mobile phones to remit money to a friend, buy airtime, or pay accounts **Latin America:** Motorola recently unveiled M-wallet a downloadable software application that allows users to pay bills, purchase products, and /or transfer money using their cell phones. The company is targeting the remittance market between the U.S. and Latin America
Electronic Payment System (deposits and withdrawals through plastic cards at ATM machines and	**Guatemala:** INCA and VISA are piloting the use of pre-paid cards for loan disbursement by partnering FINCA

(Contd...)

Innovation	*Current status*
at participating merchants, Debit, credit and prepaid cards)	Guatemala and Nicaragua with VISA member banks **Peru:** Mibanco has become a VISA member bank, and had introduced VISA products including: Miahorro (a savings account with debit card), VISA Empresarial card which can be used at ATMs and a credit card, all launched in 2006.
Point of sale devices (POS): installed at local retailers, allow clients to make withdrawals and deposits closer to home	**Uganda:** Uganda Microfinance Limited is piloting the use of POS devices to extend rural outreach **Senegal:**FERLO is piloting a similar POS initiative **India:** ICICI and SEWA bank are conducting a pilot whereby loan officers use POS devices at group meetingsColombia: 45 cooperatives with different core banking systems are using a single POS solution
Management Information System for client tracking	**USA:** the microfinance open source (MIFOS) project established by the Grameen Technology Center for management information system using open source framework **India:** FINO an initiative of ICICI Bank, is a private company established to provide outsourced MIS services to MFIs, including core banking system and distribution set up. **Andean Region:** ACCION has coordinated an effort by BancoSol (Bolivia), Banco Solidario (Ecuador), and Mibanco (Perus) to create a unified credit methodology supported by a common MIS with technology by BanTotal.
PDAs assist in on-site credit assessment	**Latin America:** At Banco Solidario (Ecuador), loan officers use Pocket PCs to conduct loan evaluation onsite with client; at BanGente (Venezuela), they use PDAs.
Credit Scoring assists in automating credit decision	Credit scores are being used for specific MFIs, but generic credit scores are not yet used and credit scoring has not been used to re-invent lending methodologies.

Source: Elisabeth Rhyne and Maria Otero, *Microfinance through the next decade: visioning the who, what, where and how,* ACCION.

11.4 Financial Inclusion and ICT

Financial Inclusion refers to providing access to financial services at affordable cost to the rural and the poor. Being remoteness, wider geographical areas, difficult terrains, sparsely populated and poor physical infrastructure in the rural areas, the biggest challenges for Financial Inclusion(FI) today is outreach to poor with cost effective. ICT has been recognized as one of the most cost effective tools for the financial inclusion.

Many of the thousands of microfinance institutions (MFIs) worldwide recognize that technology is essential, not only to reach new people, but also to make the business of microfinance more cost-effective and sustainable. Mobile phones, ATM machines, and a host of new innovations promise to help MFIs more efficiently provide services to people typically considered "unbankable".

With wireless communications networks growing and technology costs falling, electronic payments (e-payments), rather than cash or cheque-based payments, have emerged as a powerful tool with which financial institutions can build national scale and manage small lending risks.[8] Banks and MFIs can use the hardware and communication networks that process e-payments transactions, such as (ATMs, POS, mobile phones and internet-base banking) and point-of sale (POS) terminals, to serve people who cannot access, or who choose not to use, bank branches.

10.5. Branchless Banking: Emerging Business Model

One of the key challenges for MFIs is providing financial services to clients in remote areas including rural areas where the population density is low, the market is smaller and providing service entails high costs. Branchless Banking through Business Correspondent (BC)/Business Facilitator (BF) model – whereby a bank links itself with third party merchants located in remote areas – has emerged as a solution for this problem of outreach. Correspondents manage transactions on behalf of the partner institution and are remunerated on a fee-for-service basis. Bank Correspondents are expected to be having long-term businesses, and should be respected and trusted in their communities. The Bank Correspondents should also be 'ICT-enabled'; generally equipped with equipments such as an Electronic Funds Transfer at Point of Sale (EFTPOS) device, barcode readers and/or keypads, a personal computer, etc. They are linked to the partner institution's servers using a telephone line, cable or satellite link. Post offices, supermarkets, general stores, grocery stores, tele centres, etc, are good examples of Banking Correspondents.

In India, commercial banking entities like State Bank of India, HDFC, have tied up with the respective Service Centre Agencies(SCAs) in the states under the framework of National e- Governance Plan (NeGP) to provide Banking Correspondent status to the Common Service Centres (CSCs) equipped with ICT infrastructure and provide microfinance services through them. Detailed guidelines and circulars on BC & BF model were also issued to all the commercial banks by RBI to mitigate various possible financial and operational risks.

Branchless banking followed by a number of nationalized banks like SBI, UBI, Indian Bank, PNB who have collaborated with technology based companies providing solutions not only to enhance outreach but also to give microfinance services through different technology options. These agencies include Financial Information Network & Operation Ltd (FINO), Zero Mass Foundation and Atom Technologies.

Many of MFIs operating in India have already tie-up with nationalized banks to act as BC in favour of parent bank. This model is purely based on sound business model which has been widely implemented in many parts of the country through active participation of banks, MFIs, technology provider, etc. It is the clear example of collaborative and convergent of many stake holders in a single platform to reach the rural mass with the help of existing ICT infrastructure.

A unique ID (identification) for each citizen would also help accelerate this model for easy identification of clients remotely as required by Know Your Customer (KYC) norms of RBI. Setting up a Unique Identification Authority of India for maintaining UID for every citizen by 2012 is a positive step for providing better services to poor. In the recent Union Budget 2010, Government of India has already made budgetary allocation of Rs.1, 900 crores for UIAI.

10.6. m-Banking: Future of Microfinance

Cellular phones, especially with GSM backbone, due to its accessibility and affordability are becoming an indispensable communication tool for the poor in the developing countries. As per the World GSM Association report, during the year 2003-2006, more than 800 million mobile phones were sold in developing countries[9]. Mobile phones in today's scenario have become the only option for communication from being one of the options because of the ubiquity of its use and popularity even among the poorer section of the society.

Mobile phones have become mobile wallets by facilitating electronic payments in exchange for goods and services. Mobile Phone Banking (m-Banking) has assumed tremendous significance under the circumstances and this development in m-Banking has positively affected the microfinance industry also with usages like facilitating savings deposits, loan repayments and other funds transfers.

Indeed, one of the most-used devices by both microfinance providers and their clients is the mobile phone. With the number of African and Asian users increasing by tens of millions each year, many organizations are looking for ways to best utilize mobile phones as a tool for microfinance.

m-Banking has the potential to be transformational because:[10]

a) It uses existing mobile communications infrastructure which already reaches unbanked people.

b) It reduces the cost and risk inherent in dealing with cash.

c) It may be driven by new players, such as telcos, with different target market from traditional banks

d) It may harness the power of new distribution network for cash transactions, such as airtime merchants, beyond the conventional merchant POS or ATM network of banks.

e) It may be cheaper than conventional banking, if the offering is competitive.

The extent to which will mobile banking will in fact be transformational in a country will depend in large measure on whether the environment is enabling.

m-Banking is the hottest area of development in the banking sector and is expected to replace the credit/debit card system in future. In past two years, m-Banking user has increased three times if we compare the use of either debit card or credit card. Moreover 85-90% mobile users do not own credit cards. There is at least 36% of population that are literate having mobile phones and have no access to credit. This is the potential market that would appreciate mobile banking solutions.

10.7. m-Money: A New Experiment

"*m-Money*" is money that can be accessed and used via mobile phone. Today, mobile subscribers in markets such as South Africa, in Kenya *(P-Pesa)*, Philippines *(G-Cash)*, Japan, and elsewhere are beginning to use mobile money for transactions and services including domestic and international remittances, bill payment, payroll deposit, loan receipt and repayment, and purchases of goods and services ranging from prepaid airtime to groceries to bus tickets to micro insurance. Some examples of m-Money are:

(a) M-Pesa, in Kenya

When Vodafone and Safaricom launched their m-payment service M-PESA in Kenya in March 2007, they gained 2.37 million subscribers in little over one year. According to Dr. Nick Hughes, Head of International Mobile Payment Solutions for Vodafone Group, this is "an uptake which has surprised us but shows the need in the marketplace for very simple, secure and low-cost services."[11]

(b) G-cash in Philippine

In the Philippines, the Central Bank collaborated closely with Globe and SMART, the country's two mobile operators, to develop a framework for mobile banking that incorporated consumer protection into mobile-operator business model. The Central Bank issued guidelines in 2005, shortly after the launch of Globe's G-Cash product, and it continues to engage with a variety of stakeholders today, including most recently the equity stake that Globe took in one of the country's saving banks.

(c) m-Chek in India

It is one of pilot project for m-Banking in India taken up by m-Chek India Payment Systems Pvt. Ltd and Grameen Koota-Micro Finance Institution to implement mobile payments in the micro credit sector. To take this beyond the pilot phase, m-Chek needs to tie up with a bank. Under Reserve Bank of India (RBI) norms, mobile payments have to be routed only through bank or credit card accounts.

There is lots of potential for harnessing benefits of m-banking technology for inclusive growth as mobile penetration in rural India has witnessed a rapid growth in the past. m-Banking is at very initiate stage of pilot testing by most of MFIs. However, some progress has been made in the recent past through collaborative efforts of banks, telecos and MFIs. In the absence of any common regulatory framework or guidelines, m-Banking in India will take some more time to pick up at national level as one of effective tools for financial inclusion. The Reserve Bank of Pakistan has taken a pro-active approach and established transparent and detailed guidelines for banking agents and mobile banking well-ahead of any large-scale implementation. It recently joined forces with the country's telecommunication authority and set up a joint regulatory committee to propose medication to the mobile banking regulatory framework. The bank also created a cross-industry, multi-sector "Stakeholders Group" to address product, operational and technical issues for mobile banking. If RBI can follow a similar collaborative, pro-active and risk-based approach to craft supportive guidelines, it would remove one the major obstacles for MFIs to develop transformational delivery channels in India.

In India, there are about 300milliom mobile subscribers in India and has witness an exponential growth of 50% pa in 2008-09. Considering large no of mobile phone subscribers in rural India, m-banking will be the *future of microfinance* in India for accelerating financial inclusion provided there is collaborative and convergent efforts of all the stakeholders such as policy makers, regulators, banks, telecos, MFIs, etc. supported by enabling environment backed up by adequate ICT infrastructure in rural India.

10.8. Issues and Challenges of Adopting New Technologies

The promise of technology to enable breakthrough in the way microfinance is delivered around the world is quite encouraging, but there is still some important obstacles to be overcome in the near future. Some of issues and challenges for adopting new technology and alternative delivery channels are discussed below:

(a) High capital cost

Generally the greatest barrier to information technology is the cost. Most of the MFIs in India are lack capital except a few big MFIs. High initial capital investment required for any technology solution has been one of big challenges for many MFIs in India. SIDBI and NABARD financial support to MFIs for new technology adoption is appreciable. Open software solution of MIFOS, Grameen Foundation which are made available to small MFIs at free of course is also one solution to this challenge. Share of resources, through common ICT infrastructure under consortium of MFIs can also drive down the cost of the solution, making it affordable to deliver financial products and services to those living in rural areas. One of such example is FINO software solutions which can provide core banking solution for all the MFIs under one platform and IT infrastructure.

(b) Technology integration and risk

Indirect channels such as ATM, agents, smart card, POS, mobile-banking, etc. require integration and data synchronization between third-party platforms and those of the MFI. For example, an MFI's banking application must 'talk' to the partner's IT system using the same communication protocol. For mobile banking, an MFI needs to connect to a mobile operator's platform either directly or, more likely, through the black box of a mobile-technology vendor that provides application development and switching capability.[12] Experience has shown that, though manageable, this is one of the biggest hurdles to overcome. The security in relaying a customer's personal and financial data to the MFI is another concern, and, depending on the risk threshold set by the RBI and the MFI's own risk unit. MFIs must ensure that an adequate level of encryption and safe storage employed so that data cannot be intercepted or otherwise compromised.

(c) Manpower problems

Many MFI's have ambitions to explore different innovations but fall short on actual execution. Small or start-up MFIs in particular is often understaffed for all the initiatives being pursued, and managers lack the bandwidth necessary to mange the milestones, budget and scope. To obtain channels expertise in the short-term, MFIs can hire external consultants. Channel consultants should ideally have a broad understanding of multiple delivery channels and their implementation so that they can recommend appropriate channel solutions for the institution and support the MFI to bring them to fruition.

In the long-run, training and capacity building for MFI staff will be necessary for multi-channel strategies to become the norm for MFIs. Some conference, such as the Mobile Money Transfer series organised by Clarion Events, now include comprehensive workshops on everything from customer adoption to technology-vendor selection for mobile banking. Other centers that already offer training such as MicroSave, Sa-Dhan etc could expand their offering or provide separate training on channel development and implementation.

(d) Regulatory constraints

Though a number of leading or large MFIs have become NBFC under RBI regulation, majority of MFIs are still unregulated thereby limiting launching of alternative channels. For example, NGOs cannot legally offer savings accounts; they cannot offer useful services, such as account-to-account transfers, utility payments, or cash-in or cash-out transactions through retail-agent channels. Thus being NGO (and sometimes being a finance company) limits the types of financial services the institution can offer and thus curtails its ability to launch transactional payment channels.

In India, for example, the regulators permit only full-fledged commercial banks to offer mobile banking services and develop banking-agent programs; even regulated non-bank finance companies are not allowed to develop these channels. One of the reasons for mobile operators to partner with banks is "regularly cover", but non-bank MFIs cannot provide this. Moreover, NGOs cannot be a member of the major payment networks, such as Visa and MasterCard, and can only access these networks through partnerships with member banks.

(e) Infrastructure bottleneck

Finally, the infrastructure in the country or region that is needed to support certain alternative channels is not always reliable. This includes sporadic power supply, a weak wireless telecom infrastructure and the limited availability of a national switch to process electronic transactions across multiple payment platforms. Almost all well-developed ATM networks, for example, rely on these three characteristics to allow customers real-time access to their funds in nearby locations.

Improving the country's energy and communications infrastructure is imperative for certain remote channels to flourish, though naturally financial inclusion is but one of the many infrastructure-dependent activities which government decision-makers must consider, and infrastructure typically takes years to improve to a satisfactory level. In meantime, MFIs may have to consider alternatives –such as back-up power generators, fixed-line communications, and multiple interfaces with bank (en lieu of a broad switch)-that allow them to offer a robust and reliable banking channel to their customers.

10.9 .Microfinance and ICT: A Way Forward

ICTs will continue to impact microfinance operations worldwide. As prices of relevant technology like ATMs, biometrics, voice recognition, smart-cards, and PDAs continue to fall, more MFIs will be able to take advantage of the benefits they offer. New technologies and applications are constantly being developed aimed at increasing the reach and efficiency of microfinance organizations. Improvement will make operations more secure, increase transparency (and thus scalability), reduce repetitive tasks, and provide data mining capabilities that will allow MFIs to compete effectively and better mange their operations.

While mobile money is now in its emerging stages, it is rapidly moving toward consolidation and growth. Industry leaders are clear that what is needed now is sustained action: experimentation and innovation by firms with mobile money business models and by government in the regulatory framework to make them possible. It is important to sustain and even diversify the opportunities for mobile network operators, banks, technology providers and other interested firms to share experience and learn about business and technology innovations in the mobile money space. At the same time, it is important to establish and support similar forums for regulators to exchange policy innovations across countries.

Many of the more promising alternative channels will require building relationships, agreements, and alliances—sometimes with parties unfamiliar to MFIs – and thus multi-sector dialogue and collaboration will be a key skill that all stakeholders will need to enhance. Ultimately, MFIs and other stakeholders need to develop mutually beneficial channel solutions that both create business value for the institution and enhance the availability, accessibility and affordability of financial services to poor.

A stable and conducive policy environment is necessary for other initiatives such as single credit bureau, biometric IDs or smart cards and weather stations. The sector at this stage needs a laissez faire environment; policy makers should be on continuous vigil and deliver concurrent improvement in policy and regulation. All organizations engaged in microfinance should be brought together under a single legal status and regulatory authority.

Providing connectivity to rural India provides the much-needed access to information and power. Active participations and collaborative efforts of various agencies like banks, MFIs, corporate houses, telecoms, Government, regulators, etc are needed for systematic integrations and harmonic synchronization between microfinance and ICT infrastructure for accelerating financial inclusion in the coming years. It will create the necessary atmosphere to create wealth and enable rural India. We now need to build on this and work towards empowering India.

NOTES

1. ITC Ltd (2004), "Report and Accounts-2004, Kolkata, quoted by Y.C.Nanda," Micro Finance- A route to Reach Rural Poor", *The Journal of Indian Institute of Banking and Finance*, October-December 2004, p26.
2. Laura I. Fredrick (2005), "Information Technology Innovations for Scaling Rural Microfinance Outreach", exchange
3. Bhatnagar, Subhash and Robert Schware (2000), *Information and Communication Technology in Development: Cases from India"*, New Delhi-Sage Publications.
4. www.trai.gov.in
5. Nirvikar Singh, *Information Technology and Rural Development in India*, University of California, Santa Cruz, USA.
6. www.itcportal.com
7. www.nabard.org
8. CGAP, *Using Electronic Payments to Build Inclusive Financial Systems* (draft), CGAP, USA 2005 (E)
9. Beth Kenkins, *Developing Mobile Money Ecosystems*, Washington, DC: IFC and the Harvard Kennedy School.
10. Department for International Development (DFID), *The Enabling Environment for Mobile Banking in Africa.*
11. Cheryl Frankiewicz, AfriCap, "Information Technology as a strategic tool for Microfinance in Africa-A seminar Report", Calmeadow.
12. David Cracknell (2004), " Electronic Banking For the Poor: Panacea, Potential and Pitfalls, Microsave.

11

Management Information System (MIS) for Microfinance Institutions (MFIs)

11.1. Introduction to MIS

Over the past 5 to 10 years, microfinance institutions (MFIs) have been paying increasing attention to information systems, particularly management information systems (MIS). As both practitioners and donors have become aware of the great need for formal and informal financial institutions to manage large amounts of data, the drive to improve the manipulation and understanding of these data has grown. Information lies at the very heart of microfinance. Whether it is by hand or by computer, microfinance institutions maintain large amounts of critical business data, from basic client information to detailed analyses of portfolio statistics. These data must be stored, manipulated, and, most important, presented coherently to system users so that they can make sound management decisions.

A management information system (MIS) is the series of processes and actions involved in capturing raw data, processing the data into usable information, and disseminating the information to users in the form needed. Having a management information system (MIS) has become essential in the operations of microfinance institutions (MFIs), as their number of clients as well as product offerings continue to grow.

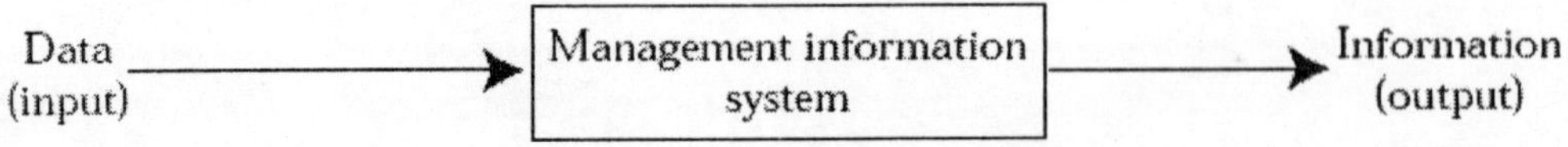

An MIS is not simply a computer program, and it involves more than just calculating numbers. Information management is first and foremost people communicating with one another about events that affect the work of their organization. The chart of accounts, all the forms used by an institution—from receipts to loan applications to staff vacation requests—meetings, reports, policies and procedures, the staffing structure, job descriptions, the planning process, and, yes, the computer software—all these and more influence the flow of information in an institution and so, together, make up the management information system.

A good information system should act as a conduit through which raw data becomes useful and useable information. A good information system is a necessary tool for managing an institution successfully. This assertion, however, begs two questions: What is a good information system? And how does one determine whether a system is good?

A high quality management information system (MIS) is a key component of any high performing microfinance institution (MFI). Information systems allow MFIs to reduce time spent on paperwork; more effectively monitor both staff and clients, and quickly roll out new products and services. Management information systems remain one of the least understood aspects of microfinance operations. MFI staff are often unaware of what an MIS should do and thus in what ways their current MIS is lacking. This confusion is compounded by the large amounts of attention paid to the latest "transformational" technology for microfinance operations, such as biometric-enabled ATMs, which often results in MFI managers chasing the latest fad rather than devoting energy to improving their core backend technology.

Management Information System can be a strategic tool in making Microfinance Institutions (MFIs) more efficient and effective. MFIs can reach more people in a more economic way by implementing the right Management Information System (MIS). While a few MFIs are making good use of technology, the majority are facing difficulties in getting the right solution. The back-office MIS is the backbone of any Information System solution and yet it has not received much attention. MFIs, whether large or small, need to have a strong back-office MIS before attempting to deploy any advanced front-end applications or delivery channels. These would be worthless without having a strong and flexible back-office MIS in place.

11.2. Benefits of MIS

A good Management Information System (MIS) is the heart of any organization and this is true for MFIs as well. For example, MFIs may have capable and motivated staff, but if they lack systematized information, they will be unable to perform up to their potential. A sound MIS is the key to achieve sustainability as it helps in providing the right type of information in achieving the sustainability. It helps in reducing default, optimal portfolio, establishing sustainable interest rates, improving operational efficiency, generating reports at various levels for various stakeholders and reviews the progress.

Some of the direct benefits of high quality MIS are given as under[1]:

a) A high quality MIS can reduce cost by doing away with time spent on paperwork.

b) It can allow for more effective monitoring of customers and MFI employees. Credit officers no longer have to sort through lists of repayment records to identify problem borrowers and MFI management no longer must wait for months for repayment and customer acquisition to filter up to them in the form of paper reports before they can get a good picture of what is going on in branch offices.

c) By increasing transparency of operations, an MIS can reduce the risk of outright fraud.

d) A quality MIS allows MFIs to modify existing products or add new products by making minor changes to the back-end software. MFIs that rely on paper-based processes often have to design entirely new forms each time a product is changed.

e) A quality MIS may lead to more, and cheaper, access to capital as banks are more willing to lend to MFI with a stable and transparent reporting system in place;

f) Lastly, a stable and robust MIS is a necessary foundation for MFIs that want to experiment with more advanced technology options such as ATMs, POSs/smartcards, or credit scoring. MFIs which adopt any of these new technologies without already having a high quality MIS in place inevitably find themselves awash in a flood of useful, yet unmanageable data.

As more and more microfinance institutions scale up their activities managers are becoming increasingly aware of the need to improve their information systems. For any institutions, methodological issues, staff development, and even financing are no longer the critical constraints to growth. Instead, the most pressing need is often a system to track the status of their portfolios in a timely and accurate manner. The reliability of such systems can make the difference between the success and failure of lending operations and therefore, of an institution. An institution that develops a system capable of producing accurate, timely and comprehensive information on operations, especially on the loan portfolio, will strengthen its financial performance and expand its clients reach.

11.3. Difficulties in Adopting MIS by MFIs

A number of MIS solutions are emerging. Currently, there are 56 MIS applications listed on the CGAP website, although more are being used by various organizations that are not publicized. Despite the advances in MIS, practical experience shows that the acquisition of a suitable MIS is not simple. Many MFIs are struggling with their MIS. Some of the reasons for these difficulties are:

a) Microfinance operations are unique and complex, compared to commercial, retail banking.

b) The Microfinance sector is still evolving and lacks standardization in its procedures, methodologies, customer characteristics, type of transactions and reporting.

c) There is no of-the-shelf software available that can address the requirements of every MFI.

d) Those MIS that are available are complex and costly for adoption by MFIs.

e) MFIs lack human and organizational capacity to develop or select an appropriate MIS.

f) MFIs operate in remote and difficult areas where communication and power infrastructure do not exist, and are therefore constrained from using IT equipment required to run MIS applications.[2]

g) Insufficient organizational and human capacity.

h) Unavailability of suitable MIS applications for microfinance.

i) Diversity in business processes and frequent changes in procedures.

j) Risk of failure of the MIS.

k) Diversity of geography and language.

l) Unavailability of vendors and their capacity to implement and support IT solutions.

m) High cost of IT solutions for MFIs.

n) Lack of commitment of management and key decision-makers within an MFI.

o) Lack of awareness about the importance of IT.

11.4. Manual vs. Computerized MIS

The microfinance sector is also quite diverse in its use of information systems. Generally there are the following three types:

1. Manual System	Some MFIs still rely on manual systems, which involve maintenance of records in forms and ledgers. Organizations having manual systems are either small micro-credit programs or NGOs.
2. Semi-automated System	More than 50% of MFIs are operating in a semi-automated mode. Within this category, the spreadsheet is the common tool being used either in conjunction with a manual system or with an MIS application that does not fulfill the information requirements of the MFI. The majority of non-regulated MFIs have semi automated systems.
3. Fully Automated System	Few MFIs are fortunate enough to have a fully automated and integrated MIS, fulfilling the whole information requirements of the organization. Such systems are existent with banks or regulated MFIs.

(a) Manual systems

Some of the disadvantages of manual Information Systems are:

a) Too laborious and time consuming.

b) Prone to errors.

c) Data manipulation and analysis is very difficult.

d) Maintenance of large amount of data is almost impossible.

e) Data and information is not secured.

f) Loosely controlled.

g) Highly inflexible (addition of new products and change in business processes can not be made).

h) Business continuity is at risk in case of damage to information due to fire, water or any other disaster.

i) Reporting is very cumbersome, time consuming and difficult.

(b) Computerized MIS

There is no doubt that "*the right information*" at "*the right time*" at "*the right place*", is crucial in decision making. Therefore, information and data is considered among the most valuable assets fundamental to the success of an organization. The primary roles of the MIS are to capture information, create new information, store information, and convey information to the user.

The two major objectives of MFIs are Outreach and Sustainability. MIS can add substantial value in achieving both the objectives:

a) A major advantage of MIS is that it provides easy access to accurate and up-to-date information. For example, loan officers get information on loans that need follow-up, branch manager's can monitor daily progress of the branch, and senior management can get a full picture of the portfolio performance and quality. Customers also get quick information on their accounts, payments and balances.

b) Detailed information is captured on customers and their activities that can then be used to assess client business to assess impact. It is also useful in tracking historical information of clients.

c) Activities, such as disbursements, repayments, deposits, withdrawals and money transfers are completed faster, better controlled and with minimum opportunity for errors.

d) Information is produced in user-required formats, which facilitates better understanding, setting priorities, objectives and strategy.

e) Key performance indicators provide an overview of the organization's performance, efficiency and effectiveness of business procedures so that timely adjustments can be made.

f) Use of Information and Communication Technology (ICT) helps make MFI services more interactive, accessible and transparent.

g) In terms of innovation, ICT provides full flexibility to structure products and services to the needs of its target group.

h) Efficiency and productivity of staff is increased, as they are able to manage more products, customers, and transactions in less time.

i) To meet target market needs, introduction of new products and setting procedures is easy and can be quickly applied throughout the branch network.

j) It can also provide the flexibility to integrate with other applications and delivery mechanisms.

k) MIS lowers transaction cost, increases productivity, reduces risk of failure, and pushes the boundaries beyond bricks and mortar infrastructure to carryout business.

11.5. Components of MIS

While the MIS needs to fulfill the business requirements of the organization, but other factors including appropriate infrastructure and hardware are also important in the success and optimal utilization of information systems. We can categorize the components of an information system solution into five areas:

1. ***Physical Architecture (Electricity/Power & communication infrastructure)***	Physical architecture consists of basic wires or cables to gateways and powerhouses. Together with buildings, offices, and computers, the architecture provides services of voice, data, image and video transmission while the consistent power supply keeps everything live and running. Every system needs electric power, and if systems are required to communicate, then there must be an appropriate communication infrastructure. Usually MFIs operate in remote and underdeveloped areas where this is lacking.
2. **Network**	Three types of environment setups could be made. ▪ Stand alone Environment; MIS is run on individual PCs and data is stored locally. ▪ Local Area Network (LAN); PCs are connected together to create a LAN. The network can be either peer-to-peer or client/server. Desirable is the Client/server network where data is stored and shared through a server in a secure way. ▪ Wide Area Network (WAN); Branch offices and operation units can be connected through a WAN. It requires proper communication infrastructure and involves high cost to establishing a WAN. For online systems WAN is critical.
3. **Hardware**	Type of hardware depends on the network environment. A client-server environment requires server and switch for connecting the workstations/ PCs.
4. **Database**	Generally databases can be categorized as local and client-server. Each category has its own strengths and weaknesses.
5. **Application**	A combination of business processes and procedures, user interface, reports and controls operate on top of the backend system. A large variety of software development and report generation tools are available and used to write software applications.

Advantages and disadvantages of local databases and client/server database are given as under:

Local databases *(Microsoft Access, FoxPro, Paradox, and file maker)*	**Client/Server databases** *(Oracle, DB2, SQL Server, MySQL, Sybase, and Informix)*
Strengths	**Strengths**
▪ Easy to set up and configure	▪ Database Management System
▪ Low hardware requirement	▪ Excellent performance under load
▪ Low cost	▪ Design to handle large data
▪ Good performance with less data load	▪ Manages large number of concurrent users ▪ Scalable with hardware ▪ Detects and corrects data corruption dynamically ▪ Rollback for incomplete and inaccurate entries ▪ Highly secured ▪ Perfect in network environment and for web applications
Weaknesses	**Weaknesses**
▪ No database management	▪ Complex to configure
▪ Unable to handle large data	▪ High cost
▪ Risk of data corruption	▪ License fee per user
▪ Data is not well protected	▪ High-end Hardware requirement
▪ Low performance when used by concurrent users and data load	▪ Requires technical skills
▪ Not scalable with hardware	
▪ Low transaction control, there is no rollback for incomplete and inaccurate entries	

11.6. Functional Parts of Core MIS

The backbone of any Information System (IS) is the core MIS as it holds the critical data, and manages the information. All other systems are add-ons. A simple core MIS comprises of two parts:

Database	Data structure; an organized set of tables designed to the needs of the business. All data of the organization resides in these tables.
Application Software	Comprises of the user interface, business processes, procedures, reports and queries.

Architecture of Computerized MIS system

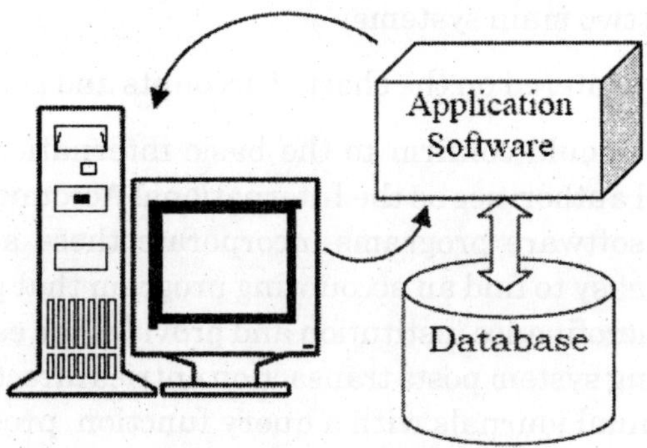

Adopting an MIS is strategically important for MFIs. They need to undertake a careful and detailed assessment of current and future needs before committing to a particular solution. Much of the system's flexibility, expandability, and robustness depend on the strength of the backend components. Strong MIS can deliver cost-effective integration of data, channels and processes, facilitating a single consolidated view of the whole portfolio. MIS can provide easy data entry for the backend database, making consolidation easy to achieve. Various studies reveal that a large number of MFIs operate manual systems despite having some kind of MIS in place. One of the reasons the MIS does not cope with the changing needs of the organization is that the backend does not have the right structure. It is important for both the MFIs and microfinance software vendors to concentrate and strengthen the MIS.

Core Functions of MIS for Microfinance

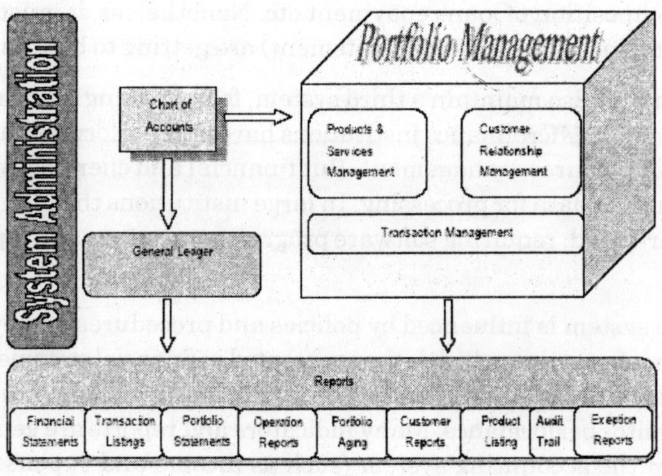

Source: Ali Ahmad, *"Management Information System (MIS) for Microfinance", the First Microfinance Bank Ltd.*

A full management information system includes all the systems an institution uses to generate the information that guides management's decisions and actions. A microfinance institution generally has two main systems:

(a) ***Accounting system:*** centered on the chart of accounts and general ledger.

Accounting systems should confirm to the basic international accounting standards developed by such central authorities as the International Accounting Standards Committee (IASC). General Ledge software programs incorporate these accounting standards and convention, so it is fairly easy to find an accounting program that performs at least the basic functions required of a microfinance institution and provides the essential accounting report. A computerized accounting system posts transaction entries directly to the general ledger. It replaces the various manual journals with a query function, producing reports as needed. Accounting systems can be cash-based (accounting for income and expenses when cash changes hands) or accrual based. Otherwise the Financial Statements will not accurately reflect the real flow of expenses. Accruing interest means calculating at month-end or year-end the interest owed but as yet unpaid. This unpaid interest is considered income for the period considered.

(b) ***Portfolio tracking system:*** covering the performance of accounts for each financial product offered by the institution.

Portfolio system, by contrast, have no standards or widely accepted guidelines for loan tracking on which to draw. And they must reflect operating procedures workflow, which vary widely from institution to institution. As a result, each software program for loan tracking differs in the information tracked, the kinds of reports generated and most important, and the features included. Key features vary widely among loan tracking software programs such as the type of lending methodology supported, the method of calculating interest and fees, the frequency and composition of loan repayment etc. Nonetheless, it must be emphasized that the report formats (including financial statement) are getting to be standardized.

Some institutions also maintain a third system, for gathering data on client impact, often at the behest of donors. Microfinance institutions have other information management needs, such as for human resource management. But financial and client activities generate by far the heaviest volume of data for processing. In large institutions the MIS tends to be mostly or entirely computer-based, requiring software programs to capture and report on the necessary information.

The portfolio system is influenced by policies and procedures and by methodology. Data are processed into information, which is then presented in financial statements and management reports. Influencing the form and content of these reports are the indicators chosen by the institution to monitor performance. Many indicators and reports are generated by combining information from the accounting system (such as income and expenses) with information from the portfolio system (such as number, amount and size of loans or number of staff). Although independent, the two systems share data and must be compatible.

Parts of MIS for MFIs

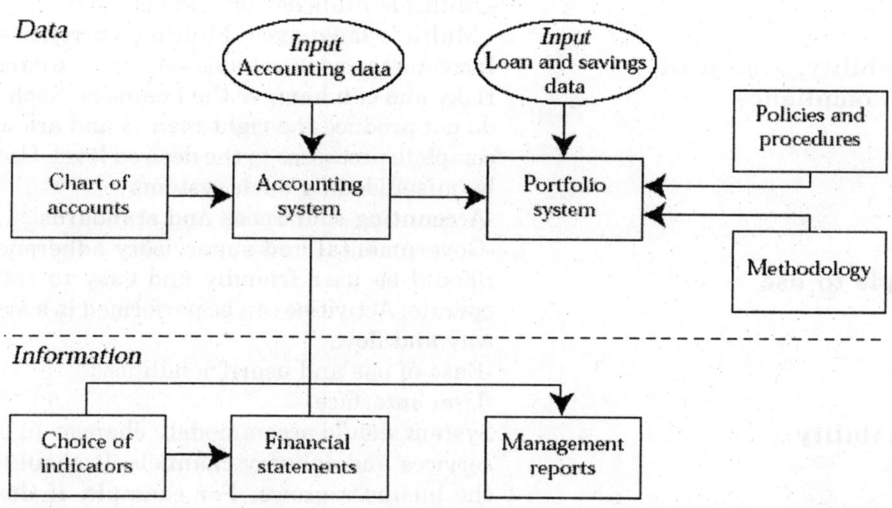

Source: *Charles Water Field and Nick Ramsing, Management Information Systems for Microfinance Institutions, CGAP*

11.7. Characteristics of a Good MIS

MFIs face great challenges in choosing the right system solution that can best fit their business needs. An MIS for microfinance must have the following characteristics:

(a) Cost effectiveness Total ownership and lifetime system operations costs, including hardware, software, network, infrastructure and human resource.
-Pricing and costs

(b) Functionality & flexibility Fulfill maximum of the current business requirement and flexible enough to incorporate future changes. Capture and generate relevant information on an individual, group, and at a consolidated level.
- Accounting package
- Portfolio tracking
- Deposit monitoring
- Customer information system
- Customer-centric vs. account-centric
- Institutional types
- Lending methodologies
- Loan interest types
- Savings and deposit account types

	- Deposit interest types - Payment types - Payment frequencies - Multiple branches or regions - Multiple languages- Multiple currencies
(c) **Reliability, standard and compliance**	Incomplete and unreliable systems are dangerously risky and can hamper the business. Such systems do not produce the right results and are unable to complete processes to the desired level. Users could be misguided by such systems -Accounting soundness and standards -Governmental and supervisory adherence
(d) **Simple to use**	Should be user friendly and easy to set up and operate. Activities can be performed in a systematic way and flow. -Ease of use and user-friendliness -User interface
(e) **Scalability**	System should accommodate changes to products, services and delivery channels. It should grow as the business grows. For example, if the system design is scalable, it can be run on an individual PC, Local Area Network (LAN) or Wide Area Network (WAN).
(f) **Integration**	Combining data from multiple sources is of great importance to microfinance. Integration of branches to get single consolidated picture should be a priority.
(g) **Administration and Support**	-Security -Backup and recovery -Fault tolerance and robustness -End-of-period processing -Support infrastructure and maintenance -Version control and upgrade strategy
(h) **Technical Specifications and Correctness**	-Technology and architecture -Performance - Number and date handling

MIS reports

Most MFIs are required to report to a broad array of outside organisations from the government to banks to donors. The MIS should have the capacity to generate all of these reports quickly and easily. A good MIS system should able to generate all the required MIS reports needed by MFIs. MIS should be able to automatically print a statement listing which centres the credit officer should visit that day and the amount each individual member of those centres should repay. This saves the credit officer time in having to calculate repayment amounts and avoids unnecessary human error. The MIS should allow credit officers to record repayment details by only entering in information for those borrowers who have not repaid the full amount on time. Because the vast majority of borrowers do repay the full amount on time, this saves the credit officer countless hours of data entry. The MIS should allow users in branch offices to easily send data updates to the head office for aggregation. In the case that some of the branches do not have internet access, the MIS should allow branch users to easily create CDs (or other storage devices) with details of recent updates and allow head office users to easily import updated information from the CD. In addition to this, the MIS should be secure, requiring all users to login with a username and password and tracking which updates are made by which users.

11.8. MIS for Different Categories of MFIs

Most microfinance institutions can be placed in one of three categories of need for information management, related to their stage of development.

(a) MIS for start up/small MFIs: In the first category are small, young institutions with fewer than, say, 2,000 and no short-term plans for significant expansion in clientele or product range. These are often multiservice nongovernmental organizations (NGOs), offering financial services as one of several service lines. Their needs are basic, and they can get by with a simple system to keep tabs on the quality of the portfolio. A simple system, too, is often all that their staff and budget can handle.

(b) MIS for growing/Medium MFIs: In the second category are medium-size institutions that have 2,000–10,000 clients and are embarking on significant growth. Many of these institutions are experiencing growing pains—they need to restructure to deal with their growth, bring in new senior managers capable of managing the increased activity and resources, and make their operating procedures more systematic. These institutions now require a much more rigorous MIS—one that has solid security features and a thorough audit trail and handles savings accounts and a large volume of transactions. But many lack the skilled staff to operate a complex and rigorous MIS, and the financial resources to purchase a commercial system or develop a customized MIS in-house. In sum, they need many of the features of a high-end system, but aren't yet ready to maintain one.

(c) MIS for Large MFIs: The third category consists of large institutions with more than 10,000 clients and plans for continued growth. These mature institutions generally have well developed operating procedures and capable staff, particularly in accounting and information systems. These institutions are so large that they can generally justify the cost of substantially modifying an existing MIS—or developing a new one— to better meet their needs. The cost can easily exceed $100,000, but the alternative would be loss of automation of some functions, with resulting inefficiencies.

Some of the popular software used by Indian MFIs are given as under:

Software Package	*Company/ Organisation*	*Cost*
FINO Core Banking Solution	FINO	Rs. 25 per account for annual maintenance fees
MIFOS	Grameen Foundation	Free
Delphix	BASIX	Free
Bankers Realm	Craft Silicon	USD 15,000/-
Micro Financier	Java Softech	Not published
Salesforce.com	Salesforce.com	Free

11.9. Challenges faced by MFIs for Implementing MIS Solution

Microfinance is a rapidly changing industry. Due to the ongoing evolution of the industry, MFIs face difficulty in defining business objectives, needs, priorities and limitations for acquisition of an MIS solution. There is lack of standardization within the microfinance sector, and business practices of MFIs differ from each other. Consequently, software developers face problems in coming-up with an MIS that can be used by most of the MFIs. Common failures are due to ill defined business process and procedures.

a) There is a shortage of skilled professionals who can understand technology as well as the microfinance industry, and be able to suggest the right solution. Such professionals can act as a bridge in filling the gap between use of ICT and microfinance operations.

b) Majority of the MFIs do not have the technical capacity and required resources to understand, adopt and implement MIS solutions.

c) Most MIS solutions are not affordable to the majority of MFIs.

d) In some cases there is a lack of vision and commitment from the management towards use of technology.

e) Integration is becoming one of the big challenges, as most of the MIS solutions for microfinance are built on weak platforms, thus not being flexible and scalable enough to integrate with emerging technologies and delivery channels.

f) There is poor information sharing on successful MIS deployments within the microfinance as well as the financial sector.

g) ICT vendors still do not see the tremendous business opportunity and growth in the microfinance industry thus are reluctant to invest and establish strategic partnerships with MFIs.

h) Power and communication infrastructure, which is the foundation for hosting ICT services, is inadequate in those areas where MFIs operate.

i) Non-availability of efficient technical support by vendors

11.10 Designing and Implementing a Computerized MIS

Designing and implementing a computerized management information system involves following:[3]

a) Discuss with the chief functionaries, advising them about the usefulness of the information system to be provided and get official permission (contract) to design and implement MIS.

b) Conduct needs assessment and requirement specification including levels of analysis mapping.

c) Identify input variables, records and information flows while modeling and diagramming microfinance processes for all levels. Finalize the necessary input documents and the periodically thereof for use in for input to reach processing center.

d) Discuss and finalize the information require at different levels e.g. client field workers, supervisors, project managers, board members, wholesalers etc. Document the above as well as necessary system analysis with necessary flow chart.

e) Define calculated variables, ratios and indicators for tracking and monitoring performance and activities at all levels.

f) Design effective reports and outputs at all levels.

g) Document all output reports, their periodicity and number of copies for use.

h) Prepare a use needs assessment and requirements specifications document to facilitate preparation of detailed requirement specifications that would form the basis for development and customization of the accounting and management information system.

i) Translate the above into program codes using appropriate front end and back end design languages.

j) Debug the software codes before installation.

k) Prepare technical and other manuals.

l) Install software at the site of client (MFI).

m) Conduct trial run and testing of the software.

n) Finalize installation of software.

o) Maintain the software for free (1 year) and with maintenance contract (later year).

11.11. MIS Reports for MFI

Reports are essential for distributing information and thus enabling users of that information to perform their jobs well and make appropriate decisions. A good MIS will therefore produce reports in a hierarchical structure, starting with detailed transaction reports, useful at the lowest level and then moving up to summarized financial statement and operational information needed by senior management and the board of directors. The report should be designed so that the detailed at one level support the summarized information at the next level.

Types of MIS Reports

Saving Activity Reports

- Saving report
- Saving Account activity
- Teller savings report
- Activity savings account by branch and product
- Dormant saving account by branch and product
- Upcoming maturing time deposits
- Saving concentration report
- General Reports

Loan Activity Report

- Loan Repayment schedule

	▪ Loan account activity ▪ Comprehensive client status report ▪ Group membership report ▪ Teller loan report ▪ Active loans by loan officer ▪ Pending clients by loans officer ▪ Daily payments report by loan officer ▪ Portfolio concentration report
Insurance Report	▪ Insurance account activity ▪ Comprehensive Client ▪ Premiums paid report ▪ Claims report-processed and pending etc
Portfolio Quality Report	▪ Detailed aging of portfolio at risk by branch ▪ Delinquent loan by loan officer ▪ Delinquent loans by branch and product ▪ Summary of portfolio at risk by Loan Officer ▪ Summary of portfolio at risk by Branch and product ▪ Detailed delinquent loan history by branch ▪ Loan write-off recuperation report ▪ Aging loans and calculation of reserve ▪ Staff incentive report
Income Statement Reports	▪ Summary income statement ▪ Detailed income statement ▪ Income statement by branch or region ▪ Income statement by program ▪ Summary actual-to-budget income statement ▪ Detailed actual-to-budget income statement ▪ Adjusted income statement
Balance Sheet Report	▪ Summary balance sheet ▪ Detailed balance sheet ▪ Programme format balance sheet ▪ Capital adequacy report
Cash Flow Report	▪ Cash Flow review ▪ Projected cash flow ▪ Gap reported
Other Reports	▪ General summary reports ▪ Salutatory reports ▪ Credit rating reports ▪ Specialized comparative reports ▪ Credit health reports

BOX-9: The challenges of integrating manual and computerized information

Systems: the experience of BRAC

BRAC is a Bangladeshi institution serving more than 1.5 million members through 330 branch offices. The head office needs to aggregate a vast amount of data, but branch offices are unable to computerize, so BRAC combines head office computerization with manual branch systems. The process is fraught with problems, but a redesign of the system is expected to solve most of them.

The high degree of standardization in BRAC's rules and procedures ensures that the branch-level manual systems work smoothly. Centralization problems and bureaucratic delays enter the picture once the information leaves the branch office.

Weekly collection forms are completed manually by the loan officers in the branch office. These forms are then checked by the branch and account supervisors before being sent to the regional office, resulting in a three-day delay. The regional office rechecks the forms and transfers the data to a new form—another five-day delay. Once the data are received at the head office, the computer department takes an average of three weeks to process them. Checking for and correcting errors—most related to borrower ID numbers—accounts for about half the time. Yet an external consultant has estimated that 40 percent of the report contents still contain errors. Adding to the large volume of information, BRAC computerizes both credit and savings data on a weekly basis for every borrower (rather than for groups or centers).

The work effort is compounded by the involvement of three departments—the computer, accounting, and MIS departments—leading to a need for regular reconciliation of numbers and to chronic irregularities. The result has been unreliable information, produced in an untimely manner and at significant staff cost. BRAC plans to pilot a new MIS to correct these flaws. The computer department will produce a pre-prepared sheet for each member with the expected weekly loan installments and savings deposits. Branch staff will simply record the exceptions.

Since most members pay on schedule, this system will vastly reduce the information that the accounting department has to enter. The automated forms will also eliminate errors in borrower ID numbers.

BRAC has learned that for computerizing data, systems must be carefully thought out to minimize the potential for data entry errors. Once introduced, errors are difficult to weed out, and doing so can result in significant staff time costs and delays in getting information to decision makers.

BOX -10: Managing Performance through Reporting and Information Systems

How SHARE did it

SHARE is a microfinance institution operating in the southern Indian state of Andhra Pradesh. Since its establishment in 1993, SHARE has seen its clientele grow to roughly 3,500. It plans to reach an active client base of 11,000 over the next few years by doubling its staff and expanding from four branches to eight.

A critical part of SHARE's expansion strategy is to replace its manual information system with a computerized one that enables management to keep a finger on the pulse of operations. SHARE decided to build a home-grown, cost-effective system from the ground up. At the end of last year it hired a local MIS specialist to design and develop the MIS, install computers in branch offices, and train staff in the use of the new system. To gain a good understanding of SHARE's operations, the specialist worked in one of its branch offices for a few months, and he sought continuous feedback from management and staff about their information reporting needs. To decentralize the system, SHARE plans to equip each of its branch offices with a Pentium computer. The staff members being trained in the use of the new system are working closely with the MIS specialist to iron out any kinks before the system is installed in all the branches. These staff members will then help train others. The old and new systems are expected to coexist for as long as six months while staff adjust to the new one.

SHARE's MIS builds on a weekly report generated by branch offices. This report contains a brief narrative from the branch manager on key statistics for the week—the number of groups forming, number and amount of loans disbursed, repayment rate, cash position, projections for the following week, and any new issues. Branch offices also prepare concise reports highlighting ongoing activities, documenting staff attendance and performance, and listing new members and groups. Branch office reports arrive every Monday morning at the head office, where the planning and monitoring department computerizes them to generate consolidated statements by Wednesday. These reports are used mainly by the planning department and the executive director. Branch managers and branch office accountants also prepare monthly balance sheets as well as reports of receipts and payments, group fund (member savings) positions, monthly progress toward targets, cash flow projections for the following month (by week), approved loan applications, and staff evaluations. An analysis of financial ratios for individual branches—all treated as profit centers—and for the institution is prepared and reviewed monthly. Quarterly and annual reports are generated by aggregating the data from the weekly and monthly reports.

The internal control system is set up so that two or three people, including the branch manager, cross-check the documentation and reporting for each group and group member. In the head office the monitoring and internal audit departments periodically supervise the flow of funds and verify the accuracy of financial records. Ultimately, the effectiveness of an MIS depends on how well it is used. SHARE uses the information its system generates to guide the actions of its management and staff in fulfilling its mission of extending financial services to extremely poor women.

NOTES

1. CMF focus note (2008), *Management Information System in Indian Microfinance.*
2. Ali Ahmad, *Management Information System (MIS) for Microfinance,* The First Microfinance Bank Ltd
3. Ramesh Arunachalam,"*Microfinance Institutions—Issue in Sustainability*-Chapter11, *Design and Implementation of MIS for MFIs.*

12

Microfinance: Issues, Challenges and Opportunities

"Micro-credit is something which is not going to disappear ...because this is a need of the people, whatever name you give it, you have to have those financial facilities coming to them because it is totally unfair... to deny the half the population of the world financial service"

- Dr. Muhammad Yunus, Founder –Bangladesh Grameen Bank, in March 2002.[1]

12.1. Industry Issues and Challenges

For the microfinance sector to expand in line with the need and demand, it is critical that MFIs achieve financial sustainability and reduce their dependence on donor funding. Despite the excellent prospects of the sector, with low loan default rates and untapped demand for financial services by low-income groups, only 1% of MFIs is self-sustainable and average Adjusted Return on Assets (AROA) is still negative across all continents.

Among the major reasons for such poor performance are MFIs' lack of access to recent technologies, their limited financial muscle and reliance on government funds, the higher costs of servicing a larger number of clients, each of them making use of very little financial services and the cost of outreaching customers in remote rural areas.[2]

Microfinance industry suffers from a number of issues that result from the fast and unorganized development.

a) Operational inefficiency of most MFIs: mainly due to their small size, fast growth, and lack of expertise of their management.

b) Information asymmetry between MFIs and their customers: Client information is costly and MFIs are reluctant to share it that makes the industry inefficient especially in competitive environments.

c) Lack of consistent information channels between industry and the investors/donors community, which result in an 'absurd gap' between supply and demand for funding.

d) Outreach poses difficulties due to lack of education of customers and their remote location.

An uncontrolled commercialization may result in an undesirable consolidation of profit oriented players at the expenses of smaller and less competitive ones targeting less profitable customer segments. This would go far beyond the 'paradigm shift' and may well lead to a destruction of the social objectives of microfinance. In order for all types of players to cohabit in the industry, each serving their respective segments in line with their specific financial and social objectives, it will be crucial that a socially responsible entity takes worldwide leadership and assists MFIs in their development, in particular by developing promoting and assisting in the implementation of cost-effective technological solutions.

Much progress has been made recently and more is promised on this count. Some of the key hurdles are anti-market measures such as price ceiling on bank loans less than $4K (Rs. 200 K) and subsidy based credit programs often promoted by state governments and supported by development agencies. The idea of a lenders forum has been mooted by SIDBI.[3] One of the main impediments to the creation of a standard credit bureau is the lack of a unique identifier e.g. national social security number. In order to nurture the sector, a review of certain structural and regulator issues is required.

Microfinance tends to be concentrated in rural areas as opposed to urban areas and in South India as opposed to North India. 58% of NABARD's clients live in one of the four states that make up South India and 78% of loans facilitated by NABARD were distributed in South India. Furthermore, 8 of the top 10 MFIs work in South India. No one is entirely sure why microfinance is more concentrated in the South, but numerous hypotheses, mostly related to socio-economic and regulatory climate, have been given. Both existing players and new comers should reach out to untapped regions.

The microfinance market in India is not well developed in relation to the potential market, in terms of number of clients, range of services and range of institutional models.

a) With a concentration of microfinance in the South, outreach remains limited (about 6 million have access to micro financial services, while some 470 million Indians live on less than $ 1 per day). The potential for microfinance industry in India is still vast. The demand, however, calculated, still far outstrips the supply of microfinance services.

b) The Self Help Group model is still and will remain for some time the dominant model for microfinance in India. The Dominance is based primarily on the fact that the Government still places emphasis on the SHG and Bank linkage programs as the best means of channelling funds to the poor in rural areas. There are however limitations in this model in terms of sustainability. The delivery channel may change.

c) Outreach will increase significantly only if various institutions are allowed to co-exist, attitudes towards microfinance are changed. Barriers to entry and growth are removed, and capacity constraints are alleviated.

d) A search for new models is underway. Industry views differ on the ideal model for a microfinance institution, but converge on the notion of a distinct microfinance institution based on a non-bank financial company adapted to microfinance. These new models are required to allow for equity capital (new ownership structures) and for public savings, both signs of a more mature microfinance market.

e) There is excess liquidity in the banking system, mopped up by government borrowing. The challenge is to move money into the rural sector. At the same time, there is a need to address the saving issue. There is an abundance of rural savings, but there is a need for a system that allows reinvestment of more of these savings into microfinance institutions.

f) Three major constraints limit outreach : i) in the light of the experience of mandated lending under government poverty programs, formal financial institutions do not see the potential of microfinance as a profitable business, ii) small microfinance provides are unable to grow because of legal and regulatory constraints, iii) institutional capacity is a problem across the board.

12.2. Reaching the Poor: Issues in Microfinance Outreach

The need for MF is overwhelming and the positives of its impact are undeniable. The macro-economic conditions, such as low inflation economy with stable interest rates, favour the growth and scaling up of sustainable MF. MFIs such as SHARE have not only made an impact on the lives of the poor, they have also made profits, providing that sustainable MF achieves excellent social results.

Experience drawn from various development initiatives suggest that subsidies credit has limited utility in terms of its effect on poverty alleviation, and as some experts hold, it also discourages mainstream financial institutions form lending to the poor.

The evidence from microfinance (MF) practices the world over is that poor can save, they are willing to repay loans at commercial prices and they display excellent repayment performance, provided the loan products are suited to their income and consumption patterns. MF has refuted the traditional wisdom that the poor need subsidized credit to change. The scaling up of MF in India, thus, should be seen as a sustainable business activity rather than a social obligation. Despite the positives, MF outreach in the country is insufficient, geographically limited and not organized-sectors which limit its impact. In order to provide enabling environment for realizing the latent potential of MF in India, a close scrutiny of policy issues such as capital constraints, legal and structural constraints and socio-cultural constraints is required.

The liquidity condition of the financial sector in India is comfortable yet the MF sector faces a crunch in terms of smooth flow of funds.

The success of MF sector in India depends on the quality of SHGs and joint liability groups. The repayment performance of groups needs to be consistently high for any MF initiative to be successful. In addition, the groups need to be well trained in maintaining records of transactions to avoid any operational frauds. At times, SHGs have to be also provided with appropriate linkages in order to take up a productive enterprise. All this required investment in terms of time, effort and money. The Ministry of Rural Development has established a norm of Rs. 10,000 per group towards group promotion expense. Thus, to form an additional one million group, the amount required is Rs.1,000 crore.

The availability as well as ensuring proper utilization of funds meant for SHG promotion is an issue that needs to be addressed. NABARD's microfinance Development Fund (MFDF), set up in year 2000-01 with Rs. 100 crore corpuses, has identified capacity building of SHGs as one of its objectives. However, the real need is much larger compared to the outlay made by MFDF. The government also makes funds available for group promotion under different development projects such as SGSY and District Poverty Initiatives project (DPIP).

However, keeping in mind the requirement of SHG creation, these initiatives are too small and spread out and need additional sources of funds. While the ideal way forward could be creating a capacity building fund for SHGs, one can look at innovative ways to reduce the grant component of capacity building. A possible solution could be extending soft loans with initial moratorium to MFIs and /or NGOs. The loan would help an MFI expand its outreach quickly, while keeping the interest burden manageable and at the same time ensuring financial discipline. The loan can be amortised over a period of six to nine years.

Equity investment in non-banking financial company providing MF services may be another prudent investment tool for meeting the capacity building needs for the sector. It is important to note that these suggestions are applicable only to mature MFIs that are close to breaking even or those that are already profitable. Grant support is a must for creating new SHGs in areas where mature MFIs are not present.

12.3. Capital Mobilisation

The biggest obstacle until recently was little access to commercial markets and the forbidding cost of capital funds. As private banks, spearheaded by ICICI Bank in 2003, entered the microfinance market, this barrier has partly disappeared and microfinance is growing at a break–neck pace on all fronts viz, loan outstanding, client outreach, product and services diversification or geographic spread. MFIs are lacking some forms of capital:

a) MFIS have not issued bonds. Bond issuance would allow MFIs to diversify their funding sources, which are dominated by a few large commercial banks and government-sponsored apex organizations like NABARD and SIDBI. For example MFIs have not yet securitized loan portfolios on the main stream financial market and a few deals have mainly been bilateral. MFIs need to securitize their loan portfolio to raise cheaper capital and to shift their credit risk onto institutions that are better fit to mange risk.

b) MFIs have been unable to access long-term debt from banks. Long –term debt would help finance expansions that may not provide net cash inflows early enough to repay short-term debt.

c) Large MFIs rarely receive equity investment. MFIs can leverage equity investment to continue current growth trajectories while maintaining capital adequacy norms. A major challenge to attract more equity is to have a recognized valuation model and a clear exit rate for investors.

The presence of thousands of small MFIs across the country indicates the demand for MF programmes. Most of theses institutions are small entities facilitating internal SHG savings and credit. Scaling up these initiatives presents a very complex challenge in terms of raising capital for expansion, often undermining their outreach potential. In the absence of scaled up operations, the small entities become grant dependent and are unviable and unsustainable.

The only option that small MFIs have to achieve scale is either large grants or commercial debt, which cannot be the sole or long-term source of funds for lending.[4]

Some capitalization alternative for scaling up operations may include:

i) Equity capital
ii) Client deposits
iii) Capital market access
iv) Foreign borrowings
v) Strategic alliance with financial institutions.

(a) Equity Capital

Equity is an ideal instrument to grow a scalable and profitable business. MF in India is still on the border of sustainability. Still, a high demand market is an opportunity to grow rapidly makes MFIs a good equity invest prospect form the investor's prospective. However, structural weaknesses in most MFIs ' operations, constraining legislation form Securities an Exchange Board of India (SEBI) on venture capital and difficult investment conditions under NBFC laws make MFIs very difficult investment vehicles for equity investors. Most of the MFIs operate as charitable trusts or societies, ruling out any kind of equity intake. Migration to Section 25 company status is not of much help as these are non-profit in nature and cannot distribute dividends. Similarly, cooperatives are not designed to attract equity participation either.

The only institutional MFI that can attract equity capital is the one operating as an NBFC. However, setting up an NBFC means meeting a net-owned fund requirement of Rs. 2 crore and most MFIs struggle to raise this start-up capital thus results a catch 22 situation.

The SEBI guidelines prohibit equity investment by venture capital in an NBFC, ruling out institutional equity to NBFC-MFIs. Social venture capital funds located outside India may have keen interest in investing in promising MFIs, but the Foreign Investment Promotion Board (FIPB) norms for financial services and the Reserve Bank of India (RBI) guidelines for NBFCs on foreign investment do not allow more than 50% holding for foreign investors for investments below US $5 million. This dissuades serious social venture capital investors' form investing in equity of Indian MFIs.

A major boost to sustainable MF can be made by reviewing the limits for foreign investment in microfinance NBFCs. This may encourage socially-conscious foreign investors to invest in young MFIs with NBFC status and provide a strong impetus to growth and scalability of the entire sector. The SKS microfinance deal with Unitus and TMSV LLC, attracting US 0.5 million as equity, is possibly the most significant equity investment from foreign social capital funds and is an evidence of global interest in the Indian MFIs sector.

Some of the solutions proposed to facilitate the flow of equity funds include setting up a national MF equity Fund for supporting MFIs entrepreneurs. As announced by Union Finance Minister Union Budget 2005-06, Microfinance Development and Equity Fund of Rs. 200 crore has been created by NABARD.

Encouraging institutional equity to MFIs from NABARD, SIDBI and NHB can help MFIs to significantly strengthen their capital structures and also bring them under the supervision of these institutions. Another option that policy makers may consider is to allow cash –rich NGOs to invest in companies uncertain MF without prejudicing their tax status. This may require an amendment in the Income Tax-Act for allowing NGOs to contribute equity to for – profit MFIs.

Some other policy initiatives that can boost the MF sector should include lowering the initial paid up capital requirement for MFIs to register as NBFCs to Rs. 25 lakh and considering extending the "sweet equity" scheme (Wherein the promoters' contribution of effort and experience is counted in monetary terms) on the MF sector.

(b) Client Deposit

Saving is a crucial service for the poor people. However, RBI regulation concerning mobilization of public deposits by MFIs allows only banks (Which require a paid-up capital of Rs. 100 crore), some NBFCs (that meet RBI norms) or member-owned institutions to raise deposits from the public. While member owned institutions can raise deposits, they suffer from problems of dual control- a cooperative bank is regulated both by the Registrar of Cooperative and RBI. The MACS Act adopted in some states, notably Andhra Pradesh, overcomes this lacuna.

The NGOs, non-deposit taking NBFCs or Section 25 Companies are unable to provide legal saving services to the poor. Funds mobilized through deposit services are at a lower cost and enable MFIs to scale up their credit operations by rotating client savings. There is a strong case for allowing MFIs to take deposit with adequate safeguards. Mahajan and Ramodal[5] have suggested that MFIs should be allowed to provide savings services with the safeguard that deposit taking by MFIs is confined only to its borrowers. Additionally, imposition of an appropriate level of statutory liquidity reserve could act as a buffer. This can be monitored on a quarterly basis and any misused can be death with by closure of the concerned MFIs. Moreover, MFIs undertaking savings may be asked to maintain high levels of capital adequacy (up to 2%) so that they approach the capitalization levels of mainstream financial institutions as they scale up and evolve. MFIs should also be provided with positive incentives to maintain a very high portfolio quality, with a regular reporting of non performing assets. The MFIs policy needs to evolve prudential norms appropriate to institutions serving the poor and should have supervision mechanisms to meet the inherent challenges.

(c) Capital and Money Market: Full Financial Integration

Evolved NBFC MFIs may look at capital markets as a solution to capital constraints. Securitisation of MFI's loan portfolio is an important initiative that provides a possible role for financial markets in addressing capital constraints that MFIs face today. Trading papers derived from securitized assets in secondary markets can possibly be an important determinant in resolving the issues of capital constraint and limited outreach for MFIs. ICICI Bank has undertaken a securitization deal with Share Microfinance Ltd worth Rs. 20 crore (US 4.3 million). The deal has enabled share to access funds at lower costs. The securitized portfolio has been rated AAA by CRISIL and traded. Such initiatives need to be encouraged and promoted.

Similarly, venture capital funding of MFIs can also help them in strengthening their capital structures.

(d) Foreign Borrowings: Potential Capital Source of Microfinance

With increased confidence in India's economy, as well as the promise shown by some MFIs in creating value, many foreign investors and donors are willing to provide loans and guarantees to Indian MFIs. However, the recent ban imposed by the Finance Ministry on accessing external commercial borrowings by financial intermediaries had major impact on the outreach plans of many MFIs, which are looking up to these funds for scaling up their operations. Hence, MFIs may be provided a special exemption for accessing foreign debts.

(e) Strategic Alliance and Partnership: Innovative Delivery Strategies

Another way to beat capital constraints for the MFIs is to enter into strategic partnership with banks. Such partnerships can allow for risk sharing between the two. The competence of the MFIs in building a high quality portfolio coupled with the access of low cost funds to a bank can lead to synergies and hence can help in overcoming outreach constraints. The ICICI Bank is also experimenting with using MFIs as management and collection agents, where the loans are always on the books of the ICICI Bank, even through the MFIs staff handles all the operations with the customers. For this, the ICICI Bank has launched a pilot project jointly with Cashpor Micro Credit , as Section 25 company specially set up for this purpose by Cashpor Financial and Technical Services Ltd, in the Chandauli district of Uttar Pradesh. However, the real returns available to the MFIs on this portfolio comes down because it has to pay service tax charged towards management and collection services and this discourages the growth of such innovative alliance.

Concerns have now shifted to growth management issues such as skilled human resources, flexible product design, reducing transaction costs, ensuring adequate management information systems, standard credit information, better use of advances in technology, accessing alternative financing, expanding into underserved areas, and dealing with regulator hurdles and political risks. There is an urgent need for structured long term financing to sector to fully address these important issues and smoothly transition into a well functioning mature industry.[6]

12.4. Sustainability of Microfinance Programme

Sustainability in simple terms refers to the long-term continuation of the Microfinance programme after the project activities have been discontinued. It entails that appropriate systems and processes have been put in place that will enable the microfinance services to be available on a continuous basis and the clients continue to benefit from these services in a routine manner. This also would mean that the programme would meet the needs of the members through resources raised on their own strength, either from among themselves or from external sources.

The different dimensions of sustainability are:

a) Institutional Sustainability

b) Mission Sustainability

c) Programme Sustainability

d) Human Resource Sustainability

e) Financial Sustainability

f) Market Sustainability

g) Policy Environment Sustainability

h) Impact Sustainability.

Datails about sustainaility in Microfinance is discused in chapter 19 separately.

Bimal Jalan's Monetary and credit policy statement of April 1999, the policy attached the importance to the work of National Bank for Agriculture and Rural Development (NABARD) and public sector banks in area of micro-credit. It announced that deregulation of interest rates on loans by banks to micro-credit organizations by these organizations to their members and beneficiaries except in the case of government sponsored programmes. The basic objective has been of mainstreaming micro-credit and accelerating the flow of bank credit to micro-finance institutions without jeopardizing their decentralized, voluntary and non-bureaucratic character.

According to RBI Mid -Term Review of Monetary and Credit Policy of 2003, the framework urged the banks to provide adequate incentives to their branches for financing SHGs, establish linkages with them, simplify the procedures while providing for total flexibility in such procedures to suit the local conditions. It was also made clear that the group dynamics of working SHGs may be left to themselves and need neither be regulated nor formal structure imposed or insisted upon.[7]

Banks were advised to consider lending to SHGs as part of their mainstream credit operations, to identify branches having potential for linkage with SHGs and provide necessary support services to such branches while including the SHG-lending within their Service Area Plan.

MFI provides other non-credit services as well such as capacity building, training, marketing of products of SHGs, micro-insurance etc. In this background, the following considerations are relevant:

a) Micro-finance would be seen to be a broader concept than micro-credit and the focus of discussion has now expanded beyond micro-credit to cover micro-finance.

b) The increasing size and growth of MFIs seems to warrant a clearer policy framework to cover operations in financial services in addition to credit, in respect of both bank and NABARD led micro finance through SHGs and micro finance institutions.

c) Delivery of non-credit financial services such as insurance and mutual funds by micro finance institutions seems to be possible but as a pre-condition, there is a need for a clear framework for the approach of different regulators to these non-bank financial services by MFIs.

d) Organisational forms of micro-finance institutions appear varied, though the activities may in some cases include non-financial services. This makes them subject to differing legal frameworks as per the organisational form.

e) Different state Governments take varying approaches to the microfinance institutions- including subsidizing interest rates. The nature and spread of micro-finance movement also differ significantly across States.

f) As per information available, a significant part of the current microfinance activity is related to credit, which is perhaps attributable to the absence of a conscious policy thrust in regard to non-credit related financial activities.

g) Developments in technology seem to provide a window of opportunity to reduce the transaction costs and thus enable microfinance to be commercially viable and profitable activity.

h) Finance Minister in his budget Speech for 2005-06 made a reference to the possibility of a suitable legislation in this regard.

The RBI felt that microfinance movement across the country involving common people has benefited immensely by its informality and flexibility. Hence, their organization, structure and methods of working should be simple and any regulation will be inconsistent with the core-spirit of the movement. It was also felt that ideally, the NABARD or the banks should devise appropriate safeguards locally in their relationship with MFIs, taking into account different organizational forms of such entities. In any case, if any statute for regulation of MFIs is contemplated, it may be at the State-level with no involvement of the RBI as a banking regulator or for extending deposit-insurance.

Internal Group of RBI on Rural Credit and Micro-Finance (Khan Committee) - 2005

The report considers the following:

a) Policy options and strategies for deepening and widening of financial services.

b) Promotion, development and rating of microfinance institutions and other outreach entities.

c) Regulatory issues and concerns.

The report will form a basis for evolving a policy framework in consultation with the Government, NABARD and other state-holders.

Taskforce on Revival of Cooperative Credit Institutions (Vaidyanathan Committee, February 2005) argued in favour of substituting RBI's regulatory jurisdiction with a separate independent national or state level regulatory body broadly in line with what as advocated by Dr. Bimal Jalan in his policy statement in 2001 in regard to Urban Cooperative Banks.

"It is necessary to recognize that we, in India, have to focus on extending financial services in both rural and urban areas for ensuring financial inclusion of all segments of the population. At the same time, one should avoid the temptation of creating one set of banking and financial institutions to cater to the poor or the

unorganized, and another for the rest. The medium to long term objective should be to ensure inclusion of all segments in the mainstream institutions while taking advantage of the flexibility of multiplicity of models of delivering a wide range of financial services. In this light, a comprehensive framework to revive the cooperative credit system, revitalize the RRBs and reorient commercial banking system needs to get a high priority while simultaneously encouraging and enabling growth of micro-finance movement in India which has been very successful".

"No doubt, a very well-crafted balance between the regulation and growth objectives would be warranted in formulating to a regulatory regime, keeping in view the big challenges of financial inclusion of a large segment of the Indian population."

Speech by Y.V. Reddy, Governor of RBI, on "Micro-Finance: Reserve Banks Approach" dated Sep 14, 2005.

12.5. Competition among MFIs

To meet the total demand of microfinance of Rs. 15,000 to 20,000 crores, the biggest challenge to promote conducive and enabling environment (i.e. policies, systems, culture and practices) in which the poor can easily access credit and other financial services quickly, easily and at minimum cost. Groups today spend 80% of their time discussing loans, recoveries and savings. Hardly 10% of time is pent on the broader issues for which the groups were first formed. At the end of day, MFIs must do report on loans, recovery and payments, but do not need to report on how empowerment has progressed.

NGOs are chronic capital shortage, dependence upon donors. Most of NGOs cannot hope to build up sufficient corpus to leverage from banks the large amount of funds that would be required for on-lending to a significant number even 5, 00,000 of BPL households. RBI is not going to let them raised these funds as public deposits. MFIs, including those established by NGOs cannot have a significant impact on their own because of the capital/fund constraint that they inevitably faced.

The linkage between the SHGs and the banks is not as smooth as the NGOs had expected. There are geographic variations in the banker's response and the NGOs' ability to link the groups.Not all the NGOs have sufficient grant fund to play the role of "Social intermediary". They are able to cross –subsidies the costs of "social intermediation" through the income from "financial intermediation'. Many NGOs are concerned about the way SHGs are made the beneficiaries' of all development programmes of the government, leading to distortion in the original concept of mutual help and affinity. This concern had led many NGOs reluctantly, to play the role of financial intermediary, and they have looked for opportunities to discontinue this role. (e.g. Federation of SHGs was one such option many opted for but this did not work as expected).

NGO has to be professionalized independently and core competencies required to be a MFI simply do not exist. One of the key questions in financial viability is the rate of interest.

12.6. Micro Insurance

In case of insurance, however, demand is usually weak but objectively the need is strong. The unexpected death of a wife and mother, leaving a debt to NGO-MFI that may not be repayable if she was the income-earner, usually pushes an uninsured household deeper into poverty. The death of a large farm animal purchased with loan funds not only deprives an uninsured household of the expected means of repayment of the loan, but also can deprive it of access to credit in future, if it is unable to repay the loan. Continuing education by NGO-MFIs is necessary to open their minds.

The most important reason is that all microfinance services including savings, credit and insurance products are needed by the poor, especially by poor women who predominate among the clients of microfinance. They need saving facilities for safe keeping and to tide them over food deficits and other periodic emergencies as well as to accumulate large amounts of funds for the marriage of their daughters and the purchase of productive assets. Micro-credit is needed for investment in income-generating activities, so as to break out of the vicious cycle of poverty. Life and large livestock insurance are needed so as not to burden survivors with debt, and to be able to cope with the death of a large farm animal purchased with loan funds.

The important reason for NGO-MFIs to provide clients with an integrated set of microfinance services is that they promote an early attainment of institutional financial break-even and sustainability , with which NGO-MFIs will not able to serve the poor for long. Not only do loan client savings provide an obvious "cushion" for timely repayment; but even more important, client savings provide basis for financial intermediation that makes possible the efficient supply of micro-credit to its clients. Normally, savings are an alternative and relatively cheap source of funds for NGO-MFIs, because the interest rates usually are less than those that have to be paid for debt. Therefore, by maximising its saving mobilization, NGO-MFI should be able to minimize its average cost of funds. This in turn should maximize its margin at any given interest rate to its clients, and thereby hasten the attainment of break-even and profitability.

From the points of view of both client and institutional benefit, therefore, NGO-MFIs should offer their clients saving facilities, micro-credit and life and large farm animal insurance. To maximize their benefits, these financial services should be integrated.

12.7. Regulatory and Legal Constraints

Currently RBI prohibits the collection of savings by any institutions except banks and NBFCs. That has been licenses to do so. The minimum capital and other requirements for attaining such a license are stiff. Thus, most of NGO-MFIs do not have access to legal savings facilities. They may confine to saving mobilisation to only from SHGs and 50% of loan outstanding to safeguard the interest of depositors.

The ongoing de-regulation of the insurance sector in India provides adequate opportunities for NGO-MFIs to arrange the needed insurance cover for their clients, by becoming agents of established insurance companies.

On the institutional side, it is of course necessary for NGO-MFIs to build the institutional capacity to provide quality savings and insurance products to their clients, including the necessary staff training and market research.

Taxation Laws

The Indian tax law does not recognize MF as a charitable activity. However, most MF initiatives are started by NGOs who invest a lot of time and effort in building these groups. For these entities to continue providing MF, the Income Tax Act would have to be amended to include MF as a charitable activity. There are suggestions from practitioners that MF should be accorded a status similar to infrastructure companies. The need for changes in tax laws to allow NGOs to invest in MFIs companies has already been stated earlier.

Liberalisation of Cooperatives

Liberalising cooperatives can also help the cause of MF. Presently, the state cooperative act of most states does not allow the setting up of district level cooperative banks other than those by the state governments. The series of scams involving cooperative banks have resulted in RBI taking a very guarded stand against cooperatives. However, such crises can be prevented in the future by improving supervision, and by ensuring that establishing cooperative outside of government control does not hinder supervision. On the other hand, this is likely to result in autonomous and better capitalized cooperative banks. The Andhra Pradesh Mutually Aided Cooperative Societies (APMACS) Act has resulted in the creation of some new mutually aided cooperative MFIs in Andhra Pradesh. These institutions are able to provide savings and credit services to their members and are fairly autonomous. There is a need to have similar laws all over the country.

12.8. Key Enablers in Building access to Financial Services[8]

In order to create an environment conducive to maximizing access to financial services, some initiatives at the sectoral level are necessary. Some of these have been identified below: Regulators and multilateral agencies have much to contribute in this area.

a) Unique Identifier: A unique identifier (social security number) is the basis on which initiatives such as credit history tracking and targeting for services such as health insurance can be implemented. This is best done by the Government or agencies such as the Employee Provident Fund Organisation (EPFO) so that the unique ID can be used for other purpose as well.

b) Credit Bureau: Credit Information tacking and sharing enables lenders to provide incentives to those with good credit history and provides a strong deterrent to wilful default. This will also facilitate transition to individual lending programmes over time. NABARD may play an important role in this initiative.

c) Rural Infrastructure: Investment in certain kinds of rural infrastructure will enable providers to offer financial services with a superior design and convenience to the client. While such investment might be too much to undertake for any one provider, such infrastructure will assume the character of public goods. Relevant examples include computerized weather stations providing real-time weather data and internet connectivity at the village level enabling ATMs and other payment devices.

d) Regular support for hybrid models: Creative responses to the challenge of access to financial services will require experimentation with several delivery formats. Regulators including the RBI, SEBI and IRDA must encourage providers to carry out pilots in order to better address the challenges. Learning from these pilots may be actively disseminated.

e) Focus on urban micro finance: Most of the micro finance outreach has been achieved among the rural poor. There are limited understanding/insights on expanding access to financial services for the urban poor. Some of this may be attributed to lack of "incentives" for formal providers in working with the urban poor. For instance, finance for urban poor housing does not qualify for priority sector benefits.

f) Discontinuation of direct subsidies: Subsidizing financial services directly (either through interest rate caps or premium caps) blunt incentives of providers to innovative in product design. A case in point is the crop insurance product where the subsidized Government programme has resulted in very limited participation from the private sector. Subsidy may be best channelled towards public goods as outline before.

12.9. Key Challenges for Growth

As microfinance activity evolves into a full fledges industry, a multitude of issues ranging from staff recruitment to advances in technology must be urgently addressed.

a) Human Resources: The pool of skilled microfinance professional in India is still quite small. It is not uncommon to find senior practitioners involved in more than one organization, serving on either the governing body or management team. Younger employees often hope organizations or leave to start new ones. Despite good pay scales, it is difficult to attract qualified graduates, accountants, MBA or IT degree holders as microfinance is still not perceived as a viable business opportunity and professional workplace.

b) Product: At present, MFIs trend to be rigid on product features such as loan amount, repayment schedule and loan tenure. MFIs need to explore new and more flexible products to satisfy latent demand.

c) Transaction Cost: MFIs currently incur very high operational costs, especially at loan origination and during monitoring because of doorstep service and little or no deployment of technology solutions. This is a critical concern in the face of rising competition, public scrutiny and political interference.

d) Technology: Technological innovations such as smart cards, biometric IDs and rural Kiosks that can help control costs are crucial for a safe and rapid scale up.

e) Finance: In fact, capital infusion is no longer a problem in India primarily because of short term loan and off balance financing via the popular partnership model. SIDBI provides grants and subsidized credit, NABARD manages microfinance development and equity fund and now private equity funds have also entered the sector.

12.10. Balancing Financial Sustainability and Social Impact

The challenge of microfinance is to be both financially sustainable and have an impact on poverty alleviation. MFIs must be sustainable to attract money from capital market. MFIS sustainability would also result in stronger competitive means against incoming players such as big commercial groups and would ensure that microfinance be served by a wide variety of institutions, differing in size, target clients, geographical reach, financial products, and development objectives, and therefore ensure maximum outreach of the microfinance industry.

Financial sustainability: Financial sustainability may be defined as ability to operate according to credit market rules and in particular to provide a return to investors adequate with the risk they take. Only financial sustainability can attract sufficient investors' money to make the industry viable in the long run.

Operational sustainability: The ability to operate in the long run with a constant amount of money no loss. It would require subsidy to initiate the activity.

Sustainable MFIs are generally characterized by:

a) They have achieved a dimension , in terms of assets and number of borrowers, that enables them to benefit from economies of scale;

b) They charge higher interest rates;

c) They serve the ' better off' among the poor; and

d) They disburse larger loans.

This suggests that there is a strong incentive for MFIs, if they want to be sustainable, to divert from poor customers to those who are better off and to divert from rural to urban markets. Thus, focusing only on financial profitability may result in a shift of microfinance from social to for profit finance. To mitigate such risk, one always needs to consider the impact.

Social impact: It may be defined as capacity of MFI to alleviate poverty effectively in its Zone of influence and in the long term. It results from the MFIs ability to reach the right clients segment and effectively improve its livelihood.

Microfinance industry suffers from the market imperfections relevant to the credit industry, in a more critically acute way. Imperfect information about clients is all the more problematic that the poor lack credit history, tract record and sometimes identification papers. Fighting loan delinquency is also a problem since the poor often lack collateral, are dispersed and remotely located.

In addition to the classical problems of credit agencies, MFIs also suffer from other difficulties specific to the microfinance model. MFIs have limited financial and human resources, they often operate in urgency and lack the skills and resources to cope with their initiate skyrocketing growth, and their management may lack the skills or the incentive to operate efficiently.

In addition, they have a great number of customers, remotely located in rural areas, sometimes uneducated and illiterate. This results in important operational costs. Also, MFIs are diverse, lack credibility in capital markets, and lack collective thinking. Finally because the microfinance industry is still young, it lacks adequate regulation.

The dilemma facing microfinance is how to achieve financial sustainability and at the same time improve impact.

12.11. Use of Technology

Issue of impact and outreach can addressed with the use of technology:

a) Technology as a tool to improve operations of MFIs;

b) Technology as a means to alleviate market imperfection within the microfinance industry, in particular the problem of information asymmetry between MFIs and their clients;

c) Technology as a means to mitigate information asymmetry between the microfinance industry and investors; and

d) Technology as a tool to increase impact and outreach.

Some of the technologies widely used in microfinance operation are briefly described here:

Smart Cards, ATMs and Fingerprint Identification

These solutions make it less costly to provide loans to customers and process their savings. Smart cards with embedded microchips, for example, allow data storage and contain all loan related and purchases information. Since smart cards contain all necessary information about a customer, cash dispensers can operate in the most remote location without a permanent network connection. Fingerprint identification enables illiterate customers to use easily the dispenser. It also protects customers from unauthorized usage in case of theft or card loss.

For example, Prodem (Bolvia) has been using smart cards and fingerprint identification devices in its ATMs within the last couple of years. This technology allowed Prodem to expand drastically its operations: in 2001, the number of customers grew from less than 1400 to almost 12000, while deposits increase from $280,000 to $ 3.6 million. The fingerprint identification played an instrumental role as many Bolivian micro entrepreneurs who are illiterate and therefore cannot sign their names. Moreover, many don't have personal identify cards, which prevented them from depositing and withdrawing funds in traditional commercial bank. Banco Solidario is another example of MFIs that implemented ATM machines.

Portable Devices Assistance (PDAS)

These small portable handheld computers reduce officer-customer transaction time in the field and in the office. Thus, loan officers can dedicate more time for existing customers increasing the quality of services or generate leads for new customers increasing outreach of MFIs programs.

The above technological solutions appear to have proven positive effect on outreach, since they significantly reduce operation costs to service customers. In addition, they improve customer service by making loan officers more efficient, reducing paperwork, providing access to information and ability to compute complex analysis on the spot.

Limitation on use of technology

However, a major limitation of these technologies is their implementation cost since profitability is achieved only with a critical mass of clients. Development of technological solutions for MFIs exceeds industry average costs for ATMs and software application since these solutions in each case need to be customized due to high diversification of MFIs and their customers. Even though Prodem found the way to manufacture ATMs for less than half a price of the industry standard, it came across great difficulties in cross-border expansion.

An important component of the cost is also the operating /maintenance cost, as new technologies require employee/customer training and support, regular servicing and maintenance.

Another difficulty is customer acceptance of technologies. Since technology is new to many customers, it bears high operational and business risk depending on the local culture. This is especially relevant when customers value personal interaction with loan officers and replacing it technological devices may scare away the poor and hamper outreach efforts of MFIs.

The microfinance industry is living a transitory period. Technological solutions to catalyze sustainability are readily available. But success of their implementation will mainly depend on the ability of microfinance players to reshape their working methods, think globally, and cooperate to establish leadership, in spite of existing idiosyncrasies.

12.12. Govt Initiatives and Policy Reforms[9]

The 1998 high –level Policy Forum in India organized by WWB ("Building India's Leadership in Microfinance) led to setting up of the microfinance task force that produced a set of recommendations in its 1999 report. Some initial steps were taken to promote the microfinance industry and notably to address legal and regulatory constraints:

a) In the March 2001, budget speech, the GOI announced the creation of a Microfinance Development Fund, operationalized by NABARD, and funded by the RBI, NABARD and participating commercial banks. It is not yet operative.

b) Easing the regulations for non-banking financial institutions engaged in microfinance (modification) of section 25 of the Companies Act via RBI circular.

c) Enabling formal financial institutions to include microfinance in their priority lending portfolios (via an RBI circular dated 2/8/2000). Banks are required to lend 40% of their portfolio to the priority sector.

d) Outside the Task Force process, the Government has introduced the obligation for banks to allocate 5% of net bank credit to women.

e) In November 2001, the Government set up groups to work further on the reform process. This "Empowered Group" is headed from the Banking Secretary. There are six sub groups: 1) Non-financial services, 2) Capacity, 3) Validated models in microfinance, 4) Resource Flow, 5) Technology to reduce costs, 6) Legal and Regulatory Framework.

Outstanding Policy Issues

a) We need a better understanding of why there has been limited development of microfinance in India in relation to the potential demand.

b) There is still the need to promote microfinance with all stakeholders, notably the Ministry of Finance, the RBI and banks. The Ministry of Finance needs to take a stand that money needs to go to the private sector.

c) There is insufficient of new model has been limited. New ownership and governance structures should be developed. (NGOs and nonblank finance companies have limited access to external funding and equity capital).

d) There is a need to develop other services, notably savings and micro insurance. Growth of the sector is held back by limitations in savings mobilization.

Several legal and regulator constraints need to be eased. These touch specific changes in legislation to accommodate existing institutions

a) The Income Tax Act limits tax exemptions for microfinance NGOs as well as the tax deductibility of loan loss provision by nonbank finance companies. It is necessary to amend the Income Tax Act to provide tax exemptions for non-profit NGOs involved in microfinance and to make tax deductible the provision and reserves by non-bank finance companies.

b) Covenants in the Reserve Bank of India Act restrict the possibility for nonprofit NGOs and nonblank finance companies to collect deposits. These restrictions need to be reviewed and licensed organizations allowed to collect savings should be allowed to use more of these saving for the provision of micro loans.

c) Minimum capital requirement are high and licensing processing is slow.

d) In multiplicity of legislation, certain statutes conflicts, especially for co-operatives. There is a need to address inconsistencies in legislation.

e) Review restriction on saving mobilization.

f) Creating a new legal form, a microfinance company with capital requirement commensurate with the size of operations. The prudential standards of new institutional models should be matched to risk. Opportunities exist for adapting the NBFC model and for using the producer company model for microfinance.

g) There is a need to clarify whether one should seek to introduce a separate chapter in the RBI Act to pass an independent MFI Act or to amend the existing acts covering microfinance. A deeper analysis of the advantages and disadvantages of these approaches is necessary.

NOTES

1. Grameen Bank in 'strongest position ever' www.news.bbc.co.uk, March 12, 2002.
2. Natalied Kulik & Patrice Molinari, "Sustainable microfinance and technology" Ford Motor Company Fellowship.
3. SIDBI speech at "Expanding Frontiers of Microfinance", *Sa-Dhan Annual Policy Conference*, 23-24 January 2006.
4. Mahajan V., & Ramola BG," Microfinance in India: Banyan Tree or Bonsai, review paper for the World Bank, August 2003.
5. Mahajan V Ramola BG, August 2003, "Microfinance in India", Banyan Tree or Bonsai".
6. *Microfinance in India: Current Trends and Challenges*, Centre for Micro Finance at Institute of Management and Research, October 2006.
7. Speech by Y.V.Reddy, Governor of RBI on "Micro-Finance: Reserve Bank's Approach" on September 14, 2005 (http: rbi.org.in).
8. Bindu Ananth, Bastavee Barooah etc., "*A Blue print for the Delivery of Comprehensive Financial Services to the Poor in India*, Centre for Micro Finance, CMR & IFMR, Working paper, December 2004.
9. Based on the India case study by Sanjay Sinha in *The Role of Central Banks in Microfinance in Asia* (ADB, 2000) and a draft World Bank Report on the microfinance industry in India.

13
Credit Rating Methodologies for MFIs

13.1. Credit Rating of MFIs

The rating evaluates the MFI or bank's creditworthiness as well as its strengths and weaknesses. It assesses the risks associated with lending to the organisation and assigns a grade based on the extent of risk. Some of the risks that form the basis of the assessment are external risk, credit risk, market risk and the risk of fraud. With reference to these, the critical aspects covered are – the quality of the governing board, the depth of management systems and financial health. For the benefit of donors, ratings also evaluate the MFI's ability to use grant funds efficiently.

Credit Rating is the evaluation or assessment of an MFI's ability to pay back financial obligations or the chances of not defaulting on the financial obligations. It is used to determine an MFI's credit risk. It is usually used to determine a bank or financial institution's credit risk. A credit rating is an opinion on the relative degree of risk associated with timely payment of interest and principal on a debt instrument. A simple alphanumeric symbol is normally used to convey a credit rating. Credit rating is done by experienced and well established credit rating agencies. Credit rating report is very used not only to lenders, donors, regulators but it is also very useful to MFIs itself.

For MFIs	▪ Provides recognized, objective, high quality assessment that assists in fund-raising ▪ Identifies areas of strength which can be built upon and areas of weakness that require correction or capacity building ▪ Enables understanding of best practices
For Investors/Lenders	▪ Professional and standardised assessment of the risk involved in lending to MFIs ▪ Lowers appraisal and transaction costs ▪ Enables more efficient utilisation of funds
For Regulators/other stakeholders	▪ Provides a tool for assessing performance.

The quality and integrity of rating of MFIs in India have been assuming increasing significance as the sector is characterized by high leverage of borrowed funds from banks and other investment institutions, absence of supervisory and regulatory framework (except NBFCs and not for profit section 25 companies) and inadequacy of transparent business practices, governance standards, internal checks and controls, risk management system, etc as mentioned above. The rating exercise generally deals with evaluation of financial and business risks covering governance, financial , HR, product delivery management, accounting, ALM, MIS, internal checks and control, performance standards, business plan and outreach and sustainability aspects. M-CRIL, CRISIL, CARE-Rating, ICRA, Planet Finance, SMERA, APMASS , etc have engaged in rating of MFIs. NABARD insists on rating of MFIs through its approved agencies while considering capital/Revolving Fund Assistance (RFA) for MFIs. RBI has a system of extending accreditation of rating agencies and the agencies concerned need to apply to RBI in this regard.

13.2. GIRAFE Rating Model

It is a rating tools developed by PlaNet Finance. The financial and organizational performance of MFIs is objectively evaluated, and the results are translated into rating reports. It is based on methodology of assessing the following areas:

G=Governance and decision making processes: It is the process by which the legal owners of the microfinance institutions guide the institution to achieve its mission and protect its assets. The rating factors in governance and decision making are planning, management team, decision making are the anticipation of risks, balancing the operational realities and strategic vision, ensuring the skills necessary to achieve the objectives and ensuring the organization's responsiveness.

I=Information and management tools: It involves the process with which the microfinance institution defines its information needs, collects and processes the data, analyze and present the data; system, information on activities, and financial and accounting information.

R=Risks analysis and control: Risk taking is very important on MFI's operations. It is important not to remove the risk entirely but to identify the risks and control those risks and react on it if the risk is too high. The evaluation of factors is internal audit. The risk identification and control includes the following:

(i) to identify and prioritize the risk,
(ii) to develop strategies to measure those risks i.e selection of one or more indicators and setting limits,
(iii) to define integrated control chain, and
(iv) to define actions for which limits are reached.

There are five types of integrated control chain and these types are prevention procedures (through formalization and standardization of procedures and separation of tasks and hierarchy), systematic control, internal audit missions, external audit and rating missions, and supervision and regulations.

A=Activities (products and services): It is necessary to assess the activities of the MFI. The accessing factors of activities are marketing and competition, portfolio management, portfolio at risk, write off ratio and credit risk coverage.

F=Funding and Liquidity: It includes the rating of the MFI's funding structure (origin of its equity, current structure and cost of its liabilities) and appropriateness of the capital structure for the activities financed. The assessment factors are financing strategy and liquidity management.

E=Efficiency and Profitability: It measures the MFI's financial sustainability that determines its operational sustainability through staff productivity, operating expenses ratio, financial self-sufficiency and return on assets.

There are two stages to the rating process:

Stage 1: *Evaluation.* After some preliminary preparation, two consultants (one of whom is a local consultant) will conduct the mission in the field during one to two weeks. The presence of a local consultant who is aware of distinctive regional characteristics is essential and peculiar to GIRAFE methodology. The evaluation takes into account the financial performance of the institution (financial statements/ portfolio follow up); it has to be completed by more qualitative information, available from other sources of the institution's information system and from personal contacts with board members, management, staff and clients. Field visits are intended to verify the financial documents and to approach sensitively the institutions' activities. Accounting and financial adjustments are carried out using a rigorous methodology in order to standardize the accounts and reintegrate various hidden costs: accountancy adjustments; inflation adjustment, and subsidized resources.

Stage 2: *Formal Rating.* Following a rating scale of 26 qualitative and quantitative factors and using a detailed questionnaire, the rating team assigns each factor a grade ranging from 0 (minimal grade) to 5 (maximal grade). After each of the 26 factors has been assigned a rough rate, a weight is applied to each of the factors to achieve a global weighted rating for each of the six areas of assessment. The final grade, on a scale of 12 is assigned by PlaNet Rating's rating committee on the basis of the scoring and the evaluation report.

This grading system results in the G.I.R.A.F.E. rating stellar graph. After each of the 26 factors has been assigned a rough rate, a weight is applied to each of the factors to achieve a global weighted rating for each of the six areas of assessment.

Synthesis

Area	*Number of Qualitative factors*	*Number of Quantitative factors*	*Total Number*	*Weight of Qualitative factors*	*Weight of Quantitative factors*	*Total Weight*
G	4	3	7	11%	7%	18%
I	3	0	3	12%	0%	12%
R	2	0	2	12%	0%	12%
A	3	2	5	14%	9%	23%
F	1	1	2	6%	6%	12%
E	1	6	7	2%	21%	23%
	14	12	26	57%	43%	100%

A GIRAFE rating is analyzed at a dual level. A global rating is given, from G1 to G5, along with a composite rating, scoring the 6 areas of assessment from "E" to "A". It allows the rater to approach fiduciary risk (G, I, R areas: analysis of governance, underperformance) and credit risk (loan portfolio management, but also counterpart risk and clientele analysis) separately.

The descriptions of the various ratings are as follows:

Grade	*Descriptions*
G5*	Outstanding performance on all areas of assessment.The institution achieved total financial and operational self-sufficiency. Minimal risk. The institution should be able to face all kind of hazard.
G5	Excellent overall performance. The institution achieved a high level of professional competency (good technical and financial self-sufficiency).Risk is very limited.
G4*	High global performance. Nevertheless, one area of assessment may be weak. Advanced professional competency. Technically self-sufficient.Low risk, related to identified areas that can be controlled (cf. composite rating)Conditional Investment/Concessional Funding.
G4	Satisfactory overall performance. Nevertheless, some areas of assessment may be weak. The institution is technically self-sufficient, but fragile.Moderate risk; related to several areas (cf. composite rating).
G3	Some weaknesses in several areas of assessment, but institutionalisation is under way; the institution has to firm up.Moderate to significant risk. Support investment, to be completed by technical assistance.Investment not recommended.
G2	Underperforming institution, not mature enough to be refinanced. The predictability of activities is low.High risk.
G1	Serious weaknesses in all areas of assessment.Substantial risk, even in the short term (institutional and credit risks).

13.3. PEARLS Rating Model

PEARL rating model was developed by World Council of Credit Unions (WOCCU). It uses a set of financial ratios to monitor the financial stability of the MFIs. These ratios provide MFIs, project staff, national federations and regulators with essential tools for monitoring, planning, standardizing, ranking and facilitating supervisory control in credit unions.

Each letter in the word PEARLS measures the key areas of MFIs operations: Protection, Effective financial structure, Asset quality, Rates of return and costs, and Liquidity and Signs of growth.

P = Protection. Protection is measured by comparing the adequacy of the provisions for loan losses against the amount of delinquent loans. A credit union has adequate protection if it has sufficient provisions to cover 100% of all delinquent loans for more than 12 months and at least 35% of loans delinquent between 1 and 12 months.

E = Effective Financial Structure. Financial structure of the credit union is the single most important factor in determining growth potential, earnings capacity and overall financial strength. The PEARLS system measures credit union assets, liabilities and capital, then recommends the "ideal" structure. Credit unions are encouraged to maximize earning assets as the means to achieve sufficient earnings.

A = Asset Quality. A non-earning asset is one that does not generate income. An excess of non-earning assets negatively affects credit union income. PEARLS indicators are used to identify the impact of non-earning assets by analyzing delinquency ratios, percentages of non-earning assets and the financing of non-earning assets.

R = Rates of Return and Costs. By segregating all of the essential components of net earnings, the PEARLS system helps management calculate investment yields and evaluate financial costs and operating expenses. PEARLS calculates yields on the basis of average outstanding investments, unlike other systems that calculate yields on the basis of average assets.

Yield is computed in four main areas: loan portfolio, liquid investments, financial investments and other non-financial investments. Operating costs are also important and broken down into three main areas: financial intermediation costs, administrative costs and unrecoverable loan costs. "By segregating in-come and expenses into the previously mentioned areas, PEARLS ratios can accurately pinpoint the reasons why a credit union is not producing sufficient net income," noted Dave Richardson, WOCCU Director of Technical Development.

L = Liquidity. Liquidity is traditionally viewed in terms of cash available to lend — a variable exclusively controlled by the credit union. With the introduction of withdrawable savings deposits, the concept of liquidity radically changes. Richardson explained, "Liquidity now refers to cash needed for withdrawals — a variable the credit union can no longer control. The maintenance of adequate liquidity reserves is essential to sound, financial management of the new credit union model." PEARLS analyzes liquidity from three perspectives: total net liquidity reserves, obligatory liquidity reserves and idle liquid funds.

S = Signs of Growth. The advantage of the PEARLS system is that it links growth to profitability, as well as to other key areas by evaluating the strength of the system as a whole. Growth is measured in seven key areas: total assets, loans, savings deposits, external credit, shares, institutional capital and membership.

13. 4. CAMEL Rating Model

The CAMEL rating model was originally adopted by North American bank regulators to evaluate the financial and managerial soundness of U.S. commercial lending institutions. Under the CAMEL rating model, five areas of financial and managerial performance are assessed. These are Capital Adequacy, Asset Quality, Management, Earnings, and Liquidity Management. Based on the conceptual framework of the original CAMEL, ACCION International developed its own instrument. Although the ACCION CAMEL reviews the same five areas as the original CAMEL, the indicators and ratings used by ACCION reflect the unique challenges and conditions facing the microfinance industry. To date, ACCION has used its CAMEL primarily as an internal assessment tool, which has contributed to setting performance standards both for the ACCION Network and for the microfinance industry as a whole.

The MFI is required to gather the following information for a CAMEL examination: (1) financial statements; (2) budgets and cash flow projections; (3) portfolio aging schedules; (4) funding sources; (5) information about the board of directors; (6) operations/staffing; and (7) macroeconomic information.

Financial statements form the basis of the CAMEL's quantitative analysis. MFIs are required to present audited financial statements from the last three years and interim statements for the most recent 12-month period. The other required materials provide programmatic information and show the evolution of the institution. These documents demonstrate to CAMEL analysts the level and structure of loan operations and the quality of the MFI's infrastructure and staffing.

Once the financial statements have been compiled, adjustments need to be made. These adjustments serve two purposes: first, they place the MFI's current financial performance in the context of a financial intermediary; second, they enable comparisons among the different institutions in the industry. The CAMEL performs six adjustments, for the scope of microfinance activity, loan loss provision, loan write-offs, explicit and implicit subsidies, effects of inflation, and accrued interest income.

The ACCION CAMEL analyzes and rates 21 key indicators, with each indicator given an individual weighting. Eight quantitative indicators account for 47 percent of the rating, and 13 qualitative indicators make up the remaining 53 percent. The final CAMEL composite rating is a number on a scale of zero to five, with five as the measure of excellence. This numerical rating, in turn, corresponds to an alphabetical rating (AAA, AA, A; BBB, BB, B; C; D; and not rated).

Based on the results of the adjusted financial statements and interviews with the MFI's management and staff, a rating of one to five is assigned to each of the CAMEL's 21 indicators and weighted accordingly. A definition of each area and the criteria ranges for determining each rating are as follows:

C=Capital Adequacy: Leverage: the relationship between the risk-weighted assets of the MFI and its equity. Ability to raise equity: assessment of an MFI's ability to respond to a need to replenish or increase equity at any given time. Adequacy of reserves: measure of the MFI's loan loss reserve and the degree to which the institution can absorb potential loan losses

A=Asset Quality: *Portfolio Quality*: Portfolio at risk: measures the portfolio past due over 30 days. Write-offs/write off policy: measures adjusted write-offs on CAMEL criteria. *Portfolio classification system:* review of portfolios aging schedules; assesses institution's policies associated with assessing portfolio risk. *Fixed Assets:* Productivity of long-term assets:

evaluates MFI's policies for investing in fixed assets; *Infrastructure:* evaluation of whether it meets the needs of both staff and clients.

M= Management : *Governance*: how well the institution's board of directors functions, including the diversity of its technical expertise, its independence from management, and its ability to make decisions flexibly and effectively. *Human Resources:* evaluates whether the department of human resources provides clear guidance and support to operations staff, including recruitment and training of new personnel, incentive systems for personnel, and performance evaluation system. Processes, controls and audit: the degree to which the MFI has formalized key processes and the effectiveness with which it controls risk throughout the organization, as measured by its control environment and the quality of its internal and external audit. *Information Technology System:* assesses whether computerized information systems are operating effectively and efficiently, and are generating reports for management purposes in a timely and accurate manner. Strategic planning and budgeting: whether the institution undertakes a comprehensive and participatory process for generating short- and long-term financial projections and whether the plan is updated as needed and used in the decision-making process.

E=Earnings: *Adjusted return on equity:* measures the ability of the institution to maintain and increase its net worth through earnings from operations. *Operational Efficiency:* measures the efficiency of the institution and monitors its progress toward achieving a cost structure that is closer to the level achieved by formal financial institutions. *Adjusted Return an Assets:* measures how well the MFI's assets are utilized, or the institution's ability to generate earnings with a given asset base. *Interest rate policy:* assess the degree to which management analyzes and adjusts the institution's interest rates on microfinance loans (and deposits if applicable), based on the cost of funds, profitability targets, and macroeconomic environment

L=Liquidity Management: *Liability structure:* review of the composition of the institution's liabilities, including their tenor, interest rate, payment terms, and sensitivity to changes in the macroeconomic environment. *Availability of funds to meet credit demands:* measures the degree to which the institution has delivered credit in a timely and agile manner. *Cash flow projections:* evaluate the degree to which the institution is successful in projecting its cash flow requirements. *Productivity of other current assets*: evaluates extent to which the MFI maximizes the use of its cash, bank accounts, and short-term investments by investing in a timely fashion and at the highest returns, commensurate with its liquidity needs.

13.5. MICROS Rating Model

MICROS stands for Management, Institutional arrangement, Capital adequacy and asset quality, Resources and asset-liability management, Operational effectiveness and Scalability and sustainability. It is methodology developed by CIRISIL for undertaking the grading of microfinance institutions (MFIs) and non-government organizations which have microfinance programme as among their key activities. This is a comprehensive framework to assess the ability of MFIs to scale up and sustain their operations. It is one of the most popular rating models used in India.

The MICROS framework considers the following elements in its analysis:[1]

M=Management

- **History & Track Record:** Number of years in micro credit, Associate entities, their performance, Growth of MFI in the past w.r.t. programmes, geography, clients and branches
- **Alliances and network:** Strategic alliances (national & international), partners contribution, MFI's gain through the relationships, Donoer agencies support, appreciation etc.
- **Documentation Levels:** Extent of documentation in terms of manual on MFI's products, policies, process, authorizations etc. Adherence of the documented policies, procedures etc, in day to day operations.
- **Management Information Systems:** Credit approval mechanism, Loan and overdue monitoring systems, Cash flow management system & fraud control
- **Use of IT in operation:** Extent of hardware and software infrastructure, Is it commensurate to the scale of operations and are there any perceived benefits after implementations? IT operations mangement, security, access levels, application control etc.
- **Human Resource Management:** Training, Role definition, Accountability & responsibility, Attrition rates
- **Process, Controls & Audit:** Head Office level controls, Group, Centre, Branch Office level control systems, Are independent audits being carried out, nature and scope fo audits, quality of such reports, experience of auditors in this field, Efficacy of internal audit, Accounting policy and procedures.
- **Social impact on environment/local impact:** Availability of Impact Assessment Studies, Credibility and conclusions of the Impact Assessment Study.

I= Institutional Arrangement

- **Management ownership & governing board:** Pedigree of promoters, their experience, recognition in this field, years of experience; Involvement in the day-to-day operations; Structure of the board, diversity of the technical expertise on the board such as finance, law, marketing etc; Professional reputation of the board members; Independence of the board from the management; Organization structure; Experience of key management personal; Management understanding of issues in MFI sector

- **Corporate Governance practices:** Are mainstream corporate governance practices sensitized in the operation; Overall assessment in terms of practices, processes and people.
- **Goals & Strategies:** Articulation of vision-medium & long term; Articulation of strategies to achieve stated goals; Strategic planning and budgeting

C=Capital Adequacy and Asset Quality

- **Capital Adequacy:** Leverage; Ability to raise equity/grants
- **Asset Quality and Portfolio at Risk:** Asset Quality, portfolio at risk; Write –off levels; Provision, Expenses and risk coverage

R=Resources

- **Ability to raise resources:** Current funding sources, adequacy of the same; Diversity in funding sources; Percentage of funding from members; Impact of the legal structure of MFI in raising resources; Ability to attract donor funds, current relationships
- **Cost of funds:** Average cost of funds; Subsidized borrowings as a % of total liabilities
- **Liquidity & Asset Liability Management:** Loans as a % of total assets; Asset liability mismatch; Debt/Equity; Cost of funds; Funding expenses

O=Operational Effectiveness

- **Office outreach and quality of infrastructure:** Geographical areas covered; Employee productivity; Client targeting practices
- **Efficiency ratios:** Staff allocation ratio; Operational efficiency; Administrative cost per loan action; Personal expenses levels; Cost per borrower

S=Scalability and sustainability

- **Resource base sustainability:** Ability to continuously access resource, Fund raising strategies in place; Are current efficiency, profitability levels sustainable at large scale of operations, diversity etc?
- **Organizational sustainability:** Legal Structure Issues; Corporate Governance Issues; Succession Issues; Human Resources
- **Programme Sustainability:** Ability to sustain operation on a larger scale; Sectoral expertise has been built; Past track record to enter new segments, geographical areas; Long term outlook of programmes are clearly envisioned.

13.6. Foreign AID Rating Methodology[2]

Rating methodology is based on five parameters Social impact, Institutional development,

Financial Efficiency and Health, Accountability and Design, Monitoring and Evaluation. The rating process is based on the following:

- Interviews with Beneficiaries and Staff
- Review of financial records and organizational procedures and documents
- Tours of organization's events and facilities
- Organizational Self-Assessment
- Evaluator's Personal Observations.

Social Impact	▪ **Beneficiary Participation** – Community contributions – Institutional Participation ▪ **Relevance, Outputs and Outcomes** – Relevance to Primary Needs – Nos. of Beneficiaries Served Annually – Outputs within Primary Needs – Program Sustainability and Follow-up – Focus (Activities and Target Groups) – Gender Sensitivity – Innovation
Institutional Development	▪ **Legality and Institutionalization** – Legal Status – Institutional Cooperation Personnel – Annual Budget ▪ **Institutional Leadership** – General Assembly – Board of Directors ▪ **Operative Management System** – Dissemination and Understanding of the Organization's Mission – Organizational Chart – Management Procedures – Integration of Personnel • **Human Resources Management** – Clearly Defined Position Responsibilities – Institutional Policy toward Personnel – Supervision of Personnel –Personal Qualifications
Financial Efficiency and Health	▪ **Financial Efficiency** – Expense Breakdown ▪ **Financial Growth** – Primary Revenue Growth – Past Budget Growth – Expected Future Budget Growth ▪ **Financial Sustainability** – Self-generated Income – Diversified Funding – Administrative Costs – Financial Planning

Accountability	▪ **Financial Management and Accounting** – Accounting Systems – Financial Analysis – Financial Controls ▪ **Transparency and Communication** – Internet Saviness – Personnel's Level of Education – Website Quality – Newsletter – Availability of Financial Reports – Quality of Financial Reports – External Audit – Disclosure
Design, Monitoring and Evalutation	M&E Information System M&E Department/Full-Time Staff M&E Use in Program Design Quality of M&E Reports.

13.7. M-CRIL Rating System

M-CRIL was established in 1998 to mitigate investors' lack of knowledge and experience of microfinance institutions and to facilitate an increased flow of funds into the microfinance sector based on professional assessments of creditworthiness. The service was based on an assessment of parameters developed specially after studying the realities of microfinance operations. M-CRIL uses a comprehensive rating tool consisting three categories of indicators.

Governance and strategy: The assessment depends on the quality and appropriateness of the board composition, its role and overall organizational strategy.

Management systems: are rated on the quality of human resources, the strength of critical systems like accounting and management information. The performance of the MFI on staff productivity and ensuring compliance is also assessed.

Financial performance: evaluation requires the rating team to construct financial statements, based on internationally accepted prudential norms, to present a fair picture of the operations. In case of organisation's doing more than one activity, the costs are allocated based on a field assessment of usage. These are then used to assess the MFIs financial strength based on aspects like repayment performance, asset quality, liquidity, Asset Liability Management (ALM) and profitability.

13.8. Micro Rate Rating Model

The objectives of Micro Rate Rating Model are used to assess the credit risks which can be used by potential investors or creditors or donors. It uses full initial evaluation, annual analysis and preliminary credit assessments.

(a) Full initial evaluation: It consists of a 3-to-5 days on-site visit by at least two staff focusing on five core areas of MFI's financial and operational performance. These five core areas are management and governance, management information systems, financial conditions, credit operations and portfolio analysis. After the full initial evaluation, the rating agency delivers of concise report showing the details of the credit worthiness, financial health, strengths and weaknesses of the financial and operational performance of the MFI.

(b) Annual Analysis: In the annual analysis, the rating agency pays at least one visit to the MFI in a calendar year. The evaluation is based on the exhaustive desk review and phone interviews. The rating agency provides regular semi-annual reports detailing the strengths and weakness of the MFI which deepen over time.

(c) Preliminary credit assessment: It is made to have a less in-depth understanding on the areas of risk in the viability of the MFI. The evaluation reports detail the financial and operational strengths and weaknesses of the MFI.

13.9. The Philippine Coalition for Microfinance Standards

The Philippines Coalition for Microfinance standards uses eight performance indicators for social and financial rating of microfinance institutions. These indicators are (i) outreach, (ii) repayment rate, (iii) Portfolio at risk, (iv) Operating cost ratio, (v) Operational self-sufficiency, (vi) financial self-sufficiency, (vii) Equity to asset ratio and (vii) current ratio.

Performance indicators	*Descriptions*
Outreach	It provides information on cliental base and active clients
Repayment Rate	The repayment rate is used as an indicator for collection efficiency with respect to the amount due. A good repayment rate is a reflection of a viable microfinance programme
Portfolio at risk	This measures portfolio quality
Operating cost ratio	Measures costs relative to average portfolio
Operational Self-Sufficiency	This indicates whether or not enough revenue has been earned to cover the institutional costs. A measure of financial efficiency equal to total operating revenues divided by total administrative and financial expenses:
Financial self sufficiency	This indicates the degree to which an organization is earning enough revenue to sufficiently cover in the long run all operating costs and maintain the value of capital.
Capital Adequacy/Leverage-Equity to asset ratio	This ratio provides information on the capital position of the MFI and its capacity to support both growths of the loan portfolio as well as potential deterioration in assets. It also measures the ability of the MFI to expand its available resources by increasing its liabilities: It is a quantitative and qualitative measure of an institution's level of equity versus the risk it incurs. This measurement shows a programme's ability to absorb loan loss.

13.10. GOOHAP Rating Model

Micro credit School of Practitioners (Microsop) Foundation, India evolved a rating tool for MFI which is based on GOOHAP i.e. Governance, Outreach, Operations, Human resources, Asset Quality & disclosure and Profitability & efficiciency parameters. The rating process involves the following steps:

a) Discussion with the Board & Senior Management personnel
b) Visits to branch units to understand the operations practiced
c) Interaction with the field staff
d) Village visits and getting feedback from SHG member-clients
e) Participatory SWOT analysis
f) Analysis of financial statements

Various parameters considered for rating are mentioned below:

Government	Board composition, Conduct of Board meetings Vision and strategic plan, Integrity & commitment of promoter directors Institutional association with other development agencies/departments
Outreach	Proximity of MFI to people, Number of villages covered, No of SHGs formed, No. of members enrolledTargeting the poorestCommitment for pro-poor approach, Geographical distribution and coverage
Operations	Nos. of years of experience in microcreditProvision of promotional support services (e.g. EDP training, skill training, marketing etc)Resource mobilization, Credit history-size of borrowings of MFITrack record of repayment of loan by MFIsSystems and Procedures in credit administration, Management Information System, Liquidity management, Range of products offered by MFI, Innovative Products/Process that resulted in cost saving to MFI or increased outreach, Amount of lent per Branches.
Human Resources	Knowledge of staff on micro finance operations/SHG promotion, Skill sets of staff, Attitude of staff towards works, Scope for upgradation of skills, Performance linked incentive schemes to staff, Professional management capacity among staff, Recruitment policy & labour laws (PF , Gratuity etc), Staff turnover
Asset Quality and Disclosure	Portfolio at Risk (PAR), Asset allocation- loan portfolio as % of total assets, Capital Adequacy Ratio, Availability of financial statements, Rating by professionals & information for public view

Profitability and Efficiency	Operational Self Sufficiency (OSS), Financial Self Sufficiency (FSS), Return on Assets (ROA), Operational Efficiency Ratio, (OER), Total Cost Ratio (TCR)

Microsop Rating Grades

Point range	*MSR Grade*	*Comments*
80 points & above	A	Prudent operative systems & procedures, Low risk, High creditworthiness, Finance can be extended
60-79-points	B	Moderate systems & procedures, Medium risk, Medium creditworthiness, Finance can be extended
50-59points	C	Systems & Procedures need to be fine tuned, High Risk, Low creditworthiness, Finance can not be extended right now. But, can be considered later, when the MFI improves certain basic requirement
Below 50	D	Systems & Procedures inadequate, Higher risk, very low creditworthiness, Finance cannot be extended.

REFERENCES

1. http://www.gdrc.org/icm/rating/rate-2.html
2. www.m-cril.com/.../M-CRIL%20Introduction%20to%20Social%20Rating.pdf–
3. www.crisil.com/pdf/ratings/CRISIL-ratings_india-top-50-mfis.pdf
4. www.planetrating.com/.
5. www.accion.org
6. www.microrate.com

14
Social Performance Management (SPM)

14.1. Social Performance Management

In the microfinance arena, performance has long been associated with financial outcomes measured by loan portfolio quality, cost recovery and profitability.[1] With significant investment of talented minds, committed organisations and donor dollars, the measures of financial performance have been tested, revised, refined and largely standardized across the industry. Yet such progress in measurement, though considerable, only tells half of the performance story in microfinance. Most microfinance institutions (MFIs) strive to meet interrelated financial and social goals, managing a double bottom line where strong financial performance facilitates the fulfillment of a social mission. Monitoring and assessing social performance is emerging as a vital activity in the industry as the practitioners increasingly acknowledge that achieving the social outcomes inherent in our missions requires more deliberate strategies and more systematic monitoring.

The renewed interest in the social goals of microfinance is part of a historical shift in industry practice from a near exclusive focus on the financial performance of institutions to a more active concern for their clients. This shift is marked by a surge of interest in various types of impact assessment, market research and product development, all directed to gain a better understanding of MFI's clients and how MFIs can best serve them. Historically, most of the MFIs kept close track of each client's repayment record, but know little about how she managed to repay the loan or how she gained from it. Such knowledge would be likely to influence MFI's operational and product decisions in her favour. As the industry matures and grows more competitive, retaining clients and attracting new ones increasingly depends on institutions' ability to meet their needs and help them make the most of the benefits they seek from using the products and services. In microfinance, social and financial performances are linked and mutually reinforcing. Those who pay attention to their mission to improve the lives of poor people are likely to improve their financial bottom line as well.

Microfinance was evolved as a tool of social empowerment, financial inclusion and poverty reduction rather than a profit making mechanism. So, social performance is an important issue for the microfinance initiative. Nowadays, most microfinance institutions (MFIs) strive to meet interrelated financial and social goals, managing a double bottom line where strong financial performance facilitates the fulfillment of a social mission.

Social performance (SP) is the effective translation of an institution's mission into practice in line with accepted social goals.[2] These include serving, increasing numbers of poor and excluded people in a sustainable manner, improving the quality and appropriateness of the financial services, improving the economic and social condition of clients, ensuring social responsibility to clients, employees and the community they serve. According to Imp-Act, Social Performance Management (SPM) is defined as the systematic assessment of performance relative to social objectives and use of this information to improve practice.

Social Performance Management is an institutionalized process which involves setting clear cut social goals and objectives, effectively tracking and assessing progress towards achieving these social goals and objectives to improve overall performance of the organization. SPM is an institutionalized process towards social mission into practice which includes setting clear social goals, monitoring progress towards these objectives and using information to improve performance and practice.[3]

Effective social performance management helps in increasing social as well as financial inclusion, reduce clients' dropouts and thereby reduce cost associated with it, improve economic returns as customer loyalty will lead to better repayment rates and effectively use the financial investments. Social performance management helps the organization/MFI to share issues and problems of clients, hence enable the organization/MFI to design social responsive products and effectively distribute it. It also helps in retaining cliental loyalty and organizational popularity and reputation.

SPM helps to build and update the understanding of clients and how they use and benefit from products and services offered by MFIs. Such information is critical to demonstrate programme impact for a range of stakeholders and improve programme services. Understanding how clients interact with microfinance programme will help MFIs to make operational and product decisions in response to their needs and preferences.

Social Performance Management (SPM) tries to find out the answer of the following questions:

a) Firstly, does the MFI have specific social objectives? Does it have specific indicators for measuring and managing progress towards those objectives?
b) Secondly, is the MFI achieving its goals for breath and depth of outreach?
c) Thirdly, is the MFI meeting the need of its clients? What does the MFI do to better meet its clients' need?
d) Finally, is the MFI having measurable impact on improving the social and economic lives of the clients?

There has been increasing realization of enforcing social performance management practices in the microfinance sector by the practitioners, donors, service providers, funding agencies and policy makers so as to promote a double bottom line that holds MFIs accountable, financially and socially.

The principle of Social Performance Management (SPM) reflects a consensus among wide range of stakeholders who commit to take proactive action to achieve their social mission by managing social performance.

a) Firstly, this process encompasses translating of mission and values into clear, measurable objectives to capture intentional social benefits;

b) Secondly, it envisages designing and implementing systems for client protection, track, understand and report on whether it is achieving its social objectives, and

c) Thirdly, it aims to align its business process to achieve both social and financial objectives and ensure that decision-making considers both social and financial outcomes.

The key elements of Social Performance include the process (governance, policies and systems), results (achievement of social goals at client & community levels) and contexts (the information available for describing the key features of MFIs and in the environment in which it operates).[4] On the other hand, in financial performance, the focus is laid on return on assets (ROA), financial self sufficiency (FSS), Operational self-sufficiency (OSS), operational expenses ratio (OER), & portfolio at risk (PAR).

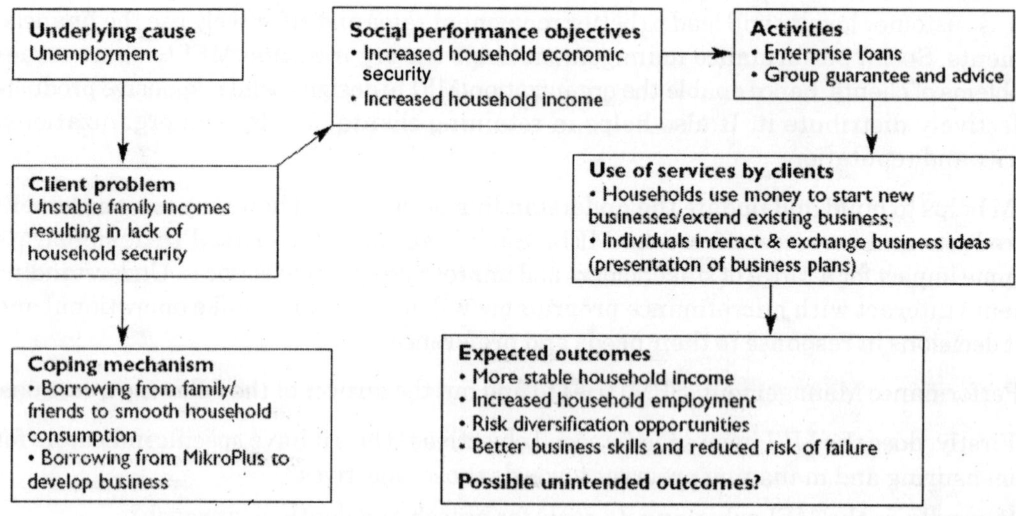

Source: Imp-Act Pathway: MikroPlus, Croatia

In the social performance, the focus is to maintain the balance between MFI's mission, mandate, social values and the strategic systems, human resource policies and information systems of the organization. The key elements of the process at the Organisational level are social performance management and social responsibility. Depending on the mission, social responsibility could encompass responsibility to clients, members, community, staff and environment. Responsibility for protection of clients is the most important and includes fair and transparent pricing, clear communication, and sensitivity to over-debiting clients, ethical behavour of staff including appropriate debt collection practices, responsiveness to clients' grievances and its redressal, etc. Social performance will also reflect the extent to which the client's financial needs are related to their capacities, and awareness and views on the package.

Finally, it is possible to assess impact of the microfinance programme with reference to program objectives and wider development objectives. In the above perspective, many development agencies as also special Microfinance Rating agencies are trying to evolve parameters for assessment of SPM and many MFIs are revisiting their mandate, process & results.

14.2. Social Rating

Microfinance rating until now has focused on organisational and financial performance related to risk assessment. Financial sustainability is vital for continuity and expansion, but is only half the story of microfinance. Most microfinance institutions (MFIs) and those who support them (investors, bankers, policy-makers, donors) have a *social mission*: such as to provide appropriate financial services in under-served areas, to families previously excluded from the banking sector, to support their micro and small enterprises, contributing to the empowerment of the poor, especially women, and meeting other financial needs, so as to reduce vulnerability and poverty. Such mission statements are seldom backed up by evidence of whether they are being achieved. Social Rating can help to address this long-felt gap in the sector, contributing to greater transparency about what MFIs are achieving. When placed alongside a Credit Rating, the Social Rating enables comparison of the social and financial performance of MFIs, providing an assessment of the double (if not triple) bottom line. It aims to assist investors and donors in making effective use of microfinance resources to achieve social/ethical as well as financial goals. It will also assist MFIs to report on and improve their social performance, just as the Credit Rating has had a positive impact on the sustainability performance of MFIs.

Why Social Rating?

a) To promote greater transparency on social performance.

b) To benchmark social performance across the microfinance industry.

c) To encourage MFIs to improve their social performance management and reporting.

d) To promote investment in MFIs with strong social performance.

Social Rating is an assessment of the likelihood of an MFI achieving social mission, in line with accepted social values. The Social Rating tool draws on the definition of social performance as the effective translation of mission into practice, in line with accepted social values. This definition (adopted by the Social Performance Task Force) emphasises that social performance is not only the end result (or impact) but a process to achieve that end; and that there are certain social values associated with microfinance in terms of goals and responsibilities (whether or not these are explicitly stated in the MFI's own mission).

The social performance assessment or rating of a MFI is done by careful assessment of the structure, system and culture of the organization (i.e. mission, vision, objectives, principles, ownership, management, human resources and intra-relationship among the staff, horizontal and vertical flow of information etc.) and by its operations in the microfinance market and community (services, products, market behaviour, relations with clients and other stakeholders etc.).[5]

The social performance can be measured by employing quantitative as well as qualitative assessment tools. The quantitative tools involve questionnaire and schedules, sample survey or population survey etc. The qualitative tools involve personal discussions, participatory appraisals, focus group discussions, discussions with key informants. Apart from that secondary sources can be used to gather information. The questionnaires should be pretested and large enough to capture all required information. Questions should be both open ended and close ended.

Social rating is helpful for MFIs in getting a clear picture on their strengths and weakness. These ratings enable MFIs to work on their strength and to improve on their weaknesses. Through social rating, MFIs can better assess their performances before any major setbacks, find out scope for improvement and can document their phase-wise improvements. Ratings are not only helpful for MFIs but also helpful for donors or bankers, and respective Governments where the MFI works. The rating of an MFI reflects its performance standards and it benchmarks the MFI in the microfinance industry or market. The rating results will act a base for understanding the social and financial performance of MFIs and the donors can use this rating information. The donors can get information on the quality and efficiency of MFIs from the rating results. Good rating results of MFIs develop confidence and security among donors and private investors. Rating of MFIs also provides information to donors and private investors who are interested to analyze the future funding to MFIs. The Government can use the rating results as the operation of MFIs comes under the financial framework of the Government. Moreover, rating creates transparency in the MFI and in the MFI sector as a whole.

14.3. Need for Social Performance Standard

In the recent years, certain undesirable practices and trends in MFIs have given rise to serious concerns. The field studies have brought to the fore certain undesirable trends.

a) The effective interest rates charged by many of the MFIs are very high, posing undue interest burden and distress on the clients. In the absence of transparent pricing of loans, the clients remain ignorant of the implication of interest rate they were subjected to.

b) The Recovery Officers are generally insensitive to the lack of capacity of the clients for repayment and often take recourse to unacceptable coercive methods in their urge to achieve 100% recovery.

c) The competing MFIs and banks operate in the same location and in the general absence of any KYC /appraisal norms/exchange of information among the lenders; the same borrowers are given multiple loans leading to their over-indebtedness.

d) In several cases, the members covered under the SHG-Bank Linkage Programme are also serviced by MFIs, often leading to splitting of SHGs. Even the basic tenets of SHG formation and graduation are relegated to the background in rush for financing SHGs.

e) In the MFI sector, there is no structured grievance redressal system for the customers, client protection mechanism, customer's education/counseling avenue to enlighten them about their rights and obligations.

f) The risk management architecture, internal checks and control system, corporate governance standards, training of staff on customers service, etc. are found to be weak and deficient.

g) The unfair competition, absence of debt restructuring/rescheduling policy, ambitious aggressive business plan leading to business expansion, absence of critical assessment under social performance have contributed to an unhealthy scenario.

Thus, the issue of Mission drift and the need for ensuring Social Performance Standards have surfaced prominently in the Indian MFIs.

14.4. Cost and Benefit of Social Performance Management

The MFI's success is closely linked to the success of its clients. In a context of greater availability of services and growing competition among providers, MFIs that do not meet the needs of their clients will lose them. Those that are focused on and responsive to their clients will retain them, and increase their share of the market. Thus, in microfinance, financial and social goals are mutually reinforcing. Strong financial performance enables an MFI to pursue its social objectives, and achieving social objectives is good for business. Through active monitoring and assessment of client interaction with products and services, SPM helps MFIs to remain faithful to their mission and maximise both sides of the performance coin.

There are costs involved in SPM, but the benefits are well worth the investment one will make over time. SPM will lead to better, client-focused services and organisational culture, more satisfied clients, stronger management and improved financial performance.

Adopting and measurement of Social Performance Management by MFIs will have the following attendant benefits:

a) Facilitates development of social performance policy, roadmap and strategies;

b) Balances and integrates financial and social objectives;

c) Institutionalizes generation of baseline information and use of social performance information;

d) It improves outreach , quality of services and products, customer's service;

e) It benefits clients by offering services suited to their needs;

f) It reduces vulnerability, increases empowerment of clients;

g) It enhances financial performance by higher retention of clients and lower operational costs;

h) It ensures transparency and makes players responsible;

i) It facilitates monitoring and assessing social performance and standardizes tools for measurement;

j) It verifies the results of the programmes and facilitates mid-term corrections;

k) It integrates intent/mission/mandates in design, internal systems, output and outcome;

l) It provides early warning signals in case of deviations and distortions; and

m) It helps and enlightens donors, funding agencies-development institutions to better appreciate the institution and channelise their funds to meet broader objectives.

Benefits to MFI's Managers	• ***Balancing financial and social objectives*** to make better business decisions based on a more thorough understanding of the trade-offs each involves. • ***Generate base line information*** that is invaluable for more in-depth assessment of social performance. • ***Track performance against targets***, both social and financial. • ***Identify problems*** at an early stage before they become damaging for the organisation.
Benefits to Clients	• Services more appropriate to their needs. • More product choices. • Better customer service. • A greater 'voice' in the programme.
To improve outreach, services and products	• ***Segmentation of portfolio*** to examine differences in performance by client characteristics, and thereby identify market niches, opportunities and problems. • ***Monitor how clients use services*** to determine how well they 'fit', addressing the question, 'Are services rendered appropriate to the needs of target clients'? • ***Innovate*** to improve client satisfaction and loyalty through better products, better customer service and greater flexibility. • ***Verify the results of programmatic changes*** to determine if they have made a difference. • ***Track intended and unintended impacts on clients' lives*** and in the wider community and understand the role that MFI plays in promoting these changes.
To improve financial performance	• ***Higher retention of clients*** through monitoring of and responsiveness to their satisfaction with the programme. Higher retention rates translate into lower costs and higher profits. • ***Programme growth*** by making MFI more attractive to potential clients because of demand driven products and services and word of mouth from current satisfied clients.

- ***Lower operational costs*** as use of resources more effectively based on better understanding of best investments.
- ***Demonstration of social performance to stakeholders***, thus improving MFI's position in a competitive funding market.

14.5. Social Performance Management Process

Monitoring and managing social performance is an ongoing process. In contrast to traditional evaluations that focus on a programme's final impact, SPM provides a framework for understanding the *process* by which social performance objectives are achieved. SPM relates to the entire organisation and its strategy. It thus focuses on how all organisational systems (human resources, information, incentives etc.) support the social mission. It also looks at how information can be gathered to support decision-making, indicating the information to collect, how to collect it and how to use it. A range of tools and methodologies are used in SPM to monitor and understand the different steps in the pathway to the social mission. SPM can include market research to determine client preferences or market opportunities, analysis of the strengths and weaknesses of the organisational systems, monitoring of client profile and changing status over time, and assessment of end results and impact. Finally, it is a framework that combines assessment with action to enhance the ability to translate social performance objectives into practice. SPM is a management-driven process comprised of the three components described below:

Components of SMP	*Descriptions*
(a) Developing a social performance strategy	MFI's social performance objectives are derived from its mission. They are the detailed translation of MFI's mission into clear and measurable objectives, which drive the design and delivery of programme activities. Social performance objectives generally fall into three categories: ▪ Outreach to clients with specific characteristics, ▪ Responsiveness to client needs, and ▪ Impact on clients, their families and communities.
(b) Monitoring and assessing social performance	Social performance is MFI's effectiveness in translating the MFI's specific social objectives into practice. Tracking progress towards each distinct objective usually requires distinct tools. For example, in-take forms or poverty assessment tools will help to assess outreach; market research tools can help to understand how effective the institution has been in meeting client needs; and finally, a rich selection of tools and processes enable MFIs to identify programme benefits to clients and the wider community. Whatever the objectives choose to assess, the process used should combine 1)

(Contd...)

Components of SMP	Descriptions
	routine monitoring that tracks basic information about client status with 2) follow-up research to explore in greater depth trends and issues highlighted by the monitoring.
(c) Institutionalising and using social performance information	The heart of SPM is information use. An SPM system needs to both collect relevant and timely information and communicate it effectively to inform organisational operations and strategy. While information can be gathered in many different ways the effort will be of little benefit unless the data is used in a systematic way to assess and improve operations, services, products, and customer relations. Actual and systematic use of data collected regularly will have widespread impact on performance of MFIs, calling for an eventual integration of SPM with other systems and processes. This "institutionalisation" of SPM can only be undertaken once MFIs are confident that the system is tracking the right information: the performance objectives that are striving to achieve.

The process of SPM starts with analysis of the declared social objective of the institution i.e. intent and design. In the next step SP includes assessment of internal systems and activities. It asks whether the institutional activities are in line to the achievement of their social goals. Are appropriate systems prevail there to meet these objectives? Are products designed to meet the flexible financial need of the poor? Finally the SP is about impact. It establishes rigorous relationship between programme participation and improvement in client's condition. So, SP looks at the entire progress by which output is created.

Intent & Design → Internal System & Activities → Output → Outcomes → Impact[6]

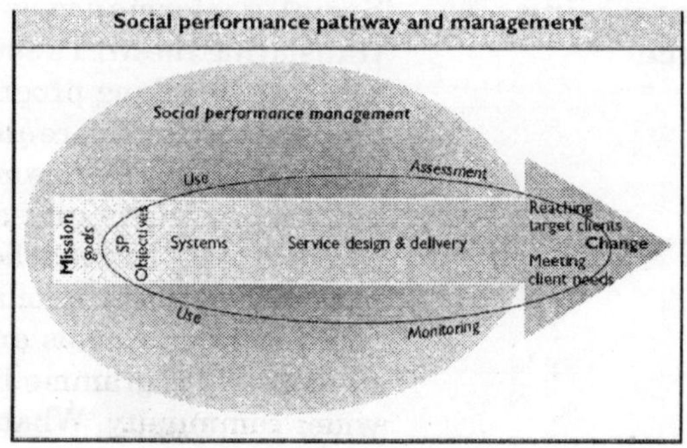

Source: Imp-Act

Above figure gives an overview of the social performance pathway, and the process of SPM. The central arrow demonstrates how an organisation's mission is translated into specific social performance objectives. Through the design of operational systems and the design and delivery of services outcomes are achieved in terms of reaching target client groups and meeting their needs. Meeting the needs of target clients leads to the desired changes relating to the social mission. Surrounding this arrow is the social performance management process. This involved monitoring and assessing progress at each stage of the arrow, and the use of information produced to feed into improved practice.

14.6. Tools for Managing Social Performance

A rich array of resources or tools is available to collect the information needed to answer social performance questions. Some tools have been developed or adapted especially for practitioners of microfinance. Market research tools, for example, such as those of *MicroSave* and SEEP/AIMS, are useful for identifying client preferences or potential products based on the financial landscape or seasonal needs for cash; others focus on how clients use your products. In-depth qualitative interviews help to understand the complex changes that may be occurring for the client in relationship to her enterprise, her family or her community. Following Figure provides an overview of how a number of commonly used tools can help MFI to answer social performance questions.

Tools for Managing Social Performance

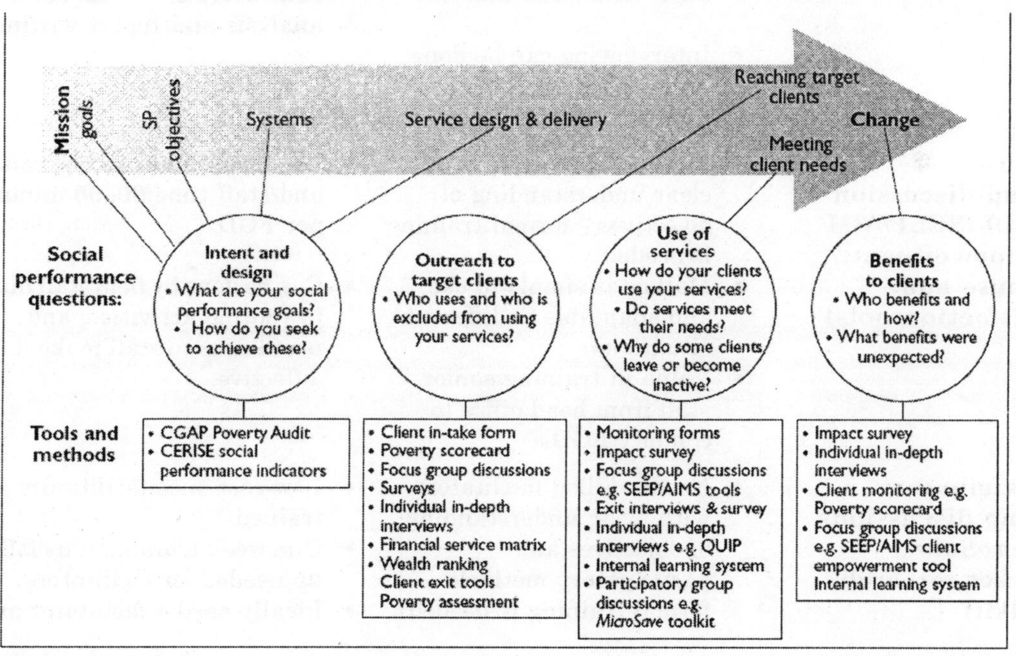

Source: Imp-Act

The choice of methods and corresponding tools will largely depend on what an MFI want to learn. It is important to relate tools to the social performance questions that an MFI wishes to answer. In designing SPM system, choice of methods and tools will have implications for cost, time required, and staffing. The type of research tool will affect the way the project is implemented in terms of logistics, human resources (number of people involved and the necessary skills) and data management. These requirements will inevitably influence the overall SPM plan.

The resource requirements of some of the main tools are summarized given below:

Skill, Cost and Resource Requirements for SPM Tools

Tool	*Staff Skill Level and Ease of Use*	*Cost and other resources*
Monitoring forms	▪ Simple to collect information with MFI staff ▪ Technically challenging to integrate into MIS	▪ If kept simple small addition to existing procedures, so not time-consuming ▪ If large sample or census then overall time inputs can be quite high ▪ Adaptation of MIS can be costly
Impact survey	▪ Requires skilled staff for design, sampling, supervision and analysis ▪ Interviewing can be done by staff with relatively little training	▪ Costly in terms of design time and input and staff time in conducting interviews, analysis and report writing.
Focus group discussion (FGD) (SEEP/AIM Sempowerment, loanuse and satisfactiontools)	▪ Needs skilled staff with clear understanding of objectives - formal training is needed ▪ Method is simple to use and adaptable to different situations ▪ Value in training senior staff from head office to conduct FGDs	▪ Low-cost – main cost is training and staff time 60–90 minutes per FGD ▪ Can be done by field staff linked to routine activities, and usefulness to staff make it cost effective.
Participatory group discussions (*MicroSave* market research toolkit)	▪ Needs skilled facilitators with clear understanding of objectives and participatory methods – formal training is needed	▪ Low-cost once facilitators are trained ▪ One week training plus follow-up needed for facilitators ▪ Ideally need a facilitator and

(Contd...)

Tool	*Staff Skill Level and Ease of Use*	*Cost and other resources*
		note-taker; about90 minutes per discussion ▪ Quick results from many people
Individual interview (QUIP)	▪ Needs skilled staff for interviews and data analysis ▪ Easy to use, but poor application will invalidate results	▪ Low-cost – main cost is training and staff time, although skill level of staff may demand relatively high salary ▪ 60 minutes per interview
Internal learningsystem	▪ Need highly skilled staff to facilitate ▪ Formal training and on-going support for staff is needed ▪ Can be used by illiterate clients	▪ Intensive tool that is time-consuming and needs to fit in with organisational approach to empowering clients ▪ Demands significant client time ▪ Can be adapted to be used in a low cost and less-intensive way

14.7. Social Performance Indicators (SPI)

Social Performance Indicators (SPI) is a set of operational indicators that seeks to measure the different dimensions and elements of social performance of MFIs.

The objectives of the SPI are:

a) To develop a conceptual framework for defining social performance in the MFI sector, and identify the dimensions and elements of social performance to be measured.

b) To suggest a set of operational indicators that seeks to measure the different dimensions and element of social performance of the MFIs.

A number of indicators have been set by different organizations for measuring Social Performance as given below:

CERISE Social Performance Indicator Tool	There are four dimensions of quantitative and qualitative data: ▪ Outreach to poor and excluded ▪ The adaptation of services and products so as to target clients ▪ Improvement of social and political capital of the clients ▪ The social responsibility of the MFIs
CGAP	▪ **Depth of outreach:** percentage (%) of clients

	living below USD1.00 per day and USD 2.00 per day; percentage(%) of clients living below the national poverty line or the absolute poverty line ▪ **Reducing poverty and hunger**: Improvement in housing structure; increases in assets (land ownership or any simple, easily visible asset); employment generation (especially lean season employment); food security and consumption smoothening (sufficient food, especially in lean seasons); crisis coping (increased resilience to cope with crises; access to emergency financing (loans and savings). ▪ **Schooling:** Primary school attendance (% of eligible children); secondary school attendance (% of eligible children) ▪ **Access to health care services:** Access to messages on preventative care and to referrals; access to clean water; immunization and parental care; use of modern medical facilities (e.g. doctors or modern health care facilities at childbirth) ▪ **Women's empowerment and social capital:** percentage (%) of women clients; women's involvement in public sphere activities (e.g. election or local adjudicating bodies); legal awareness (divorce, inheritance); women's networks (development of social networks outside kin groups)
MicroSave	▪ How poor are clients? ▪ How satisfied are the clients with the services provided? ▪ What different are services making in the lives of clients?
AIMS/SEEP[7] empowersment tool	▪ Whether the clients have grown more confident and gained more self esteem while participating in the programme? ▪ How these qualities have translated into specific changes in behavior that demonstrate power?
CGAP-FORD	▪ Whether the MFIs are reaching the very poor? ▪ Whether the clients are increasing incomes and building assets? ▪ Whether clients' social conditions are improving
IFAD[8]	▪ Does the MFI have the available means to attain its social objective? ▪ Who are the MFI's clients? ▪ How the products and services offered by an MFI are used by the clients? ▪ Are the clients satisfied with the services? ▪ What relationship do the clients have with MFI and the products and services it offers?

	▪ How do the socio-economic situation of clients and their families evolve? ▪ How do MFIs financial services fit into a local economy?
ACCION[9]	▪ Social Mission ▪ Outreach ▪ Client service ▪ Information transparency ▪ Association with community ▪ Labour climate.
M-Cril	▪ **The intent & design**: mission, clarity, communication, governance; ▪ **Alignment of systems:** service delivery model, market strategy, area, clients, products, approach to product development, HR, information & reporting; ▪ **Social Responsibility:** indebtedness, transparency in pricing, appraisal, collection practices, staff behaviour, grievance redressal, client data privacy ▪ **Non financial services:** gender approach, responsibility to staff, community and environment.

14.8. Common Framework for Social Performance Indicators (SPI)

In April-May 2007, the social Performance Task Force Sub-Committee for Social Performance Core Indicators surveyed and created indicators for microfinance after analyzing and evaluation.[10] Indicators measuring achievements of social objectives are grouped into ten categories:

a) Outreach to very poor and poor people.

b) Social objectives.

c) Outreach to small and medium enterprises;

d) Outreach to underdeveloped areas;

e) Outreach to women;

f) Outreach to socially marginalized and /or excluded groups of people

g) Indirect outreach-supporting employment

h) Outcome-change in lives of clients and households

i) Outcome-change in local communities

j) Other social objectives.

14.9. M-Cril's Social Performance Framework

Social Rating covers context information about the MFI, the steps involved in translating social mission into practice and compliance with principles of social responsibility. The key dimensions are outlined below. Rating usually depends on data available with the MFI. However, MFI data is geared primarily to portfolio reporting for financial performance. To assess social performance results at the client level, M-CRIL offers the option of a field sample survey as part of the Social Rating, to cover outreach and client feedback [SGO and SGS below]. The advantage of this is that it provides a valid basis for assessment of some of the results of microfinance services. An additional advantage is that the rating survey can be used as a baseline for later follow-up of the same sample to assess change over time [SGC below]. If, on the other hand, the MFI does have fresh available data on results (including impact related reports), these will be verified and used as part of the Social Rating.

Social Rating of MFIs by M-Cril is based on three major indicators and these major indicators are (i) context (ii) process and (iii) results. The context includes organization's profile, and financial services and access. The broad indicator "process" includes social performance management and social responsibility. Similarly, the broad indicator "results" focus on social goal which includes outreach, appropriate services and effect/impact.[11]

Dimensions covered by Social Rating of M-Cril[12]

Context	Profile of operating environment (secondary data), MFI profile, services and client data.
Social Performance Management [SPM]	Mission definition and whether management systems (including targeting, incentives and reporting) are strategically aligned to MFI's stated social objectives.
Social Responsibility [SR]	Client protection – code of conduct and systems to comply; includes (where applicable) Gender Approach, Member Governance, and Non-Financial Services; other dimensions of SR (to community, staff, environment) may be included
Social Goal Outreach [SGO]	Depth and width: distribution of clients in underdeveloped areas, depth ratio (based on portfolio data); direct client level information profiling poverty, household income levels and quality of life indicators (recently joined clients – no impact yet); hired (non-family) employment in credit supported enterprises (for 'indirect' outreach)
Social Goal Services [SGS]	Range of services; client feedback on client protection issues (awareness and experience), client satisfaction; drop-out rates and reasons for drop-out.
Social Goal Change [SGC]	Any evidence on outcomes or impact from available reports (including indicators relevant to MFI's social objectives, as well as those contributing to the MDGs).

These dimensions are scored as part of M-CRIL's Social Rating; other dimensions may be described without scoring.

14.10. Sa-Dhan's Voluntary Code of Conduct of MFIs[13]

Sa-Dhan, the Association of Community Development Finance Institutions has developed core values and voluntary mutual code of conduct for member MFIs. All members are expected to unanimously and whole-heartedly agree to abide by the core values and code of conduct. The core values in microfinance focus on the following:

Integirity: to service low income clients—women and men and their families, providing them short term and or long term access to financial services, that are client-focused, designed to enhance their well-being, and delivered in a manner that is ethical, dignified, equitable and cost-effective

Quality of Services: to believe that the clients deserve fair and efficient micro-finance services and provide these services to them with convenience, in participatory and in timely manner as much as possible.

Transparency: to give the clients complete and accurate information and educate them about the terms of financial services offered in a manner that is understandable by them.

Fair Practices: to ensure that the services to the clients are not unethical and deceptive, in providing microfinance services including lending and collection of dues, with commitment to fair practices, which balance respect of client's dignity and an understanding of a client's vulnerable situation and with reasonable pursuit of recovery of loans.

Privacy of client Information: to safeguard personal information of clients and allow disclosures and exchange of such information to others authorized to see it with the knowledge and consent of clients.

Integrating social values into operations: to maintain high standards of governance, participation, management and reporting are critical to our mission to serve the clients and to uphold core social values.

Feedback Mechanism: to provide the clients formal and informal channels for their feedback and suggestions for building competencies to serve the clients better.

14.11. Road Map for Social Performance Standards[14]

a) The umbrella organizations in MFI sector need to play a more pro-active role in preventing the MFIs to drift from their social mandate and facilitating them to various commonly acceptable codes of standards and fair practices, particularly social performance standards.

b) The Credit Rating Agencies (CRA) need to strive to internalize and integrate the social rating with financial rating. They need to continue the efforts to evolve/improve the measurement parameters, processes and tools for social rating to facilitate implementation of the same with speed, cost-effectiveness and efficiency. Notwithstanding the additional burden in terms of cost, time and efforts involved for the purpose for both MFIs & CRAs, all players may have to take up the emerging challenge and implement the same in the due course.

c) NABARD, SIDBI and other Apex Development Institutions as also financial institutions need to insist on compliance to social performance standards while considering sanction of loan, grant, capital or other forms of financial assistance to MFIs.

d) The banks, development agencies and Credit Rating Agencies need to be sensitized about the scope and significance of 'social performance standards' for MFIs and ways and means to assess the same.

e) The Research Organisations and other development organizations engaged in research and studies may evolve parameters for measuring socio-economic impact of the programmes and projects implemented by MFIs.

f) ICFAI and other authorities connected with development of audit system need to capture the social audit system and sensitize the Chartered Accountants and Auditor's community in this regard.

g) The concept of self-regulation may be propagated among MFIs and its adoption facilitated by the Umbrella Organization/Association of MFIs/Community-Based Organizations and also development agencies and financial institutions. All MFIs and banks have to evolve and adopt fair competition code.

h) Lending Agencies should develop coordination, understanding and information-sharing convention with a view to enforcing responsible finance discipline among the MFIs. A consensus with regard to the following could be pursued by them in a bid to enforcing social performance standards in the MFI Sector.

   - Maximum effective interest rate to be levied by the MFIs to their clients;
   - Insistence on social rating by Rating Agencies;
   - Internalization of social performance parameters in the internal appraisal system;
   - Putting sanction terms and conditions on the website; and
   - Introduction of common reporting format on social aspects by MFIs.

i) The international donor agencies may focus on adherence to social performance standards obligation by the assisted agencies.

j) MFIs may consider introducing suitable staff incentive system for encouraging adherence to client/client protection standards, effective and appropriate communication with customers, customer-friendly ethical behavour.

k) Media may play a crucial role in showcasing the success stories of microfinance and could increasingly portray the aspirations, dreams and difficulties of disadvantaged people serviced by MFIs in a responsible manner.

l) The investors/lending Agencies may take upon institution-building, human capital building system, system development within MFIs, apart from undertaking financial deals with MFIs.

m) All stakeholders in MFIs need to embark upon customers' education for facilitating sensitization about their rights and obligations under microfinance services. The Board of Management of the MFIs have critical role in directing the organization to ensure social performance management systems and incorporate governance standards.

The issue of adherence to social performance standards by MFIs has drawn the attention of the Government of India, State Governments, Regulator, Policy-making and development institutions like RBI, NABARD, SIDBI, Association of MFIs, Credit Rating Agencies and general public. The GOI is contemplating to introduce Microfinance (Development and Regulation) Bill which is expected to ensure prudential standards, system and discipline in the functioning of MFIs and ultimately facilitate responsible microfinance services.

NOTES

1. Imp-Act (2005), *Social Performance Management in Microfinance- Guideline.*
2. CGAP, "Beyond Good Intentions," *Measuring the Social Performance of Microfinance Institutions.*
3. Thomas, T.K. (2007), *Social Performance in development Interventions-Giving Life to Organisation's Mission*, Microfinance Community Visioning Workshop, October 11, 2007, Solution Exchange, New Delhi.
4. Francis Sinha (2006), *Social Rating & Social Performance-Reporting in Microfinance-Towards a Common Framework*, Argidius Foundation
5. www.imp-act.org and www.cerise-microfinance.org
6. The SEEP network and Alternative Credit Technologies, *Measuring Performance of Microfinance Institutions, A framework for reporting, analysis and monitoring.*
7. Gaiha, Raghav & Thapa, Ganesh (2006), A *methodology for assessment of the impact of microfinance and vulnerability*, IFAD. and IFAD (2006), *Assessing and managing social performance in microfinance.*
8. ACCION *Insights (*November 2007, Number 24), *Guideline to Evaluate Social Performance*
9. Social Performance Task Force (MIX website)
10. www.m-cril.com
11. Sinha, S. Pathak, N. Iyer, B. and Grover, G. (2006), *Financing Microfinance in India*, Technical Note 4, Micro-credit Rating International Limited, Gurgaon, India.
12. Sa-Dhan's Publicagtions, www.sa-dhan.org
13. Biswabandhu Mohanty, NABARD, *Social Performance Management in Microfinance Institutions (MFIs)-Issues, Initiatives and perspectives,* Microfinance Enabling Empowerment, Pondichery University.

15

Micro Insurance in India

15.1. Introduction to Micro Insurance

One of the major problems confronting the poor households is the lack of adequate income and assets to deal with several risk situations such as major illness, accidents, irregular employment, death of the main earner and so on. What happens when a poor family's breadwinner dies, when a child in a disadvantaged household is hospitalized, or the home of a vulnerable family is destroyed by fire or natural disaster? Every serious illness, every accident and every natural disaster threatens the very existence of poor people and usually leads to deeper poverty. That's where "micro insurance" comes in.

Microinsurance is the term used to refer the insurance to the low income people as it is different from insurance in general where Microinsurance is a low value product with less premium and benefits. According to Consultative Group to Assist the Poor (CGAP) working group on micro-insurance defines "*micro-insurance as the protection of low-income people against specific peril in exchange for regular premium payments proportionate and cost of the risk involved*".[1]

Micro-insurance refers to protection of assets and lives against insurable risks of target populations such as micro-entrepreneurs, small farmers and the landless, women and low-income people through formal, semiformal and informal institutions. Such products are often bundled with micro-savings and micro-credit, thereby allocating scarce resources to micro-investments with the highest marginal rates of return. Micro insurance is the most underdeveloped part of microfinance. Yet various schemes exist that are viable, benefiting both the institutions and their clients. Such schemes have generally served two major purposes: (i) they have contributed to loan security; and (ii) they have served as instruments of resource mobilization. The greatest challenge for micro insurance lies in the combination of viability and sustainability with outreach.

Micro insurance can boost resources for the rural poor, governments and private sector. The entire economy gains as the insurance industry matures further as well. There is a need for Microinsurance in India's poverty reduction strategy. Micro insurance is a tool for investment savings and as a measure of social security. It increases the livelihood of the poor where they can eat well, have good health since they wouldn't have to save as much for emergencies.

Micro insurance is a key element in the financial services package for people at the bottom of the pyramid. The poor face more risks than the well-off, but more importantly they are more vulnerable to the same risk. Usually, the poor face two types of risks – idiosyncratic (specific to the household) and covariate (common, e.g., drought, epidemic, etc.).

Major risks usually faced by low-income people are given below:

a) Health and incapacity for work (e.g., illness, disability, accidents –either occupational or non-occupational);

b) Life cycle risks (e.g., death, old age);

c) Economic risks (e.g., unemployment, loss of property, crop failure); and

d) Natural disasters (e.g., floods, droughts, earthquakes).

To combat these risks, the poor do pro-active risk management – grain storage, savings, asset accumulation (specially bullocks), loans from friends and relatives, etc. However, the prevalent forms of risk management (in kind savings, self-insurance, mutual insurance) which were appropriate earlier are no longer adequate.

Savings and credit products are better suited for the events that will occur with certainty such as old age, marriage, education, purchase of income generating asset etc. The uncertain events such as sickness, accident, theft, fire, flood, etc which make the poor incur irregular or unplanned for costs, are better met by insurance especially where the amount required to mitigate or cope with the event is high.

The micro and small entrepreneurs, whether in urban or rural area, are time and again choked by uncertain events, but they have not taken recourse to buying insurance from formal insurers for a variety of reasons. The reasons for this include lack of knowledge, the inaccessibility of the existing insurance schemes, inflexibility and uncertainty about benefits. This has led some of the Microfinance Institutions (MFIs) to develop in house Micro insurance programmes and some others to act as facilitators between the formal insurance companies and their clients.

The main difference between Micro insurance and regular insurance is that the first is specifically targeted at low-income people, who have limited financial resources and often irregular income flows. Thus, the product design is adapted to these people's needs and financial capabilities. Consequently, Micro insurance products possess some distinguishing features in all dimensions of the scheme, namely design of the coverage, premiums, delivery channels, terms and benefits.

Microinsurance especially designed for low income households and it is a critical tool to eradicate the poverty. Risks are common to all individuals when compare to the risks with the common individuals poor experience the risks frequently with greater financial impact.

Poverty is not just a state of deprivation but has latent vulnerability. Microinsurance should, therefore, provide greater economic and psychological security to the poor as it reduces exposure to multiple risks and cushions the impact of a disaster. There is an overwhelming demand for social protection among the poor. Microinsurance in conjunction with micro savings and micro credit could, therefore, go a long way in keeping this segment away from the poverty trap and would truly be an integral component of financial inclusion.

15.2. Insurance Industry in India

In India insurance is a big opportunity where large untapped population is there.

The total premium of the insurance industry has grown at a CAGR of 24.6 per cent from 2002–03 to 2008–09 to reach US$ 52.6 billion in 2008–09.

Increasing insurance penetration contributed 4.00 percent to GDP in terms of premium volume of life insurance business. Increased consumer awareness helped the industry to grow and tap the untapped market. Increased competition brought innovative product with competitive price with good service. This created an impact on the insurance industry.

The overall insurance industry in India is still yet to be developed. Till now approximately 10 percent of population is covered with insurance. In 2005, total global insurance premium is estimated at US$3,426 billion, India's share accounted for 0.73 percent. This shows that the coverage of the population in terms of insurance business is low.

In India till recently the insurance industry was state owned. The life insurance business was managed exclusively by Life Insurance Corporation of India (LIC) and the non life insurance products were managed by General Insurance Company and its four subsidiaries. With the recent opening of insurance sector for private companies, there are 13 entrants/prospective entrants in life insurance business and 11 new/prospective entrants in the non-life sector.

LIC is a giant with 2046 branches. Life Insurance Corporation has nearly 62 products covering various needs such as old age pension, child education, marriage, life cover etc., Though almost all the 62 products of LIC are suitable for SMEs, it is seen that the poorer families are not covered by insurance. LIC also implements subsidised group insurance schemes aimed at socially vulnerable classes which cover many of the poor MSEs, but the coverage is very limited. New entrants to life insurance would have to compete against LIC's large distribution and marketing network with all India presence.

General Insurance Corporation and its public sector associates had the monopoly of non-life insurance till the sector opened up recently. The general insurance companies have 150 products on offer. Only 30 of them contribute about 80% of premium income. General insurance has a low presence in rural India where majority of the population lives. Only 5.2% of premia is generated from rural areas. Despite a wide product range offered in the rural areas (from insurance of large commercial plantations to individual cattle), fewer policies have been written compared to the potential. Insistence of banks on borrowers taking insurance cover on assets bought out of loans has accounted for a significant part of rural non-life insurance business.

The Indian Insurance market is still not a mature one. A fatalistic attitude, stoic acceptance of risks and a lack of faith in risk cover are some of the distinct cultural features of the people. The low levels of literacy and high levels of superstitious beliefs create additional hazards in marketing of insurance products. In the midst of such a culture, marketing insurance products is a challenge. Premia paid for insurance are viewed more as an investment and wherever possible returns on premia are sought. In fact life insurance has been driven by the tax rebates on income tax offered by the government to the policy holders on the premia payments and to a lesser extent by the insistence of lenders of term loans that the borrowers must assign life insurance policies as collateral.

In the case of general insurance, the legal requirements and banking requirements have compelled most of the policy holders into taking risk cover. Voluntary non-life insurance among individuals and small enterprise is rare. Penetration in the rural areas especially to the poor is low, due to lack of awareness on the part of the people and absence of concerted marketing of customer friendly products suited to rural economic activities. Some specific insurance products (poultry insurance) for rural areas are uneconomic from the insurer's point of view. Adverse selection, moral hazard and at times fraud affect the general insurers in rural business on account of their lack of presence in the rural areas.

The procedural hurdles and exacting legal requirements have made it difficult for policy holders to get their claims settled in time. The somewhat poor claim settlement record has exacerbated the negative sentiment on insurance coverage. On the other extreme, due to the vast geographical spread, the monitoring of the policies and investigation of claims has been difficult. Over the last five years changes in the market are increasingly evident. The demand for a wide range of products and customization of policies has been increasing. Increasing sophistication of products that are newly introduced point to the changes in the profile of customers and their awareness of role of insurance in their lives. The opening up of the sector has provided a fillip to product innovations and sustained dissemination campaigns to educate the customer about the need for insurance.

15.3. Regulation of Insurance Industry

(a) Insurance Regulation and Development Authority (IRDA)

The opening up of the insurance sector for private investments has made it necessary for the government to move away from control of the sector into regulation. The Indian Insurance Companies Act formulated in 1938 was amended in 1950 resulting in far reaching changes in the insurance sector. These included a statutory requirement of equity capital for companies carrying on life insurance business, ceiling on share holdings in such companies, stricter control on investments, submission of periodical returns relating to investments and such other information to the controller. The controller could also call for appointment of administrators and put a ceiling on expenses of management and agency commission for mismanaged companies.

IRDA is set up as an authority to protect the interests of holders of insurance policies, to regulate, promote and ensure orderly growth of insurance industry. The aspects of insurance industry that IRDA would seek to regulate are given below:

i) Entry of new players through entry norms and licensing

ii) Stipulations of minimum business in rural and socially disadvantage sections

iii) Norms on investment of insurance funds, both from social sector obligations and prudential requirements point of view

iv) Reinsurance and spreading of risks

v) Regulating entry of foreign insurer

vi) Accounting and audit of insurance companies to ensure policy holders protection.

vii. Norms for agents in terms of education, professional competence.

Some of the important entry regulations relate to foreign entities. They can hold a maximum of 26 % of equity. The remaining equity should be held by Indian shareholders. Even the Indian promoters should divest their equity over a ten year period and should hold not more than 26% at the end of the period.[2] The same insurance company cannot take up both life and non-life business. At 26% equity, while a key stake is available, controlling interest vests with some other party. Foreign entities with insurance expertise may not freely enter and offer their products and experience to the local ventures when the equity stake is so low. Apart from IRDA, Reserve Bank of India has also stipulated norms for banks wanting to enter insurance business. Banks desirous of promoting insurance companies should have a positive net worth of Rs 5 billion and meet capital adequacy norms. The level of NPA should be reasonable. The norms are to ensure that first class banks only enter the business.

IRDA has the powers of making regulations and imposing fines on those who violate its norms. It can also cancel licenses issued for repeated violations. Overall, it is expected that IRDA's interventions should prove useful in regulating the insurance industry.

(b) Registration with IRDA

All the existing insurance providers as well as new insurers should register with IRDA.

To obtain the certificate of Registration from IRDA, among other provisions the insurers should have the following:

i) Evidence of having rupees ten billion ($21 million) paid share capital.

ii) Original certificate of registration of the company.

iii) Fees of rupees thousand ($1050) for each class of business.

The high initial capital norm is to ensure that promoters not only bring in high net worth, but also demonstrate their willingness to stay invested in the business. The breakeven period of insurance is seven years or more depending on the business model and the products; hence a high initial capital is necessary to provide the necessary financial depth and confidence to clients about ability of insurer to settle claims.

(c) Prudential norms of IRDA

i) The insurers, both Life and Non-Life, should not invest more than 15% of the total capital employed in equity shares and debentures.

ii) Loans are not to form more than 10% of the estimated annual accretion of funds.

iii) Accounting system of insurance companies to ensure availability of separate statements for any activity that yields 10 per cent or more revenue.

iv) To ensure that there is never a lack of audit in the insurance company, there will be two auditors, one with a tenure of four years and the second with a tenure of five-years.

The investment norms seek to ensure that risky investments with an eye on high returns are kept at low levels, so that insurance funds do not fall prey to speculative forces. Audit norms would secure good governance practices.

(d) Norms for insurance in the rural, social and disadvantaged sector

Insurance in rural India has significance since nearly 70% of the population lives in rural areas. The non life insurance companies should increase their rural coverage, reaching a level of 5 percent of total policies written, over a three year period. Similarly, life insurance companies should increase their rural business to reach a level of 15 percent of policies written over a five year period.

The stipulation seeks to enhance the coverage of rural population which presently has a low access to insurance. The emphasis on number of policies alone would not provide meaningful coverage in the rural areas. Meaningful coverage could be ensured only by stipulating a combination of minimum percentage of number of policies and amounts underwritten.

With their existing marketing and distribution chains even the LIC and GIC have not been very successful in this market so far. The transaction costs of marketing and servicing insurance products in rural and social sector could be high on account of low sums assured per policy. The NGOs and Voluntary agencies have a strong committed customer base in the rural area. They could group their clients for taking out insurance cover and thus help in lowering transaction costs, as is the case in microfinance. They would be able to leverage on their network and distribute insurance products for the benefit of their constituents and financial gains for themselves.

(e) Norms for certification and appointment of agents

IRDA has stipulated that persons should pass an examination to be certified fit for acting as insurance agents. The insurance companies can appoint as agents only those who have been duly certified as such. There is a provision for corporate agency, under which institutions pursuing a commercial objective can take up insurance marketing on behalf of insurance companies. However, NGOs who are not usually corporate cannot act as agents as per the present norms. The same criteria will apply to MFIs which are not corporate entities. This is a setback to the micro insurance sector as marketing insurance products to rural people is not an easy task. NGOs, who work with rural people already, would be in a much better position offer products best suited to rural clients. They have the credibility and skills of communication in the local idiom which are relevant in marketing risk cover. The denial of agency business to NGOs/MFIs has led to alternatives such as NGOs/MFIs acting as facilitators and advisors to insurance companies, without due remuneration for the work.

(f) Opening up of the sector and what it means for micro insurance

Competition is the driving force in any economy. Overall the Indian insurance industry is poised to witness the following trends:

i) Increase in the bargaining power of buyers

ii) Decrease in the bargaining power of suppliers

iii) Greater threat to new entrants

iv) Medium strong possibilities for substitute products

v) Intense rivalry among the various industry players

vi) Introduction of new product

vii) Greater innovation in delivery mechanism that cater to segments such as rural, urban poor and MSEs.

(g) IRDA's Regulations on Micro-Insurance

Building on the recommendations of the consultative group, IRDA notified Micro-Insurance Regulations on 10th November 2005 with the following key features to promote and regulate micro-insurance products. The regulations focus on the direction, design and delivery of the products:

i) A tie-up between life and non life insurance players for integration of product to address risks to the individual, his family, his assets and habitat,

ii) Monitoring product design through "file and use",

iii) Breakthrough in distribution channels with inclusion of NGOs, SHGs, MFIs and MACS to provide micro-insurance, with appropriate compensation for their services,

iv) Enlarged servicing activities entrusted to micro-insurance agents, and

v) Issue of policy documents in simple vernacular language.

Currently the IRDA regulations do not favor composite insurance (i.e., life and non-life insurances by the same company) and also limit the agency tie-up to one life and one non-life insurer. However, in recognition of the uniqueness of micro insurance, these regulations enable life and non-life companies to tie-up for offering a combined policy in rural areas. Further, the IRDA has allowed insurers to issue policies with a maximum cover of Rs. 50,000 for general and life insurance under these regulations. The regulations have also eased the norms for entry of agents relating to training and pre-recruitment examination. As an attraction, remuneration to agents has also been leveled across the term of the policy.

Another striking feature of the regulation is the provision of extending coverage to the family as a unit as against the system of insurance coverage to individual lives. The insurer has to take IRDA's prior approval for launching Microinsurance products through the "file and use" mode. The maximum cover will be Rs. 30,000 per annum for a dwelling and contents or livestock or tools or implements or other named assets or crop insurance against all perils. For individual and group health insurance, the maximum cover is Rs. 30,000 per annum per individual. For personal accident policies the maximum Rs. 50,000 per annum and is open to 5-70 age group.

In case of life micro-insurance products, the cover amount for term insurance ranges between Rs. 5,000-50,000 for a minimum term of five years and maximum of 15 years. The entry age for this product is kept between 18-60. Endowment insurance policy provides cover for Rs. 5,000-30,000 for a minimum five years and maximum 15 years for people aged between 18 and 60. Further, an insurer can collect the premium for both life and general insurance components directly from the consumer or agents.

At the time of opening of the insurance sector, IRDA had decided that all insurers, including the new entrants, should fulfill certain obligations to spread insurance in rural areas. Specific regulations have been issued prescribing targets in terms of quantum of policies to be written in the rural sector consistent with the years of their operations and also certain quantified target for coverage of lives in the social sector. With a view to encouraging the insurers to meet these obligations and give a fillip to micro-insurance products, IRDA also decided that all micro-insurance products may be reckoned for the purpose of fulfillment of the social obligation and where such policy are issued in rural area they could also be reckoned for rural sector obligation. IRDA has also proposed to benchmark the above obligations with reference to quantified limits of sums assured under micro-insurance policies. The above approach would ensure the faster development of the micro-insurance market and take the insurance penetration to rural areas.

The Committee wholly subscribes to the initiatives of IRDA in widening outreach of micro-insurance products to the rural poor and recommends that the same may be implemented with renewed zeal as providing micro-insurance is a necessary and essential adjunct in the inclusive process. The IRDA should continue to impose Rural and Social Sector Obligations but there should be no unreasonable caps on premiums and channel commissions. This is in line with the de-traffing process in other sectors also. In the long run, it is only when the insurance companies find it profitable to serve this market that they will do so on their own.

15.4. Micro Insurance in India

Micro-insurance in India is a new concept and in the real sense, is yet to be tested for its conduciveness to the needs of the target segment. The most significant constraint is the lack of base line data on potential claims that can help the insurers to design or price products. The consumption and saving patterns are also a critical aid to assess the insurance needs. The issue of moral hazard and adverse selection is a matter of concern for the insurer. Above all, spreading awareness among this segment of insurable population and capacity building of the delivery organisations are major challenges.

In 2003, GOI constituted a Consultative Group on Micro-Insurance to examine existing insurance schemes for rural and urban poor with specific reference to outreach, pricing, products, servicing and promotion and to examine existing regulations with a view to promoting micro-insurance organisations with specific reference to capital requirements, licensing, monitoring and review, etc. The report of the consultative group has brought out the following key issues:

a) Micro-insurance is not viable as a stand alone insurance product.

b) Micro-insurance has not penetrated rural markets. Traditional insurers have not made much headway in bringing micro-insurance products to the rural poor. (In addition, the Committee feels that micro insurance has not penetrated even among the urban poor).

c) Partnership between an insurer and a social organisation like NGO would be desirable to promote micro-insurance by drawing on their mutual strengths.

d) Design of micro-insurance products must have the features of simplicity, availability, affordability, accessibility and flexibility.

The market for Microinsurance is enormous and remains untapped. Micro insurance in India is given the greater policy stimuli, commercial interests and has growing track record of local successes. India's Microinsurance Industry is going for rapid growth in the coming days.

A study commissioned by the United Nations Development Programme (UNDP) titled "Building Security for the Poor - Potential and Prospects for Microinsurance in India" states that 90% of the Indian population - some 950 million people - are not covered by insurance and signify an untapped market of nearly US$ 2 billion. This enormous "missing market" is ready for customized life and non-life insurance, but first, serious mismatches between the needs of the insured and the insurers must be overcome, pitting priorities against profits.

The UNDP study estimates the potential market size for Micro insurance in India to be between Rs.62000 and Rs. 84000 million. The potential for life insurance is estimated to range from Rs. 15393 to Rs. 20141 million. The population used for this estimation is 40-50 percent of the potentially economically active and earning less than US$1 a day. This is about to grow as Microinsurance is better understood and demand grows with appropriate supply.

Low-income persons live in risky environments, vulnerable to numerous perils, including illness, accidental death and disability, loss of poverty due to theft or fire, agricultural losses and disasters of both the natural and man-made varieties. The poor are more vulnerable to many of these risks than the rest of the population.

According to the Consultative Group to Assist the Poor (CGAP) working group on Microinsurance appointed by Government of India defined the term as the "the protection of low income households against specific perils in exchange for premium payments proportionate to the likelihood and cost of the risk involved".

15.5. Micro Insurance for Social Protection

Social protection generally consists of policies and programs designed to reduce poverty and vulnerability by promoting efficient labour markets, diminishing people's exposure to risks, enhancing their capacity to protect themselves against hazards and interruption/loss of income. The five main areas that are there in the social protection are i) Labour Market ii) Social Insurance iii) Social Assistance iv) Child protection v) Poverty reduction (Micro and area based schemes).[3] In social protection, to reduce poverty we are diminishing people's risk and improving their capacity to protect themselves. Social protection refers to the benefits that society provides for its members including:

a) Unemployment and disability benefits

b) Universal healthcare

c) Maternity benefits

d) Old-age pensions

e) Protection for children and disabled.

Social protection reduces the poverty through its positive impact on economic performance and productivity. It helps the poor to cope with important risks and loss of income. It also enhances the principles such as solidarity, dignity and equality.

According to the ILO (2000), social security is the protection which society provides for its members through a series of public measures:

a) To compensate for the absence or substantial reduction of income from work resulting from various contingencies (notably sickness, maternity, employment injury, unemployment, invalidity, old age and death of the breadwinner);

b) To provide people with healthcare; and

c) To provide benefits for families with children.

15.6 Micro Insurance Products in India

(a) Life micro-insurance Product: A *life micro-insurance product*" means any term insurance contract with or without return of premium, any endowment insurance contract or health insurance contract, with or without an accident benefit rider, either on individual or group basis, as per terms stated in the Table below, filed with the IRDA:

Type of Cover	*Minimum Amount of Cover*	*Maximum Amount of Cover*	*Term of Cover Min.*	*Term of Cover Max.*	*Minimum Age at entry*	*Maximum age at entry*
Term Insurance with or without return of premium	Rs. 10,000	Rs. 50,000	5 year	7 years	18	60
Endowment Insurance	Rs. 10,000	Rs. 50,000	5 year	7 years	18	60
Health Insurance Contract	Rs. 10,000	Rs. 15,000	1 year	7 year	18	60
Accident Benefit as rider	Rs. 10,000	Rs. 50,000	1 year	5 years	18	60

Life insurance is the most obvious choice for micro insurance. The consequences of death are always significant for poor households so there is a constant demand. The exclusion of suicide reduces moral hazard problems. By selling to groups that are involved in some activity adverse selection can be reduced. Mortality rates are often easier to obtain than, for example, rates of different types of illnesses. A death certificate or an identification of corpse makes verification for claims easier. With a one-time payout the system is relatively easy to administrate. For this reason, the vast majority of all micro insurance products, in India and worldwide, are life products. Because poor people are frequently involved in hazardous jobs, there is a significant demand in India for disability insurance. Although termed disability insurance, in practice it is often dismemberment insurance because the latter is easier to verify than general disability.

Tables below provide a sample of some of the kinds of micro insurance products on the market.[4]

Examples of Life Insurance Product in India

Name of product	*Insurance provider*	*Premium*	*Benefits and exclusions*
1	*2*	*3*	*4*
Social Development Plan	Birla Sun LifeInsurance	Premium rates vary according to group size and average age of the members of the group	▪ The beneficiary receives full sum assured (50% partial disablement) ▪ Life: Both natural and accidental death of the policyholder ▪ Disability: Permanent total disability due to accident (loss of two limbs or two eyes) ▪ Permanent partial disability due to accident (loss of one limb or one eye) ▪ Exclusions: Accidental dismemberment benefit can be claimed only once
Social Development Plan	SBI Life Insurance	Rs. 300 per person per annum for a sum insured of Rs. 50,000. Rs. 600 per person per annum for a sum insured of Rs. 100,000	▪ The beneficiary receives full sum insured. In case of total permanent disability resulting from an accident, a sum double the sum insured is paid to the policyholder ▪ Life: Both natural and accidental death of the policyholder ▪ Disability: Permanent total disability due to accident (loss of two limbs or two eyes) ▪ Exclusions: Does not cover suicide
Janata Personal Accident Policy	Royal Sundaram Alliance Insurance	Premium rates vary depending on the size of the group	▪ Accidental death: Death resulting from an accident ▪ Disability: Disability resulting from an accident ▪ In case of accidental death of

(Contd...)

1	*2*	*3*	*4*
		and on the sum insured Standard premium rate is Rs. 25 for a benefit sum of Rs. 25,000	policyholder, 100% of insured sum is paid to the nominee ▪ In case of disability due to accident, 50% of insured sum is paid to the policyholder ▪ (depending on the nature of the disability) ▪ Exclusions: Does not cover suicide; War and nuclear perils
Janata Personal Accident Insurance	Reliance General Insurance	Premium rates vary depending on the size of the group, the sum insured and the term period Standard premium rate is Rs. 15 for benefit sum of Rs. 25,000	▪ Accidental death: Death resulting from an accident ▪ Disability: Total or partial permanent disability resulting from an accident§ In case of death of the policyholder due to accident, 100% of sum insured is paid to the nominee ▪ In case of loss of two limbs, two eyes or one limb/sight of one eye, 100% of sum ▪ Insured is paid to the policyholder ▪ In case of permanent total disablement due to accident, 100% of sum insured is paid to the policyholder ▪ In case of total and irrecoverable loss of one limb/ sight of one eye due to accident, 50% of sum insured is paid to the policyholder ▪ Exclusions: ▪ Does not cover suicide ▪ Does not cover compensation for more than one injury during the term period ▪ Pregnancy-related claims ▪ War and nuclear perils
Sankat Haran Group Insurance Policy	IFFCO Tokyo General Insurance	No separate premium to be paid as the farmer is covered immediately upon	▪ Accidental death: Death resulting from an accident ▪ Disability: Total or partial permanent disability resulting from an accident caused by:

(Contd...)

1	*2*	*3*	*4*
		purchase of a 50 kg fertilizer bag from any of the agent companies	▪ Road, rail and air accidents; Injury due to any collision/fall; Bursting of gas cylinder; ▪ Snake bite; Frostbite; Burn injury; Drowning; Poisoning ▪ In case of death of the farmer, Rs. 4,000 are paid to the nominee ▪ In case of total permanent disablement or loss of two limbs, two eyes or one limb and one eye, Rs 2,000 are paid to the farmer ▪ In case of loss of one limb or one eye, Rs. 1,000 are paid to the farmer ▪ Exclusions: Does not cover suicide; Any existing disablement; War and nuclear perils; ▪ Pregnancy or childbirth; Any breach of law with criminal intent
Janashree BimaYojana	Life Insurance Corporation	For an individual: Rs. 200 per annum (50%, or 100% subsidy to be borne by the Social Security Fund) Experience rating adjustment allowed after year 3: possible reduction of premium related to claim ratio/ group size	▪ Life: Natural and accidental death of the policyholder ▪ Disability: Permanent total disability due to accident (loss of two limbs or two eyes); ▪ Permanent partial disability due to accident (loss of one limb or one eye) ▪ Rs. 20,000 payable in case of natural death ▪ Rs. 50,000 payable in case of accidental death ▪ Rs. 50,000 in case of total permanent disability resulting from an accident ▪ Rs. 50,000 payable in case of loss of two limbs or one eye and one limb resulting from an accident ▪ Rs. 25,000 payable in case of loss of one limb or one eye

(Contd...)

1	*2*	*3*	*4*
Group Personal Accident Policy	HDFC Chubb General Insurance	Premium rates vary according to group size, sum insured and the past claims history of the group to be insured Premium fixed at Rs. 60–70 for Rs. 100,000 per annum	▪ Accidental death: Death resulting from an accident ▪ Disability: Total or partial permanent disability resulting from an accident; Loss of some essential capacities resulting from an accident ▪ Education: One-time child education benefit in case of death or permanent disability of parent resulting from an accident ▪ In case of death of the policy holder due to accident, 100% of insured sum is paid to the nominee ▪ In case of total permanent disablement including loss of two limbs, two eyes or one limb and one eye: 100% insured sum ▪ In case of loss of one limb or one eye, the policyholder receives 50% of the insured sum ▪ In case of incurable insanity, permanent loss of speech, complete removal of lower jaw, permanent total loss of mastication, permanent total loss of central nervous system or the thorax and all abdominal organs resulting in the complete inability to engage in any job and to carry out daily activities essential to life without full-time assistance, 100% of insured sum is paid to policyholder ▪ In case of permanent loss of hearing in both ears, 75% of sum insured is paid to policyholder ▪ Additional 25% of sum insured given on account of the

(Contd...)

1	2	3	4
			following: dependent daughter's wedding costs and child education benefit ▪ Exclusions:; Does not cover suicide or self-injury ; Does not cover for any prior disablement
Accident Insurance Policy	Cholomandalam MsGeneral Insurance	Currently sold as a value-added product for which no extra-payment is charged Sold along with some of the products manufactured by the group's sister companies Premium rates in year 2 vary according to size of the group and sum insured	▪ Accidental death: Compensation in case of death due to accident ▪ Disability: Covers both permanent harm and temporary disability ▪ Accident expenses: Compensation for injury caused by an accident ▪ Covers, up to a maximum stipulated amount:; Loss of life due to an accident; ▪ Ambulance hiring charges; Broken bones (fractures); Medical reimbursement; ▪ Modification of residential accommodation and vehicle; Transportation of mortal remains ▪ Exclusions:; Does not cover suicide; Does not cover self-injury
Krishi Shramik Samajik Suraksha Yojana	Life Insurance Corporation	For an individual: Rs. 365 perannum	▪ Life: On natural death of the member (before age 60); On accidental death of the member ▪ Lump sum survival benefits provided after each 10th year into the scheme ▪ Disability: Permanent total disability due to accident; Permanent partial disability due to accident ▪ Pension: Pension paid to the member on reaching age 60

(Contd...)

1	2	3	4
			▪ Rs. 20,000 payable in case of natural death, along with return of accumulated amount + interest ▪ Rs. 50,000 payable in case of accidental death, along with return of accumulated amount + interest ▪ Rs. 50,000 payable in case of total permanent disability resulting from an accident ▪ Rs. 25,000 payable in case of partial disability resulting from an accident ▪ Lump sum survival benefits depending on the accumulated amount in his/her account ▪ Pension paid depending on the accumulated balance in his/her account ▪ If member has paid for a minimum period of 10 years, at least Rs. 100 will be payable each month ▪ Exclusions: Does not cover suicide
Amartya Siksha Yojana Policy	National Insurance Company	The premium rates vary depending on the number of years for which the policy is taken out and the number of students (in case of a group policy) Minimum individual premium is	▪ Accidental death: Death caused by an accident ▪ Disability: Total permanent disability resulting from an accident ▪ Education: Covers the various following education costs:; Tuition fees; Boarding ▪ expenses; Cost of books; Examination fees; Compulsory uniform; Any other ▪ compulsory expenses to be borne under the recommendation of the head

(Contd...)

1	2	3	4
		Rs. 50 and for group policy thePremium rate is Rs. 100	of department/institution ▪ Accident expenses: Reimbursement of hospitalization expenses arising out of an accident ▪ Exclusions: Does not cover any other benefits
Shakthi Security Shield	Royal Sundaram Alliance Insurance	Rs. 25 per annum for the basiccover Rs. 35 per annum when extended to cover accidentaldeath for a woman	▪ Accidental death: Accidental death of spouse (optional: accidental death of women) ▪ Loss of income: Cash relief for the period when the woman is temporarily or totally disabled ▪ Assets: Loss or damage to dwellings and personal belongings due to fire or flood ▪ Accident expenses: Reimbursement of hospitalization expenses arising out of an accident ▪ Cash relief in case of disablement of woman engaged in some kind of work: Rs. 100 per week (maximum Rs. 1,500) ▪ Rs. 25,000 in case of accidental death of spouse/parent/ guardian ▪ Up to Rs. 1,000 for hospitalization expenses due to an accident ▪ Up to Rs. 1,000 for loss or damage to dwelling ▪ Up to Rs. 500 for loss or damage to personal goods ▪ Up to Rs. 25,000 in case of accidental death of woman (optional) ▪ Exclusions: Does not cover pregnancy-related expenses

(b) General Micro-insurance Product: By "*general micro-insurance product*" we mean any health insurance contract, any contract covering the belongings such as hut, livestock, any personal accident contract, or tools or instruments, either on individual or group basis, as per terms stated in the Table below, filed with the IRDA:[5]

Type of Cover	*Minimum Amount of Cover*	*Maximum Amount of Cover*	*Term of Cover Min.*	*Term of Cover Max.*	*Minimum Age at entry*	*Maximum age at entry*
Hut or livestock or Tools or implements or other assets—against all perils	Rs. 10,000	Rs. 20,000	1 year	1 year	18	70
Health Insurance Contract	Rs. 10,000	Rs. 15,000	1 year	1 year	18	60
Personal Accident	Rs. 10,000	Rs. 50,000	1 year	1 year	18	60

Examples of Hut and Personal Possessions Insurance

Name of product	*Insurance provider*	*Premium*	*Benefits and exclusions*
1	*2*	*3*	*4*
Packageinsurance forcredit society	New India Insurance Company	Premium rates vary according tothe size of thegroup and sum insured	▪ Package policy covering 7 sections as follows: ▪ Loss or damage to buildings and its contents personal belongings due to Fire or flood, Explosion, Aircraft damage, Bursting of water tanks, Earthquake, Typhoon, Cyclone ▪ Impact damage by any rail/ road vehicle or animal Furniture, fixtures, fittings and electrical appliances Money and valuables ▪ Accidental death, disability ▪ Fire and other perils including theft and burglary ▪ Accidental damage to plate glass and sanitary fittings ▪ Hospitalization expenses due to illness, disease or injury
Shakthi Security Shield	Royal Sundaram Alliance	Rs. 25 per annum for the basic cover Rs. 35 per annum when extended to cover accidental death for a woman	▪ Cash relief in case of disablement of woman engaged in some kind of work: Rs. 100 per week (maximum Rs.1,500) ▪ Rs. 25,000 in case of

(Contd...)

1	*2*	*3*	*4*
			accidental death of spouse/ parent/guardian ▪ Up to Rs. 1,000 for hospitalization expenses due to an accident ▪ Up to Rs. 1,000 for loss or damage to dwelling due to fire or flood ▪ Up to Rs. 500 for loss or damage t o personal goods ▪ Up to Rs. 25,000 in case of accidental death of policy holder

[5]IRDA (2004)," *Concept paper on need for developing Micro-Insurance in India"*

Examples of Livestock Insurance Product in India

Name of product	*Insurance provider*	*Premium*	*Benefits and exclusions*
Cattleinsurance	UIIC	4% of the animal's value (2.25% goesto UIIC)	Value of the animal (usually amount of Rs. 10,000) upon natural and accidental death Exclusions: Intentional death caused by owner
Cattleinsurance	New India Assurance	5% of the animal's value	Value of the animal (usually amount of Rs. 10,000) upon natural and accidental deathExclusions: Intentional death caused by owner

Examples of Weather Insurance in India

Perhaps the most significant innovation in India is the introduction of weather insurance by ICICI Lombard in collaboration with BASIX, a Hyderabad -based MFI. This is also known as index-based insurance, in this case using rainfall levels as a claims trigger. Because clients cannot affect rainfall levels there is no moral hazard problem. There could be fraud problems, however, if clients can affect the reported levels of rainfall.

Claims are processed as soon as the rainfall levels are known, and clients do not need to send in claims forms. HDFC-Chubb is now also experimenting with weather insurance. Although this is an interesting innovation, and worthy of further investigation, national roll -out of weather based insurance would not be immediately possible because only part of India has reliable weather stations.

Examples of Low-premium Health Products in India

Name of product	*Insurance provider*	*Premium*	*Benefits and exclusions*
1	*2*	*3*	*4*
ShakthiHealth Scheme	Royal Sundaram Alliance Insurance Company	Below 18 years Rs. 6518–45 years Rs. 125 45–60 years Rs. 175	Reimbursement of hospitalization expenses up to Rs.7,000:Rooms, boarding expenses Nursing expenses, surgeonAnaesthetist, specialist fees Blood, oxygen Operation theatre charge Medicines and drugs Exclusions: Pre-existing diseases Voluntary medical termination of pregnancy General check-up, vaccination, inoculation
Health Insurance policy	Choloman dalam MSGeneral	Premium rates vary according tothe number in thegroup	Hospitalization expenses resulting from illness or accident Pre-hospitalization expenses (60 days prior to hospitalization) Post-hospitalization expenses (90 days after discharge) Covers 130 minor surgeries that require fewer than 24 hours of hospitalization Ambulance services to the nearest hospital where emergency health facilities are available Exclusions: Pre-existing diseases Pregnancy/ voluntary termination of pregnancy Cataracts, dental and cosmetic surgery Obesity Naturopathy treatment Drug and alcohol abuse HIV/AIDS and all related medical conditions
Advanced medical insurance	ICICI Lombard	Rs. 10 per personper month (if the whole family joins the scheme); Rs. 14 per person per month for an individual	Free outpatient services at the recognized network hospitals Investigation at fixed discounted rates Access to drugs/medicines at special prices from network hospitals Coverage for main diseases and for surgical interventions Maximum of 3 days admission at network hospitals Benefit amount payable

(Contd...)

1	*2*	*3*	*4*
			on diagnosis and hospitalization for any ailment covered under the policy and on completion of survival period
Group UniMicro Health Insurance7	United India Insurance Company (UIIC)	Rs. 100 (Rs. 84 goes to UIIC), additional Rs. 20 charged for thatched roof houses	Rs. 5,000 for hospitalization Rs. 15,000 for accidental death Rs. 15,000 for permanent disability Rs. 250/month up to max. Rs. 750/month for temporary disability (up to 3 months) Rs. 5,000 for house fire and allied perilsExclusions:Health insurance: Waiting period 30 days Maternity benefits are not covered Pre-existing disease is not covered in the first year. After the first year there is no exclusion

15.7. Delivery Mechanism: Micro-Insurance Models

Micro-insurance products are low-value and high volume business. Major challenge of insurance providers is delivery of micro insurance products to rural people located at remote location at the cheaper cost. Therefore, it requires innovation delivery channels to provide insurance to low-income populations. A key concern in the pricing of an insurance product is the element of cost of acquisition and its delivery. Obviously, the delivery costs have to be contained to keep the cost of insurance sufficiently low to attract the poor and to incentivise the insurer to venture into this segment viewing it as a genuine market opportunity. Four different models for delivering micro-insurance services to the targeted clientele are:

Partner - Agent Model	Insurers utilize MFIs' delivery mechanism to provide sales and basic services to clients. There is no risk and limited administrative burden for MFIs.
Full Service Model	The provider is responsible for all aspects of product design, sales, servicing, and claims assessment. The insurers are responsible for all insurance-related costs and losses and they retain all profits.
Community Based Model	The policy holders own and manage the insurance program, and negotiate with external health care providers.
Provider Model	The service provider and the insurer are the same, i.e., hospitals or doctors offer policies to individuals or groups.

In India, following three models are generally emerged:

- Partnership model
- Agency model
- Micro-agent model

a) Partnership Model

Under this model, micro-insurance products are distributed through a partnership between an insurer and an agent that provides some kind of financial service to large numbers of low-income people. An agent could be a microfinance organization, an NGO, or a business that supplies precuts to large numbers of low - income people, such as a fertilizer supplier. This party is an agent, selling insurance policies to the clients on behalf of the insurance provider (usually) in exchange for a commission or fee. The insurance provider utilizes the established distribution channels of this agent and its financial transactions with low-income groups that would otherwise be too costly to set up.

Under this partnership model, it uses the comparative advantage of each partner so that each can focus on its core business: the insurance provider is responsible for designing and pricing the product, the final claims management, and the investment of reserves, and absorbs all the insurance risks. In addition to selling the policies, the agent offers its infrastructure for product servicing such as marketing the product, premium collection, and assists in claims management.

Advantages

i) Better synergies between each partner's strength and core competency resulting easier penetration of clients at cheaper cost.

ii) Requires fewer skills for the agent than an in-house model.

iii) Uses legally recognized insurance companies that have adequate reserves, adhere to capital requirements, employ certified insurance professionals, and operate under the insurance law.

iv) Insurer has access to reinsurance.

v) The overhead costs of both the organizations, the agent and the insurance company, are reduced: the agent can use its infrastructure for collecting premiums, etc.; the insurer provides the expertise on product development, etc.

vi) It reduces the need to build the capacity of agents such as NGOs and MFIs to sell insurance because the insurer can do some of this.

vii) The insurer assumes all the risks.

(viii) Information asymmetries are minimized as the agent is familiar with the needs of clients and their situations, which reduces the time needed for claims verification and settlement, while receiving feedback on client satisfaction and product design, etc.

(ix) The agent earns commission without risk, while the insurer earns profits.

Disadvantages

i) Because of the quota system, the most well-known agents are already taken and have existing relationships with insurers.

ii) The insurance provider is dependent on the quality of the agent.

iii) Conflicts of interest may occur, especially when working with non-financial institutions.

BOX-11: A Partnership Model in India

BASIX is an NGO working in livelihood promotion in several arid and backward districts spread over seven states. BASIX works towards its mission of livelihood promotion by providing a comprehensive set of services, which include Livelihood Financial Services (Savings, Credit and Insurance) and Institutional Development Services. BASIX is headquartered at Hyderabad.

As part of its mission to deliver comprehensive financial services to rural customers, BASIX began its initiatives to deliver insurance services four years age, coinciding with the opening up of the insurance sector. From the beginning, BASIX has actively partnered with multiple insurance companies to design insurance products for rural customers. In the area of life insurance BASIX began by working with ICICI Prudential and currently works with AVIVA Life Insurance Company. BASIX has worked with Royal Sundaram general insurance company for the delivery of livestock insurance and ICICI Lombard for rainfall insurance. BASIX is also actively working with these and other insurers to design a suitable health insurance product for its rural clients. In 2003, BASIX was also given a Corporate Agency license by the IRDA to distribute retail life insurance products from AVIVA.

b) Agency Model

Under this model, the micro-insurance products are distributed by individual insurance agents or corporate insurance agents or insurance brokers. In this model the insurer uses its normal agency office and sells micro insurance products directly. The client comes to the agency office for sales and servicing of the product.

Advantages

i) Does not require much additional investment in infrastructure;

ii) Better control of the quality of the agent than with the partnership model.

Disadvantages

i) Difficult to reach large numbers especially in rural areas where clients may be unwilling to travel to the office;

ii) Agents will need special training in dealing with low-income clients;

iii) Offices may intimidate poor clients;

iv) Individual policies only would be sold; generally such micro-insurance policies have not proved commercially viable.

(c) Micro-Agent Model

Under this model, Non Government Organisations (NGO) or Self Help Groups (SHGs) act as agent of Insurance Company and provide micro-insurance products to low-income people in favour of insurance company for a commission fee. A Non Government Organisation (NGO) shall be a registered non-profit organization under the Society's Act, 1968 with a proven track record of working with marginalised groups with clearly stated aims and objectives, transparency, and accountability outlined in its memorandum, rules and regulations and demonstrates involvement of committed people. Self Help Group (SHG) may be an informal group or registered under Societies Act, State Co-operative Act or as a partnership firm, consisting of 10 to 20 with a proven track record of working with marginalised groups with clearly stated aims and objectives, transparency, and accountability outlined in its memorandum, rules and regulations and demonstrates involvement of committed people. The minimum number of members comprising a group should be atleast ten for insurance of individuals, and atleast fifty for group insurance.

Advantages

i) The model creates an insurance distribution infrastructure in low-income neighbourhoods.

ii) In addition, it creates a new profession, that of micro -agent, with new livelihood opportunities in his/her vicinity;

iii) Because the position is a commercial one with financial incentives, it will last in the long term, facilitating the sale of long -term products.

Disadvantages

i) Training is costly, especially in relation to premium values;

ii) The transaction costs of the sales agent are cheap at first but increase as soon as the agent has sold to all the peoples/he knows and needs to sell to strangers, especially to those living far away;

iii) In many cases in the partnership model, when a claim arises, the MFI or NGO investigates the claim, pays the benefit immediately, and then claims it back from the insurer;

iv) Immediate payment of claims helps maintain client confidence, and this is not possible under the micro-agent system; and

v) This model is new, and much more experience is needed before it can be reasonably evaluated.

15.8. Problems, Issues and Challenges in Micro Insurance

Micro insurance is a low-price, high-volume business and its success and market sustainability is dependent on keeping the transaction costs down. Hardly any satisfactory state-run programme of insurance benefits is now available for poor population groups, people working in the informal sector and other disadvantaged individuals—and private-sector programmes are even rarer. A number of constraints make micro insurance look unattractive, including a lack of political will, scarcity of public funds and absence of a viable business model. The costs of marketing and processing appear to be too high and in view of the extremely low purchasing power of the consumer base; it cannot be easily apportioned to the target group. Such constraints make micro insurance unattractive at the cursory level. Market analysis suggests that progress can be made particularly when public and private sector work together in generating demand-based and innovative products.

The UNDP report has analysed six key issues pertinent to the growth of the micro-insurance industry in India, capturing the concerns of different stakeholders as indicated below:

a) There are specific reasons for low demand for insurance in spite of intense need. Suppliers have their own concerns which help to explain why there have been so little efforts at market development. Consequently, the rural market is characterized by limited and inappropriate services, inadequate information and capacity gaps.

b) There are challenges in product design, which has resulted in a mismatch between needs and standard products on offer. Efforts at product development / diversification have been limited.

c) Pricing, including willingness to pay and the availability of subsidies, influence the market. In the absence of a historical data base on claims, premium calculations are based on remote macro aggregates and overcautious margins. Building and sharing claims histories can help in aligning pricing decisions with actual calculations, thereby reducing prices.

d) Difficulty in distribution is one of the most cited reasons for absence of rural insurance. The high costs of penetrating rural markets, combined with underutilization of available distribution channels, hinder the growth of rural insurance services. This adds to costs, both, managerial and financial. Like inclusive credit, inclusive insurance is expected to be a "low ticket" business, requiring volumes for viability.

e) Cumbersome and inappropriate procedures inhibit the development of this sector.

f) Contrasting perspectives of the insured and the insurers, lead to low customization of products and low demand for what is available.

The UNDP report further states that micro-insurance solutions should, therefore, attempt at addressing key issues that will improve customer satisfaction (demand-supply gaps, appropriate products and pricing), provide distribution efficiencies for better outreach and remove procedural hassles facilitating easier renewals and claim settlements. With a view to reduce costs, the report has also suggested that the premia payable on micro-insurance be exempted from payment of service tax, which will also enable greater penetration in rural markets.

a) Problems of Microinsurance

The present problems that micro insurers face are:

a) High transaction costs – on account of small value policies
b) Lack of significant experience with different kinds of insurance products
c) Irregular household income flows
a) High level of premiums
b) Limited understanding of insurance needs of clients
c) Limited financing options for MFIs to make forays into micro-insurance
d) Lack of technical (actuarial) expertise.

b) Issues of micro insurance

a) The contemporary insurance paradigm is not geared to serve the poor-high costs, restrictive access and low transparency being the chief reasons.
b) Lack of unfamiliarity and trust on the service providers.
c) The penetration of Micro insurance to the low income groups has not been successful and its promotion by MFIs has not yet realized its full potential.
d) When it comes to insuring the poorest, two important issues are referred to often-whose benefit should Micro insurance target? The second issue is who should pay the Microinsurance premiums?
e) Lack of awareness about value of Micro insurance.
f) Difficulties in understanding technology introduced by the service providers.
g) Irregular cash flows of households where they are unable to pay the premiums.
h) Big challenge in educating the market and overcoming the bias on insurance.
i) For illiterate, it is very difficult to understand the terms and conditions of the insurance policy.

(c) Challenges

a) Creating an awareness among their constituents regarding insurance as a risk management mechanism
b) Demystifying insurance related beliefs and superstitions
c) Matching product design to customer requirements
d) Ensuring regularity of premia collections in the face of irregular income flows of MSEs
e) Skill building of their own staff.

15.9. Micro Insurance: Taking Forward

In order to increase the insurance coverage of low-income group, the following innovative methods and design can be implemented:

a) Increasing the partnerships between MFIs, Government, and other societies to reach the under covered market.

b) Government Sponsored schemes

c) Community based programmes that pools funds

d) Customer focused approach at the time of new product design

e) Educating the market in their local language through media, information kiosks, social meetings etc

f) Designing the product that is operated in the particular Microinsurance environment.

g) Minimizing the documentations and developing efficient, transparent claims processing systems

h) Risk prevention strategies

i) Product should be affordable to the poor

j) Flexibility in premium.

The MSEs in India are prone to a variety of risks. They adopt a range of risk management and coping mechanisms to deal with uncertainties faced in their businesses as well as the household. ILO (2002) study reveals that[1]

a) Savings is the popular instrument and many households report that they save to manage emergencies.

b) Borrowing is another mechanism to smoothen their liquidity affected by risk-induced shocks. They borrow mostly from informal sources, being the quickest and timely means of raising funds.

c) Of formal insurance products, life insurance is more popular among the households; agents of the formal insurance company being resident in the villages facilitating easy sales of insurance policies.

d) Coverage of women is less even in life insurance; Sales of policies to mostly men perhaps stems from the gender stereotyping relating to finance being a men subject. The concept of insurance is still not popular among the women.

e) Non-life insurance is usually viewed as a no return investment.

Insurance both life and general, are widely recognized to lack market orientation and customer service. Non-life insurance has not touched most MSEs in any significant way, especially in the informal sector. With the advent of new players and the stipulations of IRDA to underwrite a minimum percentage of business from rural areas there might be an improvement in design and delivery of appropriate products.

The problems that exist in insurance cover for MSEs and rural sector need to be addressed to expand this market. The perception that insurance is an investment should be dispelled. The difference between risk hedging and investing for returns should be made clear to the clients. The fact that insurance does not permit the customer to undertake risk inducing behaviour needs to be clearly established. The structure and periodicity of premia should closely follow the cash flows of clients. The method of collection should enable easy transaction to the client. Incentives for continued cover, year after year needs to be built in. An element of compulsion may be necessary in the initial years for covering large numbers, which provide the strength for negotiating with insurers on product design and premium. The compulsion may be built in through the different development projects that are undertaken for the clients, or banks. The problem of lack of direct interaction between insurers and insured should be dealt with systematically.

Provision of insurance services to the poor can be ridden with problems especially of moral hazard and adverse selection. The low level supervision over clients especially with those with risky behaviours can result in escalation of claims. Similarly the chances of adverse selection can also affect the insurers. For example, among the survey respondents who were to keen to take up health insurance were those who were suffering or recently suffered from illnesses. These aspects can be taken care of at the design stage. One possibility is to bunch a number of risks together and insure for the same. The second could be to cover wider clients which results in deepening of risk pool. Thus instead of covering only the sick person in the family the entire family needs to be covered under health insurance. The group methodology adopted by the MFIs can also help in tackling this issue. The groups and MFIs can be made to work as watchdogs especially in the larger interest of the success of the schemes and future benefits especially in terms of lower premium for groups with lesser claims.

As per the present regulations of IRDA, MFIs and NGOs cannot carry out direct insurance business as principals. As per the regulations, NGOs, MFIs (except where they are incorporated as companies) cannot be certified as agents. But there is a definite opportunity for microfinance institutions and NGOs dealing with the MSEs to act as a facilitator to fulfill the insurance needs of MSE (Micro Small Enterprised) households. The IRDA norms with emphasis on rural sector and the disadvantaged people and the social sector obligations would in fact help NGOs/MFIs to approach insurance companies with confidence. They would be of great help as facilitators and partners in enabling companies meet their obligations under the IRDA norms. The role of NGOs/MFIs could be very significant in product design suitable for MSEs and poor households. They could also facilitate the interface between the insurer and insured, in fulfilling the formalities of taking cover and making claims. With a large number of insurers to choose from, they can bring the best products at best premia rates to the rural areas.

Presently there are some NGOs and MFIs offering insurance products on their own to their constituents. This contravenes the IRDA act and regulations. The insurance providers must obtain a license from IRDA for which they should satisfy certain financial and organisational norms. None of the NGOs/MFIs are in a position to satisfy the norms. If the laws are stringently applied, they have to stop the insurance business and look to distributing products from registered insurers. Some of the MFIs and NGOs are currently offering insurance as welfare package to their constituents and are not mentioning the word insurance in their scheme details though in essence they are offering insurance services to their clients.

If contravening the law is one major aspect, being able to satisfy the conditions of the explicit/implicit contract that they have entered into with their clients is the other concern. Many of the NGO/MFIs, lack financial strength, but are in the 'insurance' type business, face the prospect of not being able to cover their possible claims liabilities, if the situation so demands. Given that many of these NGO/MFIs don't have any form of re-insurance, the risk of not complying with their contractual obligations is high. In the event of defaults on the part of MFI to settle all the claims, there will be very serious repercussions for the sector as whole – while admittedly, clients will suffer (because of not being able to get their insurance), the other products offered by NGO/MFIs will also lose their credibility, thereby resulting in erosion of the good will already earned.

Given this scenario, the partner agent model seems to be best suited for NGOs and MFIs wanting to enter insurance sector. However, the present norms do not permit an NGO/MFI to become an agent unless they register a company. Many of them are currently registered as trusts, societies and co-operatives. None of these legal forms are permitted to be agents of insurance companies. NGOs/ MFIs have to lobby for their needs with IRDA to modify the present norms.

There is a possibility that NGOs and MFIs might network and set up a dedicated insurance company to serve the sectors that they are active in. But the initial capital requirement of Rs 10 billion (US$0.22 billion) is too high; it is difficult to conclude that the volume of business in the initial years, that would be generated from these sectors would be sufficient to provide a return on the capital to be invested. It might be difficult to find resources of this magnitude, with a very long payback period.

The provision of demand based insurance services to the poor could serve as the beginning for ushering in a new era in micro-insurance in India, one where the bargaining power of the buyers is high and the invisible hand (of the market) regulates to its best ability.

NOTES

1. Craig Churchill, *'What is insurance for the poor?"* International Labour Organization 2006, (ILO).
2. Pant Niranjan, Insurance Regulation and Development Bill. An appraisal, *Economic and Political Weekly*, 6, November, 1999, Mumbai.
3. Thankom Arun, Susan Steiner, *"Micro-Insurance in the Context of Social Protection"*, Brooks World Poverty Institute Working Paper 55, Oct, 2008.
4. Allianz AG, GTZ and UNDP (2006), *Microinsurance-Demand and Market Prospect – India.*
5. IRDA (2004), *Concept paper on need for developing Micro-Insurance in India.*
6. Girija Srinivasan and Ramesh S. Arunachalam (2002), *Microinsurance in India*, A study funded by International Labour Organisation (ILO).

16

Measuring Performance of MFIs

16.1. Basic Financial Ratios

Ratio is nothing more than relationships between numbers. They are generally calculated by dividing the numerator by a denominator. The result is expressed as percentage. In a financial institution, financial ratios are among the most significant management tools available. There are many ratios used in banking and microfinance. When ratios are used primarily for benchmark purposes or comparative purposes, the focus tends to be on the ratio itself and its movement and performance over time. Analytical tools or indicators for financial and portfolio analysis can be divided into four key areas. Each measure is one important aspect of the financial organization. When combined, the key areas give a well-rounded global perspective of the financial situation. The key categories are:

Profitability/ Sustainability	It shows the financial returns to the use of the capital and assets employed. The profit level also shows the MFI's self-sufficiency in relation to covering costs and building its equity. It answers the question of MFI's survival and future growth.
Asset/Liability Management	These ratios illustrate the ability of the MFI to manage its financial obligations when they become due, while maximizing the utilization of assets for profitability as possible, while paying its expenses, debts and obligations on time without borrowing funds.
Portfolio Quality	It measures the health of the loan outstanding in terms of its risk of being default in repayment.
Efficiency & Productivity	These ratios measure the costs of an MFI's operation in relation to its output. It indicates how well an MFI is efficiently operating.

16.2. Profitability and Sustainability Ratios

Profitability and Sustainability ratios reflect the MFI's ability to continue operating and grow in the future. Most reputable MFIs are striving for sustainability, regardless of their nonprofit or for profit status; donors and investors alike look to fund sustainable institutions.

Several factors can affect profitability and sustainability. Although startup or rapid growing institutions may have low profitability, they are building the basis for a sustainable future. Some Tips for Managing Profitability and sustainability are given below:

a) The primary focus in a young MFI is to achieve break-even and ensure that financial revenues exceed all operating expenses, include financial costs and the provision for loan losses. A high quality portfolio that generates high yields but operates with low financial expenses and efficient operations is the priority.

b) MFI that receive high levels of donations and grants need to maximize by investing primarily in a productive portfolio that generates high level of revenues. As they break-even and become more profitable, their Return on Assets and Return on Equity may be as high as or higher than commercial or for-profit MFIs.

The key ratios to measure profitability and sustainability are given below:

(a) Operational Self-Sufficiency (OSS): OSS is the most basic measurement of sustainability, indicating whether revenues from operations are sufficient to cover all operating expenses. It measures how well an MFI can cover its costs through operating revenues. Operating self-sufficiency is a percentage (%), which indicates whether or not enough revenue has been generated to cover the MFIs total costs-i.e. operational expenses, loan loss provision and financial cost. OSS can be calculated by using the following formula:

$$\text{OSS} = \frac{\textbf{Financial Revenue or Operating Income}}{\textbf{(Operating Expense + Loan Loss Provision + Financial Expenses)}}$$

Trend: An increasing Operating Self-Sufficiency is positive

Operating Income is the sum of all the operating income (unadjusted for subsidies, inflation etc). It comprises of interest income from loans, loan fees, service charges, late fees and interest earned from investments. Loan Loss Provision is the provision made for bad debt out of profit earned. Financial expenses mean cost of the capital or interest on borrowings by the MFI.

OSS focuses on revenues and expenses from the MFI's core business, excluding non-operating revenues and donations. OSS reflects the MFI's ability to continue its operations if it receives no further subsidies or grants. Any MFI having OSS of more than 100% implies that operation of MFI is sustainable. Some of drivers of OSS are larger loan sizes, high yields, low financial expenses, or efficient operation. If an MFI does not reach operational self-sufficiency, eventually its equity (loan fund capital) will be reduced by losses (unless additional grants can be raised to cover the operating shortfalls). This means that there will be a smaller amount of funds to loan to borrowers (which could lead to closing the MFI once the funds run out).

(b) Financial Self-Sufficiency (FSS): FSS is the adjusted OSS. It is an important measure of sustainability of the lending operations after adjusting the cost of capital. It indicates whether or not enough revenue has been earned to cover both direct costs-including financing costs, provisions for loan losses and operating expenses and indirect costs including the adjusted cost of capital. The formula for calculation of FSS is:

$$\text{FSS} = \frac{\textbf{Financial Revenue or Operating Income}}{\textbf{(Operating Expense + Loan Loss Provision + Financial Expenses + Adjusted cost of capital)}}$$

Trend: An increasing Financial Self-Sufficiency is positive

The Adjusted cost of capital is the cost of maintaining the value of the equity relative to inflation or the market rate of equity, and the cost of accessing commercial rate liabilities rather than concessional loans. It is calculated by the following formula:

Adjusted Cost of Capital = **[(Inflation rate x (Average equity-Average fixed assets)] + [(Average funding liabilities x market rate of debt)]**

Here, the fixed assets are subtracted based on the assumption that property and buildings generally enhance their value relative to inflation.

The difference between OSS and FSS is that FSS measures not only an MFI's ability to cover its operating costs but also its ability to maintain the value of its equity capital relative to inflation and to operate and expand without subsidies. Broadly speaking, OSS measures ability to survive while FSS is a better indicator of ability to grow. Unless 100% Financial Self-Sufficiency is reached, the long-term provision of credit services will ultimately be undermined by the impact of inflation and the continued necessity to rely on donor funds.

(c) Return on Asset: It is a percentage (%), which measures the net income earned on the assets of the MFI. Return on Assets (ROA) indicates how well an MFI is managing its assets to optimize its profitability. The ratio includes not only the return on the loan portfolio, but also all other revenue generated from investments and other operating activities. ROA measures profitability regardless of the institution's underlying funding structure; it does not discriminate against MFIs that are funded primarily through equity. Therefore, it is a good measurement to compare commercial and non-commercial MFIs. In fact, non-commercial MFIs with low debt/equity ratios can often achieve higher ROA than their commercial counterparts because they have low financial expenses and pay fewer taxes.

Formula

$$\text{ROA} = \frac{\textbf{Net Operating Income (excluding donations) -Taxes}}{\textbf{Average Assets}}$$

Trend: An increasing Return on Asset is positive

Thus, ROA is an overall measure of profitability that reflects both the profit margin and the efficiency of the institution. For calculating this ratio, average total assets are used, rather than performing assets. This is because, the entire organization is being measured on its total financial performance, including decisions made to purchase fixed assets or invest in land and buildings or invest in securities.

Analysis of this ratio will improve the ability of an MFI to determine the revenue impact of policy changes, improved delinquency management, or the addition of products.

(d) Return on Equity (ROE): Return on Equity Ratio is a percentage (%) of net operating income to average equity. The return on Equity (ROE) Ratio provides information on how much net income was earned on the equity of a MFI. In other words, ROE reflects how much the MFI has earned on the funds invested by the shareholders/donors. ROE can be calculated using the following formula:

$$\text{ROE} = \frac{\textbf{Net Operating Income (excluding donations) -Taxes}}{\textbf{Average Equity}}$$

Trend: An increasing Return on Equity is positive

In a for-profit MFI, Return on Equity (ROE) is the most important profitability indicator; it measures an MFI's ability to reward its shareholders' investment, build its equity base through retained earnings, and raise additional equity investment. For a non-profit MFI, MOE indicates its ability to build equity through retained earnings, and increase equity enables the MFI to leverage more financing to grow its portfolio. By excluding donations and non-operating revenues, this ratio demonstrates an institution's ability to generate income from its core financial service activity. Thus, ROE is interest to present or prospective shareholders (and donors), and is also of concern to management, because this measure is viewed as an important indicator of the shareholder value creation.

Return on Equity Ratio provides management and investors with the rate of return earned on the invested equity. It differs from the return on assets ratio as it measures the return on funds that are owned by the MFI rather than total assets. This ratio will also vary greatly depending on the capital structure of the MFI. MFIs that find their assets primarily with equity will show lower return than those that fund the: assets primarily with liabilities. In other words, debt-equity ratio or leverage has a significant impact on return on equity ratio. The ROE ratio would increase if the profit of the MFI increases and/or its leverage (debt) increases.

16.3. Asset/Liability Management Ratios

The basis of financial intermediation is the ability to manage assets (the use of funds) and liabilities (the source of funds). Asset/liability management is required on the following several levels:[1]

a) Interest Rate Management	The MFI must make sure that the use of funds generates more revenue than the cost of funds, operational costs and the provision for loan losses. The margin between the yield on portfolio and the cost of funds is the amount available for other operational expenses. Rates that are intentionally subsidized or unintentionally too low, do not sustain services in the long term for clients.

b) Asset Management	Funds should be used to create assets that produce the most revenue (are most 'productive")
c) Leverage	The MFI seeks to borrow funds to increase assets and thereby increase revenue and net profit. At the same time, the MFI must manage the cost and use of its borrowings so that it generates more revenue than it pays in interest and fee expenses on those. Finding the right balance between debt and equity funding is not always straight forward. Borrowing funds for growth and expansion may be recommended, provided that more revenue is generated than the cost and use of borrowing.
d) Liquidity Management	The MFI must also make sure that it has sufficient funds available (liquid) to meet any short-term obligations
e) Foreign Currency Management	This occurs when an MFI lends, invests or borrows in a foreign currency. The risk is greatest when a mismatch exists between the value of foreign currency assets and liabilities, leaving the MFI exposed to either a decline in the value of its assets or an increase in balance of its funding liabilities when a significant movement in exchange rates occurs.

a) Portfolio Yield: Portfolio Yield is a percentage (%) of income of loan portfolio to average loan portfolio outstanding. It shows the average gross returns as proportion of the portfolio outstanding. Generally speaking, Portfolio Yield is the initial indicator of an institution's ability to generate revenue with which to cover its financial and operating expenses. It measures how much the MFI actually received in cash interest payments and Fees and commissions from its clients during the period. This ratio is indicator of an MFI's ability to generate cash for operations from the Gross Loan Portfolio. Portfolio Yield can be determined by using following formula:

$$\text{Portfolio Yield} = \frac{\textbf{Cash Received from Interest, Fees and Commissions on Loan Portfolio during the period}}{\textbf{Average Gross Loan Portfolio during the period}}$$

Trend: An increasing Portfolio Yield is positive although it will level off as it nears the effective interest rate.

Portfolio Yield also provides an insight into portfolio quality. If the MFIs use cash accounting, Portfolio Yield will not include the accrued interest and fees income that delinquent loans should have generated. Cash receipts from the Gross Loan Portfolio are vital for an MFI's survival. As a cash measure, this indicator is distorted by neither unrealistic accrual or deferral policies nor by loan refinancing nor other means of non-cash payment that can hide loan delinquency problems.

Portfolio yield must be understood in the context of the local market and prevailing interest rates. Yields should not fluctuate significantly unless the MFI frequently changes its loan terms and conditions. If the Portfolio Yield is significantly lower than the effective interest rate, it may indicate problems with loan collections.

If the Portfolio Yield is showing increasing trend, it is considered positive. The Ratio is affected by growth in portfolio. Portfolio Yield is an easy way to calculate the actual effective interest rate charged by an MFI. It shows how much on average, the MFI receives in interest payments on its loans.

(b) Portfolio to Assets: This ratio shows how well an MFI allocates its assets to its primary business i.e. giving loans. Portfolio to Assets measures how well the MFI is deploying its funds into high-yielding micro loans. It is the ratio of total Gross Portfolio to Total Assets. Mathematically, it can be expressed by:

$$\textbf{Portfolio to Assets} = \frac{\textbf{Gross Loan Portfolio}}{\textbf{Assets}}$$

Trend: An increasing trend is positive

The Gross Loan Portfolio can fluctuate from month to month if the MFI experiences seasonal demand for loans. This ratio can be used to identify fluctuations that may result from structural or operational rigidities that cause a high number of loans to be disbursed or repaid at the same time. Depending on the context, this ratio could indicate the need for additional funding or be a sign of excess liquidity. MFI that rely on savings to fund their portfolio tend to be more efficient at maintaining a high and steady Portfolio to Asset ratio. High Portfolio to Asset is considered good as most of assets are invested in loan portfolio having higher return.

(c) Cost of Funds: It is the ratio of total financial expenses on funding liabilities to total funding liabilities (deposits + borrowings). This ratio gives a blended interest rate for all the MFI's average funding liabilities, deposits, and borrowings. Cost of Funds is calculated by the following formula:

$$\textbf{Cost of Funds} = \frac{\textbf{Financial Expenses on Funding Liabilities}}{\textbf{(Average Deposts + Average Borrowings)}}$$

Trend: The cost of Funds may indicate a level of maturity of the MFI. A decreasing Cost of Funds ratio is generally positive. When Financial Expenses are adjusted to include free or subsidized funding, the ratio will show the actual financial cost of funds needed to fund or capitals the MFI.

Financial institutions strive to minimize cost of funds and maximize Yield. Ideally, a low cost of Funds results from an MFI gaining access to Deposits and or Borrowings at a reasonable cost because depositors and lenders considered it creditworthy. The more creditworthy the MFI, the lower the cost will be. Cost of funds could be quite low because the MFI has access to subsidized borrowings. The Cost of funds depends on the market and also by type of institutions and legal status. It is most valuable to compare cost of funds with Portfolio Yield and MFI should seek to maintain a sufficient financial spread between the Cost of Funds and Yield.

(d) Debt Equity Ratio (DER): It is the simplest and best known measure of capital adequacy as it measures the overall leverage of the institution. DER indicates the safety cushion the institution has to absorb losses before the creditors are at risk. It also shows how well the MFI is able to leverage its Equity to increase assets through borrowing and is frequently called the leverage ratio. This ratio is usually important for investors and lenders. It is calculated as ratio of total Debt to Equity.

$$\text{DER} = \frac{\textbf{Liabilities (Debt)}}{\textbf{Equity}}$$

Trend: An increasing debt/equity ratio indicates the MFI's capacity to attract debt funding based on its capital strength of its own equity. Too low at ratio might indicate that the MFI is not maximizing its equity base. Too high a factor may be risky for investors, and may spell cash flow challenges during difficult times.

Deposit taking MFIs and saving-based organizations will usually have higher ratios than noncommercial MFIs. In many environments, Debt/Equity levels may be limited by local regulations or indirectly controlled through borrowing restrictions.

(e) Liquid Ratio: The liquid ratio is one measurement of the sufficiency of cash resources to pay the short-term obligations to depositors, lenders, and other creditors. Financial institutions are particularly vulnerable to cash shortages because their entire business is based on the proper management of cash inflows and outflows.

$$\text{Liquid Ratio} = \frac{\textbf{Cash + Trade Investments}}{\textbf{Short-term Liabilities (deposits, borrowings, interest payable, account payable etc.)}}$$

Trend: No single ratio or trend provides the "correct" or "adequate" means to monitor cash levels. MFIs must have clear policies in place to ensure that cash is available when needed for all MFI operations and activities. Banking requirement and risk tolerance will affect the ratio.

Here short-term refers to assets and liabilities that can be turned into cash within a year from the date of statement or report not from the date of disbursement, issuance or purchase.

For MFIs, maintaining sufficient cash is important not only to pay bills, salaries or creditors but also to uphold its promise to provide repeat loans to clients, which is a major incentive for clients to repay loans. Similarly, any MFI that fails to repay client deposits on time is likely to lose client confidence and access to future funding. MFI should have cash management policies so as to maintain comfortable liquid ratio and to ensure sufficient cash is available on time to all branches and agencies.

16.4. Portfolio Quality Ratios

The primary asset of an MFI is its loan portfolio. Portfolio quality is important to the financial success of any microfinance institution. Drop in portfolio quality could mean decline in customer satisfaction and, therefore, may presage a low retention rate resulting in higher costs to recruit new clients. Drops may also signal problems in staff supervision and control. In any case, poor asset quality will result in additional costs and lower income. Financial health of the MFI will also largely depend on portfolio quality. To maintain good portfolio quality, MFI should have system and policies for effective management of loan portfolio. Client selection, products design and delivery, collection mechanism, quality of staffs, etc. are some of important factors for determining portfolio quality. It measures how well an MFI is managing its loan portfolio and is very important ratio for lenders and donors. Some of the tips for managing for portfolio quality are given below:[2]

a) Loan recovery begins with providing services that clients value, through efficient and effective loan administration.

b) Loan recovery is possible through good, thorough loan assessment that looks at the willingness and capacity of the client to repay

c) Effective loan recovery is strengthened through good management information system that provides relevant, timely and accurate information about the loan's status.

d) Immediate late loan follow up and effective delinquency management that uses incentives as well as dis-incentives is critical for preventing chronic problems or high write-offs.

e) The MFI needs to establish clear accounting policies to account for portfolio aging, the provision for loan losses, and write-offs for loans that are considered uncollectable.

f) The MFI should provide clear and transparent disclosure of financial information related to its portfolio quality, its accounting policies for the portfolio, and actual performance for the reporting period.

(a) Portfolio at Risk (PAR): Portfolio at Risk (PAR) is one of the most important tools used to assess the asset quality (loan portfolio) of an MFI. It is a percentage (%) of total gross outstanding loan portfolio that is at default risk. PAR measures a pessimistic estimate of the default risk in an MFI's portfolio. It is important because it indicates the potential for future losses based on the current performance of the loan portfolio.

Formula for calculation of PAR is:

$$\text{PAR} > 30 \text{ days} = \frac{\text{Portfolio at Risk} > 30 \text{ days} + \text{Regenerated/Rescheduled Loans}}{\text{Total Gross Outstanding Loan (Principal) Portfolio}}$$

Trend: A decreasing Portfolio at Risk is positive

PAR ratio is the most widely accepted measure of loan performance in the microfinance industry. PAR>30 days is often used as the threshold beyond which loans are considered to be at higher risk. This ratio also includes renegotiated loans. This not only prevents hiding troubled loans through rescheduling or refinancing, but also indicates a higher level of risk associated with clients who have had repayment problems. This ratio should be low and fairly stable. When referring to PAR, the MFI should always specify the number of days.

As far as trends for PAR is concerned, a decreasing Portfolio at Risk is positive. However, this trend can be misleading, because a lower ratio can be obtained by decreasing the numerator and/or increasing the denominator. In other words, sudden and large disbursements of loans could mask the actual default risk. Likewise, re-scheduling, refinancing and loan write-offs can portray a lower PAR ratio while default risk may still be high.

PAR for past due loans with different ages are usually calculated as given under:[3]

PAR > 1 Day	Sum of PAR 1-30 days + PAR 31-60 days + ...+ PAR >365 days
PAR>30 Days	Sum of PAR 31-60 days + PAR 61-90days +........+ PAR >365 days
PAR > 60 Days	Sum of PAR 61-90days + PAR 91-120days +....+PAR>365 days
PAR> 90 Days	Sum of PAR 91-120days +PAR 121-180 days....+PAR>365 days
PAR>180 Days	Sum of PAR 181-365days+PAR>365 days
PAR>365 Days	Sum of PAR>365 days

(b) Write-Off Ratio

Write off Ratio indicates the past quality of the Gross Loan Portfolio. Write-offs are the greatest threat to an MFI because they result in a reduction in the MFI's assets and its current and future earning potentials. A high ratio may indicate a problem in the MFI's collection efforts.

$$\textbf{Write-Off Ratio} = \frac{\textbf{Principal Amount Written Off during Period}}{\textbf{Average Gross Outstanding Loan Portfolio}}$$

Trend: A decreasing Write-off Ratio is positive.

Write-offs are an accounting device to remove persistently delinquent loans from the books. This ratio is highly dependent on an MFI's write-off policy. An MFI should disclose its write-offs policy, which should be clearly defined, followed and monitored by the board. An MFI's write-offs should be minimal; however, most MFI's write-off ratios are remarkably low. The Write-off ratio is based on the Average Gross Loan Portfolio because write-offs are usually recorded throughout a period. An aggressive write-off policy reduces the PAR Ratio. For this reason, the PAR Ratio and Write-off Ratio should be viewed together. An aggressive write-off policy should be accompanied by strong loan recovery efforts. Recoveries of loan written-off should be closely monitored.

(c) Risk Coverage Ratio or Loan Loss Reserve Ratio: Risk Coverage Ratio measures how adequate the Impairment Loss Allowance is to account for potential loan losses. Because the Impairment Loss Allowance represents the MFI's preparation for loan losses, the Risk Coverage Ratio is an approximate indicator of how prepared an institution is to absorb loan loses in the worst-case scenario ; that is PAR>days became uncollectable.

$$\textbf{Risk Coverage Ratio} = \frac{\textbf{Impairment Loss Allowance}}{\textbf{Portfolio at Risk > 30 days}}$$

Trend: A fairly constant, stable ratio is desired. Sudden changes usually indicate a deterioration or improvement in portfolio quality or an excess or shortage in the Allowance for Loan Losses account.

Impairment Loss Allowance depends on the aging of loan portfolio having past dues and also policy of the MFI. Local regulators or tax authorities may dictate the required risk ratios by dictating allowable loan-loss provision expenses.

(d) Cumulative Repayment Rate (CRR): measures repayment performance over a long period of time. The formula to calculate CRR is

$$\textbf{Cumulative Repayment Rate (CRR)} = \frac{\textbf{Total amount due from Clients till date}}{\textbf{Total amount repaid so far by Clients X 100}}$$

Trend: An increasing trend is positive

It provides a sense of the overall delinquency in the MFI especially over the years. From a historical perspective, cumulative repayment rate is also required as it provides an overall measure of what proportion of the amount due till date has been paid by clients. In other words, it gives an overall estimate of the amount past due for the programme through the years. It is useful for assessing the performance of an MFI over a long period of time.

The sequence of allocating client repayments-interest first versus principal first has an impact on repayment rates. It is suggested that client repayments should be allocated in the following sequence-first to interest overdues, then to interest due, then to principal overdue and finally to principal due. When aggregating repayments from the various clients, prepayments of some clients could cover the non-repayment by other clients. Hence, prepayments should always be subtracted while calculating repayment rates.

16.5. Efficiency and Productivity Indicators

Efficiency and productivity indicators reflect how well an MFI uses its resources, particularly its assets and personal. MFIs use many different efficiency and productivity indicators, tailoring them to reflect their own organizational structure, product lines and monitoring priorities.

It is important to note that the efficiency ratios must be used carefully. They are highly dependent on the loan methodology used, the number of products and services offered, staffing structure, the physical context (rural or urban) and the maturity level of the MFI. Efficiency ratios should also be examined in conjunction with Portfolio Quality ratios, since a quality portfolio should not be sacrificed for high efficiencies. Some of the tips for Managing for Efficiency and Productivity are given below:

a) Develop and fine-tune the products and services to suit the clients, an for the locations in which MFI operate.

b) Use of technology that will decrease operating and transaction costs.

c) Implement effective incentive systems for staff performance.

d) Continually monitor portfolio quality to ensure that efficiency is not compromised by increasing delinquency.

e) Be careful in analyzing and comparing ratios with other MFIs.

a) Operating Expense Ratio (OER): Operating Expense Ratio measures the operating expenses (administrative and personnel expenses) incurred for giving micro loans. It is the ratio of operating expenses to average gross loan portfolio.

$$\textbf{Operating Expense Ratio (OER)} = \frac{\textbf{Operating Expense}}{\textbf{Average Gross Loan Portfolio}}$$

Trend: A decreasing Operating Expense Ratio is positive.

OER highlights the efficiency of managing the loan portfolio i.e. lower OER, the greater the efficiency. It is affected by increasing or decreasing operational expenses relative to the average loan portfolio outstanding. MFI should try to keep the OER low. This can be achieved either by minimizing or controlling the operating expenses or increase the loan portfolio size. This indicator is particularly sensitive to lending conditions and methodologies, and despite its popularity, should not be used in cross-programme comparison. Making small loans and delivering financial services in underserved /remote areas is an expensive business. The delivery mechanism that an MFI chooses can significantly add to the cost per active client. If an MFI selects an efficient methodology and employs a highly productive staff, the OER will drop, resulting in a more sustainable institution. A downward trend in this Ratio highlights the increasing efficiency.

b) Cost per Client: Cost per Client Ratio indicates how much an MFI spends in personal and administrative expenses to serve a single client. It informs the MFI how much it must earn from each client to be profitable. Cost per Client Ratio can be calculated as:

$$\textbf{Cost per Client} = \frac{\textbf{Operating Expense}}{\textbf{Average Number of Active Clients}}$$

Trend: A decreasing Cost per Client is positive.

This ratio can be used to compare institutions of different sizes because the Average Gross Portfolio is not part of the calculation. Comparing the cost per client with the local GNI per capita provides a rough proxy of labour costs in the local market. Because local labour costs are largely beyond the MFI's control, MFI can determine if a reduction in cost per client is the result of reduced cost of labour or more efficient use of labour.

c) Borrowers per Loan Officer: This ratio is often used by MFIs because it helps measure personnel productivity of the loan staff. Creating caseload target for loan officers is useful in planning, and this ratio is an easy and effective way to measure progress against such target.

$$\textbf{Borrowers per Loan Officer} = \frac{\textbf{Number of Active Borrowers}}{\textbf{Number of Loan Officers}}$$

Trend: An increasing ratio is positive.

This ratio will increase until it reaches the optimal range and then plateaus. It should be monitor on a monthly basis. Plateaus can be surpassed through structural or technological changes such as streamlining the methodology or introducing technology. Plateaus also may be overcome by increasing staff incentives for efficiency, such as loan officer bonuses. This ratio depends on the local environment, such as population density and ease of access to clients. It can also vary drastically due to product terms and conditions (e.g. individual lending versus group lending) and methodology (frequency of meetings). MFIs should monitor gains with an eye on the portfolio at risk to ensure that productivity gains are not achieved at the expenses of asset quality.

d) Active Clients per Staff Members: This ratio measures the overall productivity of the staff. This helps in examining the ability of the MFI's personnel to manage all its clients, including borrowers, voluntary savers and other clients.

$$\textbf{Active Clients per Staff Member} = \frac{\textbf{Number of Active Clients}}{\textbf{Number of Personnel}}$$

Trend: An increasing ratio is positive.

As MFI's also offer more products to meet their clients' diverse financial needs, Active client per staff members is more relevant that Borrowers per Loan Officers as the primary productivity ratio for personnel. Internal issues such as excess paperwork or procedures, or external factors such as remote service locations, contribute to lower productivity. Each MFI will have its own optimal number of clients per staff person and should set this target in its business plan.

e) Client Turnover: The Client Turnover Ratio is frequently used by MFIs to determine the level of client satisfaction with the MFI's products and services.

$$\textbf{Client Turnover} = \frac{\textbf{Number of Active Clients at Beginning of Period + Number of New Clients During Period – Number of Active Clients at end of period}}{\textbf{Average Number of Active Clients}}$$

Trend: A decreasing trend is positive

Studies indicate that lack of flexible and demand-driven products continues to be a major cause of client drop out. The cost of retaining clients is significantly lower than the cost of recruiting new clients.[4] Therefore, measuring client turnover is a valuable management tools to understand when clients are leaving. The term *turnover* rather than Loss is used for this ratio because although some clients may leave or become inactive for a period of time, not all these clients are lost to the MFI. If inactive clients can be brought back into activity, loans to them tend to be less risky and require less staff time. MFI should have sound policies to retain good clients and make it easier for returning good clients to access loans and other services.

f) Average Portfolio per Loan Officer: Average Portfolio per loan officer is a currency number ratio. In simple terms, it highlights the "loan portfolio outstanding (or volume of business) generated by loan /credit officer. This ratio is useful primarily for the internal management of productivity and must be used cautiously, when comparing productivity to other microfinance institutions (MFIs).

Formula for calculation of Average Portfolio per loan officer is:

$$\textbf{Average Portfolio per Loan Officer} = \frac{\textbf{Average value of Loan Outstanding}}{\textbf{Average Number of Loan Officers}}$$

Trend: An increasing trend is positive.

The amount loan portfolio per loan officer is a key indicator of financial viability, since higher portfolio per officer will generate more revenue when staff costs are held down. Some MFIs are indeed beginning to consider loan officers as profit centers and evaluate them as such. This Ratio has an increasing interrelationship with the loan officer caseload: in that as load size drops, a loan officer must manage larger caseloads (i.e. more clients) in order to maintain the same amount of loan portfolio.

If an institution fails to maintain high loan portfolio per loan officer then that institution would be forced to charge higher interest rates in order to generate the same amount of revenue.

g) Average Outstanding Loan Size: The average outstanding loan size is one proxy for an MFI to measure its ability to reach poorer clients. It is the ratio of total loan portfolio to total numbers of loans outstanding. It is still widely used by MFIs to monitor the depth of outreach among lower-income clients. Loan size is also a major driver of profitability and can be used by MFIs to project portfolio growth.

$$\textbf{Average Outstanding Loan Size} = \frac{\textbf{Gross Loan Portfolio}}{\textbf{Number of Loans Outstanding}}$$

Trend: This ratio may fluctuate for many reasons-seasonality, change in methodology, disbursement patterns and loan size. It is important to compare against the MFI's business plan.

Although several factors other than income level of the client contribute to small outstanding loan sizes, a correlation exists between this ratio and the average income level of the areas served. It is informative for MFI to monitor this ratio in light of the GNI per capita and the Cost per Client.

16.6 .Sa-Dhan's Minimum Standards[5] with Indicators and Benchmarked Values

Sl. No.	*Indicator*	*Benchmark*	*Formula*
SUSTAINABILITY PERFORMANCE STANDARDS			
1	Operational Self-Sufficiency	At least 100%	Operating Income / (Operating Costs + Loan Loss Provisions + Financing Costs)
ASSET QUALITY PERFORMANCE STANDARD			
2	Portfolio at Risk > 60 Days Past Due	Less than 10%	Unpaid Principal Balance of Past Due Loans (with Overdue > 60 days of age) / Total Gross Outstanding Portfolio
3	Current Repayment Rate	Greater than 90%	Total Amount (Principal) Collected for the Period – Prepayments / Total Amount (Principal) Due (to be collected during period)
EFFICIENCY PERFORMANCE STANDARDS			
4	Operating Cost Ratio	Less than 20%	Total Operating Costs / Average Outstanding Portfolio
5	Total Cost Ratio	Less than 30%	Total Costs / Average Outstanding Portfolio
6	Active Borrowers Per Credit Officers	Between 250-350	Average Number of Active Borrowers / Average Number of Credit Officers

NOTES

1. The SEEP Network (2005) *Measuring Performance of Microfinance Institutions: A Framework for Reporting, Analysis and Monitoring.*
2. MicroSave (2008), *Basic Financial Management and Ratio Analysis for MFIs Toolkit.*
3. Sa-Dhan Microfinance Manager Series: Technical Note #1.
4. Brigit Helms and Imran Matin, 2000, "Those who lease and those who never join: Insights from East African Microfinance Institutions", *Focus* Note 16 (Washington, DC, CGAP).
5. The Sa-Dhan , *Operational Manuals on Performance Standards.*

17

Risk Management for MFI

17.1. Risk Management

All the MFIs are exposed to a great number of risks, both internal and external, that threaten effective services to clients, financial stability, and future sustainability. As MFIs grow and become more complex, the need for periodic reviews of risk management systems becomes greater. It is the responsibility of management of MFI to assess the institution's level of exposure, to prioritize areas of greatest vulnerability, and to ensure that proper controls are in place to minimize MFI's exposure to various types of risks. Risk is the potential that current and future events, expected or unanticipated may have an adverse or harmful impact on the institution's capital, earnings or achievement of its objectives.

Risk management is the process of taking calculated risks, a systematic approach that identifies and prioritizes the risks and implements strategies to mitigate the risks. This approach includes both the **prevention** of potential problems and the early **detection** of actual problems. It is a continuous process that involves staff at all levels of the organization.

Risk management is the process of balancing risk-taking and capital against a well-designed control environment. Managing risks includes identifying, prioritizing and selecting responses to risks. Managing risks effectively reduces the likelihood that a loss will occur and minimizes the scale of the loss should it occur. Risk management includes both the prevention of potential problems, the early detection of actual problems when they occur, and the correction of the policies and procedures that permitted the occurrence.[1]

Risk management is an ongoing process because internal and external vulnerabilities keep changing.

17.2. Types of Risks

MFIs face many risks that threaten their financial viability and long-term sustainability. Some of the most serious risks come from the external environment in which the MFI operates, including the risk of natural disaster, economic crisis, or war. While the MFI cannot control these risks directly, there are many ways in which the MFI can prepare itself and minimize their potential for negative impact. Some of the common risks come from internal policy and environment of MFIs are namely operational, credit, liquidity, interest rate, and fraud risks. Thus risks can be broadly categories into two groups i.e internal risks and external risks. Details are given as under:

a) Internal Risks

Institutional Risks

- **Social mission risk:** the provision of appropriate financial services to the intended clientele
- **Commercial mission risk:** to manage the organisation as a business to allow it to exist for the long term.
- **Dependency risk:** continuing need for strategic, financial and operational support from an external organisation.

Operational Risks

- **Credit Risk:** lending money and not getting it back
- **Fraud Risk:** intentional deception for personal gain illegal or irregular means
- **Error Risk:** Unintentional errors that create unreliable information and reports, or the loss of assets
- **Security Risk:** risk of theft or harm to property or person

Financial Management Risks

- **Asset and liability Risk:** management of interest rate, liquidity, and foreign exchange. These risks increase and become more complex as the MFI grows, and broadens its range of financial services to include savings.
- **Inefficiency Risk:** management of costs per unit of output, affected by both cost controls and level of outreach.
- **System integrity risk**: the integrity of the information systems, whether computerized or manual.

b) External Risks

Microfinance institutions can have relatively strong management and staff, and adequate systems and controls, but still experience major problems due to the environment in which it operates. It is important that these risks are recognized as challenges to be addressed rather than excuses for poor performance.

Regulatory Risk

Awareness of regulations in banking, labour laws, contract enforcement, and other policies that affect MFIs. Some Central Bank prohibit the collection, mobilization and use of client savings unless the MFI is registered and licensed to do so. In India, some of the partnership loans offered by a large bank to

	several MFIs were not renewed, severely resulted in reduced portfolio growth.
Competition Risk	Familiarity with the services of others to position, price. Competition for staff is also a huge risk.
Demographic risk	Assessing characteristics of the target market. This could look at special social issues, including health, aging and migration. The HIV/AIDS pandemic is a threat to productive middle aged people, posing risks to the MFI's targeted market and their staff.
Physical environment Risk	Natural disasters, physical infrastructure. Some rural areas (e.g. Bihar, Assam in India) may be prone to floods nearly every year. Droughts will also affect the rural poor who are dependent on agriculture or agri-businesses; these natural disasters will not only affect clients and their business, but the MFIs that serve them.
Macroeconomic risk	Currently devaluation and inflation and effect on both the institution and the clients. A regular interest rate increase of bank loans to MFIs will reduce the margins available to MFIs and force them to cut operating cost. The market or regularity environment may be too competitive to increase rates, leaving them little choice to do otherwise.
Political/Governmental risk	Political instability, civil unrest, etc.
Reputation risk	An MFI's image amongst clients in the community it servers is critical to strong repayment and repeat business. Image and reputation in the community does not only come from actual and factual information about the MFI. It is about client perceptions and the satisfaction they feel about the institution, about how they feel they are treated, and whether they value the services provided.

17.3. Risk Assessment Framework

Most microfinance institutions are small, unprofitable, and operate without proper systems to reduce risk exposure. Although the microfinance literature focuses on this industry's success stories, such as BancoSol in Bolivia or BRI's microfinance units in Indonesia, these organizations are the exceptions rather than the rule. For microfinance programs that are striving to fulfill their **dual mission** of sustainability and outreach to the poor, CARE suggests the implementation of the risk assessment framework described below:

i) **Financial Health** and ii) **Institutional Development**

A standard risk assessment of a financial institution typically addresses the first issue only. In assessing the financial health of a bank or other financial institution, one would consider the organization's asset and liability management, including credit risk, as well as operational risks such as fraud and inefficiency. While this traditional approach is incorporated into the CARE framework, microfinance risk assessment also needs to embrace an institutional development perspective. As the microfinance industry evolves from donor dependency into a commercial approach, clear vision, reliable systems, effective governance, and staff capacity become critical factors in an institution's ability to manage risk. This integrated risk assessment framework for microfinance institutions, which analyzes both institutional development and financial health issues, is organized into four categories of risk: institutional, operational, financial, and external. This framework provides managers and directors of microfinance institutions with a step-by-step means of assessing their organization's current and potential vulnerabilities.

Categories of Microfinance Risks

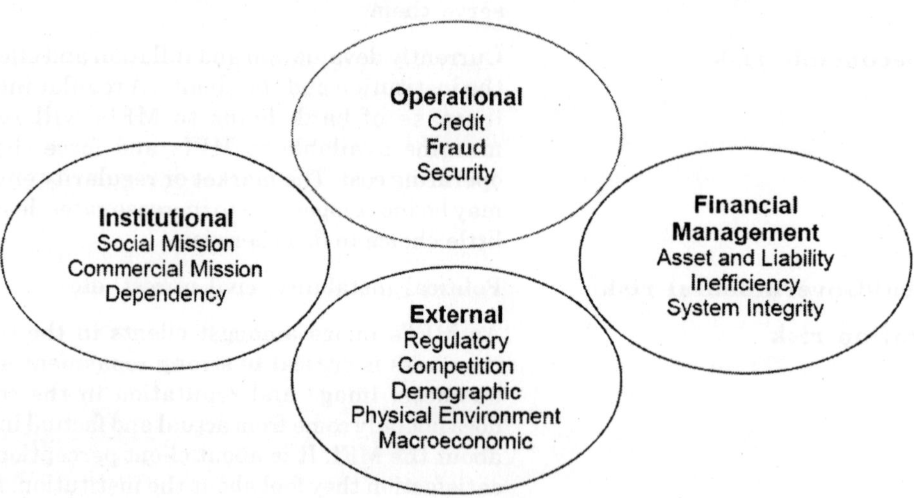

Source: Adapted from Craig Churchill and Dan Coster, *CARE Risk Management Handbook* (Washington D.C.: CARE and Pact Publications, 2001).

(a) Institutional risks are those that threaten the loss of either the social or the commercial mission of the institution: change in the target client, continued donor dependency.

(b) Operational risks are the vulnerabilities faced in daily operations: credit, fraud, inefficiency, security.

(c)Financial management risks include asset-liability management issues, liquidity, and system integrity.

(d) External risks are more often out of the MFI's control but must be recognized and mitigated: regulatory, competitive, demographic, macroeconomic, etc.

For many institutions, operational risk is the most relevant type of risk because it is in this area that an MFI stands to lose the most.

17.4. Risk Management Process

The risk management approach implies a shift in responsibility for internal control from the traditional back-office and support functions to the board and chief executive officer. Only by involving the board of directors and senior management can an MFI develop and integrate a strong culture of risk management into all areas of operation. To reach its fullest potential, MFIs need to recognize risk management as an important ongoing internal function rather than view it as the role of the annual external audit. Outside assessments are often too limited in scope and arrive too late to provide the depth and timeliness of feedback needed to protect the MFI from significant financial loss. Risk management is the process of controlling the likelihood and potential severity of an adverse event. While taking risks is a natural part of lending and finance, MFIs should attempt to plan for risk and avoid unnecessary surprises, i.e., unforeseen events that can threaten their viability. Risk management is a systematic approach to identifying, measuring, monitoring, and managing business risks in an institution. While each of the following six steps of risk management involves different employees of the MFI, collectively they integrate all employees into the process.

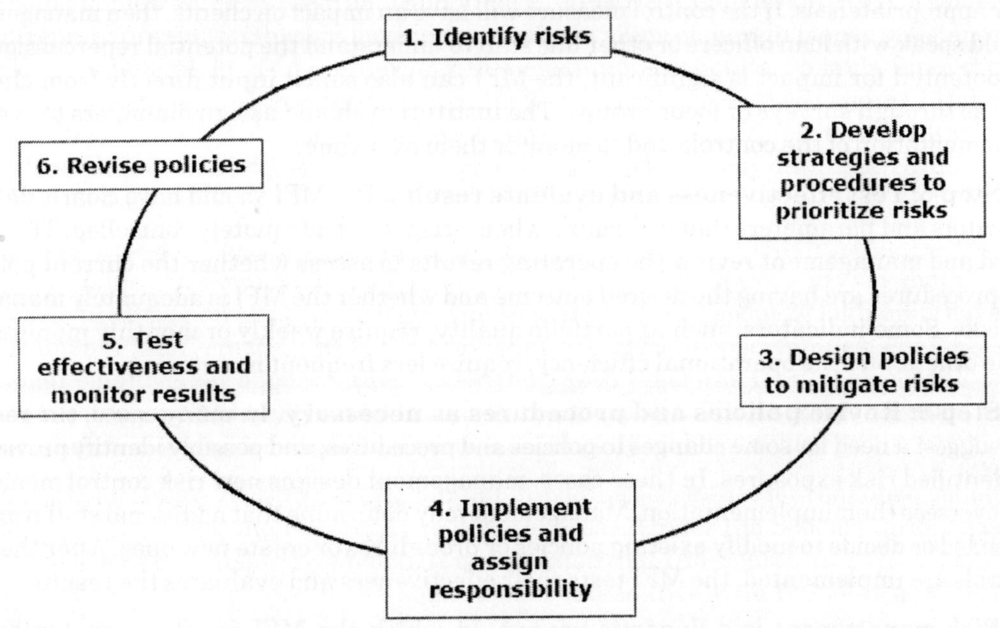

Source: Adapted from Anita Campion, *Improving Interal Control: A Practical Guide for Microfinance Institutions*, Technical Guide No. 1 (Washington D.C.: Microfinance Network and GTZ, 2000).

Step-1: Identify, assess and prioritize risks. The risk management process begins with management identifying and prioritizing the key risks, which are reviewed and approved by the board of directors. This step requires the board and management to determine the degree of risk the MFI should tolerate and to conduct assessments for each risk of the potential negative impact if it is not controlled. The most significant risks faced by microfinance institutions include operational risk, credit risk, liquidity risk, interest rate risk and fraud risk, which are described above.

Step-2: Develop strategies to measure risks. The board approves policies for measuring and tracking risks and monitors the MFI's adherence to them. Management identifies key indicators and ratios that can be tracked and analyzed regularly to assess the MFI's exposure to risk in each area of operations. Management sets the acceptable range for each indicator, outside of which would indicate excessive risk exposure. Management also determines the frequency with which each indicator should be monitored and analyzed.

Step-3: Design policies and procedures to mitigate risks. Next, management develops sound procedures and operational guidelines to mitigate each risk to the degree desired. Sound policies and procedures clearly instruct employees how to conduct transactions and incorporate effective internal control measures.

Step- 4: Implement controls into operations and assign responsibility. Management now selects cost-effective controls and seeks input from operational staff on their appropriateness. If the control measure will have an impact on clients, then management should speak with loan officers or other line staff to understand the potential repercussions. If the potential for impact is significant, the MFI can also solicit input directly from clients, such as through surveys or focus groups. The institution should assign managers to oversee implementation of the controls and to monitor them over time.

Step-5: Test effectiveness and evaluate results. The MFI should have clearly defined indicators and parameters that determine when a risk is not adequately controlled. Then, the board and management review the operating results to assess whether the current policies and procedures are having the desired outcome and whether the MFI is adequately managing its risks. Some indicators, such as portfolio quality, require weekly or monthly monitoring, while others, such as operational efficiency, require less frequent monitoring.

Step-6: Revise policies and procedures as necessary. In many cases, the results will suggest a need for some changes to policies and procedures, and possibly identify previously unidentified risk exposures. In these cases, management designs new risk control measures and oversees their implementation. Management may determine that additional staff training is needed or decide to modify existing policies or procedures or create new ones. After the new controls are implemented, the MFI tests their effectiveness and evaluates the results.

Risk management is a dynamic process, in which the MFI regularly evaluates the effectiveness of its policies and procedures in controlling risks and makes adjustments as necessary. Even if an evaluation finds that the MFI is adequately controlling its risks, the risk management process does not end; it continues with regular, ongoing evaluations. Each successive evaluation not only tests the effectiveness of new controls but also includes a review of previously tested controls. Because MFIs operate in ever-changing risk environments, the risk management process is never-ending. Creating an infrastructure and system to incorporate risk management into the MFI's culture ensures that all staff focuses on identifying and anticipating potential risks. The process ensures a continual "feedback loop" from and back to the board and senior managers to ensure they receive the information they need, that the information is accurate and that it is consistent with the risk parameters set by the MFI.

17.5. Internal Control and Internal Audit

As microfinance institutions (MFIs) grow and more operate as regulated financial intermediaries, internal control becomes essential to long-term institutional viability. The number and types of stakeholders concerned with the MFI's financial well-being increases: donors desire to support sustainable microfinance projects; board members want to protect their reputations and fulfill their obligations; investors are interested in preserving capital; borrowers are concerned with continuous access to loans; depositors want to ensure the safety of their savings; and regulators want to protect the financial environment and depositors' interests. To remain competitive, MFIs are undertaking product and geographical expansion, which introduce new risks and challenges imposed by rapid growth. An effective system of internal control allows the MFI to assume additional risks in a calculated manner while minimizing financial surprises and protecting itself from significant financial loss. Thus, internal control is an integral component of risk management.

What is Internal Control?

According to the Basle Committee on Banking Supervision, the primary objectives of the internal control process in a financial institution are:

1. To verify the efficiency and effectiveness of the operations;
2. To ensure the reliability and completeness of financial and management information;
2. and
3. To comply with applicable laws and regulations.

Internal Controls (ICs)

Internal controls are all of the resources and procedures used by managers to properly control their activities. Using the process allows the management and its personnel to be reasonably sure that their objectives have been met. ICs help correct contradictions and detect anomalies that occur among different decision centers that have varying degrees of autonomy.

Internal controls can be:

Preventive – designed and installed to prevent undesirable outcomes *before* they happen.

Detective – designed to identify undesirable outcomes when they *do* happen. Detective ICs identify errors *after* they occur.

Corrective – designed to make sure that corrective action is taken to reverse the undesirable outcomes or to see that they do not recur. Corrective ICs are exercised to correct the identified errors. All of them, in concert, function to ensure that some management objective or goal will be met.

Internal Audit

Internal auditing is an independent appraisal function that is established within an organization to examine and evaluate its activities. The objective of internal auditing is to provide a service to the organization by assisting members of the organization in the effective discharge of their responsibilities. To this end, internal auditing furnishes them with analyses, appraisals, recommendations, counsel, and information concerning the activities reviewed. The audit objective includes promoting effective control at reasonable cost. At some levels it serves to monitor and evaluate the applications of established controls. Occasionally an MFI may contract an external auditor or firm to conduct its internal audit function

The primary goal of the financial internal audit is to determine whether the risks to the organisation are identified by checking to see if:

a) Financial and operating information is accurate (for internal and external purposes);

b) Internal policies and procedures are being followed;

c) Management's risk identification, prioritization and mitigation is appropriate; and

d) Any new risks become evident or previously identified risks remain unaddressed.

The MFI Internal Auditor contributes to the monitoring component in the internal control system. The Internal Auditor monitors compliance to policies, procedures and systems that have been put in place to prevent loss and minimize operating risks. The Internal Auditor is also a key contributor to the communication and information flow that is integral to the functioning of a strong internal control system. However, the Internal Auditor is not part and parcel of daily operational activities. The Internal Auditor is the objective perspective that the Board and senior management need to know what is actually happening in the field with clients, in the field officers and in branch operations.

External Audit

An *external audit* is conducted by an individual or firm that is independent of the company being audited. These independent auditors audit the books of a company generally once per year after the completion of the company's fiscal year. Their role is to give an opinion of the financial statement's reflection of the status and operations of the company being audited. Depending on what they witness during the audit, external auditors will also produce a management letter for use by management and the board, Although a financial statement audit is the most common type of external audit, external auditors may also conduct special-purpose audits, which might include performing specific tests and procedures and reporting on the results, performing a less intensive review (donors commonly request such a review), and doing compilations.

Difference between Internal and External Auditors[2]

Internal Auditor	*External Auditor*
Can be an employee of the organisation	Is an independent contractor
Serves the needs of the organisation	Also serves third parties who need reliable financial information and reports
Focuses on future events by evaluating controls that ensure the achievement of the organisation's objectives	Focuses on whether financial statements reflect historical events clearly and accurately
Is directly concerned with preventing fraud	Is incidentally concerned with fraud controls in general, but is directly concerned only when the financial statements are affected
Audit work is continuous throughout the year	Audit work is done annually at the end of the fiscal year.

Practitioners often confuse internal control with internal audit, which is an integral part of internal control. While internal audit focuses solely on evaluating risk management "ex-post" (after operations), internal control comprises both the "ex-ante" and "ex-post" (before and after operations) measures to control risks. In other words, internal audit is just one component of the internal control process.

Internal controls are systems and procedures that seek to prevent problems and institutional loss. The internal audit function may meet external regulatory requirements for MFIs. It is a management tool to monitor to the implementation of internal controls. Internal audits seek to detect problems before they become large and destructive, and they provide assistance and communication to management that its systems are in place, are functioning and are building the MFI's capacity to deliver its products and services sustainability to the community.

Microfinance practitioners often confuse internal control with internal audit. Practitioners often define internal audit too narrowly, following a simple paper trail to verify financial data. Microfinance institutions use internal control mechanisms to ensure that staff respects their organizational policies and procedures. However, internal control alone cannot ensure that the MFI is adequately minimizing its risk exposures. Only if the MFI's risk management strategies are effectively integrated into its policies and procedures can the internal control function support risk minimization. For example, an MFI experiencing increasing arrears might decide to reduce its exposure to credit risks by developing stricter lending requirements or limiting increases in loan sizes for renewals. The MFI links internal control to risk management by creating mechanisms to evaluate the results of these delinquency reduction efforts, such as by requiring branches to regularly monitor portfolio quality and conduct client visits to verify loan officers' adherence to the new policies.

Internal control is the institution's mechanisms to monitor risks before and after operations. Internal audit is a systematic "ex-post" appraisal of an institution's operations and financial reports.

Internal control and internal audit play important roles in the risk management feedback loop, in which the information generated in the internal control process is reported back to the board and management. Internal control mechanisms work to improve decision making by ensuring that information is accurate, complete, and timely, so the board and management can respond to control issues promptly as they arise. In addition, if the MFI links its internal control mechanisms to risk management, internal control can identify remaining risk exposures and inform management.

Traditionally, internal control systems have focused primarily on detecting and then resolving problems. A risk management approach to the development of internal controls instead emphasizes problem identification and prevention before a loss occurs. In the past, many MFIs have viewed internal control as a peripheral function, separate from operations. An effective system of internal control links risk identification at the branch level back to the board and management. Therefore, for internal control to play a role in mitigating risk, MFIs must institutionalize risk management into their organizational culture and at all levels of their operations. MFIs demonstrate effective risk management by mitigating the risks that pose the greatest threat to their financial health and long-term sustainability.

Internal control is an integral component of the risk management process. An effective internal control system links risk management into the design, implementation and testing of operational procedures, and policies.

17.6. Common Risk Management Practices

(a) Peer lending – Peer or group lending reduces credit risk by spreading the risk of lending without collateral over a larger number of borrowers and transferring the burdens of encouraging repayment and collection from loan officers to clients. For example, several MFIs use a 2-2-1 disbursal mechanism, which encourages the clients in the group who have not yet received a loan to put pressure on the first two members to repay their loans, thereby ensuring their access to a loan.

(b) Character assessment – Microfinance institutions develop expertise at assessing the character of borrowers and become familiar with those characteristics that reduce the risk of future loan default due to credit risk or fraud risk. For example, MFIs consider clients who have reputations for being honest and hardworking to be lower credit and fraud risks.

(c) Forced savings or co-signature requirements – Forced savings and co-signature requirements act as collateral substitutes, which reduce the risk of default by transferring part of the risk to the borrower or third party.

(e) Small loan sizes – By making many small loans, the microfinance institution reduces its credit and liquidity risk exposure by diversifying its loan portfolio.

(f) Varied loan terms – By disbursing loans regularly or by issuing loans with different term lengths, the MFI reduces its liquidity risk exposure by having loans mature and renew frequently.

(g) Limits on loan size increases – Microfinance institutions reduce credit risk by increasing loan sizes in strict increments to ensure that clients can manage gradually larger loan sizes. In addition, MFIs manage risk by basing loan sizes on clients' demonstrated capacity to repay.

(h) Loan approval processes – Some MFIs require a credit committee to approve larger loans, which reduces the chance of poor loan decisions being made (operational or fraud risk) and increases the control for loans that pose a greater financial risk to the institution (credit risk).

(i) Center collections – Some microfinance institutions transfer the risk associated with handling cash to clients by making clients responsible for collecting loan payments and depositing them at a formal financial institution. This reduces operational and fraud risk simultaneously.

MFIs with strong risk management maintain quality loan portfolios, avoid liquidity crises, reduce the risk of loss caused by fraud and human error, and minimize the effects of interest rate fluctuations over the long term.

In addition to risk management practices within the microfinance methodology, MFIs that effectively mitigate risk also integrate risk management strategies into their normal operations. There are five additional key elements prevalent in MFIs that can reduce risks. They are given below:

(1) a conducive environment, (2) transparency, (3) simplicity, (4) individual accountability, and (5) security.

Consciously or not, management sets the tone for employees' and clients' tolerance and attitude toward risk. Management can create an effective control environment by communicating the MFI's commitment to risk management through both words and actions. In a small microfinance institution, the example set by the managing director is perhaps the strongest form of communication. As the MFI grows, veteran employees communicate the MFI's attitude toward risk, as well as corresponding appropriate behavior, to new employees.

Management can work to overcome negative perceptions by encouraging employee participation in the internal control system, stressing the benefits of risk mitigation, and emphasizing solutions to problems rather than placing blame.

Creating a supportive atmosphere or culture that has a low risk tolerance is especially important for an MFI that operates in an environment with a high tolerance for fraud. If the MFI operates in a country that condones fraud, management must work hard to distinguish the culture of the MFI from the surrounding environment. In Kenya, a country where corruption is common, K-Rep has successfully employed this approach by screening employees and clients based on character and by strictly enforcing a policy by which Microfinance institutions exist to fulfill a dual mission-financial sustainability and positive social impact on the urban and rural poor in urban of the communities that they serve. However, too many MFIs are pre-occupied with expansion, out-smarting their competition, or reducing their operational costs to take time to look interest estimates.

NOTES

1. MicroSave (2007), *MFI Internal Audit and Control Toolkit*.
2. MicroSave, *MFI Internal Audit and Control Toolkit*, August 2007.

18

Impact Assessment of Microfinance

18.1. Introduction to Impact Assessment

Microfinance holds a big promise to generate income and employment and alleviate poverty in developing countries. This, in turn, can have positive social effects at different levels of society, from the personal, to the community, to the regional level. The whole discussion about the social impact of Microfinance has just started. International bodies (namely, CGAP, UNCTAD and others), development agencies, academic institutions etc. are all engaged in deepening the understanding about the social impact of Microfinance and a series of social impact studies at local and regional level are under way. All Microfinance institutions and projects contribute at all levels and with the same strength. On the contrary, it is equally important to constantly monitor also potential negative impacts, such as over-indebtedness of clients or risks of corruption and illegal use of credits. At the same time, it is to be understood that Microfinance is not the solution to all the problems in developing countries, but should be focused on economically active poor, who can afford to borrow and repay money as part of their normal budget and who are not living in an emergency situation.

According to Hulme "Impact Assessments assess the difference in the values of key variables between the outcomes on "agents" (individuals, enterprises, households, populations, policymakers, etc.) which have experienced an intervention against the values of those variables that would have occurred had there been no intervention. The fact that no agent can both experience an intervention and at the same time not experience an intervention generates many methodological problems."

Impact Assessment is the structured study, which measures the impact on employment, income generation, nutrition, education, health, consumption, business development (micro entrepreneurship) and gender equity on MFI's clients.[1] Impact assessment refers to the assessment of "how financial products and services affected the lives of the poor. Impact assessment is the measurement of the income growth, assets growth and vulnerability reduction of the poor by the microfinance programme. The indicators for impact assessment are not limited to economic development but extended to development growth like health, education, empowerment, gender etc.

18.2. Objectives of Impact Assessment

According to Social Performance Working Group, SEEP Network, Impact Assessment is a research activity undertaken with objective of attributing observed outcomes to organizational activity. Impact is determined by counterfactual. Determining the counterfactual in turn requires comparing the treatment group to a valid control group.

Impact assessment in microfinance programmes should focus on the profile of the institution implementing microfinance programmes. The institution profile should include mission, structure, operations, methodologies and policies of the institution. Also impact assessment should focus on institutional needs and context. The institutional needs cover current problems, needs and strategic plan of the institution; while the institutional context includes poverty characteristics, socio-economic situations and politically stability of the area.

Impact assessment is not only benefiting the implementing MFIs, but it also useful for donors, Government and clients. It helps donors and investors to validate their investment, and it enables the MFIs to track whether they are able to meet their mission and objectives. Moreover, impact assessments help MFIs to better understand their organisation and improving the organizational practices, products and services, and accountability to clients.

According to Simanowitz (2001),[2] the objectives of impact assessment in microfinance are:

a) Improving methodology/assessment

b) Internal Learning

c) Internal Management and

d) External Proving and advocacy.

IAs have become an increasingly significant activity for recipient agencies due to their popularity with donor agencies. In part this reflects a cosmetic change, with the term IA simply being substituted for evaluation; however, it has also been associated with a greater focus on the outcomes of interventions, rather than inputs and outputs. IAs can be viewed as laying on a continuum between 'proving impacts' and 'improving practice'.

While the goals of IA studies commonly incorporate both 'proving' impacts and 'improving' interventions,

Explicitly	IAs are promoted by both the sponsors and implementers of programs so that they can learn what is being achieved and improves the effectiveness and efficiency of their activities.
Implicitly	IAs are a method by which sponsors seek to gather more information about program effectiveness than is available from the routine accountability systems of implementing organizations.

IAs are also of significance to aid agencies in terms of meeting the ever-increasing accountability demands of their governments and for contesting the rhetoric of the anti-aid lobby. A strong case can be made that IA is too donor driven and externally-oriented. If recipients perceive that the IA standards expected of 'them' are higher than donors expect of themselves, then IA will be seen as an external imposition rather than a shared opportunity.

18.3. Components of Impact Assessment

Broadly, there are three categories of impact due to microfinance programme and these categories are:

a) **Economic Impact**	Change in income, accumulation of wealth, reducing vulnerability, outcome level of enterprises etc.
b) **Social impact**	Change in power(status position), shift of economic decision making from men to women, social and cultural diversity etc.
c) **Psychological impact**	Women empowerment, psychological strength due to financial strength, political empowerment etc.

The components of the impact assessment are:

a) **Poverty reduction**	Change in income, saving, assets positions, consumptions (food, social obligations, clothes, education, entertainment, etc).
b) **Gender mainstreaming**	Women in decision making, participation, business or income generation, network building etc.
c) **Social development**	Employment generation, education, health, migration etc.
d) **Institutional development**	Improvement of practices, products and services, efficiency, productivity, meeting social objectives etc.

The table below lists the four variables that form the basis of the model along with the key indicators that act as the processes to initiate social change.

a) **Livelihoods** (Lifestyle and empowerment)

- Factors that influence the way people behave and relate to individuals, family, friends and cohorts on a day-to-day basis.
- Attitudes and perceptions towards family and friendship networks.
- Gender equality and empowerment issues
- Participation in social activities
- Self-reliance
- Residential stability
- Concerns about social well-being
- Sense of place
- Aesthetics and heritage
- Perception of belonging
- Security and liveability
- Aspirations for the future

b) **Literacy** (Knowledge and awareness)

- Children's schooling
- Adult literacy
- Manual skills
- Indigenous knowledge

c) **Community** (Social and cultural interaction)	▪ The size, level of activity, infrastructure and services of voluntary associations, religious organizations and interests groups and how these institutions relate to one another. ▪ Social well-being Activity networks and cohesion ▪ Shared customs ▪ Social and cultural obligations ▪ Social values Language ▪ Religious beliefs and other elements which make a social or ethnic group distinct ▪ Social support networks
d) **Health** (Physical and mental well-being).	▪ Mental and physical health ▪ Nutrition ▪ Hygiene and sanitation facilities ▪ Family planning ▪ HIV/AIDS prevention ▪ Child Survival ▪ Reproductive Health

18.4. Levels of Impact Assessment

Microfinance programmes impact at three levels i.e. individual level, household level and enterprise level.

Impact of Microfinance in Different Levels[1]

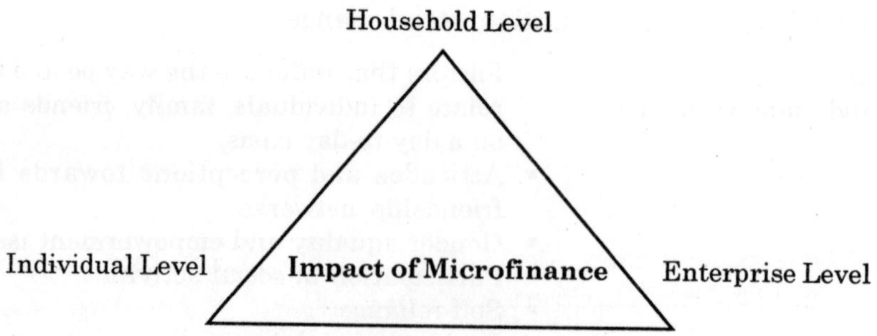

a) Household Level: The impact assessment programmes should capture the changes in the household level due to microfinance programme. The household economic positions like income, expenditure, asset position, livelihood portfolio etc. may be changed over time due to the increasing access of households to microfinance products and services. The socio-psycho changes can be experienced at the household level i.e. change in literacy, migration, gender equality, health, social status etc.

- increase in the level of household income;

- greater diversification in the sources of household income;
- increase in household assets, including
- improvements in housing;
- increases in major household appliances and transport vehicles, and
- increases in microenterprise fixed assets;
- increase in expenditures on children's education;
- increase in expenditures on food, especially among the very poor; and
- increase in the household's effectiveness in coping with shocks.

b) Individual Level: In general, effective microfinance programmes bring a positive change in individual level. It develops managerial ability among the beneficiaries and increase status and position not only in the society but also in the house/family. The increase in capacity development due to microfinance programmes leads to a change in individual income level, expenditure pattern, living condition, literacy position, awareness, accessibility, and equity and equality to the household and community assets etc.

- increase in the client's control over resources and income within the household economic portfolio;
- increased self-esteem and respect from others;
- increased incidence of personal savings;
- better position from which to deal with the future through more proactive behavior; and
- increased in confidence level.

a) Enterprise Level: Microfinance programmes influence microenterprise operations i.e. change in profits, scale of operations, diversifications etc.

- increase in microenterprise revenue;
- increase in enterprise fixed assets, especially among repeat borrowers;
- increase in the paid and unpaid employment generated by the enterprise; and
- improvements in the transactional relationships of the enterprise.

Impact assessment can be carried out on different levels such as individual, enterprise, household, community, institutional impact and household economic portfolios. Advantages and disadvantages of these units of assessment are highlighted below:

AIMS Conceptual Framework: Levels and Domain of Impact

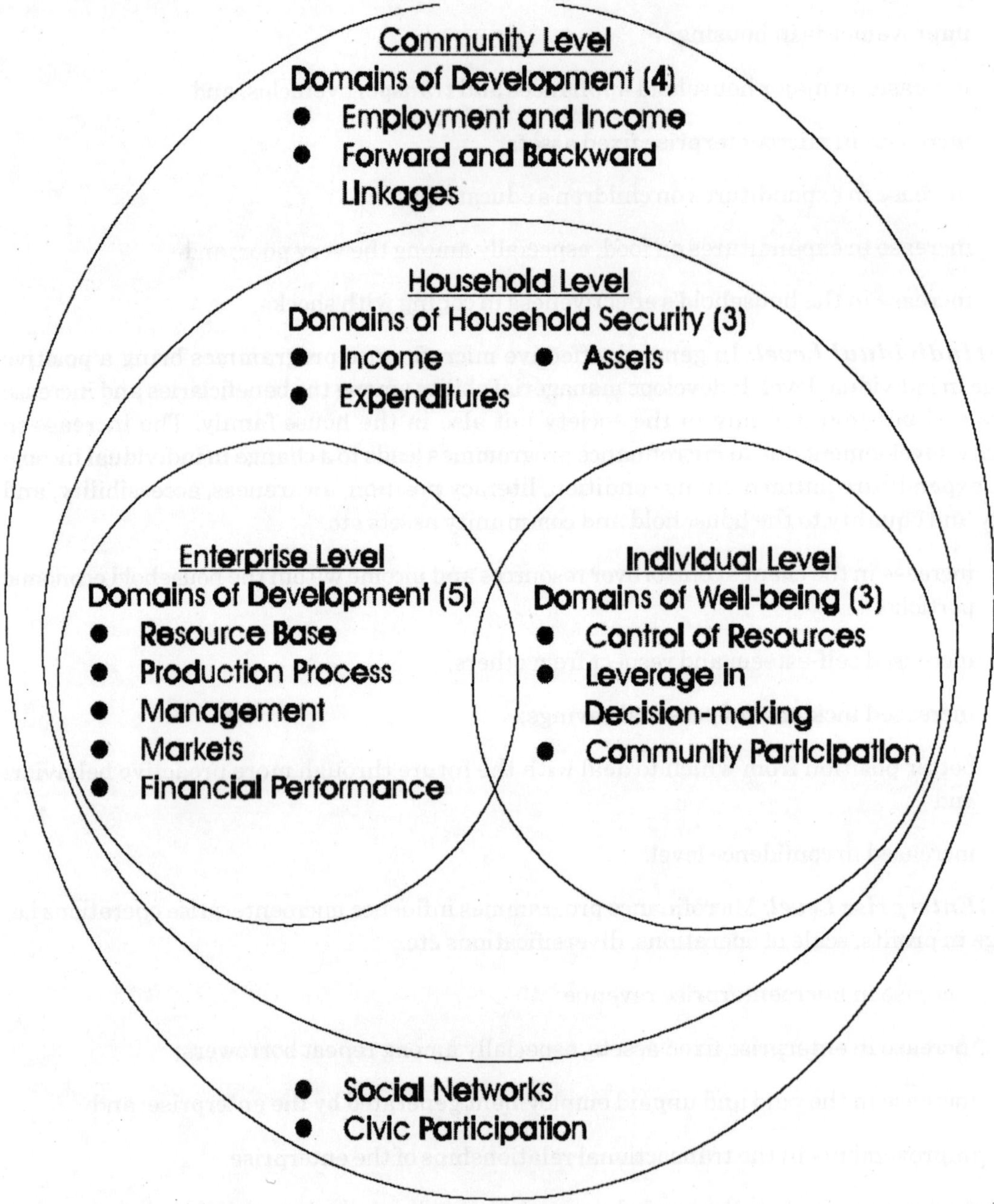

Source: Linda Mayoux (2001), *Impact Assessment of Microfinace: Towards a sustainable learning process, EDIAIS: Application guidance note, Oct 01*

Unit of Assessment	*Advantages*	*Disadvantages*
Individual	Easily defined and identified	Most interventions have impactsbeyond the individual Difficulties of disaggregating group impacts and impacts on'relations'
Enterprise	Availability of analytical tools (profitability, return on difficult in microenterprises investment etc)	Definition and identification is difficultMuch microfinance is used for other enterprises and/ orconsumption Links between enterpriseperformance and livelihoods need careful validation
Household	Relatively easily defined, Permits an appreciation of livelihood impacts, Permits an appreciation of interlinkages of different enterprises and consumption	Sometimes exact membership identified difficult to gauge
Community	Permits major externalities of interventions to be captured	Quantitative data is difficult to gather Definition of its boundary isarbitrary
Institutional Impacts	Availability of data Availability of analytical tools the (profitability, SDIs, transaction costs)	How valid are inferences about outcomes produced by institutional activity?
Household Economic Portfolio (household, enterprise, individual and community)	Comprehensive coverage of impacts, Appreciation of linkages between different units	Complexity, High costs, Demands sophisticated analytical skills Time consuming

18.5. Impact Assessment Methodologies

Impact assessment can be done through using qualitative as well as quantitative data collection tools. The qualitative tools are Participatory Rural Assessment (PRA), Rapid Rural Appraisal (RRA), personal discussions, observations etc. Qualitative impact assessment provides a broad idea, mostly open-ended, on the impact of microfinance programmes.

The quantitative data collection tools are the schedule and structured questionnaires for household survey. Data from secondary sources complement the primary data. Quantitative impact assessment requires various mathematical, statistical and econometric models for analysis of data. In many microfinance programmes, both qualitative and quantitative methods are jointly used for overall impact assessment.

Features	*Qualitative Impact Assessment*	*Quantitative Impact Assessment*
Method of data gathering	semi-structured questionnaires and schedules, one-to-one discussion and group discussions	Structured questionnaires and schedules
Quality of data	Open ended, detailed and difficult to comprehend	Close ended; specific and measurable; easy comprehended but does not provide detail information
Cost	Costly	Less costly
Time period	Requires more time for gathering	Requires less time for gathering information
Use of tools for data analysis	Cause-effect relationship, root cause effect, case study and simple compilation of information	Statistical, mathematical and econometric models
Respondents	Small and homogenous groups	Samples selected from the whole population based on a statistical sampling technique
Results	Words and descriptions	Codified results which can be compiled and measured statistically

The commonest methods used in impact assessment are sample surveys, rapid appraisal, participant observation, case studies and participatory learning and action.[1]

Method	*Key Features*
1	*2*
Sample Surveys	Collect quantifiable data through questionnaires. Usually a random sample and a matched control group are used to measure predetermined indicators before and after intervention
Rapid Appraisal	A range of tools and techniques developed originally as rapid rural appraisal (RRA). It involves the use of focus groups, semi-structured interview with key informants, case studies, participant observation and secondary sources
Participation Observation	Extended residence in a program community by field

(Contd...)

1	2
	researchers using qualitative techniques and mini-scale sample surveys
Case Studies	Involving open-ended detailed studies of a specific unit (a group, locality or organization) questioning and the preparation of 'histories'
Participatory Learning and Action	The preparation by the intended beneficiaries of a program of timelines, impact flow charts, village and resource maps, well-being and wealth ranking, seasonal diagrams, problem ranking and institutional assessments through group processes assisted by a facilitator.

Impact assessments are "as much an art as they are a science." The "scientific" improvements relate to improving standards of measurement, sampling and analytical technique; whereas the "art" of impact assessments has at least three standards:

- making more systematic and informed judgments about the overall design of IAs in relation to their costs, specific objectives and contexts;
- deciding what mixes of impact assessment methods are most appropriate for any given study; and
- increasing our understanding of the ways in which the results of IA studies influence MFI policy-makers and managers.

In impact assessments, the resource persons engaged in data gathering should focus on:

i) What information is required to collect?

ii) How this information will be collected?

iii) How gathered information will be stored?

iv) How the gathered information can be compiled for further analysis?

18.6. Impact Assessment Method: Scientific (Target Group vs. Control Group)

Scientific method seeks to ensure that effects can be attributed to causes through experimentation. A particular stimulus to a particular object in a rigorously controlled environment is judged to be the cause of the observed effect. The experimental approach is virtually infeasible in the social sciences, because of the nature of the subject matter, and so the approach has been adapted into quasi-experiments. Quasi-experiments seek to compare the outcomes of an intervention with a simulation of what the outcomes would have been, had there been no intervention. One method for this is multiple regressions, but this has rarely been used in microfinance IA because of its enormous demands for data on other possible causal factors and its assumptions. A second approach is the *control group* method which has been widely used. This requires a before and after comparison of a population that received a specific treatment (i.e. a microfinance program) and an identical population (or as near as possible) that did not receive the treatment.

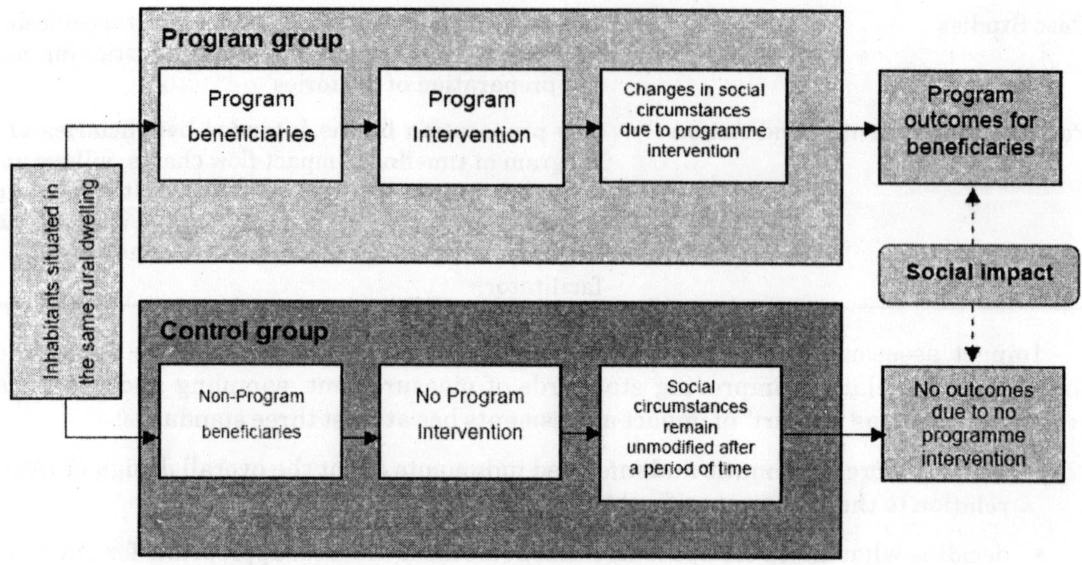

Source: Asad Kamran Ghalic, *"Measuring the Impact of Microfinance intervendtion—A conceptual Framework of social impact assessment"*, The Singapore Economic Review Conference, 2007.

Under this method, two sets of groups i.e. target group and control group are employed, both from the same rural dwelling and living in identical economic and social conditions. Target Group is compared with that of control group taking various parameters or variables. The target group is the set of household/clients who are subjected to microfinance intervention (i.e. participating in the microfinance programme) whereas the control group is set of clients who are not directly participating in the microfinance programme. This method is a good approach in understanding the extent and magnitude of success and failure of the microfinance programme.

After a while, the program borrowers start to show signs of improvement in terms of literacy, health, gender-related issues and community relations. Subjects of the control group, on the contrary, continue to lead lives as before. The difference in the quality of lives, between the two measured against a set of social impact variables and indicators, exhibits the impact that has taken place due to the microfinance intervention. Needless to say, there will a wide range of factors that come into play, and social impact being a highly complex phenomenon is not an entity that can be quantified in mathematical and econometric terms. As mentioned earlier, the model assumes that other conditions remain the same and the loan is utilized for the purpose that it is taken out for.

This method has one serious demerit i.e. selection bias of control group. Selection bias may occur because of

i) difficulties in finding a location at which the control group's economic, physical and social environment matches that of the treatment group;

ii) the treatment group systematically possessing an 'invisible' attribute which the control group lacks (most commonly identified as entrepreneurial drive and ability);

iii) receiving any form of intervention may result in a short-term positive response from the treatment group (the Hawthorne effect);

iv) the control group becoming contaminated by contact with the treatment group (though this could be a long term program goal!); and

v) the fungibility of the treatment (e.g. when a loan is transferred from a borrower to someone else or when the loan is not used in the planned way);

Problems (i) and (iv) can be tackled by more careful selection of the control group. This applies particularly to controlling for access to infrastructure (which has a key influence on input and output prices as well as other variables) and ensuring that the control group is located far away from the treatment group. Problems (ii) and (iii) are more intractable, but in many cases they can be tackled by using program-accepted 'clients-to-be', who have not yet received microfinance services, as the control group. It must be noted, however, that this approach will not be valid when the take up of microfinance services is based on diffusion through a heterogeneous population.

The mis-specification of underlying causal relationships arises most commonly because of the assumption that causality is a one-way process. This may be a reasonable assumption in the physical sciences (though it does not go unchallenged by contemporary philosophers of science). For human activity it is commonly invalid, as causation may also run from impact back to costs. It will only be feasible on very rare occasions. For most researchers adopting the scientific method, reverse causality is a problem to be coped with rather than overcome. The main means of dealing with it are:

(i) tracing dropouts from both the treated and control groups;
(ii) only conducting IAs on relatively mature programs;
(iii) interim impact monitoring activities to gather qualitative information about the complexity of causality; and
(iv) retrospective in-depth interviews with clients.

18.7. Impact Assessment Method: Before and After Intervention

Under this method, the status of the sample units (person/household/village etc) before microfinance intervention is compared with that of the after microfinance intervention; taking the various parameters or variables. This method is good for assessment of the actual impact; but this method has a limitation. It becomes difficult to get the data (related to various variables) on before microfinance intervention from samples, as the impact assessment study is commissioned at the end of the programme.

Some of the microfinance programme compared the "Baseline Study" with the "Endline Study" for impact assessment. In the "Baseline Study" and "Endline Study" either the donor or the implementer designs a structured mapping of all the socio-economic characteristics related to a microfinance programme. The "Baseline Study" and the "Endline Study" are two similar studies conducted taking the same components or variables; but the "Baseline Study" is conducted just before beginning of the microfinance programme; and the "Endline Study" is conducted just after ending the microfinance programme.

Before and After Intervention Method

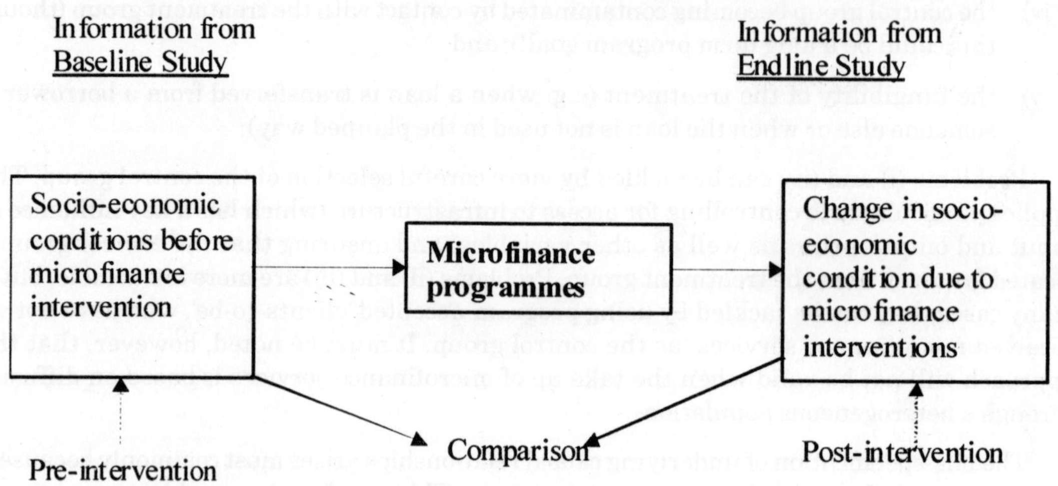

Source: Debadutta K. Panda (2009), *Understanding Microfinance*, Wiley India

18.8. Impact Assessment Method: Participatory Learning and Action (PLA)

In the last five years participatory approaches to development planning and management have moved from being a fringe activity to centre stage. While many donor agencies, have simply added a bit of PLA to their existing procedures, it can be argued that this is inappropriate as conceptually participatory approaches challenge the validity and utility of the scientific method as applied to developmental problems. According to this line of argument the scientific method fails as: it ignores the complexity, diversity and contingency of winning a livelihood; it reduces causality to simple unidirectional chains, rather than complex webs; it measures the irrelevant or pretends to measure the immeasurable; and, it empowers professionals, policymakers and elites, thus reinforcing the *status quo* and directly retarding the achievement of development goals.

At heart, PLA theorists do not believe that ultimately there is one objective reality that must be understood. Rather, there are multiple realities and before any analysis or action is taken the individuals concerned must ask themselves, 'whose reality counts?' Their answer is that the perceived reality of the poor must take pride of place as, if development is about 'empowering the poor' or 'empowering women' (as virtually all development agencies now say), then the first step towards empowerment is ensuring that 'the poor' or 'women' take the lead in problem identification and analysis and knowledge creation. By this means two objectives may be achieved (i) better impact assessments, and (ii) intended beneficiaries will be empowered through the research process itself. In practice, the art of participatory impact assessment (PIA) is in its infancy and a pragmatic rather than a purist approach has been common.

Agencies such as Proshika in Bangladesh have begun to use PLA methods extensively for their assessment and planning exercises. The reliability of participatory methods varies enormously, as with 'scientific' surveys, depending largely on the motivation and skills of facilitators and those investigated and the ways in which informants' perceptions of the consequences of research are addressed. Nevertheless, it is argued that a number of rigorous comparative studies has shown that, when well-conducted, participatory methods can be more reliable than conventional surveys. To date the literature on PLA and PIA has only partially addressed the issue of attribution.

From a scientific perspective PIA has grave problems because of the subjectivity of its conceptualizations of impact; the subjectivity of the data used to assess impact; the variables and measures used vary from case to case and do not permit comparison; its pluralist approach may lead to a number of mutually conflicting accounts being generated about causality; and, the assumption that because lots of people are taking part in an exercise means that all are able to 'voice' their concerns (so that opinions are representative) is naive about the nature of local power relations. From the perspective of a 'new professional' then such a set of accounts is unproblematic, as it reflects the complexity and contingency of causality in the real world. In addition, it can be argued that PIA contributes to program goals (perhaps particularly in terms of empowering women and the poor) by not facilitating the continued dominance of target groups by powerful outsiders.

18.9. Impact Assessment Method: Household Economic Portfolio (HHEP) Model

The household economic portfolio (HHEP) model is based on a conceptualization of the microenterprise as part of a larger portfolio of household economic activities. Decisions about microenterprises are made in the context of options and trade offs within the overall household economy. The HHEP model provides a framework for developing hypotheses about the cause-and-effect relationships between microenterprise services and impacts. It is measures the impacts, or changes, at the household, the microenterprise, and the individual levels.

The model of the household economic portfolio builds on three key developments in the analysis of households by economists, anthropologists, and feminist scholars. First, it recognizes that there may be negotiation, bargaining, and (even) conflict within the household. Second, it presents the household as a permeable unit, rather than a bounded unit, which is embedded in wider social units, networks, and processes. And, third, it recognizes that there is enormous variability in household composition, structure, and functions both between and within societies and over time.

The household portfolio model is premised on the fact that individuals within the household have one or more socially ascribed identities: notably gender but also seniority, marital status, parental status, and others. And that individuals or categories of individuals within the household may have separate (even competing) preferences, interests, needs, resources, and constraints and may, therefore, take separate (even competing) decisions and actions. For instance, men and women within the same household may engage in different enterprises; may engage in joint enterprises; or may share resources and income across separate enterprises. Depending on the pattern they follow within a given household, men and women can be expected to respond differently to microenterprise services. The model allows for the systematic investigation of the implications of socially defined divisions within the household.

The *household economic portfolio* can be defined as a) the set of household resources, b) the set of household activities, and c) the circular flow of interaction between household resources and household activities.[5] A model of the household economic portfolio is illustrated in below:

Conceptual Model of Household Economic Portfolio

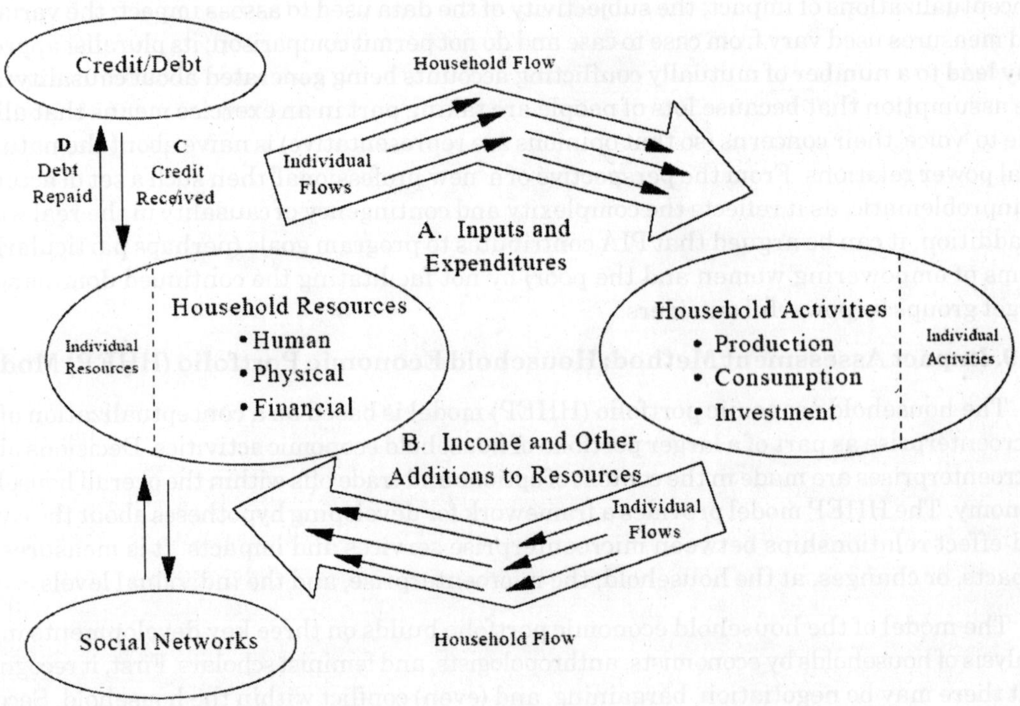

Source: Martha Alter Chen and Elizabeth Dunn (1996), *"Household Economic Portfolios"*, AIMS

In this model, resources may be held jointly by the household members, or they may be held separately by individual members of the household. In addition, it is important to note that resources may be owned or they may be accessed through borrowing or through social relationships and *social networks*. That is, the set of resources available to the household may include more than just the resources that are individually or jointly "owned" by the household members. Households may have access to significant resources through social networks or through a common resource pool. Social relationships and networks can be drawn upon for securing human, physical, or financial resources on a reciprocal or nonreciprocal basis. Examples of social networks, which can vary greatly by setting, include family and kin networks, patron-client relationships, factional or political loyalties, and wider pooling or exchange networks. In addition, the household may have access to collective goods or common resources through the public sector or from common property resources.

Household resources are the set of human, physical, and financial resources available for use by the household in a given period of time. The human resources include the time, labor power, and skills of household members, which depend on the household composition. Physical resources include any tangible items that are at the disposal of the household members such as land, buildings, tools, raw materials, input stocks, inventory, equipment, livestock, personal items, and so on. Financial resources include cash and other forms of liquid savings.

Household activities are the set of consumption, production, and investment activities that the members of the household undertake in a given period of time.

Consumption activities are defined as the satisfaction of material wants and needs through the provision of items such as food, clothing, medical services, liquor, ceremonies, and amusements. Consumption activities are not generally expected to contribute to the physical or financial resource base of the household. However, consumption does play a critical role in maintaining the health and vigor of the human resource.

Production activities can be broken down into three categories: 1) income generating activities; 2) household maintenance activities; and 3) wage and outside work.

Income generating activities are any productive enterprises that generate a marketable good or service. This category would include all types of microenterprises, as well as activities such as the renting out of land and housing. The product of an income generating activity may be agricultural or nonagricultural, and it may be sold or consumed by the household.

Investment activities involve the use of household resources in order to create the potential for additional income in future periods. The products of investment activities are the resulting investments, or assets. These investments can take many forms, both tangible and intangible, but they are characterized both by their expected endurance into the next period and by their enhancement of the resource base of the household in future periods. The products of investment activities may be real property (i.e. land, housing), physical stores of wealth (i.e. jewelry, livestock), financial stocks or interest bearing accounts (i.e. savings accounts, money loaned out), productive assets (i.e. sewing machine, truck, inventories), strengthened social networks, or improvements in human capital through training or education. To the extent that durable consumer goods such as bicycles, stoves, and refrigerators are used in income generating activities or household maintenance activities, they can also be considered as investments. In summary, investment activities act to build up the resources and asset base of the household.

18.10. Poverty Assessment

Poverty assessment was the basic requirement for undertaking analysis of the outreach of the micro finance programme and variations in its impact on different poverty groups. A combination of Participatory Wealth Ranking (PWR) and Household Index-based Ranking (IBR) was used to arrive at Household Wealth Rank. While PWR reflects local perceptions of community, IBR enables standardised ranking relative to local conditions and indicators relating to employment status, housing status, household and transport assets. The indicators for wealth rank categories are given in below:

Indicators for Different Wealth Rank Categories[3]

Indicator	*Very Poor*	*Poor*	*Borderline*	*Self-sufficient*	*Surplus*
Housing	Homeless, or small Kutccha/ thatched houses	Small houses, kutccha, or semi-pucca	Medium size houses, semi-pucca or pucca	Medium-large mixed type of houses	Large pucca houses
Assets	No land, 1-2 goats, basic utensils	Marginal land (< 1acre, few milch animals, fan/radio, bicycle	Small Lands (1-5 acres), 1-2 milch/ draught animals, fan/radio, B&W TV, bicycle, some furniture, old two wheeler	Large land (5-10 acres), 1-2 milch/ draught animals, well/tube-well, B&W TV, telephone, fridge motorcycle	Large land (> 10 acres), more than 2 milch/draught animals, wells, lorry/ tractors, colour TV, telephone, fridge, motorcycle, car
Employment	Low paid casual wage labour,single earner	Regular casual wage labour, one-two earners	Skilled wage labour/ seasonal business/ low paid salaried job	Adequate income source, small agriculture, small regular business, medium paid job	Assured income source, commercial agriculture, established business, high paid job

Longitudinal methodology of poverty assessment by SIDBI

The quantitative data of sample households was analysed to find out percentages, averages and frequencies for various indicators. The results were subjected to longitudinal analysis for three types of comparisons, i.e. client v/s non-client for endline data and baseline v/s endline results for clients and non-clients, and the same were tested for statistical significance. The results of comparisons were studied/superimposed to find out whether the behaviour of a particular indicator supports the micro finance intervention as the cause of change. The quantitative results were supplemented by qualitative observations obtained from Case Studies, Focus Group Discussions and Semi-structured interviews. Comparison between baseline and endline data/results revealed changes in the socio-economic conditions of the clients and non-clients. The impact of the microfinance programme on the beneficiaries was assessed in terms of Outreach, Access, Credit Use, Entrepreneurial Activities, Income, Employment, Human Capital, Vulnerability and Women Empowerment.

18.11. Challenges of Impact Assessment

There are a number of conceptual challenges associated with conducting impact assessments in the social sciences. These challenges affect not only the design of impact assessments but, ultimately, the usefulness and credibility of the results. The common challenges while designing the impact assessment methodology are challenges of fungibility, attribution, and selection bias.

(a) Fungibility

Fungibility is a basic characteristic of money. It means that monetary units are interchangeable and can be used for a wide variety of purposes. The money that a client receives as a program loan may be used within the intended microenterprise, but some or all of the money might also be used in a different microenterprise or used to purchase property, pay school fees, or buy groceries. Not only can money be used in a variety of ways, it is usually very difficult to accurately trace how a household allocates loan funds.

In the past, the fungibility of money was considered a major impediment to conducting impact assessments of microenterprise services. According to this view, the fact that a client may not spend all of the loan proceeds on the intended microenterprise meant that an unknown amount of loan funds were reaching the microenterprise. In addition, the household might mobilize other (non-program) funds to support the enterprise. This made it difficult to link any changes in the enterprise to the financial services received, thus undermining the premise of impact assessment.

The problem of fungibility can be addressed by widening the unit of analysis for the impact assessment. Instead of focusing only on the microenterprise, the unit of analysis should be expanded to include the entire economic portfolio within which the fungible capital might be used. In this way, there is no longer a need to assume that all of the loan funds are spent on the intended enterprise or, alternatively, to attempt to track how loan funds are actually spent.

(b) Attribution

Another important conceptual challenge in evaluating the impact of microfinance programme is the problem of establishing a strong, plausible case for attribution. The attribution problem is a general one, affecting impact evaluation in all the social sciences. Basically, the problem arises from two causes.

a) First, the statistical methods used to measure impacts can establish statistical correlation, but they cannot be used to prove the existence of a cause-and-effect relationship.

b) Second, controlled experiments in which all factors except the treatment (intervention) are held constant are very difficult to conduct in the social sciences.

The result is that it can never be proven incontrovertibly that the treatment led to the impact. Instead, the best that can be done is to establish a strong case in favor of attribution. One of the ways to build a plausible case for attribution is to base the research on an internally consistent conceptual model that links the intervention to the impact in a plausible cause-and effect relationship. The household economic portfolio model, described below, provides just such a conceptual framework. It can be used to model the ways that households, and the individuals within households, use microenterprise services to protect, manage, and increase their resources and activities, including their microenterprises.

Another way to strengthen the case for attribution is to use qualitative research to identify and document the chain of events, ordered in time, that lead from the program services to the impact. Qualitative research can also be used to eliminate the possibility of alternative explanations for the impacts that are observed. Any one of these approaches—qualitative evidence, a logically consistent conceptual model, statistical results indicating association between variables—could be used alone to build a plausible case for attribution. By combining them, however, the mixed method approach builds a much stronger case for attribution.

(c) Selection Bias

A third important challenge to the design of an impact assessment is selection bias. Selection bias can occur for two reasons.

a) First, it can occur because people self-select whether or not they will apply for microenterprise services.

b) Selection bias can also occur because program managers select service areas on the basis of the probability of program success and credit agents select individual clients on the perceived creditworthiness of these potential clients.

The problem with selection bias is that it can exaggerate the measured impacts. When samples of clients and non-clients are drawn, the observed differences in outcomes might be due either to the impact of participation in credit program (i.e., the "true" impact) or the differences might be due to the fact that the people who applied for credit were already different in some way(s) that would have led them to have greater success anyway.

The use of a quasi-experimental design combined with panel data permitted the removal of some, but not all, of the influence of selection bias on the results. With the ANCOVA approach, it was possible to control for the starting values of the impact variables and to statistically match similar observations in the treatment and control groups based on their characteristics. In addition, the comparison of outcomes for client groups receiving different levels of program services helped to clarify the distinction between program impacts and differences related to selection bias.

18.12. Choice of Appropriate Impact Assessment Method

All impact assessments have a conceptual frame based on (a) a model of the impact chain; (b) the identification of units (levels of assessment); and (b) the specification of the types of impact to be assessed. The range of methods used for IA have extended over the last decade — sample surveys, rapid appraisals, participant observation, case studies and participatory learning and action - and each method has particular strengths and weaknesses. The choice of methods must be based on objectives, costs and feasibility. Cost and complexity do not automatically equate with rigor and, for example, a large survey can be poorly designed while a good PLA can yield highly accurate data about impact. The main need in contemporary IA studies is for simple IA approaches that achieve a relatively high degree of plausibility. This can be done by using a mix of methods, focusing on a small set of key hypotheses, developing time series data, documenting triangulation, using the same methods for later studies and assessing comparison groups.

The major conceptual problems that confront the IA of microfinance relate to attribution and fungibility. Problems of attribution can be greatly reduced by skilled survey design in complex IA approaches and by triangulation in other designs. Studies that focus on impact at several levels can overcome many of the difficulties associated with fungibility.

Among the principle problems facing effective impact assessment are the following:

a) cost and confidence;

b) respondent motivation;

c) consultant and interviewer quality and availability; and

d) avoiding low-impact IAs.

The key task for the IA designer is to select an approach that can meet the objectives of the specific assessment at an acceptable level of rigor that is compatible with the program's context, that is feasible in terms of costs, timing and human resource availability and that avoids the problems identified above. Whenever possible, an IA methodology should be piloted before full implementation. The questions that s/he must answer can be summarized as follows:

a) What are the objectives of the assessment?

b) How is the information to be used and by whom?;

c) What level of reliability is required?;

d) How complex is the program, what type of program is it, and what is already know about it?; and

e) What resources (money, human and time) are available?

The complexity of impact assessment means that improvements in IA must be based on raising the capacity of impact assessors, particularly the army of people who design and run simple IAs.

18.13. Characteristics for Effective Impact Assessment[4]

a) Mix of qualitative and quantitative approach by using a wide range of tools;

b) Emphasis on cross-varification of information gathered for the impact assessment for more reliability and credibility;

c) Designing the impact assessment for a wide range of objectives including both primary and secondary objectives; and

d) Carrying out impact assessment on-going basis rather than a one-time activity.

The methods, process and tools of impact assessment should not be rigid rather should be flexible to meet the organizational requirement. The cost and time factor should be focused for designing impact assessments. The impact assessments are not only important to donors or funders to understand the appropriateness of the use of their fund, but IA are equally important to understand organisations/MFIs. IA enables MFI's staff and board members to understand whether the interventions are actually meeting their organizational mission and objectives. It helps MFIs to assess internally and externally, analyze the consequences, consolidate on their weaknesses and reorganize their operational practices for further improvement. Moreover, IA results work as market research for MFIs.

NOTES

1. Debadutta K . Panda (2009), *Understanding Microfinance,* Wiley India.
2. Simanowitz, A (2001), "From Event to Process: Current Trends in Microfinance Impact Assessment", *Guideline* No.5, Imp-Act.
3. Cohen, M. Bourjorjee,D. (2003), "Impact of Microfinance", *Donor Brief No. 13, CGAP.*
4. Prof. David Hulme, *Impact Assessment Methodologies for Microfinance-A review,* AIMS.
5. Martha Alter Chen and Elizabeth Dunn (1996), *Household Economic Portfolios,* AIMS.
6. SIDBI(2008), *Assessing the Development Impact of Microfinance: Findings and Policy Implications from a National Study of Indian Micro Finance Sector*.
7. Simanowitz, A (2001), "From Event to Process: Current Trends in Microfinance Impact Assessment", *Guideline* No.5, Imp-Act.

19

Sustainability in Microfinance

19.1. What is Sustainability?

Sustainability in simple terms refers to the long-term continuation of the Microfinance programme after the project activities have been discontinued. It entails that appropriate systems and processes have been put in place that will enable the microfinance services to be available on a continuous basis and the clients continue to benefit from these services in a routine manner. This also would mean that the programme would meet the needs of the members through resources raised on their own strength, either from among themselves or from external sources.

Though sustainability does get understood immediately in the financial terms or the resource terms, it actually has broader dimensions, of which financial sustainability is only one major dimension. The different dimensions of sustainability are given below:

a) Institutional sustainability;

b) Market Sustainability;

c) Legal Policy environment sustainability; and

d) Impact sustainability.

19.2. Institutional Sustainability

Institutional sustainability looks at those dimensions of the organisation, which deals with the internal organizational environment. These are dimensions that make organisation a wholesome, vibrant and a going concern. Institutional sustainability can be studied in four broad categories: i) Mission sustainability, ii) Programme sustainability, iii) Human Resource sustainability, and iv) Financial sustainability.

Mission sustainability: Sustainability of its mission is what will keep the organisation in its chosen path in the long term. Activities that the organisation is engaged in have to be constantly evaluated for its compatibility with the defined mission of the organisation. If changes are brought about in the mission, it would be through a well articulated and participatory process in the organisation

Programme sustainability: Programme sustainability occurs when stakeholders (clients) perceive that the services that they are receiving are of sufficient importance and value and are willing to assume responsibility and ownership for them. When this occurs the MFI can develop a phasing out strategy because the programme remains client supported and no externally subsidies support is sought.

Human Resource Sustainability: It refers to MFI's ability to recruit, induct, train and maintain well-qualified staffs, who are capable of delivering the services as required. Also the staffs are able to monitor and maintain the organisation on the right track, keeping in mind all the other parameters of sustainability.

Financial Sustainability: Financial sustainability means that the MFI is able to cover all its present costs and the costs incurred in growth, if it expands operations. It would mean that the MFI is able to meet its operating costs, its financial costs adjusted for inflation and costs incurred in growth. Financial sustainability is a tangible parameter and can be measured and monitored continually through a set of indicators given below:

Ratio	*Formula*	*Purpose*
Return on performing assets	Financial income/ Average Performing Assets	Indicates financial productivity of credit services and investment activities
Financial cost ratio	Financial cost/Average Performing Assets	Shows cost of funds, affected by mix of soft loan, hard loans and networth
Loan Loss provision ratio	Loan Loss Provision/ Average Performing Assets	Indicates provisioning requirement on loan portfolio of the current period
Operating cost Ratio	Operating expenses/ Average Performing Assets	Key indicator of efficiency of lending operation
Donations and Grants Ratio	Donations/Grants/Average Performing Asssets	Shows dependency of institution on outside funding for operation
Operating self-sufficiency	Financial income/ (Financial & operating costs + loan loss provision)	Shows ability of institution to cover costs of operation
Financial Self-sufficiency	Financial Income/ (Financial & Operating costs + Loan loss provision + adjusted cost of capital)	Shows whether revenue earned is sufficient to cover all operating, financial and loan expenses as well as to maintain the value of equity.
Adjusted cost of capital	Inflation x (average net worth-average fixed assets) + (Inflation-interest rate paid)x concessional loans/ average performing assets	Shows the cost of maintaining the value of the net worth of the organization

The key sustainability financially is to charge an interest rate that is high enough to cover operating costs, loan losses and interest and adjusted expenses. However, MFIs must operate efficiently enough that reasonable, affordable and competitive interest rates can be charged to cover these costs. Therefore long term sustainability requires MFIs to manage delinquency, keep their cost of capital low (by mobilizing savings), rotate their portfolio efficiently, keep operating costs to a minimum and most importantly, set interest rates to cover all these costs.

19.3. Market Sustainability

Market sustainability deals with the whole gamut of issues that deal with demand and supply of microfinance. It deals with issues relating to the different types of the clientele, their differing types of needs, and designing products that suit the needs of this clientele.

Servicing these needs in the most client friendly manner will lead to the sustainability of the demand. A sustainable supply of resources will need that the MFI is financially self-sufficient and meet all its costs from operations and has access to resources raised from the clients and from external sources at commercially viable rate of interest.

Market sustainability is also about availability of a large number of choices to the clientele. The MFIs sustain purely on the effectiveness and efficiency of its services and not due to artificially created perfections.

19.4. Legal and Policy Environment Sustainability

Market sustainability as described above assumes the existence of a stable and friendly legal and policy environment that will enable the proliferation of a large number of organisations involved in the delivery of microfinance services. It would deal with issues relating to legal forms of organisations, interest rates, saving mobilization, resource mobilization from capital markets, from overseas commercial sources, etc.

19.5. Impact Sustainability

Microfinance has emerged as an effective methodology for alleviation of poverty among the disadvantaged sections. Thus it is necessary that the services delivered by the different organisations have a positive impact on poverty. The positive changes that occur in the life the poor family have be sustained over the long term for the family to gradually emerge out of the state of poverty.

REFERENCES

1. www.sa-dhan.net/.../Microfinance/.../SustainabilityInMicrofinance.pdf
2. www.unescap.org/drpad/publication/fin_2206/part5.pdf -
3. www.mdf.org.rs/pdf/MF-Principles.pdf
4. www.microfinance.com/English/Papers/Thinking_about_Sustainability.pdf
5. www.unescap.org/drpad/publication/fin_2206/part5.pdf
6. www.fdc.org.au/.../1%20Mathison.pdf
7. www.ruralfinance.org/cds.../1117490855207_Nair_SHGs_and_feds.pdf
8. www.edamba.eu/userfiles/file/Evans%20Quang%20Luong%20.pdf

20

Microfinance and Women Empowerment

" Women constitute half of the world's population, perform nearly two-third of its work, receive one tenth of the world's income and own less than-hundredth of the world's property", U.N. Report (1980).

20.1. Definition of Empowerment

The concept of empowerment has been evolving over the years since the nineteenth century. In the broadest sense empowerment means expansion of freedom of choice and action which comes with increasing one's authority and control over the resources and decisions that affect one's life. Empowerment is more closely related to the people who are disempowered or powerless due to some socio-economic and cultural barriers in the society of which they are part. The choices of these powerless people are extremely limited due to lack of resources and lack of better negotiations with the range of formal and informal institutions. Thus empowerment can also be defined as the process through which those who currently disadvantaged achieve equal rights, resource and power. Empowerment implies the overall positive change in the physical quality of life, this positive change for better encompasses economic as well as social impact.

Empowerment is an abstract and complex concepts and it is interpreted in many ways. According to the *Random House Dictionary*, the word 'empowerment' comes from the term 'empower' which means, to give power or authority and enable or permit. Empowerment is a multifaceted process, involving the policy of resources to achieve collective strength and countervailing power and entailing the improvement of manual and technical skills; administrative managerial and planning capacities and analytical abilities.

The literally meaning of "Empowerment" is defines to give the power in the hands of the group which is powerless , no right to decision, no access, choices and considered as the silent observer in the society. The World Bank defines empowerment "as the process of increasing the capacity of individuals or groups to make choices and to transform those choices into desired actions and outcomes. It also identifies four key elements of empowerment to draft institutional reforms: access to information, inclusion and participation, accountability; local organizational capacity.

In the development literature the term 'empowerment' has gained priority since last two decades. The realization of need for equality of women and their importance in socio-economic development resulted in several organized efforts across the world to uplift women. The usage of term 'empowerment' in the context of women was thus born. A review of women studies would reveal that the efforts to bring women into mainstream of socio-economic progress have undergone paradigm shifts. Empowerment is an ongoing process and policy for the advancement of women.

Marginalized people who have no opportunities for self-sufficiency become, dependent on charity or welfare. They lose their self-confidence because they cannot be fully self-supporting. The opportunities denied them also deprive them of the pride of accomplishment which others, who have those opportunities, can develop for themselves. Empowerment is then the process of obtaining these basic opportunities for marginalized people, either directly by those people, or through the help of non-marginalized others who share their own access to these opportunities.

Empowerment is defined as the processes by which poor take control and ownership of their lives through expansion of their choices. Thus, it is the process of acquiring the ability to make strategic life choices in a context where this ability has previously been denied. The core elements of empowerment have been defined as agency (the ability to define one's goals and act upon them), awareness of gendered power structures, self-esteem and self-confidence.[1]

Empowerment is something to do with getting power and also sharing the power and remaining in power, exercising power, and controlling power, leading to a democratic and inclusive growth. It is not just financial independence, nor access to education, but a combination of increasing their social, political, economic and spiritual strength, both individually and collectively, removing the obstacles that penalized and prevented women from being integrated into their respective societies – from being subordinate, marginalized, deprived, oppressed, suppressed, victimized, etc. and getting out of the internalization of values of patriarchy.

The empowerment of women is one of the central issues in the process of development of countries all over the world. . Improving their status and empowering them would go a long way in accomplishing egalitarian gender relations in society. Women who are hitherto constrained by their social structure for their self-expression constitute the target of most development programs, which aim at bringing them into the mainstream of development process. Giving access to credit would be a step towards empowering them.

The Secretariat of the United Nations defines women's empowerment as having five components: first a belief in individual self-worth; second, the right to make decisions, third, the power to access opportunities and resources; fourth, the ability to control their public and private lives and fifth, the opportunity to engage within society in order to influence nations and the world.

According to Rowlands (1997), empowerment is defined as a process whereby women become able to organize themselves to increase their own self-reliance, to asset their right to make independent choices and to control resources which will assist in challenging and eliminating their own subordination.[2]

According to Mayoux (2003), empowerment is a multidimensional social process that helps people gain control over their own lives. It is a process that fosters power in people for use in their own lives, their communities and in their society, by acting on issues they define as important.[3]

Sen and Grown stated that women's empowerment is the transformation of the structures of subordinations, including changes in law, civil codes, property and inheritance rights, control over women's bodies and labour and legal social institutions that endorse male's control.[4] Women's empowerment as a concept was introduced at the International Women's Conference in 1985 at Nairobi, which defined it as "redistribution of social power and control of resources in favour of women. The concept of empowerment received fresh impetus in the early 1990s.

According to Sharma (1992), "empowerment' in its simplest form is redistribution of power that challenges the male dominances.[5] This does not however mean that empowerment process adopts an 'antagonist' approach. It is only to enable women to supplement and co-ordinate with men. It is an active process of enabling women to realize their potential and power in all spheres of their lives.

Batiwala(1994) observes that 'women empowerment' is the process by which women gain greater control over material and intellectual resources and challenges the ideology of patriarchy and gender-based discrimination against women in all institutions and structures of the society.[6]

Kabeer (1999) asserts that 'empowerment; is the expansion in people's ability to make strategic life choices in a context where this ability was previously denied to them.[7] In the same line Narayan(2002) observes that 'empowerment' broadly refers to expansion of freedom of choice and action to shape one's life. It implies control over resources and decisions.

To Beteille (1999) much of the literature on empowerment is control-driven and is about radical social transformation, oppressed-oppressor relationship, redistribution of power and social change. The critical question, according to him, is linked with the nature of social transformation and its measurability.[8]

Bansal and Chauhan (2002) have defined empowerment as giving legal and moral power to an individual in all spheres of life; social, economic, political, psychological religion and spiritual, which are essential for survival and overall development of mankind.[9]

Sinha (2004) defines empowerment as a process of change by which individuals or groups gain power and ability to take control over their lives. It involves increased well-being, access to resources, increased self-confidence, self-esteem and increased participation in decision making and bargaining power and increased self-control over benefits, resources and own-life.[10]

Malhotra (2004) opines that 'empowerment' is conceptualized differently by different writers. However, for all of them goal of empowerment is to address the issues relating to women's subordination inequality and inequity. Furthermore women's empowerment is seen as entailing a shift from position of powerlessness towards strategic social, economic and political participation.[11]

To Sunny (2006), 'empowerment' of women in most basic sense implies strengthening the recourse base viz financial, social, education, skill etc so as to take on challenges of discrimination and to bridge the gap between men and women.[12]

Empowerment is a multi-faceted, multi-dimensional and multi-layered concept. Women's empowerment is a process in which women gain greater share of control over resources - material, human and intellectual like knowledge, information, ideas and financial resources like money - and access to money and control over decision-making in the home, community, society and nation, and to gain 'power'. The process of empower aims at realization of individual potentiality and ensures equality with men. It is also evident from the views of different scholars that empowerment has different dimensions like social, political and economic etc. Thus, women's empowerment is to give the power to act, participate, make decision, raise voice against social evils, and fight against right and above all make conscious of their own rights and privileges and sensitize both men and women to recognize the potential of women.

Box-12: Global Conference on Women's Empowerment

The first World conference on women took place in Mexico City in 1975 to address the issue of gender inequality. This was followed by second world conference on women at Copenhagen in 1980 and a third in Nairobi in 1985. To provide a clear blue print for action fourth world conference on women took place in Beijing in 1995. In that conference, it was declared that women are central to the success of the poverty alleviation effort; hence the importance of women's empowerment and their full participation on the basis of equality in all spheres of society is crucial. Empowerment is the best means to solve problems, which cannot be resolved by legal procedures. The Beijing platform states unequivocally that women empowerment is "fundamental for achieving equality, development and peace". During 1990s a series of UN World conferences were held to set standards and directions that would take policy, planning and practice into the next century. Women emerged as a global force for shaping international debates and providing a gender perspective on all developmental issued. The Global conference of women's empowerment (1998) highlighted empowerment as the surest way of making women partners of development.

20.2. Forms of Empowerment

One of the most popular goals of most of the development programmes and especially of microfinance programme is empowerment of women. Even then the methodology to evaluate the level of empowerment is not yet fully developed. Empowerment is closely related to the concept of power which can be understood in terms of "power to", "power within", "power with" and "power over". Empowerment can be judged at various levels such as individual level, family level and collective level.

Four forms of powers are identified in the empowerment literature. They are 'power over', 'power within', 'power to' and 'power with'.

Power within	Enabling women to articulate their own aspirations and strategies for change. It is a personal or psychological power in the minds of the people which focuses on their sense of

	self-confidence, self-esteem, self-respect and helps in consciousness raising. Main objective of developing this power is to develop a sense of ability to overcome internalized oppression. It arises from a recognition that one is not helpless, not the source of one's own problems.
Power to	Enabling women to develop the necessary skills and access the necessary resources to achieve their aspirations. It involves capacity building, supporting individual, decision making and leadership. It is the capacity to take action.Involves access to a full range of women activities and potential. It is creative and enabling as women reconstruct and reinvent themselves.
Power with	Enabling the women to examine and articulate their collective interests, to organize and achieve them and to link with other organisations for change. It involves social mobilization, building alliances and coalitions. It is a collective force where people cooperate with each other to solve problems and to achieve goals.It is the capacity to achieve with other that one could not achieve alone. People's ability to associate with each other becomes critical to economic life.
Power over	Enabling women to change the underlying inequalities in power and resources which constrain women's aspirations and their ability to achieve them. It is the process of one person or group to get another person or group to do something against their will.

Thus the "power over" is the controlling power; "power to" is the generative or productive power creating new possibilities and actions; "Power with" is relational and "power within" is seen in terms of self-reliance and self –esteem. The three levels of empowerment which are closely interlinked such as "power within", "power to" and "power to" help women to tackle "Power over" . Empowerment process addresses various combinations of these dimensions by affecting at various levels such as household, community, national and international.

Personal empowerment or "power within" is the key to the entire empowerment process as it plays a very important role in bringing out change in gender conditioning and renegotiating her role within the family and community. At the same time without collective empowerment, i.e. power with" it is very difficult for women to achieve personal empowerment. In fact there is a circular relationship between the two. Thus empowerment is not only about opening up the access to decision making, but also must include processes that lead people to perceive themselves as able and entitled to occupy that decision-making space.

Power within is crucial as primary step of empowerment which arises out of reflections and analysis of women's subordination and acts as a new form of consciousness. It helps women to make strategic life choices which are crucial for their lives. Thus she believes that the change in self-perception that involves undoing negative social construction and believing in oneself as having the capacity and right to act is essential for empowerment. Collective action is important in bringing out this consciousness in the individual as well as in social and political empowerment.

20.3. Elements of Empowerment

Since social, cultural, political, and economic conditions vary and institutions are context-specific, reform strategies must vary as well. Although there is no single institutional model for empowerment, experience shows that certain elements are almost very present when empowerment efforts are successful. These elements are in synergy and strengthen the demand side of governance.

There are four key elements of empowerment that must underlie institutional reform:[13]

Access to information: It refers to two-way information flows from government to citizens and from citizens to government and it is critical for responsible citizenship and responsive and accountable governance. Critical areas where information is most important include state and private sector performance, financial services and market, and rules and rights regarding basic services. Information and communication technologies often play a pivotal role in broadening access to information.

Inclusion/participation: An empowering approach to participation treats poor people as co-producers, with authority and control over decisions and resources developed to the lowest appropriate level. Inclusion of poor people and other excluded groups in decision-making is critical to ensure that limited public resources build on local knowledge and priorities, and brings about commitment to change. However, in order to sustain inclusion and informed participation, it is usually necessary to change rules and processes to create space for people to debate issues, participate in local and national priority setting and budget formation, and access basic and financial services.

Accountability: State officials, public employees, private providers, employers, and politicians must be held to account, making them answerable for their policies and actions that affect the well-being of citizens. There are three main types of accountability mechanism. Political accountability of political parties and representatives takes place increasingly through elections. Administrative accountability of government agencies is ensured through internal accountability mechanisms, both horizontal and vertical, within and between agencies. Social or public accountability mechanisms hold agencies accountable to citizens, and can reinforce both political and administrative accountability.

Local organisation capacity: This refers to the ability of people to work together, organize them, and mobilize resources to solve problems of common interest. Organised groups and communities are more likely to have their voices heard and their demand met. When such membership-based groups federate at higher levels, they can gain voice and representation in policy Dialogues and decisions that affect their wellbeing.

A critical component to achieve economic independence is access and control over productive resources. A second component of empowerment is knowledge and awareness, of one's self and society, and of personnel needs, health issues, legal rights, technological innovations and the availability of social and economic resources and how to take advantage of them.

The third component is self-image. This includes realization of one's capabilities and potential and confidence to take action in one's life. Both economic independence and knowledge help create a positive self-image but confidence in one's self can also facilitate the acquisition of further knowledge and action towards attaining greater economic independence. The last component is autonomy, which in its ultimate realization is empowerment at the level of society, for women empowerment is the restructuring of gender relations within both the family and in society at large and it is society's recognition of women's equality with men in terms of their worth society as independent persons.[14]

20.4. Women Empowerment through Microfinance

Microfinance has brought tremendous change in the life of women at the grass root. Microfinance, it is believed, contributes to economic empowerment in different ways. First, the provision of savings facility to the members enables them to contribute small savings regularly and the savings amounts, thus accumulated, provide a sense of security to them and reduce their vulnerability. Second, the programmes make it possible for the members to create a credit fund from which they can avail loans for consumption purposes such as purchase of food, accessing health and education services, performing social functions and so on. This is expected to have positive impact on their well-being, and access to basic needs. Third, the facility to borrow for Income Generating Activities (IGA's) either through savings fund or funds mobilized from donors, government and banks enables the members to undertake those activities which are expected to contribute to employment generation, income increase and asset acquisition. Fourth, the non-credit support in the form of training on how to undertake feasible and viable IGAs, facilitating linkages between the target group and services providers in the government such as agricultural extension services, facilitating the provision of insurance is expected to contribute to the satiability of employment and income security. This, in turn, leads to household food security.

Box-13: A Widow became Self-reliant and Financially Stable

C. Rama Subbamma became a widow at the tender age of 18 years with two children to feed. With courage and determination she started a roadside 'dosa' stall and earned a meagre sum of Rs. 15 to Rs. 20 a day. She was unable to invest more and moneylenders were not willing to help her because she was a widow.

Fortunately, on hearing about the MFI, she enrolled herself as a member and availed of her first loan of Rs. 5000. With the amount she purchased a small bunk, serving eatables and tit-bits to children, continuing her original trade of serving 'dosa'. Her income rose to Rs. 50 per day, and she was able to clear off the first loan and availed of a second loan of Rs. 10,000. With this second loan, she opened a provision and a sweet shop and this further increased her income to Rs. 150 per day and helped her in clearing the second loan. Subsequently, she took the 3rd and 4th loan of Rs. 11,000 and Rs. 15,000 respectively, purchased a shop to help her son and daughter-in-law to set up business and also expanded her own business. The total business turnover increased, leaving her with a surplus of Rs. 300 per day. Her standard of living and that of her family improved immensely. Apart from saving a sum of Rs. 50,000, she also constructed her own house and opened her own saving account in a bank, saving an amount of Rs. 100 per day. The case revealed C. Rama Subbamma's strong will power in the face of adversity, coupled with the social empowerment instilled by SHG/MFI activities and timely availability of successive FI credit that succeeded in giving the family the much desired financial stability.

Source: SIDBI, *Assessing Development Impact of Microfinance Programme*

The Fourth World Conference on Women in Beijing (1995), put women's access to credit on the international agenda. Since then, the number of women receiving microfinance has increased rapidly. By 1999, the number of poor women receiving micro loans had more than doubled to 10.3 million poor, and by 2005, this had jumped to 69 million, or 84 per cent of the total number of poor people receiving microfinance. Women have now gained an international reputation for their excellent credit performance, making them a priority for poverty-oriented credit programs. For the majority of women borrowers, credit is much more than access to money: it is about women lifting themselves out of poverty, and achieving economic and political empowerment within their homes, their villages, and their countries. For example.

a) 40 per cent of poverty alleviation in rural Bangladesh has been attributed to the role of microcredit.[15]

b) Combining education and financial services programmes in Nepal has empowered women to ensure female children have equal access to food, schooling, and medical care, and given women a stronger role in property transactions, and domestic and familial choices.[16]

Microcredit and achieving the MDGs

One of the major objectives of the International Year of Microcredit (2005) was to promote the role of microfinance in achieving the Millennium Development Goals. The General Assembly adopted a resolution, recognising the importance of microfinance in achieving the MDGs, especially goals 1 (reducing poverty), and 3 (gender equality and women's empowerment). The resolution calls on Member States, the UN system and International Financial Institutions to maximize efforts and adopt policies to facilitate the expansion of microfinance to help meet the demands of the poor. The most successful microfinance schemes have been complemented by access to other resources such as land and property, finance and marketing skills, as well as services that reduce women's household and care-giving burden. Creating an enabling environment for microfinance and women's empowerment can be achieved with the help of the following activities:

(a) Promoting women's access to public services and employment opportunities. Public policy should promote social inclusion and equal opportunities for poor women. Women can become powerful catalysts for development when empowered through microfinance, but require access to childcare, health, education and skills, employment opportunities, and greater control over their fertility and children's education to enable them to take advantage of the opportunities that microfinance can provide.

(b) Establishing stronger partnerships between the private banking sector and microfinance institutions so that the market plays a more effective role in contributing to poverty alleviation. Multinational banks that provide micro-loans have greater access to resources, banking technology, and broader range of financial services. These potential benefits however, need to be balanced against concerns arising from corporate lending practices and competition with microfinance institutions serving the poor.

(c) Providing complementary services with microfinance such as literacy classes, business training and childcare. These are significant factors in improving both repayment rates and women's empowerment; therefore it is important to resist pressures on microfinance programmes to reduce operational costs by cutting back on such essential complementary services.

(d) Including women's empowerment indicators in the design and evaluation of microcredit programmes. Best practices has shown that microfinance is more effective when assets used as collateral or purchased with loans are solely or jointly in women's names; a range of savings products and facilities offering higher interest rates are made available; the lending process includes participatory consultations, including for non-business loans such as health, education, and housing.

Microfinance has been instrumental in empowering grass root women in several areas. Evidences from different regions revealed that there are positive improvements realized in terms of all the group members becoming literate; mitigating village disputes, improving health and education of children and keep the village roads clean, giving exposure to all the members of the group to carry on the bank's transactions, etc. It has helped in many ways: in replacing moneylenders, changing cropping pattern, increasing use of organic pesticides and fertilizers, creating seed banks; and creating a better awareness on nutrition, health and hygiene. It has also prompted the involvement of people in regular saving and internal lending, helped them initiate micro enterprises and manage lending schemes, avail government credit, operate savings accounts and communal funds and maintain financial records. Besides, microfinance have been instrumental in people becoming environmentally conscious, using Ecoscan toilets, constructing and using and repairing rainwater harvesting structures, participating in politics. Women have gained technical skills, and basic principles of management, and group building. The SHG groups are also getting federated and as such the help women of different regions to unite collectively for a common cause.

A woman's practical needs are closely linked to the socially defined gender roles, responsibilities, and social structures, which contribute to a tension between meeting women's practical needs in the short-term and promoting long-term strategic change. By helping women meet their practical needs and increase their efficacy in their traditional roles, microfinance may in fact help women to gain respect and achieve more in their socially defined roles, which in turn may lead to increased esteem and self-confidence.

20.5. Approaches to Women Empowerment

From the early 1970s, women's movement in a number of countries identified credit as a major constraint on women's ability to earn an income and became increasingly interested in the degree to which poverty-focused credit programs and credit cooperatives were actually, being used by women. Self Employed Women's Association (SEWA) in India, for example set up credit programs as part of a multi-pronged strategy for an organisation of informal sector women workers. Since the 1970s, many women's organisations worldwide have included credit and savings, both as a way of increasing women's incomes and to being women together to address wider gender issues. The 1980s saw the emergence of poverty-targeted microfinance institutions like Grameen Bank and ACCION and others. Many of these programs see themselves as empowerment-oriented. In the 1990s, a combination of evidence of high female repayment rates and the rising influence of gender lobbies within donor agencies and NGOs led to increase emphasis on targeting women in microfinance programs.

Following are the some of the reasons for targeting women under various development programmes in general and in micro finance in particular:

a) Firstly, women contribute one half of the segment of population in India. So we cannot afford to keep them out of the mainstream.

b) Secondly, women are vital and productive workers in India's national economy and they make one by three of the labour force.

c) Thirdly, there is a significant gap between women's especially rural women's potential and actual productivity. The productivity gap of the poor women will gain proportionately more, if investment allocation and development efforts are shifted in their favour.

d) Fourthly, women's earnings have positive correlation with children's health, productive, income and quality of life. Therefore, women SHGs and microfinance imply multidimensional contribution to overall growth and development.

Women have been shown to spend more of their income on their households; therefore, when women are helped to increase their incomes, the welfare of the whole family is improved. The Special Unit on Microfinance of the UNCDF in its report on its survey findings explains "Women's success benefits more than one person. Several institutions confirmed the well-documented fact that women are more likely than men to spend their profits on household and family needs. Assisting women therefore, generates a multiplier effect that enlarges the impact of the institution's activities".[17]

Different perception exists regarding the ability of microfinance to contribute to women empowerment. There are three different approaches to microfinance used around the world. They are i) Financially sustainable approach ii) Poverty Alleviation approach and iii) Feminist empowerment approach.[18]

Financially sustainable approach: Financially sustainable approach often referred to as financial system approach or sustainability approach underlies the models of microfinance promoted since the mid 1990s, by most of the donor agencies like USAID, World Bank, UNDP and CGAP. The insight of the approach is that, in order to reach the millions of poor people needing microfinance services, microfinance institution must eventually be profitable and fully self-supporting. Here it's assumed that increasing women's access to microfinance services itself lead to individual and economic empowerment, thereby social and political empowerment.

Poverty alleviation approach: This approach of empowerment is seen in terms of community and self-sufficiency. It is a paradigm based on the principle of self-help to build sustainable livelihood and sustainable communities. The idea of this approach is that, increasing women's access to microfinance will enable women to make greater contribution to household income. This raises the status in the household, which will in turn give women the support they need to enable women together with men to bring about wider changes in gender inequality in the community.

Feminist empowerment approach: This paradigm seeks to promote microfinance as an early point in the context of wider strategy for women's economic and socio-political empowerment. Further development of sustainable and participatory women's organisation is seen as an end in itself in order to bring about the change in gender relation at both micro and macro levels. The feminist empowerment firmly rooted in the earliest microfinance program in India like, SEWA in Gujarat. Here the underlying goals are gender equality and women's human rights.

The policy framework and strategies for women development and empowerment gradually evolved, over time. In the earlier phase of developmental planning, the concept of women's development was mainly welfare-oriented. During the sixties, women's education received priority. During the seventies, there was a definite shift in the approach from 'welfare' to 'development' which started recognizing women as participants of development. The eighties adopted a multi-disciplinary approach, with a special thrust on the three core sectors viz, health, education and employment. The early nineties made a beginning in concentrating on training-cum-income generation programmes for women with the ultimate objective of making them economically independent and self-reliant.

20.6. Dimensions of Empowerment and its Attainment

Though women represent half of the human resource, they are often not recognized and regarded so, due to their positioning in the society. Women themselves have failed to recognize that they are working though they are not paid. For the first time in 1981 the Indian Census included certain kinds of work which have market value on opportunity cost or imputation basis and succeeded in bringing activities such as fetching fuel wood, making pickle, etc. were included. However, even if women's work does get included will they command any value or recognition?

There is a tendency in general to relate women and their role predominantly to reproduction particularly biological reproduction. Women perform in addition to biological reproduction, several other tasks, but often, they are not visible. It is their biology and their reproductive role that overwhelms their productive role of earning and meeting livelihood needs. Realizing this third Millennium Development Goal [MDG] has included women's empowerment and promoting gender equality among the eight MDGs. However, given the nature of impact of gender equity in society, it need not be spelt out as a separate goal. Rather it should have been included as an integral component of each and every goal, as there is gender discrimination existing in every aspect be it education, empowerment, health, environment, etc. There is a need to change the power relations from domination and subordination to equality. This can be done only by changing the institutions which try to maintain and reinforce gender inequalities including patriarchy, culture, religion, family, educational institutions, state, market, media, law, religions rituals, traditional practices, stereotyping of such practices and expectations.

There are four major dimensions of women empowerment. They are:

a) Economic Empowerment (e.g. rights and accessibility and to the productive resources)

b) Social empowerment (e.g. accessibility to basic education);

c) Political empowerment: refers to the equitable representation of women in decision-making structures, both formal and informal, and their voice in the formulation of policies affecting their societies. (e.g. participatory action in development, voice in decision-making)

d) Legal empowerment (e.g. information of legal machinery to protect the interest of women).

There are four processes involved in empowering. They are growth in people's awareness and confidence, ability to articulate problems gaining access to resources as well as public facilities and negotiating over relations between different social groups.[19]

The poor women need a range of assets and capabilities to increase their well-being and security, as well as their self-confidence, so that they get power and can negotiate with those who are powerful. Power itself can be simply defined as control over resources and capabilities. The resources and assets over which control can be exercised fall in four broad categories, namely;

1) Physical resources (land, water, forest etc.).
2) Human resources (people, their bodies, their labour and skills).
3) Intellectual resources (knowledge, information or idea).
4) Financial resources (money or access to money).

Capabilities on the other hand, are inherent in the people and enable them to use their assets in different ways to increase their well-being. Human capabilities include good health, education etc. Social capabilities include social belongingness, leadership, relation of trust and sense of identity, values that give meaning to life and capacity to organize. Political capability includes capacity to represent oneself and others, access to information from association and participate in political life of a community or country.

20.7. Indicators of Women Empowerment

Women's poverty is directly related to absence of economic opportunities and autonomy, lack of access to economic resources including credit, land ownership and inheritance, lack of access to education and support services and their minimal participation in the decision-making process. Thus the lower status of women mostly stem from their low economic status and subsequent dependence and lack of decision-making power.[20]

Various case studies show that there is a positive correlation between credit availability and women's empowerment. It is believed that economic strength is the basis of social, economic, political and psychological power in the society. The economic empowerment of women requires transfer of skills of management and control of economic activities to women's groups over a period of time to enable women to feel confident and empowered. Once economic empowerment is achieved it would have a major implycations on the over all empowerment of women. Availability of timely and adequate credit is essential for women to undertake any economic activity rather than credit subsidy.

Over 90 per cent of rural women, workers are unskilled and hence they are mainly engaged in informal/unorganized sector. Wage rates for women in agriculture have been, on an average. 30-35% less than those paid to men. Women shoulder almost the entire burden of household activities and children responsibilities, and a large proportion of women's work time is spent on such activities. This leaves little time for women to engage themselves in income generating activities. Female casual labourers in rural India show the highest incidence of poverty of any occupational category male or female.

Women's economic independence is highly stressed by many authors. They argued that money in the hands of man is spent quite differently from the money in the hands of women. An ILO study finds that men tends to spend 60 per cent of their income for their home and 40 per cent on themselves where as a women spends 90 per cent of her income on her family and only 10 per cent herself thus if a women controls the household income the family flourishes more and develops.[21]

Once economic empowerment is achieved it would have major implications on the over all empowerment of women. Intra-family relationships and domestic work culture would change resulting in social empowerment and participation in decision-making leadership and active participation in group culture would improve political wisdom and help towards political empowerment in turn would result in more representative planning for women and sustaining the process of overall empowerment of women.

Beijing Conference 1995 Indicators of Women Empowerment, Qualitative & Quantitative

Qualitative Indicators

a) increase in self-esteem, individual and collective confidence;

b) increase in articulation, knowledge and awareness on health, nutrition reproductive rights, law and literacy;

c) increase an decrease in personal leisure time and time for child care;

d) increase on decrease of work loads in new programmes;

e) change in roles and responsibility in family and community;

f) visible increase on decrease in violence on women and girls;

g) responses to, changes in social customs like child marriage, dowry, discrimination against widows;

h) visible changes in women's participation level attending meeting, participating and demanding participation;

i) increase in bargaining and negotiating power at home, in community and the collective;

j) increase access to and ability to gather information;

k) formation of women collectives;

l) positive changes in social attitudes;

m) awareness and recognition of women's economic contribution within and outside the household; and

n) women's decision-making over her work and income.

Quantitative indicators

a) demographic trends (maternal mortality rate, fertility rate, sex ratio, life expectancy at birth, average age of marriage)

b) Number of women participating in different development programmers

c) Greater access and control over community resources/government schemes-crèche, credit cooperative, non formal education

d) Visible change in physical health status and nutritional level

e) Change in literacy and enrollment levels

f) Participation levels of women in political process.

Indicators of Economic Empowerment

Some of the indicators of economic empowerment are:

a) Level of earning and savings

b) Control over earned income

c) Increase of women's share in household income

d) Increase in household expenditure (food, cloths, consumer durables, health care, education etc.)

e) Access and control over credit facility

f) Greater participation in decision-making within and outside the home

g) Participation in the paid employment

h) Enhanced knowledge, ability and bargaining power in areas like marketing, wage and price negotiation.

Some of the indicators of empowerment at individual level are given as under:

Decision-making ability	▪ Decision-making ability over the use of income ▪ Decision-making ability over the use of loan taken from SHG ▪ Decision-making ability over the expenditure of the household ▪ Decision-making ability related to other issues such as education of children etc. ▪ Overall decision-making ability
Self development	▪ Overall awareness about self

	▪ Economic independence ▪ Self-confidence ▪ Self-esteem ▪ Leadership development ▪ Risk-taking ability
Improvement in Social Status	▪ Mobile and social status ▪ Physical mobility ▪ Social status within the household ▪ Social status within the neighbourhood

Although increased self-confidence does not automatically lead to empowerment, it may contribute decisively to a woman's ability and willingness to challenge the social injustices and discriminatory systems that they face. This implies that as women become financially better-off their self confidence and bargaining power within the household increases and this indirectly leads to their empowerment. Finally, given that empowerment is a process, the impact of the microfinance program may take a long time before it is significantly reflected on the observable measures of women empowerment.

Box-14: Empowerment of Women through Microfinance: Indian Experience

Women enjoyed full liberty in saving with the group and saving in their name without any inhibition. They were able to influence their husbands to contribute to savings. Many were happy to say that savings in their name gave some social status at home and in the community.

- Regarding utilisation of savings for purchase of assets or ornaments women had the power, but none of them (excepting single women households), wanted to take decision without consulting their husbands or other elder members in the house. However, many of them reported that they enjoyed freedom of spending the savings on purchase of clothes and other household goods.
- Decisions regarding utilisation of loan, whether for husband's business or new activity or repayment of loan, were taken jointly by husband and wife.
- Savings out of income from business were spent on education of children and purchase of assets. The decision to spend the savings was taken jointly.
- One of the women participants, who availed of an individual loan of Rs. 1.00 lakh for business purpose, had got her son educated as an engineer. Her son completed the engineering course and wanted to go for MS course in US.
- The women told that they earned prestige and importance in their homes and their family members also helped them in domestic work. Their spouses listened to them and consulted them in domestic decision making.
- Women, however, commented that the burden of their domestic work had not been reduced, their earlier spare time was now utilized for business purpose.

Source: SIDBI, *Assessing Development Impact of Microfinance Programme*

Women's empowerment cannot be achieved through economic independence alone. It should also be accompanied by other social, political empowerment to attain the MDG and gender equality. Women must get proper education, skill training, exposure to information, training to use modern technology apply the technology through mainstreaming to all members including women in the family.

Social empowerment of women includes changes in the socialization process, without any discrimination on gender in day to day affairs, gender sensitization and inculcating a feeling of equality instead of subordination among women. On a rights perspective equal right to be born, equal literacy, equal education, equal employment, equal property right, equal participation in decision making at home, at work place, policy making, committees, politics, etc. are to be included.

Another important component is political empowerment. If economic and social empowerment is to be achieved, political empowerment should include equal participation and power to take decision, no subordination, nor domination of men or women, recognition of work of both men and women as equals, and so on.

20.8. Government Initiatives for Women Empowerment in India

As women's empowerment is the key to socioeconomic development of the community, bringing women into the mainstream of national development has been a major concern of government. The Government of India has made Empowerment of Women as one of the principal objectives of the Ninth Five Year Plan (1997-2002) and also declared 2001 as the year of 'Women's Empowerment'. These issues of gender equality are discussed in World Conferences, National and International Conferences, etc. Our Constitution has conferred and guaranteed equality before law, universal adult franchise and equal opportunities for men and women as fundamental rights. The imperative of gender partnership in matters of development has been recognised. In order to give a fillip to empowerment of women and appropriate institutional mechanisms and interventions have been consciously built into the development design. Separate institutions for women and child development, departments at the Central and State levels, creation of the National Commission for Women and also State Commission for Women in several States are some of the important developments for the betterment and prosperity of women. The launching of Rashtriya Mahila Kosh, Indira Mahila Yojana, Mahila Samridhi Yojana, reserving of one third of the number of seats in Panchayats and the local bodies are programmes launched with a view to improve and empower women socially, economically and in political frontiers.

The Ministry of Rural development has special components for women in its programmes. Funds are earmarked as "Women's component" to ensure flow of adequate resources for the same. Besides Swarnagayanti Grameen Swarazgar Yojona (SGSY), Ministry of Rural Development is implementing other scheme having women's component .They are the Indira Awas Yojona (IAJ), National Social Assistance Programme (NSAP), Restructured Rural Sanitation Programme, Accelerated Rural Water Supply programme (ARWSP) the (erstwhile) Integrated Rural Development Programme (IRDP), the (erstwhile) Development of Women and Children in Rural Areas (DWCRA) and the Jawahar Rozgar Yojana (JRY).

India being the signatory of UN efforts to move towards achieving the Millennium Development Goals (MDGs), it is necessary to understand the measures taken by government of India in achieving the MDGs with particular reference to attaining gender equality. It may be possible to realize through the following.

- Economic, social, cultural and political empowerment and feeling of gender equality and promotion of the same is the way out.
- Equal employment and recognition of women's work at home, at work place, etc.
- Self employment to those who do not wish to be employed.
- Control over resources, freedom to spend the income earned.
- Increase in WPR in non-farm sector, in non-wage operations.

Government Initiatives: In order to attain the MDGs the government of India and other state government have introduced several gender positive initiatives.

Gender Budget Initiatives: Gender budget initiatives analyse how governments raise and spend public money, with the aim of securing gender equality in decision-making about public resource allocation; gender equality in the distribution of the impact of government budgets, both in their benefits and in their burden. The impact of government budgets on the most disadvantaged groups of women is a focus of special attention. Gender budgeting is an exercise to translate stated gender commitments of the government into budgetary commitments and a strategy for ensuring gender sensitive resource allocation and a tool for engendering macro economic policy. It entails affirmative action for empowering women and covers assessment of gender differential impact of government budgets and policies by enabling tracking and allocating resources for women empowerment. It is an opportunity to determine the real value of resources allocated to women.

National Policy for Empowerment of Women: Another important initiative of the Government of India is the enactment of a national policy of empowerment of women. The objective of the policy is to move women towards advancement, development and empowerment, elimination of discrimination.

Parliamentary Committee on Empowerment of Women: This is looking into the aspects of gender budgeting and also reservation in parliamentary elections. There have been other initiatives also.

Tenth Plan Initiatives: The Tenth Plan indicates that 42.9 per cent of the gross budgetary support in 15 women-related ministries/departments has gone towards a commitment to gender budgeting to establish its gender-differential impact and to translate gender commitments into budgetary commitments. The Plan aims at initiating immediate action in tying up the two effective concepts of the women's component plan (WCP) and gender budgeting plays a complementary thus ensuring both preventive and post-facto action in enabling women to receive their rightful share from all the women-related general development sectors.

Monitorable targets for the Tenth Plan and beyond had certain key issues related to gender. The key issues are given below:

a) All children in school by 2003; all children to complete five years of schooling by 2007.

b) Reduction of gender gaps in literacy and wage rates by at least 50% by 2007.

c) Reduction of IMR to 45 per 1000 live births by 2007 and 28 by 2012.

d) Reduction of maternal mortality ratio (MMR) to 2 per 1000 live births by 2007 onto to by 2012.

Box-15: Social Measures of the Government to Protect and Empower Women

Article 15 of the constitution empowers state to enact the legislation to protect women and promote the welfare and progress of SCs/STs. Various Laws have been passed to protect women at different times-The Special Marriage Act 1954; Hindi Marriage Act 1955; The Medical Termination of Pregnancy Act 1971; The Child Marriage Restraint (Amendment) Act 1976; The Maternity Benefit Act 1976; The Equal Remuneration Act 1976; Indecent Representation of Women (Prohibition) Act 1986;The Commision of Sati (Prevention) Act 1987; National Commission for Women Act 1991. The Pre-natal Diagnostic Technique (Regulation and Prevention of Misuse) Act 1994 etc.

Various social measures of the state to uplift the women are implementation of National Plan for Women (1988) to facilitate mainstreaming of women's issues in policies and programmes. Implementation of National Plan of Action for Girl Child (1991-2000).Declaring the Census 1991 as Gender sensitization Census and efforts made to capture for the first time women's work in the informal sector. Setting up National Commision for Women (1992) to review the Constitutional and legal safeguards for women. The 73rd and the 74th Amendment Act of 1993 for providing 1/3 reservation seats for women in local bodies and municipalities. Publication of Legal Literacy Manual (LLMs) in 1992 by the Government to educate women about their basic needs (GOI, 1995). Declaration of the year 2001 as Women's Empowerment Year.

Source: Jyasheela, Prasad, and Dinesha (2009), *Microfinance in India A tool for Women Empowerment*, Serials Publications, New Delhi

NOTES

1. Kabeer, N, " *Resources, agency, Achievement: Reflection on the Measurement of women's Empowerment", Development and Change*, Vol 30, July 1999 , pp. 435-464.
2. Rowlands, J (1997), *"Questioning Empowerment: working with women in Honduras"*, Oxford; Oxfam.
3. Mayoux, Linda (2003), "Women's Empowerment and Participation in Micro-finance: Evidence, Issues and ways Ahead". In Linda Mayoux (ed.), *Sustainable Learning for Women's Empowerment*, New Delhi, SAMSKRITI.
4. Sen and Grown (1987), *"Development, Crisis and Alternative Visions: Third World Women's Perspectives"*, Monthly Review Press, USA
5. Sharma, Kumud (1992), *"Grass Roots Organisation and Women's Empowerment: Some Issues in Contemporary Debate"*. Centre for Women's Development Studies, New Delhi.

6. Batiwala Srilata (1994), "The Meaning of Women's Empowerment: New Concepts from Action". In Gita Sen *et al* (ed), *Population Policies Reconsidered: Health, empowerment and Rights*, Harward Centre for Population and Development Studies, London.
7. Kabeer, Naila (1999), "Resources, Agency, Achievements: Relfection on Measurement of Women's Empowerment", *Development and Change*, Vol 30, No1,pp 435-464.
8. Beteille, Andre (1999), "Empowerment", *Economic and Political Weekly*, Vol.34, No.10 & 11, March 6-13, pp.589-597.
9. Bansal, Gaurav and Chauhan, Shyam Sunder Singh (2002), "Various Dimensions of Women's Empowerment", *Social Welfare*, April Vol.8, No.1, pp.10-16.
10. Sinha, Archana (2004), *"Micro-finance and Women's Empowerment: A Perspective"*, *Kurukhshetra*, Vol.16, No.10, April, pp.31-38.
11. Malhotra, Meenakshi (2004), *Empowerment of Women*, Vol.1, Isha Books, New Delhi.
12. Sunny, Dolly (2006), "Women's Empowerment and sustainable Development through SHG-A tale of selected states of India", *Samyukta-A Journal of Women's Studies*, Vol.5, No1, pp. 153-166.
13. Narayan Deepa (2002), *Empowerment and Poverty-A Source Book*, World Bank, Washington D.C.
14. Holly M. Hapke (1992), "An Experiment in Empowerment". In Ranjana Kumari (ed), *Women in Decision-making*, Vikash Publishing House, New Delhi pp.19-37.
15. Khandker, Shahidur R. *"Microfinance and Poverty: Evidence Using Panel Data from Bangladesh,"* *World Bank Economic Review*, vol.19, no.2, 2005
16. UNCDF website
17. Susy Cheston and Lisa Kahn(2002), *Empowering Women.*
18. Linda Mayoax (2003), *Sustainable Learning for Women's Empowerment*, SAMSKRITI, New Delhi.
19. Reddy G.N.(2002), "Empowering Women Through SHGs and Micro Credit: The Case of NIRD Action Research Projects", *Journal of Rural Development*, Vol.21, No.4
20. Sunil Goyal (2004), "Women Entrepreneurship and Empowerment", *Social Welfare*, March, pp 19-20.
21. Padmavathi, D. (2004), "DWACRA agent of Women's Empowerment, Perspectives", *Social Welfare*, March, pp. 9-12.

Bibliography

"Microfinance in India Current Trends and Challenges", CMF & IFMR, October 2006.

A report of the Review Group on the Working of the Local Area Bank Scheme headed by Shri G.Ramachandran , Former Finance Secretary, Government of India, Reserve Bank of India, September 2002.

Alfred Hanning, *How to Regulate and Supervise Microfinance: Key Issues in an Internal Perspective,* The case of India (by Prakash Bakshi), High Level Policy Workshop, World Bank, Kampala, November 1999.

ASA (2002): *Annual Report 2001.*

Bangladesh Bank(2002): *Annual Report 2000-01.*

Based on the India case study by Sanjay Sinha in *The Role of Central Banks in Microfinance in Asia* (ADB, 2000) and a draft World bank report on the microfinance industry in India.

Bindu Ananth, Bastavee Barooah etc., *A Blueprint for the Delivery of Comprehensive Financial Services to the Poor in India,* Centre for Micro Finance, CMR & IFMR, Working paper, December 2004.

Bindu Ananth, Bastavee Barooah etc, *A Blueprint for the delivery of comprehensive Financial Services to the poor in India,* CMR & IFMR, Centre of Micro Finance Working Paper, December 2004.

BRAC (2002): *Annual Report 2001.*

C.P.Mohan,"Microfinance & India's RRBs: The Best Fit", *Cab Calling,* Jan-Mar-2005, p. 27.

Centre for Micro Finance at Institute of Management and Research, *Microfinance in India: Current Trends and Challenges,* October 2006.

Chidambaram P., *Governement of India Union Budget 2004-05.*

Deb Kalipada, "Development and Disparities, Rawat Publications, Jaipur, 2001.

Directorate of Economics & Statistics of all NE states.

Dr. A.N. Sarkar, "Innovation in MicroFinance" *Kurukshetra,* 2Dec-2001.p. 7.

Dr. A.N. Starker," Innovations in Microfinance, *Kurukshetra,* December 2001, p. 2.

Dr. A.R. Patel, "Micro-Finance and Micro-finance institutions –need for bank's initiative and commitment", *National Bank News Reviews,* April-June 2002, p. 35.

Dr. Amal Mandal, "Poverty Eradication in Rural India: Relfection on Methodology", *Kurukshetra*, August, 2003, p. 5.

Dr. Amrit Patel, "Micro-Credit and Role of Banks- Need for Initiatives and Commitment", *Kurukshetra*, February 2004, p. 6.

Dr. Ashutosh Raravikar, "Union Budget 2005-06: A lead towards Bharat Nirman", *Cab Calling*, January-March 2005.pp. 44-45.

Dr. Bimla Kumari, "Amartya Sen's Strategy of Poverty Reduction and its relevance to India", *Poverty and Sustainable Development*, p. 39. B

Dr. H.D.Dwarakanath, "Savings and credit movement in Andhra Pradesh-Participation of Rural Women", *Kurukshetra*, August 2003. p. 31.

Dr. K. Sivaloganathan, "Problems in the recovery of rural credit", *Kurukshetra*, Feb-04, p. 36.

Dr. Manoj Shankar Gupta, "Poverty Eradication through Micro-Finance/SHG", *Poverty and Sustainable Development*, p. 379.

Dr. Medha Dubhashi, "Expert Committee on Rural Credit", *Kurukshetra*, 2004, p 29. (http://www.un.org.in/iawg/icecd/section1.htm)

Dr. N.K.Thingalaya, *Rural Financing: Compatibility of Regional Rural Banks*, October-December 2004, p. 31.

Dr. Om Raj Singh, "Role of NGOs in Fostering Self Help Groups: A case study of MYRADA", *Kurukshetra*, February 2003, pp. 33-34.

Dr. Sabanna S.Talwar ," SHG, Women and Poverty Alleviation in Karnataka State", *Poverty and Sustainable Development*, p. 636.

Dr. T. Srinivas Prasad, "Regional rural Banks: Performance Evaluation", *Kurukshetra*, August 2003, p. 20.

Draft Paper of Women's World Banking "Micro Environment and legal regulatory Framework India, March 2002. and a draft report on World Bank Report on the Microfinance Industry in India.

Duggal and Singhal, " Extending Banking to the poor in India", *Working Paper Series*, www.icicisocialinitiatives.org.March 2002.

Economic Survey 2004-05.

Economic Survey: 2003-04 & 2004-05, Government of India and Union Budget 2005-06, Government of India.

Extracts from an article written and presented at APRACA Seminar at Manila on Regulation of MFIs in July 2004 by K.Muralidhara Rao, General Manager, NABARD, Mumbai. (http://www.nabard.org/microfinance/mf_institution.asp).

Fisher T, Sriram MS: 2002, *Beyond Micro-credit*, Vistaar Publication.

G.K.Murthy, Micro Finance in India, *Banking Finance*, October 2005 p. 23.

G.Srinivasan, " Rural Credit Delivery: Reaching the Unreached", *Kurukshetra*,Vol 51, No 10, August 2003.p. 11

Grameen Bank in 'strongest position ever' (www.news.bbc.co.uk, March 12, 2002.).

Grameen Bank: *Annual Report 2001.*

Grameen Communications 1998 updated 2002.

H.S.Shylendra, "The SHG-Bank Linkage programme: An assessment and future strategies", *Journal of Rural Development*, Vol 23(4), pp 411-433 (2004), NIRD Hyderabad.

Helzi Noponen, "The Internal Learning System for participatory Impact assessment of Microfinance", *National Bank News Reviews*, April-June 2002, p. 53.

http:www.databank.nedfi.com.

ITC Ltd (2004), "Report and Accounts-2004, Kolkata, quoted by Y.C.Nanda," Micro Finance-A route to Reach Rural Poor", *The Journal of Indian Institute of Banking and Finance*, October-December 2004,p26.(www.itcportal.com).

J.C.Mishra & R.K.Thanvi, "Indian Banking System and Microfinance", *Kurukshetra*, February 2004, p. 13.

Jagdish Capoor, "Development Issues in Micro Credit", *RBI*, Mar 16, 2001 (http://rbi.org.in)

Jayanta Kr. Gogoi, "Rural Credit Scenario in North East India", *Kurukshetra*, February-04, pp. 39-42.

Jayaraman, B (2001): *Occational Paper 20-Micro Finance Retrospect and Prospects*, NABARD, Mumbai.

Jha A.K. (2000), "Lending to the poor: Designs for credit", *Economic and Political Weekly*, 35 (8 and 9):606-209 ,

Jonathan J. Murdoch, "Empowerment of Women through Government", *Focus*, p. 7.

Journal of Rural Development, Vol 23(4), pp 411-433 (2004), NIRD Hyderabad. Basu, Priya, Lead Economist, Finance & Private Sector, World, Debate: Cap the interest rate on microfinance? *The Economic Times* 21 March 2006.

Krishna, Norman Up off & Milton Jessant ed. *Reasons for Hope: Instructive Experience in Rural Development*, pp. 9-24, Connecticut: Kumara Press.

Mahajan, Vijay and Bharti Gupta Romola (2003) "Microfinance in India: Banyan Tree and Bonsai." *A review Paper for World Bank*, New Delhi, World Bank (Unpublished),

Md. Saifulislam, "Who Benefits, How benefits": The political Economy of Grameen Bank's

Mehan, Jennifer," Tapping Financial Markets for Microfinance", Grameen Foundation USA Publication Series, 2005.

Micro credit Programme in Rural Bangladesh: A theoretical Overview, Indian Journal of Social Development, Vol-4 No 1, Jun-04, pp. 1-17.

Microfinance Institutions of Bangladesh: Lessons for India, *Kurukshetra*, and February 2004.

NABARD (1996), " Linking of Self Help Groups with Banks, Mumbai. NABARD 2002,"Micro Credit Innovations Department (MCID) update." Mumbai (http://nabard.org/roles/mcid/introduction.htm)

NABARD 2002, " MF in India-An Overview," Mumbai (http://nabard.org/roles/mcid/section1.htm

NABARD 2002,"Micro Credit Innovations Department (MCID) update." Mumbai (http://nabard.org/roles/mcid/introduction.htm)

NABARD 2004, "NABARD and Microfinance." Mumbai (htpp://nabard.org/roles/mcid/introduction.htm).

Index

■■■